SIDE-LIGHTS ON MARYLAND HISTORY
VOLUME I

KING CHARLES FIRST

*After Van Dyck.   Shown through the courtesy of **Mr. Thomas F. Ryan** of New York from his collection at "Oakridge," Va.*

SIDE-LIGHTS
ON
MARYLAND HISTORY

WITH

SKETCHES OF EARLY MARYLAND FAMILIES

BY

HESTER DORSEY RICHARDSON

Special Executive Historian to represent Maryland in Historic Work at The Jamestown Exposition, 1907; President Public Records Commission of Maryland 1904-6; Vice-President of the Maryland Original Research Society; Member of The American Historical Association; The Maryland Historical Society; President of The Order of Colonial Lords of Manors in America; A Fellow of The Manorial Society of England.

Originally published: Baltimore, 1913
Reprinted by Genealogical Publishing Co., Inc.
Baltimore, 1967, 1995
Library of Congress Catalogue Card Number 67-31022
International Standard Book Number, Volume I: 0-8063-1467-2
Set Number: 0-8063-0296-8
Made in the United States of America

AN ACKNOWLEDGMENT

The Author gratefully acknowledges the courtesy of those who have added interest to her work by the contribution of specially prepared photographs, or by giving the privilege of using exclusive ones loaned for illustrations. These include, Mrs. Edward Shippen, Mrs. Kirby Flower Smith, Mrs. Graham Gordon, Miss Eileen Hemsley, Mr. Douglas H. Thomas, Ex-Governor Edwin Warfield, Mr. J. Charles Brogden, Mr. Richard Mareen Duvall of Baltimore, Mrs. Thomas Cradock of Baltimore, Mrs. Francis H. Darnall of Portland Manor, Mrs. Frederick Sasscer of Prince George's County, Miss Mary V. Dorsey and Miss Nellie Calvert Carroll of Dorchester County, Mrs. Horace Massey of Chestertown, Md., Mrs. Jesse Habersham, Mr. John Read Magruder, and the Misses Walton of Annapolis, Miss Rebecca L. Webster of Rochester, N. Y., U. S. Senator William P. Jackson of Salisbury, Maryland; Mr. Herbert L. Satterlee, Mr. Thomas F. Ryan, Mr. H. Mason Raborg of New York, General Coleman DuPont of Wilmington, Delaware.

her that Maryland, the Palatinate of the Lords Baltimore, in which they possessed royal rights and privileges, was not one of "Their Majesties' Plantations" to which convicts were transported by royal mandate, and established beyond question that Maryland was not a penal colony, but was settled by "gentlemen adventurers" in very large numbers. Instead of convicts there were ladies of high degree, and courtiers from the English capital; instead of a penal colony, she found that the Lords Baltimore had a little kingdom "beyond seas" to which the "Conditions of Plantations," offered by the Proprietary, attracted many land-hungry young Englishmen of good blood and adventurous spirit—the spirit of the pioneer—while the religious liberty proclaimed to all men gathered here from all parts of the world the persecuted for "conscience' sake." "The Land of Sanctuary" was the peaceful name by which our early Province was known.

Realizing that in the nearly three centuries that have elapsed since the settlement of Maryland, the meaning of words has in many instances undergone radical changes, the author investigated these changes in ancient English authorities, with interesting results; and in addition studied the conditions in England as they affected the people in the seventeenth century rather than the rulers; and was well repaid, in the new light gained on certain very essential points relating to the moral, educational and social status of the early settlers of Maryland.

Glowing with enthusiastic love of the State in which her blood has been deep-rooted in the soil for nine generations, the writer sought expression for her new vision of Maryland people in the Colonial period. The History Movement had not yet been inaugurated, and the leading papers were not in sympathy with the suggestion of a series of historical articles. It was due to the appreciation of Mr. Lynn R. Meekins, that the writer was encouraged to put in print the results of her gleanings, her first article appearing in March, 1903, in the Baltimore Sunday "Herald;" and through the influence of Mr. O. P. Baldwin, editor of the Baltimore Sunday "Sun," the "Side-Lights on Maryland History" were contributed to that Journal, beginning with May 17, 1903.

From its inception, this effort to show the best in Maryland's past struck a responsive chord in the hearts of many thousand descendants of the old blood of the State, and their tributes of appreciation are still preserved as valued evidences of good will. Among these are two from Maryland's distinguished historian, Dr. William Hand Browne, one of which conveys his thanks for the page reference in the rare "Relation of Maryland" from which the author of "Side-Lights" had brought to light the fact that bricks were being made in Maryland in the year 1635, an interesting discovery made by her, disproving the old tradition of "Bricks imported from England," which so many have believed.

BALTIMORE, May 26, 1903.

DEAR MADAM:

I am greatly obliged to you for your note. The "Relation of Maryland" I read long ago, but it, I mean the reference to brick making, had escaped my memory. I do not know whether I have seen the Shea pamphlet.

I have always maintained, partly from positive and partly from *a priori* reasons, that the importation of brick in Colonial times was a fable.

May I suggest to you that in future numbers of your highly interesting historical papers, you give the titles of your authorities, MS. or printed. There may be some, like myself, who wish to read further and to make notes.

So many idle tales and popular traditions are written about Maryland, that it is a pleasure to hear from a writer who has the historical sense, and can distinguish between fact and fable.

Very respectfully,
(Signed) WM. HAND BROWNE.

Mrs. Hester Dorsey Richardson."

The next from Dr. Browne was written after the "Side-Lights" had appeared weekly regularly for nearly seven months, and was particularly gratifying to the writer.

Baltimore Sunday "Sun," November 1, 1903.
Messrs. Editors:

Allow me to express the hope that Mrs. Richardson may see her way to bring out in book form her very accurate and interesting 'Side-Lights on Maryland History.' I am sure that there are many, who, either from historical or genealogical reasons would, like myself, be glad, to have such a book.

Baltimore.   (Signed)   WM. HAND BROWNE.

With such cordial endorsement from the distinguished author of "Maryland, the History of a Palatinate," and Professor of English Literature at the Johns Hopkins University, the author could forgive those disciples of Scharf, who, accepting his ignorant estimate of Maryland people in the Colonial period, rushed into anonymous and scurrilous criticisms of the "Reformer in the field of Maryland History." Pleading guilty to their accusations of rewriting Maryland History the author has had the gratification of recognizing the influence of her view point in the productions of those who have come after her.

The first official recognition which came to the writer as a result of bringing to light the best in Maryland's past, was conferred by Governor Edwin Warfield, when he issued a commission to her as Chairman of the Public Records Commission of Maryland, May 19, 1904. The conferring of this honor was on the occasion of a reception to the Daughters of the American Revolution in the Old Senate Chamber at Annapolis, the Capital of Maryland, made nationally historic by Washington's resigning his Commission there.

The Baltimore "Sun," in an editorial on May 21, 1904. under the caption "A graceful recognition of good work," said: "Governor Warfield made a proper and most graceful recognition of the historical work of Mrs. Hester Dorsey Richardson, whose series of articles entitled 'Side-Lights on Maryland History,' were written by her for the Baltimore Sunday 'Sun.' These articles, because of their historic value, have attracted widespread attention and excited the deepest interest among Maryland people at home and abroad. . . . In the pursuit of information Mrs. Richardson goes to the original sources, and her work is judicious, interesting and accurate. She has given to the future historian of the State, in the 'Sun's' articles, an admirable magazine of information."

Realizing that the Jamestown Exposition was an opportunity to have the true Colonial history of Maryland emphasized, Governor Warfield again gave official endorsement to the original research of the author by appointing her to make the Memorial Collection for exhibition in the Maryland Building, now a permanent exhibit in the State House at Annapolis. To this end the Governor issued the following commission to her, dated November 9, 1906.

"Be it known that you are hereby appointed Special Executive Historian to represent the Executive Department of the State of Maryland in connection with the historic work of the Jamestown Exposition. To collect and put in shape such historic data and documents as will redound to the fame and glory of Maryland."

Such a commission from the Governor of Maryland, distinguished for high ideals in official life and State pride, was an inspiration to one who welcomed the opportunity to exhibit the proofs that our grand old Commonwealth was of far nobler record than ever had been believed.

No higher tribute could have been paid the Executive Exhibit than its preservation as a whole in the State House at the State Capital, where it still fulfills its mission in proclaiming the glory and honor of Maryland.

The first list of the adventurers who came to Maryland on the *Ark* and the *Dove* in the year 1633 was compiled by the author of "Side-Lights" from the original (then unindexed) manuscript records of the Province. This list has since been published by others, with many additional names, not entitled to recognition as first settlers.

In the compilation of so much material, and the lapse of more than ten years since its preparation, errors (through haste) may have been overlooked. For these the author asks consideration. But honesty of purpose has been her watch word, and intentional errors of fact are not to be found in her work.

The rare, printed "Relation of Maryland," the "Instructions of Cecilius Calvert," photographed and exhibited at Jamestown by the writer: Leonard Calvert's letters; Alsop's "Maryland," and Seventeenth Century tracts, from which the author drew many unfamiliar facts in the preparation of "Side-Lights" in 1903-4, have recently (1910) been brought together in book form by another, under the title of "Early Maryland Narratives," forming a valuable source-reference volume to those not familiar with them at first hand.

Many of the unindexed manuscript records, which were examined with such difficulty when gleaning the data collated in these volumes, have since been indexed, and made easy of access. This progressive work was done by an appropriation from the Maryland Legislature, in response to the interest aroused in the records by the History Movement inaugurated by the "Side-Lights on Maryland History" published in the Baltimore Sunday "Sun"—which inaugural movement spread to national proportions, and has been reflected in many leading journals throughout the United States.

If the gleanings, now gathered into more permanent form, continue to fulfill their mission by adding luster to the early history of our people and to the Commonwealth of Maryland, the author will not have written in vain.

HESTER DORSEY RICHARDSON.

Baltimore, Maryland, 1913.

DEDICATION

To those who love their native State, and whose blood is deep-rooted in the soil, these pages are addressed.

To the dwellers afar, who have sought in vain for a more intimate knowledge of Maryland people, and a true presentation of their character and quality in the early days. "Side-Lights" are commended.

And to Dorsey Richardson, the loyal young son of Maryland, who has been his mother's inspiration in her efforts to preserve the true and best in Maryland's past, these volumes are lovingly dedicated by

THE AUTHOR.

CONTENTS

	PAGE
Chapter I. The *Ark* and the *Dove*	1
Chapter II. The First Maryland Settlers	6
Chapter III. The Voyage to Maryland	16
Chapter IV. Christmas on the *Ark*, A. D. 1633	25
Chapter V. Leonard Calvert's First Letter from Maryland.	30
Chapter VI. Goods Brought by First Settlers	36
Chapter VII. An Ancient Bill of Lading	40
Chapter VIII. Colonial Life and Aristocracy	45
Chapter IX. A Glimpse through Colonial Doorways	49
Chapter X. The Transported Settlers	53
Chapter XI. Maryland Not a Penal Colony	56
Chapter XII. First Prison in Maryland	62
Chapter XIII. The Lords and Ladies of the Manors	65
Chapter XIV. Leisurely Ways of the Colonial Court	72
Chapter XV. The Puritans from Virginia	75
Chapter XVI. The Oldest Church in Maryland	78
Chapter XVII. A Property Qualification	82
Chapter XVIII. Removal of the Capital to Annapolis	85
Chapter XIX. The Old Tuesday Club	89
Chapter XX. Mail Service in Provincial Times	95
Chapter XXI. Colors of the Counties	99
Chapter XXII. The Birthplace of Religious Liberty	102
Chapter XXIII. The Curious Law of Deodand	106
Chapter XXIV. The Palace of Lord Baltimore	109
Chapter XXV. Somerset County and the Presbyterians	115
Chapter XXVI. A Colonial Lending Library	119
Chapter XXVII. Colonial Currency	124
Chapter XXVIII. The Dutch on the Delaware	129
Chapter XXIX. The Origin of Lynch Law	133
Chapter XXX. The Gentle Hearted Indian	135
Chapter XXXI. Witchcraft in Maryland	141
Chapter XXXII. The First Theatre in America	144

CONTENTS

	PAGE
Chapter XXXIII. A Colonial Business Woman	147
Chapter XXXIV. New Light on Claiborne's Claim to Kent Island	151
Chapter XXXV. Origin of the Ground Rent	161
Chapter XXXVI. Education in the Province	165
Chapter XXXVII. First Free School in Maryland	169
Chapter XXXVIII. Renaissance of Antiques	177
Chapter XXXIX. Preston-on-the-Patuxent	181
Chapter XL. Coming of the Swedes	188
Chapter XLI. A Provincial Poet's Lines	191
Chapter XLII. The First Steamboat	193
Chapter XLIII. Old South River Club	197
Chapter XLIV. Losing the Flitch of Bacon	205
Chapter XLV. The King's Rebels	209
Chapter XLVI. The Scotch Exiles	213
Chapter XLVII. The Fountain Pen in the Time of Charles II	216
Chapter XLVIII. Early Divorce Law	218
Chapter XLIX. Quakers not persecuted in Maryland	220
Chapter L. Early Parishes	225
Chapter LI. Diversity in Spelling Colonial Names	228
Chapter LII. A Colonial Sanitarium	231
Chapter LIII. Establishment of the Land Office	234
Chapter LIV. The First Labor-saving Invention in Maryland	238
Chapter LV. A Poet Laureate in Colonial Maryland	243
Chapter LVI. Life on Colonial Plantations	246
Chapter LVII. Maryland—The Promised Land to the Persecuted	249
Chapter LVIII. Old Towns of the Eastern Shore	251
Chapter LIX. Giving Names to Lands	257
Chapter LX. Proprietaries and their Representatives	260
Chapter LXI. Lords of the Manor in Colonial Maryland, with their original Land Surveys taken from Lord Baltimore's Rent Rolls	263
Chapter LXII. Maryland Colonial Militia	267
Chapter LXIII. Names of one thousand early Settlers, with their earliest Land Surveys	287

CONTENTS

	PAGE
Chapter LXIV. The Sons of Liberty	356
Chapter LXV. The Burning of the *Peggy Stewart*	361
Chapter LXVI. Maryland's Declaration of Independence..	371
Chapter LXVII. The Ride of Lieutenant-Colonel Tench Tilghman	378
Chapter LXVIII. Where Washington resigned his Commission	383
Chapter LXIX. The Society of the Cincinnati in Maryland.	387
Chapter LXX. Unsung Heroes of the Revolution	394
Chapter LXXI. The Value of Family Traditions	397
Chapter LXXII. "Maryland, My Maryland"	401
Chapter LXXIII. The Mural Paintings in Baltimore Court House	405
Chapter LXXIV. An Inaccurate List of the *Ark* and *Dove* Adventurers	411
Chapter LXXV. Maryland Executive Exhibit	419

LIST OF ILLUSTRATIONS

FACING PAGE

King Charles I, Van Dyck	Frontispiece
Queen Henrietta Maria after Van Dyck	2
Caecilius Calvert, Second Lord Baltimore	6
Leonard Calvert, First Governor of Maryland	16
Rare Autographs of Some First Adventurers	30
Charles Calvert, Third Lord Baltimore	42
Benedict Leonard Calvert, Fourth Lord Baltimore	55
Charles Calvert, Fifth Lord Baltimore	69
Old Trinity Church, Dorchester County	78
Seventeenth Century Jacobean Communion Table	80
Queen Anne Kneeling Cushion	80
Eighteenth Century Chalice from Old Trinity Church, Dorchester County	80
Dorsey House at Annapolis	85
Frederick Calvert, Sixth Lord Baltimore	96
Rare Autographs of Those Who Passed the Act of Religious Toleration	104
Original Assignment of Homewood to Charles Carroll	139
Homewood	165
St. John's College	169
Old Staffordshire and Salt-Glaze "Sportive Innocence" Pictures	178
Statue of John Hanson	188
Contee Silver Bowl Engraved with Contee Arms	201
General Otho Holland Williams	210
Communion Silver Presented to St. Anne's Church, Annapolis, by William III	225
Rare Autographs of High Colonial Officials	236
Cooke's Point, Estate of Ebenezer Cooke	243
Mackubin Family Silver	252
Fort McHenry	277
General John Eager Howard	290
Governor Thomas Johnson and Family	306

LIST OF ILLUSTRATIONS

FACING PAGE

The Wife and Daughters of Chief Justice Samuel Chase..... 320
Whitehall, Home of Governor Horatio Sharp................ 330
Old St. Paul's Church, Baltimore......................... 341
The Peggy Stewart House, Annapolis....................... 361
Mrs. Anthony Stewart, Mother of Peggy Stewart............ 364
Anthony Stewart, Owner of the Brig *The Peggy Stewart*..... 368
Samuel Chase... 372
Lieutenant-Colonel Tench Tilghman........................ 378
Old State House, Annapolis............................... 383
General William Smallwood................................ 389
Unfamiliar Portrait of George Washington................. 390

SIDE-LIGHTS ON MARYLAND HISTORY

CHAPTER I

THE "ARK" AND THE "DOVE"

To THE student of colonial history an account of the first emigration to Maryland will be a "twice-told tale," but to those among us who have quite recently asked "What is the *Ark* and the *Dove*?" (as if they were a sort of composite affair), and for any others, either young or old, to whom these words suggest only "The Ark of the Covenant," we address this sketch.

Maryland has herself to blame for the embarrassing knowledge that whereas the *Mayflower* and the landing of the Pilgrims are familiar to her children, the names of the vessels that brought the first settlers to Maryland are not known to the average grown person.

It is time, therefore, that we look for all of interest concerning the *Ark* and the *Dove*, the two staunch little vessels which sailed from Gravesend in October, 1633, and after spending some time at Barbadoes finally landed their cargoes of hopeful adventurers at what became "ye Citie of St. Marie's" in Maryland.

Cæcilius Calvert, upon the death of his father, Sir George Calvert, acquired the charter of Maryland which had not passed the great seal before the death of Sir George Calvert. The charter was confirmed and published on June 20, 1632, and it is evident that Lord Baltimore at once began his preparations toward colonization. A year later the *Ark* and the *Dove*, having been fitted out at Lord Baltimore's personal expense, said to have been £40,000, the party, consisting of about 320 persons was ready to start for Maryland. Cæcilius sent his two brothers, Leonard and George, with the colonists, appointing the elder, Leonard, as lieutenant-governor under him.

* * * * *

Many troubles delayed the expedition. First the planters of Virginia petitioned the King to cancel Lord Baltimore's charter as interfering with their rights. After considerable discussion the privy council, on July 3, 1633, decided that the Lord Baltimore should be allowed to enjoy the privileges granted him by the King.

An order was thereupon issued by the King's Council at London as follows: "Whereas the good ship called the *Ark* of Maryland, of the burden of about 350 tons, whereof one Lowe is master, is set forth by our very good lord, the Lord Baltimore, for his lordship's plantation at Maryland, in America, and manned with about forty men. For as much as his lordship hath desired that the men belonging to his said ship may be free from press or interruption, these are to will and require you to forbear to take up or press any—the officers, seamen, mariners, or others belonging to his lordship's said ship—either in her voyage to Maryland or in her return for England, and that you permit and suffer her quietly to pass and return without any let or hindrance, stay or interruption whatever."

Considering this as sufficient authority upon which to embark, Lord Baltimore's party set sail about the middle of October for their new home. But again new troubles

QUEEN HENRIETTA MARIA

After Van Dyck portrait. From the Author's Collection

awaited them, for on October 19 we find an order was issued by Lord Coke, British Secretary of State, to Admiral Pennington to have the *Ark*, Richard Lowe, master, and the pinnace called the *Dove*, of fifty tons, commanded by Captain Wintour, turned back from their course as the company on board had not taken the oath of allegiance to the King.

* * * * *

Consequently the little vessels were returned to Gravesend and Edward Watkins, the "London Searcher," as he is called, administered the following oath to all on board:

"I do truly and sincerely acknowledge, profess, testify and declare in my conscience before God and the world that our sovereign lord, King Charles, is lawful and rightful King of this realm and of all other of His Majesty's dominions and countrie, and that the Pope, neither of himself nor by any authority by the church or See of Rome, or by any other means with any other, hath any power or authority to depose the King or to dispose of any of His Majesty's kingdoms or dominions, or to authorize any foreign prince to invade or annoy him or his countries, or to discharge any of his subjects of their allegiance and obedience to His Majesty, or to give license or leave to any of them to bear arms, raise tumults or to offer any violence, or hurt to His Majesty's royal person, state or government, or to any of his Majesty's subjects within His Majesty's domains.

And I do swear from my heart that, notwithstanding any declaration or sentence of excommunication or deprivation made or granted by the Pope or his successors, or by any authority derived, or pretended to be derived from him or his See, against the said King, his heir or successors, or any absolution of the said subjects from their obedience, I will bear faith and true allegiance to His Majesty, his heirs and successors, and him and them will defend to the uttermost of my power against all conspiracies and attempts whatsoever, which shall be made against his or their persons, their crown and dignity, by reason or color of any such sentence or declaration or otherwise, and will do my best to disclose and make known unto His Majesty, his heirs and successors all treasons or traitorous conspiracies which I shall know or hear of to be against him or any of them.

* * * * *

And I do further swear that I do from my heart abhor, detest and abjure as impious and heretical this damnable doctrine and position that princes which be excommunicated or deprived by the Pope may be deposed or murthered by their subjects or any other whatsoever.

And I do believe, and in conscience am resolved that neither Pope nor any person whatsoever hath power to absolve me of this oath, or any part thereof, which I acknowledge by good and full authority to be lawfully ministered unto me, and do renounce all pardons and dispensations to the contrary. And all these things I do plainly and sincerely acknowledge and swear according to these express words by me spoke, and according to the plain common sense and understanding of the same words, without any equivocation or mental evasion or secret reservation whatsoever. And I do make this recognition and acknowledgement heartily, willingly and truly upon the true faith of a Christian. So help me God."

Father White and others who forsook the ship upon its detention, boarded her at the Isle of Wight, thus perhaps saving their consciences by eluding the "Searcher." After a months delay they sailed from Cowes, Isle of Wight November 22, 1633.

* * * * *

The names of those who came to Maryland with the Calverts in 1633 have not been preserved as a whole. Even the number which actually came is uncertain, for while Lord Baltimore, in a letter written to the Earl of Stafford after his vessels had finally started, says: "There were near 320," the "London Searcher," in his report to the King's privy council, gives the number of persons on board as "about 128."

CHAPTER II

THE FIRST MARYLAND SETTLERS

So CHERISHED has become the tradition in many Maryland families that the immigrant ancestors "came over in the *Ark* with Lord Baltimore" that I am as loath to controvert it as I am to demolish the Colonial mansions and churches built of "brick brought from England."

The truth is that Lord Baltimore did not come in the *Ark*, but Leonard Calvert, the Lieutenant-Governor, came as the representative of his brother, Caecilius Calvert, second Lord Baltimore. It was not until some years later that Charles, third Lord Baltimore, arrived in Maryland. Hence those who came in the ship with him were not among the first adventurers.

As the result of much research in original sources in the interest of a permanent contribution to Maryland history bearing upon the first settlers and their origin, much new light has been thrown upon this very interesting period of our provincial life. Because Caecilius Calvert in his "Relation of Maryland with Conditions of Plantations" mentions only "twenty gentlemen of very good fashion," the idea has gone abroad that only this limited number of gentlemen were in the party. This is, however, positively erroneous.

Some of these twenty gentlemen themselves were parties to the "Conditions of Plantations" to the extent of letting others of the company receive land for paying their passages over.

CAECILIUS CALVERT, SECOND LORD BALTIMORE AND
FIRST PROPRIETARY OF MARYLAND

After a line engraving by Abraham Blooteling. From the Author's Collection

These were "Richard Orchard, master of the *Dove;*" "Samuel Lawson, mate;" "Richard Kenton, boatswain;" "John Games, gunner;" "John Curke and Nicholas Perrie," employes, duties not specified.

"Mr. Robert Smithson" was mentioned in Leonard Calvert's letter to Sir Richard Letchford as having come in the *Ark* with the first adventurers (he was also a gentleman of quality).

Mr. Barefoot, mentioned by Father White, Calvert Papers No. 35 as "one faithful servant of my Lorde, who died on the *Ark* en route."

The first list of adventurers on the *Ark* and *Dove* was published by the author in August, 1903, it being her pioneer work in the manuscript records of Maryland to establish the names of those who came in the first adventure to Maryland. At that time 1634 was accepted as the year of settlement, and those who were entered on the records as having come in that year were included by the author in her first published list, and these were also included in the original list prepared for the Special Executive Exhibit, which later was revised in the final analysis, and is now the first and only official List of Maryland's First Settlers as the following will make evident.

The first Maryland adventurers who arrived in Maryland water on March 3, 1633, and landed on St. Clement's Island, March 25, 1634, the first day of the new year (old style).

Governor Leonard Calvert and George Calvert, brothers to His Lordship. The Commissioners, Mr. Jerome Hawley, Thomas Cornwallis, Esq., Richard Lowe, Master of the *Ark;* John Bowlter, Purser of the *Ark;* Richard

Edwards, chirurgeon of the *Ark;* Captain Wintour, commander of the *Dove;* Richard Orchard, master of the *Dove;* Samuel Lawson, mate of the *Dove;* John Games, gunner of the *Dove;* Richard Kenton, boatswain of the *Dove;* John Curke, Crew on the *Dove;* Nicholas Parrie, Crew on the *Dove.*

PASSENGERS

Mr. John Althem, William Ashmore, William Andrews, John Ashmore, Thomas Allen, Mathew Burrowes, Anam Bonam, John Bryant, Thomas Beckworth, William Browne, Ralph Beane, Thomas Gervais, John Hillierd, John Hill, Thomas Heath, Nicholas Hervey, John Hollis, Thomas Hodges, Richard Hills, John Halfhead, Benjamin Hodges, James Heckley, John Holdern, Timothy Hays (Father), Robert Sherly, John Saunders, William Saire, Thomas Smith, Stephen Sammon, Smith (lost by the way), Robt. Smithson, James Thornton, John Thomson, Richard Thompson, Mathias Tousa (a mulatto), Richard Bradley, John Baxter, Henry Briscoe, Mr. Barefoot, Thomas Cooper, Christopher Carnock, Thomas Charinton, Richard Cole, Edward Cranfield, Mrs. Ann Cox, Richard Duke, Peter Draper, Thomas Dorrell, William Edwin, Robert Edwards, William Edwyn, John Elkin, Nicholas Fairfax (died on the *Ark*), Lewis Ffremonds, William Ffitter, John Hallowes, Capt. John Hill, Mary Jennings, Henry James, Josias (drowned afterwards), James (killed later at Mattaponi), Richard Loe, Richard Lusthead, John Marlburgh, Thomas Mimus, Chas. Middleton, John Metcalf, Roger Morgan, Richard Nevill, John Nevill, John Price (black), John Price (white), Lodowick Price, Robert Pike, Roger Walter, Rev. Andrew White, Frederick

Wintour, Edward Wintour, Henry Wiseman, Evan Watkins, John Ward, Thomas Grigsta, Richard Gerard, Thomas Gregson, Richard Gilbert, Stephen Gore, Thomas Green, Henry Greene, Mr. Rogers, John Robinson, Francis Rabnett, William Smith, Thomas Statham, Robert Simpson. (End of list).

The following from the Land Records proves that there were other arrivals in the year 1634, after those who landed on the first day, this being March 25 (old style), the finding of which entry caused the writer to revise the executive list before publishing.

Liber A. B. H., page 67. "October 15th, 1639, Mr. Thomas Green demandeth land due to him by the conditions of plantations—that is to say in his own right for himself, and two servants, Anam Bonam and Thomas Cooper, brought into the Province Anno 1633—and one servant, Thomas Wills, brought into the Province 1634."

The assignments here given in abstract, illustrate the repetition of the same lists of transported settlers, according to records found in "Warrants" and A. B. H., and give some idea of the difficulty the author had when gleaning the names of the first adventurers, from these transcribed and unindexed books, when unassisted she in the year 1903 collected the first list ever compiled from original sources in Maryland, and which, with a few very slight changes, stands today practically unaltered.

Liber 1, pages 19 and 20. "Entered by Mr. Copley. Brought in the year 1633." (Copley himself did not come until 1636.)

"Mr. Andrew White, Mr. John Althem, Thomas Statham, Robert Simpson, Mary Jennings, Mathias Tousa, John Hillerd, Robert Sherly, Mr. Rogers, John Hill, Christopher Carnock, John Bryant, William Ashmore, Richard Lusthead, Nicholas Hervey, Robert Edwards, Thomas Charinton, William Edwyn, Thomas Grigsta, Richard Duke, Henry Bishop, Thomas Heath, John Thomson, James Thornton, Lewis Fremonds, Richard Nevill, John Hollis, Richard Cole, John Elkin, Thomas Hodges."

Liber 1, page 17. "Entered by Mr. Thomas Green the first year, 1633, brought into the Province, Mr. Green in his own right and two servants, Anam Bonam in his own right, in right of Mr. Fairfax his person as his assignee, Mr. Smith as his assignee and for Thomas Wills in his (Mr. Green's) own right." (Father White says Nicholas Fairfax died on the *Ark*.)

Warrants, Liber 1, folio 26. "Thomas Cornwalleys, Esq., demandeth 2,000 acres by first conditions of Plantations for transporting five able men in the year 1633, viz.: John Hollowes, John Holdern, Roger Walter, Roger Morgan and Josias, that was drowned afterwards."

Liber 1, page 37. "Mr. Fernando Pulton demandeth land due by conditions of Plantations and these several titles following, that is to say for men brought in by several persons whose assignee, the said Fernando Pulton, is and for men brought in in his own right; as assignee of Mr. Andrew White brought into the Province Anno 1633.

"Mr. Andrew White, Mr. John Altheme, Thomas Statham, Robert Simpson, Henry Briscoe, Thomas Heath, Lewis Fremond, Richard Thompson, Mathias Sousa, a mulatto, Richard Lusthead, William Ashmore, Robert Sherley, Anno 1634, Mr. Rogers, John Hill, John Briant, Nicholas Hervey, Xtofer Carnock, A. Smith lost by the way.

"As assignee of Mr. John Saunders, Benjamin Hodges,

John Elkin, Richard Cole, Richard Nevill, John Marlburgh." Brought in 1633.

Ibid. "As assignee of Mr. Edward Wintour, Black Mimus, Thomas Gregston, Robert Edwards, John Ward, William Edwin." Brought in 1633.

Ibid. "As assignee of Mr. Edward Wintour, Black John Price, White John Price, Francis Rabnett, Thomas Smith, Richard Duke, Henry James, Thomas Carinton. 1633.

Ibid., folio 38. "Fernando Pulton, Esq., demandeth 260 acres of Town land, due by conditions of Plantations for transporting 26 able men into the province to plant and inhabit there in the year 1633—that is to say in the year 1633: Henry Bishop, Thomas Heath, Lewis Fremond, Richard Thompson, Richard Lusthead, William Ashmore, Robert Sherley, Benjamin Hodges, John Elkin, Richard Cole, Richard Nevill, John Marlburgh, Thomas Muuns, Thomas Grigson, Robert Edwards, John Ward, William Edwin, John Price, Senior, als. black John Price, John Price, Junior, als. white John Price, Francis Rabnett, Thomas Smith, Richard Duke, Henry James, Thomas Harrington, Robert Simpson, Mathias Tousa."

Annapolis Land Records. Liber 1, folio 110. "Thomas Cornwalleys, Esq., demandeth 4,000 acres of land due by first conditions of Plantations for transporting into the Province, in the year 1633, ten able men-servants—that is to say 2d June, 1633: Thomas Beckworth, Matthew Burrowes, Samuel, that was brought from St. Xtpofer, Cuthbird Ffenwick, Richard Loe, William Ffitter, John Robinson, Carpt., William Browne, Stephen Gore, Stephen Jammison."

"I would have you to lay out for Capt. Thomas Cornwalleys 2 Manors, each of 2,000 acres of land, next to St. Inego's land to draw a Patent for them. And this shall be your warrant."

Liber 1, page 121. Land Warrants, Annapolis. August 13, 1641. "Leonard Calvert, Esq., demandeth 6,000 acres of land due by conditions of first Plantation for transporting 15 able men into the Province in the year 1633, and likewise 100 acres of Town land for the said title, viz.: Peter Draper, Robert Pike, James Heckley, Richard Gilbert, John Ashmore, Thomas Allen, Charles Middleton, John Andrews, Ralph Beane, Evan Watkins, Richard Hills, John Nevill, Lodowick Price."

Liber 1, page 166. "Thomas Copley demandeth land; transported in 1633: Mr. Andrew White, Mr. John Althem, Robert Simpson, Mary Jennings, Henry Bishop, Richard Lusted, Thomas Heath, William Ashmore, Robert Sherley, John Hilliard, Mathias Zause (a mulatto), Lewis Ffreman, James (killed at Mattaponie.)"

Annapolis Land Records. Liber A. B. H., page 65. Mr. Fernando Pulton demandeth land due by conditions of Plantation under these several titles following—that is to say, for men brought in by the several persons whose assignees the said Fernando Pulton is, and for men brought in in his own right:

"As assignee of Mr. Andrew White, brought into the Province Anno 1633: Mr. Andrew White, Mr. John Alcome, Thomas Statham, Robert Simpson, Henry Briscoe, Thomas Heath, Lewis Freemond, Richard Thompson, Mathias Tousa (a mulatto), Richard Lusthead, William Ashmore.

"Robert Sherly as assignee of Mr. John Saunders Anno 1633: Benamin Hodges, John Elkin, Richard Cole, Richard Nevill, John Marlburgh.

"As assignee of Mr. Richard Gerrard Ano. Eod.: Thomas Mimus, Thomas Gregson, Robert Edwards, John Ward, William Edwin.

"As assignee of Messrs. Edward and Frederick Wintour Ano. Eod.: Black, John Price, white, John Price, Francis Rabnet, Thomas Smith, Richard Duke, Henry James, Thomas Charinton.

"Anno 1634: Mr. Rogers, John Hill, John Briant, Nicholas Harvey, Christopher Carnot, A. Smith lost by the way."

Annapolis Land Records. Liber A. B. H., folio 94.
"Thomas Cornwalleys, Esq., demandeth 4,000 acres of land due by first conditions of Plantations for transporting into the Province in the year 1633 10 able menservants—that is to say: Thomas Beckworth, Matthew Burrowes, Sam, that was brought from St. Xtophers, Cuthbert Fenwick, Richard Loe, William Fitter, John Robinson, Carp., William Brown, Stephen Gore, Stephen Sammon."

The order to lay out land for the above Cornwalleys was issued and recorded on page 94, September 9, 1639.

Again on page 244, Liber A. B. H., Land Warrants, the following proves that Cuthbert Fenwick did not come over in the *Ark*. In the year 1652 the same names are entered, viz.:

"A list of persons brought into the Province of Maryland at the cost and charges of me, Thomas Cornwalleys, Esq., since the first seating in Anno 1634, to this year, 1652, for which I demand land according to the conditions of Plantations from time to time; Anno 1634, transported in the *Ark* myself and 12 servants. By my partner Mr. John Sanders, who dying gave me that year, 5 servants. Brought the same year and exported from Virginia, four servants, viz: Cuthbert Fenwick, Christopher Martin, John Norton, Senior, John Norton, Junior, so in all that year, 2 and 20 persons, for which I was, by conditions of Plantations then set forth by the Lord Baltimore, to have for every 5 persons a mannor of 2,000 acres and 100 acres of Town land, and for the old persons 200 acres each. So there is due unto me the first year's account 8,800 acres."

Although the Land Warrants at Annapolis mention settlers "entered by Thomas Copley" in the years 1633. which naturally caused him to be accepted as a first settler, the fact that he remained in England until 1636, has just been discovered by the author, in the history of the "Early Jesuits in Maryland," by Rev. William P. Tracey, to whom we are also indebted for the names of "Father" Timothy Hayes, and "Brother" Thomas Gervaise, as first adventurers in the *Ark* and *Dove* expedition, included in the above list.

On December 5, 1633, Thomas Copley Gentleman, an alien, and a recusant, was given a warrant by the King "at our palace of Westminster," granting him freedom of action, in the performance of his occupation. This was nearly a month after the *Ark* and *Dove* had sailed. In 1636 Father Thomas Copley was, under the alias of Philip Fisher, appointed Superior of the Maryland Missions, in which year he came to the Province.

CHAPTER III

THE VOYAGE TO MARYLAND

THE following account was sent by Leonard Calvert on the return trip of the *Ark* to a friend in England. In referring to it he says: "This I have sent you was writ by a most honest and discreet gentleman, wherefore you may be confident of the truth of it."

It will be noted in this it is stated that they entered the "Potomac" River on March 3, leaving an interval of over three weeks before they landed at all.

From the reference he makes to the Indians being excited against them, and from the additional and more detailed account given by one of the gentleman adventurers of the 1,500 bowmen who, upon the appearance of the *Ark* and the *Dove*, swarmed to the shore, we can only conclude that the colonists were prevented from landing by the hostile Indians. This belief is borne out by the fact that after sailing about for so long a time they finally chose an island occupied only by wild heron as a safe spot for landing. Finding that this was not satisfactory nor conducive to the growth of the colony we learn that Governor Calvert went to make peace with the King of the Piscataways before attempting to settle on the mainland.

Hence it is quite evident that after bringing his party of adventurers across 3,000 miles of trackless sea it was no easy thing to plant the colony, and that he was for more than three weeks kept from taking possession of

LEONARD CALVERT, FIRST GOVERNOR OF MARYLAND

After rare original portrait owned by Mr. H. Mason Raborg of New York, shown through his courtesy

the land which was the Land of Promise to these weary travelers.

The account of the voyage which was evidently sent to Caecilius, second Lord Baltimore, by his brother, who had accompanied the first adventurers to Maryland is as follows:

"On St. Cecilius' day, the 22d of November, 1633, with a gentle northern gale, we set sale from the Cowes about 10 in the morninge toward the Needles, being rockes at the south end of Ile of Whight, till by default of winde we were forced to ankor at Yarmouth, which very kindly saluted us, howbeit we were not out of feare, for the seamen secretly reported that they expected the post with letters from the Counsell of London, but God would tende the matter and sent the night soe strong a faire winde as forced a French barke from her anker-hold, driving her foule upon our pinnace, forced her to set saile with losse of an ankor and take to sea, that being a dangerous place to floate in, whereby we were necessarily to follow, least we should part companie, and thus God fruŝtrated the plot of our seamen. This was the 23 of Novemb., on St. Clement's day, who wonne his crown by being cast into the sea fastened to an ankor. That morning by 10 o'clocke we came to Hurste Castle, and thence saluted with a shot, and soe passed the dangerous Needles, being certaine sharpe rockes at the end of the island, much feared by seamen for a double tyde which she carried to shipwrecke, one upon the rockes, tother upon the sand, so with our danger passed Yarmouth, where by dragging ankors in a strong winde and tide we almost runne our shipp aground. All this Saturday and the night following the winde served us so well that next day by 9 of clocke we got beyond the westerne cape of England and so steered along so strongly as we might because of our pinnace slow saileinge, whom we feared to leave behind for feare she might meet with Turkes or some other pirates, though we see nowe by this meanes a faire shipp of London overtook us of 600 tunne. Here we had a great recreation to see that shipp and ours runne for the same with all the clothe they could make an hower's space with faire winde and weather and pleasant sound of trumpets, but ours gave the other a topsaile and yet held with her. This done we stroke one course of our sailes and staied for our pinnace, which was farre short of us out of sight that evening. Soe all Sunday and Monday the 24th and 25th of November, we sailed afore the winde till night, when the winde changed to northwest so violent and tempestuous as the dragon was forced backe to ffamouth, not able to keep the sea, being yet not to goe southwest, but right south to Angola, and our pinnace mistrusting her strength came up to us to tell that if shee were in distress shee would shew two lights in her shroode, our master was a very sufficient seaman, and shipp as strong as could be, made of oake and iron; 400 tonne, King built; making faire weather in great stormes; now the master had his choise whether he would returne England as the draggon did on saile so close up to the winde, as if he should not hold it he must necessarily fall upon the Irish shoare, so infamous for rockes of greater danger—of these two out of a certaine hardiness and desire to trie the goodnesse of his shipp, in which he had never been at sea afore, he resolved to keep the sea, with great danger, wanting sea roome.

"The winde grew still louder and louder, making a

boysterous sea, and about midnight we espied our pinnace with her two lights, as she had forewarned us in the shroode, from which time till six weeks we never see her more, thinkeing she shall assuredly beene foundered and lost in those huge seas, but it happened otherwise, for before she came to the Irish channell, where we were now tossinge, she returned for England, and entered into the Scilley Isles, whence afterward in the dragons Company shee came to the long reach and Canarie Isles. God findeing a convenient guard for that small vessel, this night thus frightfull being past, the winde came about to Southwest full against us, though not very stronge, so that with many tackes about we scarce crept on our way, soe all 26, 27 and 28 days the winde altered little. On the 29th the winde were all day a gathering and toward night poured forth such a sea of winde as if they would have blowen our shipp under water at every blast; all next day beinge the blessed Apostle St. Andrewe's day, the like cloude gathered in fearful manner terrible to the beholders, so that ere it began to blow it seemed all the sprightes and witches of Maryland were now set in battaill array against us. This evning the master saw the sunne fish to swimme against the sunne's course, a thing evidently shewing fearful stormes to come. About 10 in the night a blacke cloud shede a pitiful shower upon us, and presently such a furious winde followed as wee were able to beare noe cloath at all, and yet before we could take in our maine course which we only carried a furious impression of winde suddently came and splitt it from top to tone, and cast one part of it into the sea. This amazed the stoutest heart, even of the sailurs, who confessed they had seene ships cast away with lesse violence of weather; all the

Catholiques fell to praier, confessions and vowes, and then the helme being bound up and ship left without sail or gouvernment to the windes and waves floated at hull like a dish till God were pleased to take pittie upon her: Thus we were in fear of imminent death all this night, never looking to see day in this world, till at length it pleased God to send some ease and by little and little still more, till we were with mild weather freed from all those horrors.

"This delivery in a manner assured us of God's mercy toward us, and those infidells conversions of Maryland his holy goodness be forever praised. Amen. From this time to our journey's end, about three months, we had not one houre of bad weather, but so proprous a nauvigation as our mariners never saw so sweet a passage; when I say three months I meane not we were so long at sea, but reckon the time spent at Barbadoes and St. Christopher's, for we were at sea only seven weeks and two daies, which is held a speedy passage."

After reciting several exciting experiences in meeting ships which they invariably believed to be filled with "Turkes," he describes their trip through the tropics, and the celebration of Christmas Day on board the *Ark*. Finding their provisions short, "we altered againe our course at St. Christopher's" continues the narrator, "and soe began to think at what season we were like to come to Maryland, and how we should secure our seed corne, as for Virginia we expected little from them but blows, although we carried the King's letters to their Governour, and the Governour himself much esteemed and loved my Lord, yet wee feared he could or would be overawed by his Councell; as for the salvages we expected to find them as our English ill-wishers would make them, and therefore affraid to build all the weale of our plantation on priced adventures, resolution was made for the Barbadoes, the granaries of the Charybbies Isles, which howbeit it was somewhat about for corne, was the surest course. In this island Mr. Hierom Hawley his brother was Gouvernour, and in his absence Mr. Acers, his brother-in-law, was deputie. Here we arrived Januar the 3 hopinge for some refreshing by convenient good dyet some few days, but in part we were deceived, for everything bore so high price that nothing could be had but it cost us our eies, a pigge six weeks old was at 5s. sterling, a turke, 50s., and a chicken at 6s. Beefe or mutton they have noe, and the inhabitants live wholy upon poane, that Indian bread. * * * The Governour told us at first corn was at 1s. the bushell but understanding that we came for corne, he called a Cousnell and decreed there should none be sould us under 2s. a bushel, and soe we found him a kinde kinsman of Mr. Hawleyes!" The adventurers had other equally disconcerting experiences, the most thrilling of which can best be told by the narrator.

"The very day we arrived (at Barbadoes) we found the island all in armes to the number of about 800 men. The servants of the island had conspired to kill their masters and make themselves free, and then handsomely to take the first ship that came and soe goe to sea. This first ship was ours, and, therefore, it was the goodnesse of God to discover the treason by a servant who was afraid to joine in the plott with them. . . . God be praised for this our deliverance." Omitting the stop at St. Christophers', "We came to Virginia February 27 much contrary to my Lord's instructions, we expected here every houre to be staied by Councell, desiring noethinge more than our ruine. At this time Captaine Clabourne was there, from whom we understood the Indians were all in armes to resist us, haveing heard that 6 Spanish ships were a comeinge to destroy them all, the rumour was most like to have begunne from himselfe. We had the King's letters, and my Lord treasures to the Governour, which made him shew to us the best usage the place afforded, with promise to furnish us with all manner of Provisions for our plantation, though much against his Councell's will. . . . . Here we staied 8 or 9 daies, not without imminent danger, under commande of the castle, and then on the 3 of March came into Chesapeake bay, at the mouth of Potomocke. This baye is the most delightfull water I ever saw between two sweet landes, with a channell 4, 5, 6, 7 and 8 fathom deepe, some 11 leagues broad, at time of years full of fish, yet it doth yield to Potomecke, which we have named St. Gregories. This is the sweetest and greatest river I have seene, so that the Thames is but a little finger to it. There are no marshes or swamps about it, but solid, firme ground, with great variety of wood, not choaked up with undershrubs, but commonly so farre distant from each other as a coach and fouer horses may travele without molestation.

"At our comeinge we found (as we were told) all in armes. The King of Pascatoway had drawne together 500 bowmen (one of the adventurers said 1,500); great fires were made by night all over the country, and the biggeness of our ship made the natives reporte we came in a canow as bigg as an island, with so many men as trees were in a wood, with great terror unto them all. Thus we sailed some 20 leagues up the river to Herne Island, so called for infinite swarmes of herenes thereon; this we called St. Clement's. Here we first came ashore; here by the overturning of a shallop which we had allmost lost our mades, which we brought along, the linnen they went to wash, was much of it lost, which is no small matter in these parts. . . . . In this place on our b. Ladies day in lent we first offered, erected a crosse, and with devotion tooke solemme possession of the country. Here our Governor was advised not to seate himself till he spoke with the Emperour of Pascatoway, and told him the cause of his comeing, to witt, to teach them a divine doctrine, whereby to lead them to Heaven, and to enrich with such ornaments of civil life as our owne country abounded, withall not doubting but this emperour beinge satisfied the other kings would be more peaceable. With this intention he tooke our pinnace and went there in higher up the river; in their way they found still all the Indians fleede from their houses, till comeing to Patomecke towne he found the king thereof a childe, governed by Archihoe, his uncle. Here by an interpretour, they had some speech with Archihoe, a grave and considerate man, and shewed his errours in part unto him, which he seemed to acknowledge, bidding them all very welcome, being of a very lovinge and kind nature. From here they went to Pascatoway, the seat of the Emperour, where 500 bowmen came to meet them at the waterside. Here the Emperour lesse feareing than the rest, came privately on board where he found kind usage, and perceiving we came with good meaneinge toward them, gave leave to us to sett downe where we pleased; the king being aboard his men by the water side feared some treason till by interpretours we assured them otherwise. Whilest the Governor was abroad the Indians began to loose feare and came to our coart of guarde and sometimes aboard our shipp, wondering where that tree should grow out of which so great a canow should be hewen, supposing it all of one peece, as their canowse use to be. . . .

"The Governor being returned from Pascatoway by Fleet's direction, we came some 9 or 10 leagues lower in the river Patomecke to a lesser river on the north side of it as bigge as Thames, which we call St. George's. This river makes 2 excellent bayes, wherein might harbour 300 saile of 1000 tunne apiece with very great safeties, the one called St. George's bay, the other more inward St. Maries. On one side of this river lives the King Yoacomaco, on the other our plantation is seated about halfe a mile from the water, and our towne we call St. Maries. To avoid all occasion of dislike and colour of wrong we bought the space of thirtie miles of ground for axes, hoes, cloth and hatchets, which we call Augusto Carolino. It made them more willing to entertaine us, for that they had warres with the Sasquasahannockos, who come sometimes upon them and waste and spoil their country, for thus they hope by our means to be safe.

"God disposeing things thus for those which were to come to bring the light of His holy law to these distressed poore infidels, so that they doe indeed like us better for coming so well provided assuring themselves of greater safety by liveing by us.

"Is not this miraculous that a nation a few daise before in generale armes against us and our enterprise, should like lambs, yield themselves, glad of our company, giveing us houses, lands and liveings for a trifle Digitus dei est hic, and some great good is meant toward this people."

CHAPTER IV

CHRISTMAS ON THE "ARK," A.D. 1633

> God rest you, merry gentlemen;
> Let nothing you dismay,
> For Jesus Christ our Saviour
> Was born upon this day.

THE first Christmas mentioned in connection with the early Maryland settlers was the one spent en route abroad the *Ark*, when we learn from one of the party that "on Christmas Day, wine being given on the *Ark*, for the celebrity of the day, it was so immoderately taken that the next day 30 sickened of fevers and whereof about a dozen died afterward."

By this we see that the "wassail bowl" of the merry English Christmas was not forgotten by the adventurous subjects of King Charles I.

During the reign of this monarch Christmas was kept with great splendor and the zenith of mirth and festivities was reached. The master of the revels was no unimportant personage at the court. The King and Queen took part in the plays and masks which constituted an important part of the entertainment.

In 1634 "Cymbeline" was performed before the court at this season and was well received, while during the reign of James I several of Shakespeare's plays were acted for the first time at the Christmas festivities before the King and his courtiers. Among these were

"Measure for Measure," "The Plaie of Errors," "King Lear" and "Love's Labor Lost."

At the very period that Maryland was first settled England was making Christmas the merriest season of the year. The King directed his noblemen and gentry to return to their landed estates and to keep up the hospitality during the period of festivity—and what the king directed for his rural gentry in England was transmitted to his subjects across the seas. Hence in Provincial Maryland as well as in old England, the great halls of the lords of the manors and of the other great houses were decked in holly and rosemary in honor of the season, the servants and other dependents were given holiday and their mirth and frolicking in the great hall was a part of every Christmas gathering. From the dimensions of the Colonial fireplace, which yawned nearly halfway across the room, it is quite certain that the yule log in Maryland, as in England, was the center of the Christmas fun. The young folk, knowing that the festivities were to be continued as long as the Christmas block, or yule log, lasted, selected a great gnarled stump of an oak tree, often grotesquely marked. This was dragged amid much merriment and rejoicing into the hall and placed on the hearth. Each one of the family sat down on the log in turn, and after singing a yule song drank to a merry Christmas and a happy New Year.

The log was then put in place ready for the Christmas lighting. Once lighted the fire was not allowed to go out, nor the fun and good cheer to diminish until the yule log was burnt out with the exception of a small piece, which was always saved to start the next year's yuletide fire.

While the logs crackled in the hall the Lords kept open house—beef, beer and bread were free to all comers. Among the pleasures provided we find "a noyse of minestrells and a Lincolnshire bagpipe were prepared— the minstrells for the great Chamber, the bagpipe for the hall, the minstrells to serve up the knights' meate and the bagpipe for the common dancing."

During the revelries at the English Court, King Charles I found gambling his favorite diversion, and thousands of pounds changed hands at the Christmastide under this monarch and the custom continued to be a kingly one till the reign of George III. In contrast to the hilarious first Christmas of the Maryland adventurers that of the Puritans in New England is peculiarly barren. Their history tells of their arrival on Christmas Day on the bleak New England coast, of the day's work toward building a house and the utter disregard of the day as a holiday.

Our friends, the Dutch of Manhattan, we are told, bore the image of St. Nicholas, on the prow of the first ship in which they emigrated to that island, and this friend of children was called the patron-saint of their infant city.

Our little English children frolicking in the great halls of Maryland's manor houses knew none of the delights of Santa Claus and the mysterious sleigh when its eight tiny reindeer and never lessening load of toys until the Dutch of New Amsterdam who came into the province brought their pretty legends and quaint customs with them.

Old Governor Stuyvesant while endorsing the observance of the Christmas season, frowned upon some of the "heathenish practices" of the time, and emphatically refused to allow the young folk to "ride the goose" at the annual feast. The Board of Burgomasters in 1654 ordered that "as the winter holidays are at hand there shall be no more ordinary meetings of this board between this date, December 14th, and three weeks after Christmas. The court messenger is ordered not to summon anyone in the meantime."

The typical merry Christmas, with its lavish hospitality its boar's head, wassail bowl, plum pudding and general feasting and jollity continued in England, and hence in Maryland until the year 1641–42, when the King's troubles with Parliament began and the Puritans made the attempt to abolish Christmas as a festival, and passed their first ordinance to suppress the performance of plays. Next ministers were forbidden to preach on the Nativity, and in June, 1647, Parliament abolished the observance of saint's days and the three grand festivals, Christmas, Easter and Whitsuntide—"any law, statute, custom, constitution or canon to the contrary in anywise notwithstanding." The King protested, but was answered.

In London much resistance was made to the new law. but might prevailed, and for twelve years the observance of Christmas ceased as a holiday.

Upon the restoration of King Charles II the festival and sacred observance of Christmas were resumed, but it is said that court revels never attained to their former splendor.

In Maryland, with the increase of population and of wealth, the pleasures of life were more and more enjoyed on the large plantations. The abundance of holly and cedar in every planter's woods enabled his young folk to adorn the home with lavish hand.

The mistletoe here, as in England, still found at the top of decaying oak trees, was the cause of much innocent merriment in Colonial mansions when Christmas decked the halls. These were the ideal Christmas times! The great house gathered beneath its wide-spreading roof all the scattered younger family branches at the Christmastide, when the feasting was a wonder to behold, quite rivaling that in the mother country, when thirty-two courses are said to have been the order of the day! And the spirit of the Yuletide was

> "Heap on the wood, the night is chill,
> But let it whistle as it will,
> We'll keep our Christmas merry still."

CHAPTER V

LEONARD CALVERT'S FIRST LETTER FROM MARYLAND

RECENT investigation has brought out fuller knowledge of the early days in Maryland—days full of adventure and industry to the newcomers. For the first time the general reader is to be given the opportunity of perusing Leonard Calvert's own account of his arrival in Maryland through his letters sent to Sir Richard Lechford of Shellwood, in the County of Surrey, Knight.

These personal communications in a most unexpected way were brought back to Maryland after an interval of nearly three centuries, and, together with abstracts of certain other letters to Caecelius Calvert sent by the gentlemen adventurers who accompanied the Lieutenant-Governor on the expedition, are full of human interest. All of these were forwarded to London on the return voyage of the *Ark*, just one month after her arrival in Maryland, in 1634, and the experiences related throw valuable and interesting side lights on the pioneer days in the province, when the red man, gorgeous in paint and feathers, was king of the forest. This "war paint," which we have supposed was always a sign of ferocity, we are told by this first Calvert was used by the Indians as a means of defense against gnats.

In his letter, dated at Point Comfort, May 30, 1634, Leonard Calvert recites how they stopped at Virginia to land some passengers there and to deliver the letters from the King to the Governor and Council, after which

Leonard Calvert

Henry Fleet

Thomas Cornwallis

Richard Duke

Jerome Hawley

Thomas Copley

John Medcalfe

John Langford

Josias Fendall

Giles Brent

Thomas Gerrard

James Neale

Cuthbert Fenwick

John Lewger, Secretary

George Evelin

Marmaduke Snow

Benjamin Gill

Edward Hill

RARE AUTOGRAPHS FROM THE AUTHOR'S COLLECTION
OF SOME FIRST ADVENTURERS, AND OTHER
EARLY SETTLERS

"we sayled for Maryland, the country wee so long looked for, in which we made choyse of the most southerly river to set down in, and (as I have found it) the fairest, beeing 7 or 8 leagues broad at the mouth, affordinge a deep channell from side to side, the land being high and free from swamps and marshes, growne over with large timber trees, and not choked up with any under shrubs, but so clear as a coach may without hindrance pass all over the country."

"At our first arrival," he continues in his letter to Sir Richard, "the Indians being astonished at the sight of so great a cannow, as they termed it, and at the number of people they imagined those to be which were heaped upon the decks, they raysed all the nations throughout the river, making from towne to towne, by which they made a general alarm as if they intended to summon all the Indians of America against us.

"This," he confides to his partner, "happened more by the ill reporte our enemies of Virginia had prepossessed them with, of our cominge to their countrye, with intention to destroy them all and take from them their country, than by any real injuries they had received from us."

Realizing the necessity of making peace with the natives, Leonard Calvert took the matter in his own hands and proved himself a man of no small courage, for which the object of showing his good intentions "and withall to view all parts of this fair river, so as to be able to make some good choice of a seat for our colony, I sailed our pinnace almost to the head of the said river, where the Emperour of Pascatoway did reside, to whom, after I had declared my good intentions in comeinge to these parts, I settled a firm peace with him, arid likewise obtained leave from him to make use of what place I would chuse for myselfe and our company to sett downe in. This done, I returned to the place where I left the great ship at anchor, viewing many parts of the shoare on each side of the river by the way, in all which tract I could not find what I most looked for, to wit, some field cleered and left by the Indians."

Passing more toward the mouth of the river, he says he found "a most convenient harbour and pleasant country lying on each side of it, with many large fields of excellent land."

"On each side of it we have seated ourselves, within one-halfe mile of the river, within a pallizado of 120 yards square, with four flankes. We have mounted one piece of ordnance and placed six murderers in parts most convenient, a fortification we think sufficient to defend against any such weake enemies as we have reason to expect here."

In this letter to his partner, who had entered with Calvert upon "an adventure of £400 13s 8d, lawful money of England, upon a voyage to be made by the said Leonard Calvert and others, etc., the said Sir Richard Lechford having put in one-fourth of the adventure," Leonard Calvert reports the first investment in Maryland of the money confided to him.

"While we were doinge these things ashore, our pinnace by our direction followed the trade of beaver thorow all parts of the precincts of this province, but by reason of our so late arrival here we came too late for the first part of the trade this year, which is the reason I have sent home so few furs (they beinge all dealt for by those of Virginia before our coming. The second part of our trade is now in hand, and is like to prove very beneficiall. The nation we trade with all at this time a yeare is called the Massawomeckes. We have lost by our late coming 3,000 skins, which others of Virginia have traded for."

In one of the letters written by a gentleman adventurer an interesting account is given of the "Solemnitie of carrying our colours on shore when the King of the Patuxent accompanying us was much taken with the ceremony.

"But the same night the *Arke's* great gunnes, to honor the day, spake aloud, which the King of the Patuxent hearing with great admiration, counseled his friends, the Yoacomoco Indians to be careful that they break not their peace with us, and said: 'When wee shoote, our Bow strings giue a twang that's heard but a little way off. But doe you not heare what cracks their Bow strings giue?' "

We have read in some of the histories that the Indians gave up their houses in part to Leonard Calvert and his company, but it has remained for one of those who partook of the red man's hospitality to describe them as "all built in a long ovall, nine or teene foote high to the middle top, where, as in ancient Temples, the light is admitted by a window halfe a yarde square, which window is also the chimney, which giveth passage to the smoke, the fire being made in the middle of the floor (as in our old halls of England), and about it they used to lie."

Remembering that the settlers had been in Maryland but a month, it is surprising to read: "Wee have planted since we came as much maize (or Indian wheat) as will suffice (if God prosper it) much more company than we have. It is up knee high above the ground all ready and wee expect return of 1000 for one, as we have reason for our hope from the experience of the yeelde in other parts of this countrey, as is very credibly related to us."

Doubtful as this yield appears to us, we cease to wonder when reading a little further on that the virgin soil is composed of "a black moulde a foote deepe, and then comes after red earth."

Alsop, writing of Maryland a few years later for the instruction of his friends in England, says: "All sorts of grain as wheat, rye, barley, oats, peas, besides several others that bore their original and birth from the fertile womb of this land [and nowhere else] they all grow, increase and thrive here in Maryland without the chargeable and laborious manuring of the land with dung, increasing in such a measure and plenty by the natural richness of the earth, with the common beneficial and convenient showers of rain that usually wait on the several fields of grain [by a natural instinct] so that famine [the dreadful ghost of penury and want] is never known with his pale visage to haunt the dominions of Maryland."

The letter which Leonard Calvert left for the Governor of Virginia from his Majesty the King caused that gentleman to welcome the settlers by an early visit, and to give them "as noble usage as the place afforded, with promise that for their cattle and hogges, corne and poultry our plantation should not want the open way to furnish ourselves from thence."

Disappointing as it may be to many who have treasured the tradition of bricks imported from England, these letters, written a few weeks after the landing at St. Mary's, inform us as well as they did Cæcilius Calvert nearly 270 years ago that "Governor Harvie told us that when his lordship should be resolved on a convient place to make himself a seat he should be able to provide him with as much brike and tile as he should have occasion to imploy until his lordship had made his own."

The next year, in the account of the plantation, the Proprietary says: "We have a loam which makes as fine bricks as any in England."

After this no one can hope to have any thoughtful person believe that bricks were ever "imported from England" to build the great old mansions and churches of Colonial days, when the little caravels had their capacity more than taxed in bringing over settlers and their household necessities.

CHAPTER VI

GOODS BROUGHT BY FIRST SETTLERS

WHILE we have known, of course, that the first settlers had to bring with them all the necessities of life, we have never known in detail what was brought, nor does it seem possible that the *Ark* and and *Dove* could carry the adventurers themselves and all of the provisions necessary for so tedious a voyage and the beginnings of life in an unfamiliar country, even though one of the party speaks of the *Ark* as our "great ship, as strong as could be made of oak and iron, 400 tonne—King built, making fair weather in great storms!"

We knew that they brought a barge in sections, which was put together after their arrival, but it is due entirely to a most unexpected find that we are privileged to know what were considered necessities in those days, and after reading the list we cannot but believe that Caecilius Calvert held the doctrine of the younger Motley that the luxuries are more essential than the necessities of life!

We must not forget, however, that Lord Baltimore and the gentlemen of his set belonged to the gay court circle of the reign of Charles I.

The following is the inventory of the articles to be brought over by each adventurer, issued by Cæcilius Calvert at London:

"A note for adventurer's memory of such things as he may carry with him either for his own better accommodation on ship-board, or for some time after his arrival in Maryland, or for trade, according to his abilitie:

"Fine wheat flour close and well packed to make puddings. Claret wine burnt. Canary sack, confernes, marmalades, suckers and spices, sallet oyle, prunes to stew, live poultry, rice, butter, Holland cheese, porke, dried meat tongues, beefe packed up in vinegar, some weather sheep, meats baked in earthen pots, leggs of mutton minced and stewed and close packed up in tried sewet or butter in earthen pots; juice of limons, etc."

Another list called "Provision for Adventurer's House" is as follows: "Iron and locks and hinges and bolts, etc., mustard seed, glasse and lead, for his windowes, mault for beere, a Hogshead of beefe or porke, two or three firkins of butter, a hundred or two of old cheeses, a gallon of honey, soap and candles, iron wedges, porkes, for rennet to make cheese—a good mastiffe, etc."

None could doubt that a man prepared the above memoranda, which run so largely to cheeses and sack—and mixed "sallet oyle" (salad oil) with live poultry and soap, and candles with a gallon of honey.

The Lord Baltimore is more in his element when giving directions as to the necessary provisions for fishing and fowling to the gentlemen adventurers. These he declares are "necessaries for a boat of 3 or 4 tunne, spokes, nayles, pitch, tarre, acorne, canvis for a sayle, ropes, anchor, iron for ruther, fishing lines for cod and mackrills, cod hookes and mackrill hookes, a sceane of basse net, herring netts, leade fowling pieces of sixe-foote, powder and shott and flint stones—a good water spaniel," etc.

Accompanying the directions for the gentlemen adventurers' supplies we find also "A particular of such necessary provisions as every adventurer must carry, according to the number of his servants."

	£.	s.	d.
2 bus. of oates	0	9	0
8 bus. of meale	2	8	0
1 bus. of pease	0	4	0
1 gal. of oyle	0	3	6
2 gal. vinegar	0	2	0
1 gal. of aqua vita	0	2	6
1 bus. of Bay salt	0	2	0
In sugar, spices and fruit	0	6	8
Total	3	17	8
In apparel for one man:			
3 Munmoth caps or hats	0	4	0
3 falling bands	0	1	3
3 shirts	0	7	6
1 waistcoate	0	2	2
1 suit of canvas	0	7	6
1 suit of frieze	0	10	0
1 suit of cloth	0	16	0
1 coarse cloth or frieze coate	0	15	0
3 paire of stockings	0	4	0
6 paire of shoes	0	13	0
Inkle for gaiters	0	0	2
One dozen points	0	0	2
Total	4	0	10
Beddings for two men:			
1 paire canvas sheets	0	16	0
7 ells of canvas to make bed and bolster to be filled in the country	0	8	0
5 ells of canvas to make a bed at see filled with straw	0	6	6
Course rug at sea	0	6	0
Total	2	2	0

One man's part one-half
  In arms:
    1 musket..............................1   0   0
    10 lbs. powder........................0   11   0
    40 lbs. lead, bullets, pistol and gross shot
        of each sort some.................0   5   0
    1 sword...............................0   5   0
    1 belt................................0   1   0
    1 bandeleere and flaske...............0   2   0
    In match..............................1   2   6
                                          —   —   —
        Total.............................2   5   6

In addition to these are lists of tools and household implements for the servants, all which in the aggregate must have taxed to the utmost the small ships of that day. The inventories from which the foregoing were taken were issued by his Lordship in the year 1635 for the information of other adventurers who wished to join those who had already gone. From the nature of their contents they bear evidence that they were prepared for those who came in the *Ark* and the *Dove,* for Cæcilius Calvert knew only too well that the natural products of Maryland and the successful planting of the first settlers made it unnecessary to carry over peas, beans, butter or meat a year after settlement.

The internal evidence, therefore, makes clear to us that these were the provisions brought over on the first voyage by the adventurers.

CHAPTER VII

AN ANCIENT BILL OF LADING

A QUAINTLY interesting bill of lading for the better securing of the goods transported by every adventurer in the *Ark* and the *Dove* and the later outgoing ships for Maryland reads: "Shipped by the grace of God in good order and well conditioned by—in and upon the good ship—called——,whereof ——is master under God for this present voyage and now riding at anchor in the harbor of ——and bound for——to stay, being marked and numbered as in the margent, and are to be delivered in like good order and well conditioned, at the port of St. Maries, in Maryland, the danger of the seas only excepted unto—— or his assigns, paying freight for the said goods, with primage and average accustomed, in witness whereof the Master or Purser of the said ship hath affirmed to three bills of lading, all of this tenure and date, the one of which three bills being accomplished, the other two stand void. And so God send the good ship to her desired Port in safety. Amen."

Thus reverently did our forefathers consign their material comforts and necessities to the dangers of the sea!

We have seen what each adventurer was required to bring for each man transported and also learned that the cost of each so-called servant in passage and provisions amounted to 20 pounds sterling, or about $100 in our money. Therefore it is especially interesting to find "a computation of a servant's labour and the profit that may rise by it, by instance in some particulars which may be put in practice the first year."

"One man may at this season," writes the Lord Baltimore, "plant so much corne as ordinarily yields of wheate 100 bushels' worth upon the place at 2 shillings a bushel £10. Of beanes and pease, 20 bushels worth at 3 shillings a bushel £3. The same man will plant tobacco bebetween 800 and 1,000 weight, which, at lowest rate, £2 the 100, is worth £20. He may also in the same year in winter make 4,000 pipe staves, worth upon the place £4 per 1,000, besides all his other labour in building, fencing. clearing ground, raising of cattle and gardening. Or if a man's labour be employed in hempe and flaxe it will yield him as much profit as tobacco at this rate. So in many other commodities whereof this country is capable."

Not only does the Proprietary set forth all these advantages to such as have the means of transporting ablebodied young men without money desiring to emigrate, but also in the most coldly calculating way calls their attention to the fact that as the charge for bringing over a servant is expended most in provisions, in case the servant die by the way or shortly after his coming thither the goods being sold in the country will return all his charge with advantage!

It is not surprising that men of wealth availed themselves of the opportunity to increase their fortunes by transporting others into the Province, where by the "Conditions of Plantations" they secured 1,000 acres of land for every five men between the ages of 16 and 50 years, each man being provided in all things necessary for a plantation, "this 1,000 acres of English measure to be erected into a manor and be conveyed to him and his heirs and assigns forever, with all such royalties and privileges as are usually belonging to manors in England."

To the person transporting less than five men 100 acres were allowed for himself and each servant.

A married man who brought over his wife and children received 100 acres each for himself and wife and 50 acres for each child.

Any woman transporting herself and children under the age of 6 years had the same conditions offered her. For every woman servant brought into the Province 60 acres of land were allowed her master.

It is easy enough to see what a paying investment it was to transport the young men seeking a chance in the new country. For every £20 paid out in charges for a servant the adventurer received, it was estimated, £49 each year, and as each man was indentured for at least four years, at the expiration of his term of service he had earned for his master not only £196 by his planting, etc., but had labored in the ways previously described, besides adding 100 acres of land to the possession of the liege lord.

The latter, on the other hand, was required not only to pay the passages of each man servant, but to find him meat, drink, apparel and lodging, with other necessaries, during the said term, but at the end of his indenture must give him a whole year's provision in corn and 50 acres of land, according to the custom of the country; and later the law included "three suites of apparel, with things necessary to them and tools to work withall, so that they are no sooner free but they are ready to set up for themselves."

CHARLES CALVERT, THIRD LORD BALTIMORE

Original portrait in England from the Author's Collection

Passing over the interesting question of the status and condition of the indentured servant in Colonial days, let us see what the first settlers found here in natural commodities when they began to explore the virgin forests of Maryland.

In the account of the successful planting of the colony, published by the Lord Proprietary in 1635, but written about six months after the first settlement, we are told:

"The temper of the ayre is very good and agrees well with the English, as appeared at their first coming, when they had no houses to shelter them and their people were enforced, not only to labor in the day, but to watch in their turns at night, yet had their healths exceeding well. The timber of these parts is very good and in abundance; it is useful for building houses and shippes. The white oak is good for pipe staves and the read oak for wainscot. There is also walnut, cedar, pine and cipresse, chestnut, elme, ashe and poplar—all which are for building and husbandry. Also there are divers sorts of fruit trees and mulberries; persimmons, with several kind of plummes, and vines in great abundance. The mast and the chestnuts and what rootes they find in the woods doe feed the swine very fat and such as is not inferior to the bacon of Westphalia. Of strawberries there is plenty, which are ripe in April, mulberries in May, raspberries in June, maracocks, which is somewhat like a limon, are ripe in August. In the spring are several sorts of herbs as corn-sallet, violets, sorrell, purslaine—all of which are very good and wholesome and by the English used for sallets and in broth."

What could be more interesting than to know that the first Colonial Dames of Maryland were so daintly aesthetic as to eat spring violets in their broth—or served up a salad of violets with the "sallet oyle" and "cheeses" upon which his Lordship laid such stress in the "list of necessities for the adventurers."

They found the country well stored with corn; they also brought with them some Indian corn from the Barbadoes, which in their first arrival they began to use, thinking fit to save their English provisions of meal and oatmeal. And the Indian women seeing their servants to be unacquainted with the manner of dressing it, would make bread thereof for them, "also a meale which they call omene; it's like our furmety, and is very savory and wholesome. It (meaning the corn) will malt and make good beree."

These accounts of the cornbread and hominy (omene) introduced to the English settlers by the Indian women disproves the general impression that the negroes first knew the art of making cornpone! To all true Marylanders it is delightful to find that we are yet purely Colonial in many of our ideas and customs, and particularly on the Eastern Shore, where today no truer evidences of cordial hospitality and welcome can be extended the visitor than the cornpone and hominy which over two centuries and a half ago were in the same spirit of loving welcome prepared for the newcomers by the dwellers in Arcadia.

CHAPTER VIII

COLONIAL LIFE AND ARISTOCRACY

WHEN King Charles I declared it his purpose to "more eminently distinguish Maryland above all other regions in America," and "to decorate it with more ample titles" by erecting it into a province, with all the royal rights and privileges of the Palatinate of Durham—we have reason to believe that he knew what he was about.

His majesty, by his royal gifts and privileges, had transplanted a little kingdom across the sea. The younger sons of the principal Secretary of State, under King James I were naturally a part of the court circle under Charles I and, accustomed as they were to the luxurious life of the English court at the zenith of the decadent splendor preceding its overthrow, had no thought of taking vows of renunciation, when, as representatives of the Lord Baltimore, they set forth for a new and fertile land, in which they were to reign supreme.

And we have reason to believe that a right gallant company of Cavaliers followed in their train, and soon changed the primeval forest into a mimic rural England.

Manor houses with outstretched wings were built to gather under their sheltering roofs the dozen or more little ones who usually came to break the stillness of the quiet days in that far-off time, when there was more of maternity than nervous energy in the world. The days before the club woman was evolved from the childless home and empty-handed mother.

In the Colonial days every mother was practically a club president—the home club composed of her growing family on the one hand, and her dependent servants on the other, left her no time for improving civic conditions. And be it remembered there were practically no civics to improve.

True to the habits and traditions of the mother country the early gentry lived in the heart of their vast possessions, which gave them the seclusion and power so dear to the Briton. These had imported not only the language, manners and legends of the English court life, but had brought over their hounds and hunters, their mahogany and plate, and other evidences of luxurious living, when the Provincial Government had become firmly established. Towns did not flourish in the early days and the manors and large plantations were the centers of the social life.

The Colonial mansions of ample dimensions which have survived stand as monuments to the hospitality so graciously dispensed in the day when family coaches filled with merry young folks, accompanied by attendant cavaliers on horseback came unbidden and remained for weeks—"the days when the music of horns and the bay of hounds were often the first intimation to a hostess that the house was soon to be filled to overflowing with the pleasure-seekers already crossing her husband's preserves." These were the days when the lords of the manor were privileged to exercise the rights of Court Baron and Leet in true lordly style.

Every woman in Colonial days could sit a horse as firmly as she could a rocking chair, as the quickest and easiest mode of travel was through the bridle paths.

Many a high-bred dame also rode to hounds with all the daring of her brother, the squire or lord of the manor, and, doffing habit, top hat and top boots, presided at her father's well-spread mahogany with the grace of one "to the manner born."

The wills of the early Colonial period give us not only glimpses of the wardrobe of a lady of that time, but throw charming sidelights on the furnishings of a Colonial home. In a typical will of a Colonial lady who died about 1665 she leaves her taffeta suit and serge coat to her stepdaughter, Teresa; also all her fine linen, her hoods and scarfs, except the great one, and her three petticoats, the tufted Holland one, the new serge and the spangled one. To her three boys she leaves "that great scarf" and all her jewels, plate and rings, except her wedding ring, which goes to Teresa. To Thomas, the Indian servant, two pairs of shoes and a match coat. To her two stepsons she leaves an ell of "taffeta."

Just what a yard and a quarter of silk was to two boys does not appear at this writing, but no doubt it had its uses to the young "macaronies" of that day.

This piece of silk reminds me of a roll of 12 yards of figured "taffeta" which has descended from one of the Colonial dames of "Myrtle Grove," Talbot county, to a no less charming and witty descendant in Cambridge.

At a loan exhibition of Colonial relics this exquisite roll of embroidered white silk was noticed by a visitor in town from Virginia.

"My!" quoth this lady of the Old Dominion to a bystander, "I wonder why this piece of silk is exhibited. My great-grandmother used to wear such as that every day!" "But my great-great-grandmother was above wearing it at all, you see," replied the fiery young aristocrat who had lent it, "since she never had it made up for every day even." She was very young and very proud of her roll of silk! In numerous wills of the Colonial gentry we find bequests of nails, brass kettles and other household utensils, along with "the plate in the house," that "came this year out of England." Occasionally we find a coat-of-arms willed to some member of the family, a "silver seal to my son," etc.

In the days when gentlemen wore white hair wigs of such flowing proportions that they were obliged to carry their cocked, gold-laced hats under their arms, they willed these costly importations with other personalities.

Indeed, as late as the nineteenth century a Baltimore gentleman of the old school bequeathed his red-hair wig and false teeth to his faithful old black body servant, who it is said proudly arrayed himself in these memorial tokens of his deceased master and wore them ever after!

CHAPTER IX

A GLIMPSE THROUGH COLONIAL DOORWAYS

THAT Caecilius Calvert, second Lord Baltimore, wished to emphasize class distinction in Colonial Maryland is evident from his instructions to his son, "that you seriously take into your consideration to finde and speedily to propose unto us some convenient way of and for making of some visible distinction and distinctions between you, our lieutenant-general, our chancellor, principal secretary, general officers, councillors, judges and justices *and the rest of the people of the said province*, either by the wearing of habits, medals or otherwise."

That this command of the Lord Proprietary was carried out we have no reason to doubt, but just what form of distinction the officers of this mimic English court disported themselves in, has not yet been brought to light.

The early inventories, however, make clear to us that the picturesque costume of the time of King Charles I was worn by those who were near to Lord Baltimore's little throne in his palatinate of Maryland. Here we find our lordly esquires in gold-banded hats, with drooping plumes, the plushed-lined coat and embroidered belt, the falchion and the rapier, lace cuffs and silken hose and garters of like richness. Signet rings adorned the white hands of the gentry and mourning rings were favorite mementoes left to friends in their early wills. Not only have these descended in many families, but one from

King Charles himself is still preserved by a descendant of one of his favorites. In the inventory of Capt. Robert Wintour, 1638, one of the twenty gentlemen adventurers who came with Leonard Calvert, we find the plush-lined "short coate" or doublet, the silver belt, laced band, gold ring and other evidences of the richness of the cavalier "habit."

The apparel of the ladies of the early Colonial period was equally rich, and all imported from London.

Then, as now, "spangled" lace was the height of fashion, brocade and velvets, dimities and silks all helped to add to the charms of the high-bred Colonial dames.

Here were daughters of English lords who presided as mistresses of the stately mansions which were reared in the centers of the great manor lands in St. Mary's County.

A retrospective glimpse through these Colonial doorways shows us the great halls, with sweeping stairways, wainscoted walls and hand-carved finishings. The dining-room, which then as now gave the keynote of the family life, was a reflex of the great English manor houses. The large open fireplace and the inglenook and corner cupboard were all there. On the high mahogany sideboards, which usually extended down two sides of the room, were the chafing dish, the porringer, the tankard and sack cup, in both pewter and silver. Great pewter platters, plates and dishes of the same metal were used daily in the great houses in Colonial Maryland, while frequent mention is made of "the silver plate now in the house, or this year to come out of England." Sometimes it is described as being engraved with the family coat of arms. The term "plate" was used to designate any piece of silver, which in that day was all "sterling."

In the inventories we find even "the covered silver skillet" and the silver drinking horn devised to individuals. After the Province had been firmly planted and the gentlemen had had their mansions built of brick of their own making—as in the first of the "Side-Lights" we found that they were "making as good brick as any in England in the year 1635"—they next turned their attention to importing, in addition to the brickmakers, artisans of every trade, until on the large manors and plantations practically every article of daily use was made. The very spoons were molded from pewter and the candles which shed their soft light from the brackets on the walls were made in the candle molds which continued to be used to the middle of the nineteenth century in the rural districts of Maryland.

There are still preserved in some old families the curious spoon molds mentioned, which speak for the ingenuity of the early settlers. There is never a fork devised, and it is therefore a rational conclusion that our Colonial dames did as good Queen Bess, who experienced the inconvenient truth that "fingers were made before forks."

Later, when a premium was put upon the home production of linen and cotton, the spinning wheel and loom began their busy hum in many households. As the customs increased on imported stuffs women became proud of wearing home-spun and took peculiar and active interest in home manufactures of every kind. The loss of the slave and the consequent desertion of the Colonial mansions has caused the passing of the ideal life in Maryland.

The tide which for so many years has been toward city life, has however, begun to turn backward, and our sense of fitness is occasionally pleased at the announcement that an ancestral estate has been recovered, some old mansion restored by some twentieth-century descendant of an early cavalier who has appreciated the fact that a name without a home can never be so strong and lasting as one which is deep-rooted in the soil!

CHAPTER X

THE TRANSPORTED SETTLERS

THE uncomfortable condition of affairs in England at the time of the settlement of Maryland made men of fine feeling and true worth anxious to leave it any cost.

Many of these having utterly impoverished themselves in the cause of religion or in the service of the King readily embraced the conditions of plantations offered by Cæcilius Calvert.

Hence many a man who had no means of paying his passage over—a matter of £20 sterling—let another transport him for their mutual benefit.

But this simple word "transported," which represented only a financial accommodation between man and man in Colonial days, has in the eyes of many of their descendants grown into a bar sinister of the deepest dye. The mere mention of the word seems to give them a sinking sensation, the feeling that their social underpinning is being ruthlessly pulled from beneath their feet. To such persons that a father "transported" his own son or daughter even implies a lowering of their social status.

If for a parent to pay the passage of his children to this country in Colonial days was a disgrace to be visited upon his descendants to the eighth and ninth generation, why is it not equally disgraceful for the twentieth-century American father to "transport" his sons or daughters to Europe each summer?

It was purely a business arrangement. The person who advanced the passage money received a goodly number of acres for each settler, while the latter himself was given a snug little farm of fifty acres to start his fortune.

Even those who entered into an indenture for a term of four years to perform some service as clerk, teacher, or to assist in cultivating the plantations, lost no social caste even in the province.

Those who have jumped to the conclusion that because a man is recorded as having been "transported" he therefore belonged to the lower strata of society have not looked very deeply into the peculiar social conditions in the province. How would such an one account for the fact that many so transported, and some even designated as "servants," within a few years were sitting in the Council or in the Assembly, and had perhaps married the daughters of other Councilors or associates of his Lordship?

This was an English settlement, and, as we well know, a Palatinate—a little kingdom with an English Lord as sovereign. Social lines, we have reason to believe, were not relaxed because of freedom of conscience. All men were not declared free and equal.

When, in the history of England, could one of the peasant class at the end of his indenture to a tradesman sit in the House of Lords or with the King's Privy Council?

When was the underling ever given the command of the military forces of the Sovereign?

There seems, then, only one logical explanation of the conditions which existed in the early settlement of Maryland, when men "transported" and "indentured," after fulfilling their services in many instances, quickly appeared

BENEDICT LEONARD CALVERT, FOURTH LORD
BALTIMORE

*From original portrait at Mt. Airy, shown through the courtesy of
Miss Rebecca L. Webster of Rochester, N. Y.*

as high dignitaries in the legislative halls and on the field—and it is this: Social caste was so immutably fixed, so absolutely stationary, that an English gentleman could be transported—could turn his hand to earning his living—and still be an English gentleman!

King Alfred played the cook at the old dame's bidding under the spur of necessity. That he turned the cakes into the fire was from lack of experience, for he was still King Alfred. So with the young men who came to Maryland, under the stress of circumstances, in subordinate positions. All who rose to places of honor in the Province can no doubt be traced to honorable lineage in England, as have many already.

The very fact that well-born young men dared to accept subordinate positions in an hour of financial embarrassment, such as then prevailed in England, proclaims the Province of Maryland a settlement of most superior gentlemen, since, instead of trying to keep such men down, history shows those high in authority sharing the honors with them. Evidently there were as few cads as there were convicts in royal old Maryland—none in the beginning certainly!

It appears that more pre-eminently here than at any known place "the gold was but the guinea's stamp and the man the man for a' that."

The spirit that prevailed in Colonial Maryland must have been the forerunner of that of the pioneer Western days, when young fellows of tender rearing would turn in and work as hard as the man brought up to manual labor; but the leadership was to the fittest, and in a few years they were the cattle kings, and "the man with the hoe" was still digging.

CHAPTER XI

MARYLAND NOT A PENAL COLONY

It has been said of Maryland that she was a penal colony at the time of her settlement and afterward. Others, no better informed, assert that she has neither history nor claims to colonial aristocracy, and even Mr. Hezekiah Butterworth in a juvenile story published many years ago in "St. Nicholas Magazine," gave his young readers the following erroneous version of the settlement:

"King Charles I you remember," said Mr. Butterworth, "founded a colony in this country in very early times in honor of his young and beautiful queen, Henrietta Maria. He called it Terra Mariae, or Maryland. He gathered fifteen hundred orphan children from the streets of London and sent them to Maryland, and there these early settlers loved to hear and recount the legends of the court of Charles I."

This is a fair sample of the general knowledge of Maryland history. The truth regarding the settlement of Maryland presents a very different picture, and one much more pleasing to the descendants of the cavaliers.

In the first place, King Charles did not settle Maryland—he granted it to Cæcilius Calvert, who, at his own expense, sent over a goodly company of persons in the year 1633. In response to the request of the King for Lord Baltimore to say what name should be inserted in the charter, the Lord Baltimore courteously replied that he "would like it to be something in honor of His Majesty's name, but was deprived of that happiness, as there was a province in those parts called Carolina." "Let us, therefore," said the King, "give it a name in honor of the Queen." He suggested first "Marianna," but Calvert objected, it being the name of a Jesuit who had written against monarchy.

King Charles then said, "Let it be Terra Maria, or Maryland," which was inserted in the grant.

In rebuttal of Mr. Butterworth's statement, and of others of similar character, let us read excerpts from the charter received by Cæcilius Calvert from his sovereign.

"Charles, by the grace of God, of England, Scotland, France and Ireland, King, Defender of the Faith, etc., to all whom these presents shall come, greeting:

Whereas our well beloved and right trusty subject Caecilius Calvert, Baron of Baltimore in our kingdom of Ireland, son and heir of George Calvert, knight, late Baron of Baltimore, in our said kingdom of Ireland, treading in the steps of his father, being animated with a laudable and pious zeal for extending the Christian religion and also the territories of our kingdom, hath humbly besought leave of us that he may transport by his own industry and expense a numerous colony of the English nation to a certain region hereinafter described in a country hitherto uncultivated and in the parts of America partly occupied by savages, having no knowledge of the Divine Being, and that all the region with some certain privileges and jurisdictions appertaining unto the wholesome government and state of his colony and region aforesaid, may, by our royal highness, be given, granted and confirmed unto him and his heirs."

After giving the boundaries, the King continues as follows:

"V. And we do by these presents for us and our heirs and successor make, create and constitute him the now Baron of Baltimore and his heirs the true and absolute lords and proprietaries of the region aforesaid, and all other premises (except the before excepted) saving always the faith and allegiance and sovereign dominion due to us, our heirs and successors, to have and to hold, possess and enjoy, the aforesaid region, islands, islets and other premises to the sole and proper behoof and use of him the now Baron of Baltimore, his heirs and assigns forever; to hold of us our heirs and successors, Kings of England, as of our castle of Windsor in our county of Berks in free and common socage by fealty only for all services and not in capite nor by knight's service, yielding, therefore, unto us our heirs and successors two Indian arrows of those parts to be delivered at the said castle of Windsor every year on Tuesday in Easter week, and also one-fifth part of all gold and silver, one which shall happen from time to time to be found within the aforesaid limits.

"VI. Now that the aforesaid region thus by us granted and described may be eminently distinguished above all other regions of that territory and decorated with more ample titles know ye that we, of our more special grace, certain knowledge and mere motion, have thought it that the said regions and islands be erected into a province, out of the plenitude of our royal power and prerogative, we do, for us, our heirs and successors, erect and incorporate the same into a province and nominate the same Maryland, by which name we will that it shall henceforth be called."

Then follows the granting to Lord Baltimore and heirs the power to make "laws of what kind soever, according to their sound discretions, whether relating to the public state of the said province or the private utility of individuals, of and with the advice, assent and approbation of the free men of the same province, or of the greater part of them or their delegates or deputies, whom we will, shall be called together for the framing of laws, etc." Omitting all that relates to the laws in detail, we come to section XIV, which must stand as direct evidence of Maryland's claims to colonial aristocracy, and disproves the many slurs regarding the standing and character of our early settlers.

"Moreover," continues King Charles I in this charter of Maryland, "lest in so remote and far distant a region every access to honours and dignities may seem to be precluded and utterly barred, to men well born who are preparing to engage in the present expedition, and desirous of deserving well, both in peace and war of us, and our kingdom for this cause we for us and heirs and successors do give free and plenary power to the aforesaid now Baron of Baltimore and to his heirs and assigns, to confer favors, rewards, honours upon such subjects inhabiting within the province aforesaid as shall be well deserving, and to adorn them with whatsoever titles and dignities they shall appoint (so that they be not such as are now used in England).

"XIX. We also by these presents do give and grant license to the same Baron of Baltimore and to his heirs, to erect any parcels of lands within the province aforesaid into manors, and in every of those manors to have and to hold a court-baron, and all things which to a court-baron do belong; and to have and to keep frank-pledge for the conservation of the peace and better government of those parts, by themselves and their stewards or by the lords for the time being to be deputed, of other of those manors when they shall be constituted, and in the same to exercise all things to the view of frank-pledge belonging."

We find then that Maryland was not a colony of England, but was a province granted to the Lords Baltimore with privileges peculiar to a Palatinate government, which the king declared it was his desire eminently to distinguish above all other regions of that territory (America).

We have seen that sons of knights and ladies came in the *Ark* and the *Dove* with the Calverts.

Later other men of birth and education were attracted by the inducements of peace and plenty in the province of Maryland, a condition strongly in contrast to the state of affairs in England during the reign of the martyr king. Many younger sons of noble families sought to better their fortunes in the new country, when England was poor and torn by dissensions.

In his Palatinate the Lord Baltimore had royal rights and privileges, license to erect courts and to create judges, and, as we have seen, the right to parcel land into manors after the English custom.

As the land is the basis of aristocracy in all monarchial countries, it naturally became so here, where the King in his charter distinctly encouraged the founding of manorial holdings on the law of primogeniture and the bestowal of titles and decorations to the well deserving.

The germ of a transplanted nobility naturally sprung up. Class distinctions were at once recognized and "gentlemen" were recorded as such. These were entitled to be addressed as esquire, and with their large landed estates corresponded to the gentry of England. All important officials, civil and military, were chosen by the Lord Baltimore from the privileged classes, who belonged to his own educated coterie, which was natural enough and not contrary to the present-day custom of political patronage.

CHAPTER XII

FIRST PRISON IN MARYLAND

More than once since the author began her original researches in which she has sought to banish some of the shadows cast upon the character of the early settlers of Maryland, has she found pleasant surprises in unfamiliar bypaths.

In looking for the much-talked-of "convicts" we have found the gallant cavalier and the lady of high degree, and while we have rejoiced within our souls to be able to approve what we had expected to deplore, there is yet another evidence of the superior character of the Maryland settlers before us, namely, the fact that the Province of Maryland existed twenty-eight years without a prison or jail within its jurisdiction.

Farewell forever, ye haunting shades of convicts, so nimbly conjured up through the haze of time by our imaginative neighbors!

Not until the year 1662 did the Assembly find it necessary to build its first prison, at the City of St. Mary's:

George Alsop, that talented young Londoner who came to Maryland in the years 1650 at the age of 20, served a four years' term of indenture to Mr. Thomas Stockett and wrote before 1662 "A Character of Maryland," printed in London in 1666, tells us that here "a man may walk in the open woods as secure from being externally dissected as in his own house. So hateful is a

Robber that if but once imagined to be so he's kept at a distance and shunned."

"Here," he continues, "the Constable hath no need of a train of Halberteers that carry more armour about them than heart to guard him.

"Heres no Newgates for pilfering Felons, nor Ludgates for Debtors, nor Bridewells to lash the soul into Repentance. For as there is none of these Prisons in Maryland so the merits of the country deserve none.

"Common ale houses. . . . those schools which train up youth as well as Age to ruine, *in this Province there are none!*"

Surely, our earliest settlers must have been a remarkably superior class of people. Their laws are equitable and give evidence of broad-minded legislation. Their suits in court are civil, and the criminal class seems conspicuously absent in this province which bore the peaceful and suggestive name of "The Sanctuary."

As there were no prisons in the early days, if a convict was to be found in Maryland it must have been incognito. A province that could thrive for a term of twenty-eight years without a jail or prison house is unique in the history of colonization. Neither drunkenness, robbery or murder stained the fair record of our annals except in isolated and rare cases.

But as the years passed and a greater influx of immigration came to our shores the "world, the flesh and the devil" became more in evidence, and in the year 1662 we find passed the following:

"A Council held at the Resurrection, 27th June, 1662. Present, Charles Calvert, Esq., Lieutenant-General of this Province; Phillip Calvert, Esq., Chancellor of said

Province; Henry Sewell, Esq., Secretary John Bateman, Baker Brookes, Esq., Councillors Ordered, that there bee a Pryson built, for the speedy effecting of which carpenters and other workmen to attend them be pressed, the charges to be defrayed accordinge to the law of England."

A little later an act of Assembly provided for a pillory, ducking stool, whipping post, stock and branding irons for each county.

Eleven years after this a prison was ordered to be built in every county in connection with local court-houses.

We must judge from that that we grew in wickedness as we waxed in strength, which, while nothing to our credit or to that of the lawbreakers of olden times, it is distinctly a gratification to know that the firstcomers were true blue and set their followers a high standard of living.

If there is any dark spot of Maryland history which should be illumined with the searchlight of truth it is the stigma of her convict settlement, and never will it be dropped by local Marylanders whose lineages reach back into those first days until all who run may read that Maryland's provincial records prove her to have been the highest-toned colony in the known world. And that in this free and gracious place of refuge he who sought a "convict" found a rebel—not a felon, but a patriot, or, perchance, a Christian martyr.

CHAPTER XIII

THE LORDS AND LADIES OF THE MANORS

THAT Lords and Ladies of the Manor did actually form the center of a social aristocracy in Colonial Maryland is a matter of fact, rather than a dream of fiction, and no more charming retrospective glimpses can be taken through Colonial doorways than those which include these personages of high degree.

And that these Lords were of the genuine English brand, tricked out in gold-banded hats with waving plumes, silk and velvet coats and much curled wigs, knee breeches and long silk hose, the inventories of their personal estates leave no doubt.

That they wore lace ruffles over their well-kept hands, invariably adorned with "the seale gold ring" which was a part of every gentleman's possessions, we also have reason to believe. These seal gold rings were important to their owners, of course, but to the modern student of family history they have a value entirely separate from their official worth on a property deed.

The impression of an old seal may mean the key to open the most charming vistas in which Old World castles and Norman knights may form the central group. Fortunately, many of these have survived the ravages of time, and as it was a criminal offense to use a crest or coat of arms not authorized by the Crown, we may be sure that they were hereditably used by our Colonial gentry and do prove the right of the bearer to the arms of the English house they stand for.

Although Maryland was settled in 1634, and the right to erect land into manors included in the charter from the King, we find no record of their actual existence until after the year 1637–38, in which the Assembly passed the bills for bounding of manors, for assigning and peopling them, and also made laws regulating the services to be performed for manors and freeholds. It is evident, however, that grants of manors had been made prior to the passing of these bills, since in a letter from Thomas Copley to Caecilius Calvert, dated 1638, he speaks of sending these bills lately passed by the Assembly, and urges his lordship not to sign them.

From his comments it appears that the burgesses enacted a law that all who held lands should relinquish them and then the inhabitants of the province should all cast lots as to where they should live.

Evidently this ingenious plan was the result of the putting together of some heads that had come into Maryland too late to secure the choice sites along the beautiful Potomac and Patuxent Rivers.

Copley says most shrewdly: "If we permite this precedent that assemblys may alter men's rights noe man shall never be sure of what he hath, but he that canne git most proxis in every assembly shall dispose of any man's estate that he pleaseth."

It was at this famous Assembly that the bill for baronies was passed, and also the one which required that everyone holding a manor must be trained as a soldier, provide munition and have in every manor fifteen freemen ready for the service of the country, whom the lord of the manor must also maintain in time of service, which was an attempt to revive the old English law of land tenure.

Other laws objectionable to Thomas Copley were carried through the third reading and forwarded to London for Lord Baltimore's approval. Among them was the one which related to woman's land rights and of which the commentator says, "Unless she marry within seven years after land fall to hir she must either dispose away hir land or else she shal forfeite it to the nexte of kinn, and if she have but one mannor, for whereas she cannot alienate it, it is gone unless she git a husband."

"For what purpose this ole law is maid your lordship, perhaps, will see better then I, for my part I see great difficultyes in it, but to what purpose I well see not."

By a curious coincidence the first patent of land recorded in Maryland is to two women—Margaret and Mary Brent, under the name of "Sisters Freehold." This patent was dated October 7, 1639.

The land was in St. Mary's county, adjoining that of their brother, Colonel Giles Brent. After the death of Governor Leonard Calvert, Mistress Margaret Brent became the lady of St. Gabriel's Manor and a most interesting record of her alienation of a part of the land by livery of seizen is still extant in the original manuscript records.

This was a custom of conveyance which antedated the recording of deeds. In this we learn that Martin Kirk was in the year 1656 given seizen of a part of the manor of St. Gabriel's by the rod, one end of which was held respectively by Martin Kirk and the steward of the manor, who, in the presence of witnesses, declares "the lord of this manor by me the steward doth hereby deliver you seizin by the rod and admit you as tenant of the premises." Then the said Kirk did his fealty to the lady of the manor in full court, swearing "Hear you, my lady, that I, Martin Kirk, shall be to you both true and faithful and shall owe my fidelity to you for the land I hold of you and lawfully shall do and perform such customs and services as my duty is to you at the terms assigned, so help me God, and all His saints." This was the oath of fealty required of all tenants of manor lands.

While little is left to perpetuate the memory of the lords of the manor in Maryland there is just enough to leave no doubt as to their actual rule and sovereign sway on the lands which have descended in many cases to their posterity. Here the lords of the manor established themselves, transferring to the lovely southern country the mimic life of rural England. On Kent Island, as the Eastern Shore was originally called, there were also several notable manors; but it is to St. Mary's county that we must turn to learn what were the rights of this privileged class in Colonial Maryland, as of all the lords who enjoyed the privilege of court baron and leet, the records of but one having, so far as known, survived the passing of the centuries. This is peculiarly interesting to us of the twentieth century, when life is based on the apartment-house plan and land is sold by the square inch in the overcrowded metropolis.

The manorial courts, which date from a time prior to Edward the Confessor, were in the Province of Maryland, as in England, peculiar to a state of society in which law-abiding men lived far apart and it was necessary to have in each community a person uniting in

CHARLES CALVERT, FIFTH LORD BALTIMORE

After portrait in the City Hall, Baltimore, Md., from the Author's Collection

himself the influence of wealth and the majesty of the land."

Manors in colonial Maryland comprised any number of thousands of acres and were occupied by freeholders, leaseholders and resiants. The lord of the manor was entitled to hold court baron and court leet. At the former the freeholders were tried by the lord of the manor and the free tenants of the manor, but if less than two of the peers of a freeholder were present the court could not sit. It was here that the tenant did fealty for his land, swearing the quaint oath: "Hear you, my Lord, that I, ——, shall be to you both true and faithful and shall owe my fidelty to you for the land I hold of you and lawfully shall do and perform such customs and services as my duty is to you, at the terms assigned. So help me God and all His saints."

Disputes between the lord of the manor and the people were settled before the court baron, while the court leet was the court of the people. Here the steward presided and the jury and officers were chosen from the residents of the manor. Its original intent was to view the Frank pledges, that is the freemen within the liberty who were mutually pledged for the good behavior of each other. The attendance of all between the ages of 16 and 65 was required. At the opening of the leet, after the steward had taken the judge's seat, the bailiff made proclamation with three "Oyez" and commanded all to draw near and answer to their names upon "pain and peril." In the early English statutes the following persons are specified as subject to trial at a court leet: "Such as have double measure, and buy by the great and sell by the less. Such as haunt taverns and no man knoweth whereon they live. Such as sleep by day and watch by night and fare well and have nothing."

Besides fixing the price of bread and ale, punishing for the sale of corrupt victuals by the butcher, it also inquired strictly into the presence of irresponsible visitors in the Province. The old English law by which a man was forbidden to take in a stranger "unless he would hold his guest to right" was enforced in the Province, where there was evidently small hope of entertaining angels unawares. In accordance with this law the constable on the manor took security of all heads of families for the keeping of the peace by strangers in their homes. This was before the days of Maryland's famous hospitality. A case in point is in the records of St. Clement's Manor, where an entry states: "We also present John Mansell for entertaining Benjamin Hamon and Cybil, his wife as inmates. It is, therefore ordered that the said Mansell do either remove his inmates or give security to save the parish harmless by the next court under payne of 1000 l. tobaco." John Mansell seemed to have been particularly hard pressed, as another entry in the same record is where Samuel Harris broke the peace "with a stick and there was blood shed on the body of John Mansell."

In the year 1648, "at a court held at St. Maries, came Mrs. Margaret Brent and requested the opinion of the court concerning the patent of Mr. Leonard Calvert in the case of the tenements appertaining to the rebels within his manors, whether or no their forfeitures belonged to the lord of the manor. The resolution of the court was that the said forfeitures did of right belong to the lord of the manor by virtue of the "Condition of Plantations," the said rights usually belonging to the lords of manors in England, and that the words in the patent expressed, viz.: All commodities, advantages, emoluments and hereditaments whatsoever (royal jurisdiction excepted) included the same."

In the first "Condition of Plantations" Cæcilius granted the privilege of erecting manors to those who took up 1000, acres, but it was not long before he stipulated that there "must be 2,000 acres of English measure to lye all together in some one place within the said Province."

Manors were called baronies in ancient times, and later were termed lordships. These were held by lords or other great personages. The demesne lands were those reserved for the lord of the manor and his servants, the other parts being distributed among tenants. In Maryland, as in England, the tenants had to swear fealty to the lord or lady of the manor in open court.

The records of St. Clement's Manor, of which Dr. Thomas Gerard was the lord, are the only ones known to be extant, although others may be hidden away in old hair-covered chests in many an attic in St. Mary's county and in the homes of the descendants of the lords of the many other manors in colonial Maryland.

In the records of the court leet and court baron, held during various years from 1659 to 1672, we find the steward and constable, the residents, free holders, leaseholders, jury and homages, and learn that "a paire of stocks, pillory and ducking stool" are to be provided by a general contribution throughout the manor, and in the Maryland Archives the law is found requiring these instruments of punishment to be kept on every manor.

CHAPTER XIV

LEISURELY WAYS OF THE COLONIAL COURT

AN INTERESTING illustration of the leisurely ways of the Colonial gentry of Maryland and Virginia appears in the early proceedings of the Provincial Court, when a christening party at home is the sole apology for delaying the prosecution of a criminal until the next court.

Mr. John Washington, of Westmoreland County, Virginia, on September 30, 1659, writes thus to Governor Josias Fendall.

"*Honnble Sir* Yours of the 29th instant this day I received. I am sorry, yet my extraordinary occasions will not premit me to be at ye next Provincial Court to be held in Maryland ye 4 of this next month. Because then, God willing, I intend to git my young sonne baptized, all ye company and gossips being all ready invited."

It appears from the records that Mr. John Washington accused one Edward Prescott of hanging a witch on board his ship enroute from England the year previous and consequently the following letter had been sent by Governor Fendall:

Mr. Washington: Upon your complaint to me that Mr. Prescott did in his voyage from England hither cause a woman to bee executed for a witch, I have caused him to bee apprehended upon suspition of felony and doe intend to bind him over to ye Provincial Court to answere it, where I doe allso expect you to make good your charge.

"He will be called upon his trial ye 4th or 5th of October next att ye Court to bee held then att Patuxent, neare Mrs. Fenwick's house, where I suppose you will not fayle to bee. Witnesses examined in Virginia will be of no vallew there in this case, for they must bee face to face with ye party accused, or they stand for nothing. I thought good to acquaynt you with this that you may not come unprovided. This at present, Sr, is all, from your friend.

JOSIAS FENDALL.

29th September.

Washington's delightful excuse to the Governor of Maryland for deferring the case until next court speaks volumes for the social conditions of that day, and throws a particularly amusing ray of light upon the attitude of his mind toward the Colonial dames in 1659.

Here the Governor of the Province of Maryland is politely, but none the less emphatically, told that the court must wait upon the pleasure of Mr. Washington! The judges must doff their wigs and gowns, while the "young sonne" donned his christening robe! "The gossips" (in the modern sense sponsors) were more to be feared than the Provincial Court judges, and well they might be, for they made no little trouble in the early days, before the era of women's clubs and the strenuous intellectual life. An instance in point is the trial of one Mrs. Blank at a court holden for the Province of Maryland October 16, 1654, at which one witness testified that he heard Mrs. Blank relate that she heard Mrs. G. had beaten her maid two hours, by the clock, and there were those that would take their oath it was an hour and a half by the clock. As the witnesses advanced the length of the time of the beating grew to two hours and a half, and the climax was reached when an enthusiastic young maid of 20 summers declared that Mrs. G.'s irate husband "tore the hair of his head and wisht that she (his wife) would kill the self same maid that she might never kill more."

As all these testimonies proved to be unsupported by satisfactory evidence the gossip, Mrs. Blank, was made to pay the charges.

Of course it is not to be supposed that such offensive persons were referred to by the ancestor of the Father of His Country when he made his excuses for not attending court because of "ye company and gossips being already invited"—"gossips" was simply the ancient name for sponsors.

The name of the ship of which Edward Prescott was captain, and on which Colonel John Washington evidently came to Virginia was *The Sarah Artch* as written in an old record in Northampton County, Virginia. The correct name was most likely the *Arch Sarah*!

CHAPTER XV

THE PURITANS FROM VIRGINIA

THE coming of the persecuted Puritans from Virginia to Maryland in the year 1649-50 brought to the Province a band of high-principled and intelligent men of the ruling class, which any community suffered in losing and whose arrival in Maryland was but another contribution to her population of men whose actions were governed by principles rather than self-seeking.

The persecution of the Puritans in England naturally extended to her Royal Colony of Virginia, whose government was subject to the King and whose Governor and Council were by royal favor.

In Maryland all was different, and Lord Baltimore secure in his chartered rights, dared open wide the doors of his little kingdom to all whom the royal mandates oppressed. Hence, when the nonconformists were driven from Virginia, they came in a large body to the only spot on the earth where the principle of "Live and let live" was the law of the land.

The Puritans settled at Providence, now Annapolis, where they laid out a town and sold lots. Among those were Richard Bennett, afterward Governor of Virginia; Edward Lloyd, Richard Preston, William Berry, William Burgess and others. All were men of ability and have left their impress upon the early history of Maryland.

The young King Charles II, though an exile, resented the action of Lord Baltimore in receiving all kinds of "sectaries and schismatics into that plantation." The uncrowned king was as apparently ignorant of Maryland's chartered rights as some of his subjects were of Virginia's annulled charter. Lord Baltimore was never pronounced disloyal by King Charles I for inviting to his palatinate, where he alone was sovereign, all who were driven from England or elsewhere for conscience' sake.

But deprived of his power at home the exiled King thought to punish Lord Baltimore by sending a royal governor to Maryland. Hence, according to Langford in June, 1650, while at Breda, Charles II issued a royal commission to Sir William Davenant as Governor of Maryland.

Certain it is that neither he nor his commission ever reached Maryland, while, on the contrary, the Parliament sent Richard Bennett and William Claiborne to reduce both Maryland and Virginia to submission. The story of their success is well known. Hence we will take a brief glance at Sir William Davenant, who was chosen for the first royal Governor of the Province. As the godson and pet of William Shakespeare, the King's choice was a compliment to the intellectual appreciation of his Maryland subjects. "This young Will Davenant, born 1606, our proposed Governor," says Bozman, "when a little schoolboy at about seven or eight years old in the town of Oxford, was so fond of Shakespeare that whenever he heard of his arrival he would fly from school to see him." The Bard of Avon stopped at the Crown Inn tavern, kept by Davenant's father.

From this patronage of Shakespeare, without doubt originated Davenant's interest in these matters, and after the restoration of the King he applied himself to writing plays and was the author of almost as many as his godfather. He was the first to introduce women as actresses on the stage. He died in 1668. Sir Wiliam Davenant was evidently very close to royal favor, as he retired with the young Prince, the Queen and other loyalists into France upon the defeat of the King.

From all accounts of the wit and ability of Sir William Davenant, the cloak of the godfather fell—if lightly—upon his shoulders. In view of this it seems rather a pity after all for Maryland, whose capital city more than a century ago was termed the "social Athens of America," to have missed the distinction of having been governed by one who had sat at the feet of the great Bard of Avon! No doubt the scintillation of his wit would have been a delightful relief after the long faces of the Puritans!

CHAPTER XVI

THE OLDEST CHURCH IN MARYLAND

THERE can be no question that the "Old Church," known until the middle of the nineteenth century as "the Church in Dorchester Parish," is the most ancient church edifice in Maryland, for while the Poplar Hill Church, in St. Mary's County, has been rebuilt, as have others in parishes of earlier settlement than that of Dorsett, the "Old Church" has never been burned or otherwise demolished. And so it stands today in a picturesque spot on the Little Choptank River, on the narrow creek to which it has given the name of Church Creek which name has in turn been transmitted to the village half a mile beyond—so that one has the rather confusing experience of seeing those who speak of their destination as "going up the Creek," deliberately turn their backs upon the sparkling waters of the stream which flows by the church and wend their way up to the village postoffice, known to the United States Government as Church Creek. The ancient little edifice was built so long ago that all memory of its date as been lost, and no record extant bears evidence of its foundation.

Certain it is, however, that this was one of the 30 parish churches (including chapels of ease) paying tithes to the Bishop of London in the year 1690, two years before the Act of Assembly which erected the counties into parishes.

OLD TRINITY CHURCH, DORCHESTER COUNTY

The oldest church edifice in Maryland, Built prior to 1692. From the Author's Collection

In the division of Dorchester into Choptank and Dorchester parishes, the inhabitants of the upper part of the county were directed to worship in the courthouse at Cambridge until a church should be built, while those below Cambridge were to worship at "Dorchester Town."

The fact that the vestrymen in both parishes were fined by his Lordship's Council in the year 1696 for disregarding the law passed by the Council prescribing that a list of marriages should be kept and returned to Annapolis is proof that the records were not kept and can readily explain the absence of entries that would be invaluable to the seeker after truth in Maryland history.

While there is no record of the deed of gift of the site of this early church, there is proof that the graveyard surrounding it was given by the maternal forebears of the Dorseys, the present owners of the outlying fields, which in part were once the glebe lands of the church in Dorchester parish.

Strange as it may seem, this longest survival of the early churches stood nameless for nearly two centuries, It was about the year 1850 that the "Old Church" was reconsecrated after its restoration from great dilapidation and a long period of silence. It was then named "Trinity" for the first time, the Rt. Rev. Bishop Whitehouse, of Illinois, officiating.

It was during this process of restoration and iconoclasm that the high box-shaped English pews were removed; also the hand carved wainscoting, which formed part of the interior decoration. The choir gallery, suspended above the main entrance and approached from the outside by a circular staircase, was removed as unsafe and unnecessary. It is not certain when the tiled floor was boarded over in the interest of health, or when the window above the reredos was bricked up, but with these changes the old church has lost many of its Colonial characteristics.

Many interesting traditions linger about this old sanctuary, which has long since become a Mecca to those who have removed from the county and to those who visit it for the first time. Two relics of its earlier life survive the ravages of time—one is a large silver communion cup, which bears the inscription, "To the Church in Dorchester Parish." The other is a red velvet cushion, of royal shape and quality, which tradition claims was the coronation cushion of Queen Anne, who sent it over to the church in connection with a communion service, which has long since disappeared. So sacred was the tradition of the cushion held, that at one period it was kept upon the altar of the Old Church, and an atmosphere of veneration grew up around it like unto a halo around a saint's head. Such was the state of affairs when a newly arrived dignitary of the church was told by one of his fold, with bated breath, to behold and do reverence to the Queen Anne cushion. "To behold" with the Bishop was to dethrone the hallowed cushion. "What is that doing here?" demanded the Bishop as he tossed the relic to the floor for his prayer cushion. "Brother," exclaimed his host, "it was Queen Anne's" "What of that? queried his Reverence. "If Queen Anne were here would you sit her on God's altar?" And so, while still held very dear, the velvet cushion of royal hue fulfils its rightful mission as a kneeling cushion in the ancient sanctuary.

This, like other Colonial Churches has the tradition of being built of "bricks imported from England," which

SEVENTEENTH CENTURY JACOBEAN COMMUNION TABLE, QUEEN ANNE KNEELING CUSHION, AND EIGHTEENTH CENTURY CHALICE FROM OLD TRINITY CHURCH, DORCHESTER COUNTY

Shown through the courtesy of Miss Mary V. Dorsey, of Dorchester County

has no more foundation than any such absurd claims. A large hollow in the grave yard bore evidence of the clay pit from which the bricks were made by English brick-makers *here,* in English moulds.

CHAPTER XVII

A PROPERTY QUALIFICATION

SURPRISING as it may be to the general reader it is none the less true that in Colonial Maryland the property qualification was essential for one having a voice in public affairs. The government of the Province was limited to freemen owning not less than 50 acres of land or "a visible personal estate of £40 sterling within the country."

As the right to vote was thus regulated according to a man's possessions the same qualification was applied to the legislative body; hence no man could sit in the Assembly or House of Burgesses unless he possessed the stipulated amount of worldly goods.

While at the first glance this seems an unjust basis it has the sanction of both the Divine law, which says: "To him that hath shall be given," and the purely sociological one which recognizes that any government to be permanent must be deep-rooted in the soil.

While the claim has been made that this is the basis of an aristocracy it is none the less true of a republic, The property qualification for the individual disseminates the power among the people and stimulates the growth of the equal rights of men and benefits the individual while helping the state.

The educational basis is egoistic, taking from the state to benefit the man, which is directly contrary to the old Roman law that the man owed his life to the state, not vice versa. So closely has the relation of the government and the land been associated for all time in England and from earliest days in Maryland that laws regulating its possession and transmission have always been conspicuous and of vital importance.

From the first settlement of the Province until the separation of the Colonies from Great Britain, lands descended in Maryland by the English law of primogeniture. The first act relating to the matter was enacted in the year 1642, by which "lands were to descend to the heir who hath right by the law of England. In the absence of the heir from the province the next in succession was entitled to possess the land as trustee for a period of seven years, at the end of which period the estate became his own if the heir had not returned.

While, according to this law, the oldest son succeeded to the entire estate in the absence of a will, we find that parents in the majority of cases devised certain tracts of land to their younger sons, and, in many cases, to their daughters as well.

It is no unusual thing to find a deed of gift from a man of large possessions to his "beloved son-in-law," in this way bestowing a marriage portion on his daughter. With few exceptions fathers bequeathed the home plantation to the eldest son—but in the absence of a will he inherited everything. The widow received one-third of the land and a dower house, which was occupied by her when the heir came of age or married and took possession of the mansion or manor house.

By the English law of entailment lands were transmitted for many generations in a direct male line, and these could not be sold or alienated without the payment of a fine to the Proprietary, until the passage of an act making it possible to "dock" the entailment. This was in 1782. But in the year 1786 the General Assembly passed a law which declared "that the law of descent in Maryland, which originated in the feudal system and military tenures in England, was contrary to justice and ought to be abolished." This ended the law of primogeniture in Maryland, although a few of her notable estates still descend to the eldest son by will, thus maintaining the prestige and influence for these families which are inseparable from large landed possessions.

To return to the property qualification in the elective franchise, the rule of "no taxation without representation" was simply reversed to read no representation without taxation!

DORSEY HOUSE AT ANNAPOLIS

Meeting place of The Assembly 1694–1704. From the Author's

CHAPTER XVIII

REMOVAL OF THE CAPITAL TO ANNAPOLIS

It was not long after the province had grown to a considerable size that the capital was removed from St. Mary's to Annapolis, on the Severn River, another center of the early aristocracy, who found it more convenient for the capital to come to them than for them to go to it, situated as it was at the extreme southern part of the State, necessitating a long journey over the roughest of roads. Several attempts had been made to remove the capital from its original site, and in the year 1683 the Assembly was held at The Ridge, Anne Arundel County but, this being found unsatisfactory in regard to accommodations, no further session was held there.

This, however, was not the first time that the Provincial Court had held its august meetings away from the scene of the Lord Baltimore's government. In the year 1654, after the commissioners appointed by the English Parliament had reduced to submission the rebellious Province of Maryland, which had shown itself favorable to a royal ruler, a petition from a hundred or more leading citizens called for the removal of the captial from the Catholic stronghold to the house of Richard Preston, the great Quaker and Commander of the Patuxent. This was accordingly done and the Preston mansion became the Provincial Court and the meeting place of the Assembly, and also the repository of the official records from this time until 1660, when the King (and at the same time the Lord Baltimore) came to his own again. The result of this change of capitals was the battle of the Severn, which begun with an attack on the Preston house with the avowed purpose of capturing Richard Preston "that we might hang him for his rebellion against the Lord Baltimore." The battle, which begun on the Patuxent, was fought to a finish at Providence, and the old Preston house, built in 1650, still stands to mark the scene of one of the most interesting events in the history of the early government.

To Governor Francis Nicholson Maryland is indebted for the permanent removal of the capital to the Port of Annapolis.

The people of St. Marie's protested with all the energy and vigor of men who recognized in this the deathblow to their ancient seat of government. Every argument was used to convince his Excellency Captain-General and Governor-in-Chief over "this their Majesties' Province and Territory of Maryland" that St. Marie's was the most suitable situation for the capital, because "almost encompassed around with harbor for shipping, where 500 sail of ships at least may securely ride at anchor before the city."

As an offset to the inconvenience of reaching it the citizens of St. Marie's offered to provide "a coach or caravan, or both, to go at all times of public meetings of Assemblies and Provincial Courts, every day daily between St. Marie's and Patuxent River, and at all other times once a week, and also to keep constantly on hand a dozen horses at least, with suitable furniture for any person or persons having occasion to ride, post or otherwise, with or without a guide, to any part of the province on the Western Shore." They further argued that their distance from the center of the province was no reason for removal, since the Imperial Court "is held at London, which is as far from the center of England as St. Marie's, in this Province; Boston, in New England; Port Royal, in Jamaica; Jamestown, in Virginia, and almost all other of their Majesties' American plantations where are still kept and continued in their first ancient stations and places the chief seat of government and courts of judicature."

The petition was referred to the House and all of the sixteen separate pleas dismissed summarily to the last. "This House conceives that the Citie of St. Marie's is very unequally rankt with London, Boston, Port Royall etc." This was a withering slap at the ambitious little city which, according to these burgesses, like Pharaoh's lean kine, devoured everything and yet attained to no size. The truth was that the seed of progress had been planted by that far-seeing and public-spirited Governor, Francis Nicholson, whose purpose to benefit the province was not to be frustrated by those who wished to further their private interests by keeping the seat of government at St. Mary's. Therefore, the House of Burgesses rejected the petition, and the Council concurring in its action the removal was effected in the year 1694. The public records of the Province were ordered to be carried in good strong bags to be secured with cordage and hides and well packed, with guards to attend them night and day, to be protected from all accidents and to be delivered to the Sheriff of Anne Arundell Town. Capt. William Holland was intrusted with their transportation. On October 18, 1694, the name of the new capital was changed from the

"Town Land at Proctors" to that of the "Town and Port of Annapolis." The first commissioners appointed were Major Edward Dorsey, Major John Hammond, Mr. John Dorsey, Hon. Nicholas Greenberry, Esq., Mr. Philip Howard, Mr. Andrew Norwood, Mr. John Bennett and Mr. John Sanders. Two years later an act was passed for keeping good rules and order in the town of Annapolis. The body corporate then appointed included Governor Francis Nicholson, the Hon. Sir Thomas Lawrence, the Hon. Thomas Tench, the Hon. Col. Nicholas Greenberry, Major Edward Dorsey, Captain Richard Hill and Mr. James Sanders. Among other interesting acts passed by the Assembly of 1696 was one for the improvement of the new capital. One of the provisions was that "an handsome pair of gates be made at ye coming in of the towne and two triangular houses built for ye Rangers. To have the way from the gate to go directly to the top of ye hill without the towne and to be ditched on each side and sett with quick setts or some such thing." The first meeting of the Assembly was held in the house of Major Edward Dorsey, which, as it was chosen for the Governor's residence and the place for the meeting of the Provincial Court and Assembly, was evidently the most commodious house in the Town and Port of Annapolis. How the quaint little city, inclosed in mediæval style behind its iron gates and its King's Rangers, grew in wealth and splendor we all know and recall with pride that Eddis in his famous letters declared that society here compared favorably with the most brilliant circles of London.

CHAPTER XIX

THE OLD TUESDAY CLUB

IN THIS day of many clubs of serious intentions, whose members are inclined to take seriously every opinion advanced, it is delightfully relaxing to take a retrospective peep at the old Tuesday Club, of Annapolis, with its unique gelastic law passed in the interest of good feeling and fun. The gelastic law, passed on the 18th of June, 1745, was that "If any subject whatever nature so ever be discussed which levels at party matters or the administration of the government of this Province, or be disagreeable to the club, no answer shall be given thereto, but after such discourse is ended the society shall laugh at the member offending in order to divert the discourse."

At the very next meeting—June 25—we find "the gelastic law was this night put in execution against Mr. Secretary Marshe, who got into a prolix harrangue about the conscience of lawyers. Order that Secretary Marshe entertain this society upon Tuesday, the 2nd of July, next ensuing."

The London "Spectator," commenting upon early clubs in England, says: "When men are thus knit together by a love of society, not by a spirit of faction, and do not meet to censure or annoy those that are absent, but to enjoy one another; when they are thus combined for their own improvement or for the good of others, or at least relax themselves from the business of the day by an innocent and cheerful conversation, there may be something very useful in these little institutions and establishments."

On the old records of the Tuesday Club appear the following list of contents:

"From the earliest ages to the transmigration of the club to America and the foundation of the Red House Club, of Annapolis, in Maryland: a succinct account of the ancient and venerable Tuesday Club, of Lannevie, in the Kingdom of Scotland, with a chonological table." Again: "From the transmigration of the club to America to the first sederunt of the ancient and honorable Tuesday Club, of Annapolis, in Maryland."

The old record book, however, upon examination proves to have none of the history referred to within its covers. Beginning, with its organization on May 14, 1745, in Annapolis, the first entry reads:

"The following gentlemen met at the house of Dr. Alexander Hamilton, and then erected themselves into a society or club under the name of the Tuesday Club, to meet weekly, and consent to the following rules."

The first four rules which were made at the initial meeting were that the club should meet weekly at each other's dwellings by turns every Tuesday throughout the year; second, that the member appointed to serve as steward shall provide a gammon of bacon or any one other dish of vittles, and no more; third, that no fresh liquor shall be made, prepared or produced after 11 o'clock at night, and every member to be at liberty to retire at pleasure; fourth, that no member be admitted without the concurrent consent of the whole society, and should such member be admitted he shall be obliged to serve the succeeding night after his admission.

The gentlemen who were the organizers at this first meeting were Robert Gordon, Esq., Rev. Mr. John Gordon, Captain William Rogers, William Cummings, Esq., Mr. John Bullen, Mr. John Lomas, Mr. William Marshe and Dr. Alexander Hamilton. From these names it is easy to see that the members were mainly, if not entirely, Scotch; but it was not long before others were elected members.

Laws continued to grow with the meetings until in a few weeks we find "That immediately after supper the ladies shall be toasted before any other toasts or healths go round.

"That such as are the bachelor members of this society may be permitted to have a cheese instead of dressed vittles." Some weeks later, however, it is

"*Resolved*, That cheese is not any more to be deemed a dish of vittles," no doubt to the regret of the bachelor minority. It was not long before the Tuesday Club, which limited its membership to fifteen, included the leaders of the day, with an honorary membership all over the State.

Among the active members we soon find the names of Mr. Charles Cole, for a long time president; Sir John Oldcastle, knight of the club; Col. Edward Lloyd; Mr. Edward Dorsey, speaker; Mr. William Thornton, attorney-general; Mr. James Calder; Mr. Jonas Green, armiger of the club; Mr. Samuel Hart, Walter Dulaney, Beale Bordley and others.

Among the strangers entertained by the club during visits to the capital city were Mr. Robert Morris and Rev. James Sterling, of Oxford, Talbot county; Messrs. Christopher and Charles Lowndes. That the Tuesday

Club was truly gallant we judge not only from the toasts to the ladies given at each meeting, but to the fact that brilliant balls in honor of the ladies were given at the Stadt House by the club.

An item of special interest is "the humble petition and remonstrance of sundry of the single females of Annapolis showeth that whereas it has been observed by sundry persons, as well as your petitioners, that a single and surprising success has all along attended such happy females as your Honor has been pleased to pitch upon as the toasts of the honorable chair, every one of whom in a short time after having been adopted by your Honor has successfully and happily been provided with a much more eligible state, your petitioners therefore earnestly pray that your Honor, instead of conferring your favors in so partial a manner would, in commiseration of our desperate situation, include us all in the circle of favor that the benign influence of your Honor's maritiferous notice may henceforth equally shine upon us all, and your petitioners shall ever pray. To the Hon. Chas. Esq., President of the Most Worshipful and ancient Tuesday Club."

The minutes of the club give many interesting glimpses into the life of the society. Mr. Charles Cole on one occasion as steward entertained the club with a large bowl of sack punch and a catch song—"The Great Bell of London."

While Mr. William Thornton, Esq., on account of his uncommon talent in singing, was by unanimous consent of the club appointed *prato musicus*, or chief musician and it is ordained that as often as he votes in the club he is to sing his vote in a musical manner, else it is to go for nothing, after which he has the privilege conferred on him of commanding any member of the club to sing after having first sung himself.

The yearly anniversary of the club's organization was an occasion of great merriment and ceremony.

Jonas Green, Esq., was the poet laureate of the Tuesday Club and prepared elaborate odes for such state occasions. We are told that the members, wearing their badges (which were sent from London by Mr. Anthony Bacon, representative of the club there), proceeded to the house of the president, marching along two by two in stately manner to the admiration of "many spectators of all sorts and ranks."

When they came within twenty paces of the honorable president's gate his honor made his appearance and did each member the honor of a salute by manupuassation, upon which they halted a little, and Jonas Greene, Esq., holding up the anniversary ode in his hand, waved it around his head in a very graceful manner, by way of salutation to his honor, who made several low bows, which were respectively returned by the master of ceremonies, Sir John Oldcastle, and the chancellor.

Then his honor the president took his place between the last two named and led the procession into his own courtyard, the way being all strewn with flowers and the ensign or flag displayed as usual.

After sitting in the courtyard of his honor's mansion the anniversaries always occurring on the 14th of May, when the season was mild and Annapolis, with its old English gardens terraced to the water, was an ideal spot —enjoying the out-of-door scene, members of the club assembled in his honor's great salon, and "as he went to take a chair with a *grand pas* a martial tune was played by the proto-musicus, and he took the chair with a *plaudite.*

Following the supper, of which we are told the "outward decoration and apparatus was as elegant and harmonious as the inward rhetoric and eloquence of the club was uncommon, many loyal healths were drunk," etc.

It is interesting to know that Mr. Robert Morris, of Oxford, sent nine bottles of English beer as a present to the Tuesday Club, over which there was considerable trouble, one member having been accused of appropriating it to his own use.

Again we find "Mr. Speaker Dorsey rising up with that gravity and action which is his peculiar talent upon all such occasions and discoursing in a nervous and elegant state which is natural to that gentleman upon all occasions." He is described as appearing dressed in his proper robes and badge of office, being a black gown and a band to be worn by him on all occasion.

Volume II of the Tuesday Club, 1755–1756, has been found by the Author. This volume, still unknown to other Maryland historical students, was presented to Colonel Peter Force by William S. Green, of Annapolis. The first volume is owned by the Maryland Historical Society.

CHAPTER XX

MAIL SERVICE IN PROVINCIAL TIMES

IN OUR modern methods of quick delivery of mail which have kept pace with the whizzing trolley car, the extension telephone, the electric button and all the labor-saving and up-to-date inventions necessary to the strenuous life of the twentieth century, it is difficult to realize the patience which must have been the chief virtue of our Colonial forebears in the early days of the postal service.

Prior to 1661 all letters in the province were sent by private individuals or by special messengers when official ones were forwarded from the government.

At the Assembly held at St. Johns in May, 1661, "an act for the conveyance of letters concerning the State and public affairs" was passed and gives an interesting glimpse of the primitive delivery of mail in those far-off days, when, as Richard Carvel says, "there was more of good will than haste in the world."

We shall see that by this act every man was a public messenger if occasion required, and while many circumstances might have arisen to prevent his performing the service in the time specified, there were only two which exempted him from a large fine should he fail to respond.

The bill as passed reads:

"*Be it enacted by the authority of this present General Assembly* That all letters whatsoever to or sent from the Governor and Council, or any of his lordships, councellors or justices of the peace, touching the publik affairs of this Province, shall without delay be sent from house to house the direct way till they be safely delivered as directed, and every person after receipt of such letter delaying to carry the said letter to the next house above the term of half an hour shall pay for a fine to the Lord Proprietary one hundred pounds of tobacco unless it were delivered so late in the day as that it could not before night be delivered at the next house, or that through violence of wind or tempest it could by no means be sent over the creek or river if any chance to bee between the house where such letter shall be delivered and the house to which it ought to be conveyed; and be it further enacted, that all the Public letters shall be superscribed by the person directing or sending the said letter upon the outside of the said letter thus, viz., to be sent from house to house, and then subscribe his name. This act to endure for three years, or to the end of the next General Assembly."

In the year 1678 we find that James Smallwood is appointed "post" to convey all public intelligence in Charles county "from thence to his Lordship and his Council upon such reasonable salary as at the Discretion of his Lordship and Council shall be allowed of during his Lordship's pleasure."

The fact that at the same meeting of the Council of Maryland it was ordered that "a fferry be settled at Ashcomb's Plantation, on Point Patience, in Pottuxen River, for wafteing over all publick messages or other persons whatsoever that shall have occasion over the said River," leads us to conclude that a special post for each county had been previously appointed to bear the official mail. Aside from the inconvenience to private individuals under

FREDERICK CALVERT, SIXTH LORD BALTIMORE

After portrait in the State House, Annapolis, Md., from the Author's Collection

the act of 1661, the danger of loss and delay must have been great.

Thomas Pew (Pue) is the first one mentioned as the Pubic Post of this Province, being allowed "6000 pounds of tobacco for his year's wages."

In the year 1695 a more extensive postal system was established, with Mr. John Perry as the postrider. His salary was fixed at £50 a year on condition that he discharge all "publique messages and pacquettes" as his Excellency shall direct, and also "discharge this Province from any expense whatever by reason of any messengers to be employed for the Country's Service."

In the agreement Mr. John Perry consents "to go eight times a year betwixt Potomac and Philadelphia in this manner—viz:—from such place on the north side of Potomac and Philadelphia to such place in Petuxent as your Excellency shall direct and so to Annapolis, from thence to Kent and so to William Stadt (Oxford), and from thence to Daniell Toas' and to Adam Petersons, and from thence to New Castle and so directly to Philadelphia and return the same way back again to Potomack, and at all those place receive, carry, bring and leave all pacquets and letters of and for the inhabitants of this province at his nearest stages, according to the directions thereof, and take no gratuity or reward for carrying any letters from this Province to Philadelphia or bringing any from Philadelphia hither, and delivering the same according to the directions at his nearest stages, and if further occasion shall require go to New Yorke, Virginia or elsewhere, as his Excellency shall direct."

The route arranged for this first public mail service began at "Newton's Point on the Wiccocomaco River in Potomac, from thence to Allen's Mill, on to Benedict, Leonard Town, across the Patuxent River to Mr. George Lingans, to Mr. Larkin's and so to South River and Annapolis," and thence to the stages above named.

Fifteen years later the first regular post-office in the colonies was established by Act of Parliament in the year 1710. By its provision a general post was established in North America.

In 1717 a regular mail system by post was started from Virginia, through Maryland and all the northern colonies, bringing and forwarding mail from Boston to Williamsburg in four weeks. Later we find the time of these mails was irregular, the postriders waiting until they had enough letters to pay the cost of going, which indicates that the old custom of a yearly salary had been done away with.

In the year of 1774 the cost of a letter was 9 pence to Philadelphia, and 7 pence to New Castle, Del.

The records show that the post routes were in fairly good condition, but were due, however, to private enterprise.

The Kent Island route was owned by the Tilghmans, the one to Rock Hall by the Hodges and Kennards, while the Ellicotts built the road from Ellicott City to Baltimore.

While there is a delightful picturesqueness about the old post chaise, which weekly swung into the old Maryland towns, at the sound of whose horn the inhabitants were thrown into a pleasant excitement, yet I feel quite sure that the weekly visitor was no more eagerly awaited than is our tridaily postman in modern shirtwaist and Rough Rider hat—a less picturesque figure, but one whose frequent comings bridge time and distance between friends apart.

CHAPTER XXI

COLORS OF THE COUNTIES

IN THIS renaissance of things Colonial, it may be of interest to know the colors borne by the militia of each county after the year 1694, at which time the Provincial Council passed an act regulating the same. Prior to this the Calvert colors were the only ones ever mentioned in connection with the Colonial militia or army. After the Protestant revolution and the accession of William and Mary the Calverts were not the governing power in the province, and soon we find the Council of the Royal Governor regulating affairs in Maryland. The militia too was reorganized, and in 1694 the Assembly ruled "that the field officers and captains of horse and foot be empowered to determine all military affairs and to issue execution for the sheriffe to serve and collect all fines and forfeitures which shall become due and forfeited, etc., ex-officio.

"And that the same be employed toward the purchasing of armes and ammunition for such persons as are poore and unable to buy, and when that is done then towards paying of drumers and trumpeters. That there be a person appointed to execute the office of muster master and adjutant on each side of the bay, who shall be obliged to muster and see exercised the several troops and companies six times every yeare, besides the general muster and that 21. tobacco p. poll be settled upon each of the said officers."

The colors authorized by the Council were: For Kent, blue: St. Mary's, red; Anne Arundel, white; Calvert, yellow; Charles, bronze; Baltimore, green; Talbot, purple; Somerset, jack flag; Dorchester, buff; Cecil, crimson. These comprised all the counties of Maryland at that date.

As the troubles with the Indians continued it was necessary to pass another act in the year 1699 for the ordering and regulating the militia of this Province, for the better defense and security thereof.

This authorized "every colonel, major or captain of foote to enlist as many as they thought necessary in their communities, not already enlisted, between the ages of 16 and 60 years; by as equal proportions of the said inhabitants as possibly they can, to be of the militia or train bands of this providence, which said persons so enlisted, they shall muster, exercise and train in and at such places and at such certain times, as to them shall seem meet or the service, safety or defence of the province shall require, or as His Excellency the Governor of this Province, for the time being, shall cause or order."

It was further directed that no person should be a trooper without he be the owner of a good serviceable horse, and that such troopers must ride their own horses, and in consideration of their "great pay," they were not only to provide suitable furnishings for their horses but to find themselves with swords, carbines, pistols, holsters and ammunition. The great pay as then stipulated by the Assembly was to every colonel of foot, 2,000 pounds of tobacco per month; to every major of foot, 1,200 pounds; to a captain of foot, 1000 pounds; to a lieutenant of foot, 700 pounds; to an ensign 600 pounds; to a sergeant, a corporal and a drummer, each 400 pounds; to every private soldier, each 300 pounds of tobacco per month; to every major-general chief-commander in the field, 3,000 pounds per month; every colonel of horse, 2,300 pounds; a major of horse, 1,500 pounds; a captain of horse, 1,300 pounds; a lieutenant of horse, 1,000; to a cornet, 900 pounds; to a quarter-master, 700 pounds; to a corporal, 700 pounds; to a trumpeter, 700 pounds; to every private trooper, 600 pounds of tobacco.

CHAPTER XXII

THE BIRTHPLACE OF RELIGIOUS LIBERTY

To MARYLAND belongs the glory of having enacted the first law embodying the true spirit of religious freedom in the civilized world.

Sects and peoples had protested and revolted against dogma and ecclesiastical tryanny in the Old World, but all and divers of them proclaimed each itself the only true religion and proscribed all others who thought and believed differently. But in the little city of St. Mary's, in the budding springtime of the year 1649, when the air was redolent of the flowering blossoms and the very atmosphere pulsated with the breath of new life and hope, sixteen men of noble purpose, the representatives of the few inhabitants of the Province of Maryland, assembled at the little capital and promulgated a policy so broad as to embrace the persecuted in the remotest ends of the earth, so noble as to instill hope into the oppressed in all lands. It was on the 21st of April in the year above mentioned that this "Act Concerning Religion" was made a law under the seal of Governor William Stone, and with the coöperation of the people's representatives.

From the fragmentary survivals of this memorable Assembly, whose session was of but twenty-five day's duration, have been gleaned the names of the men who passed the Act of Religious Toleration.

The provisions of this act of Assembly were to secure

absolute harmony among the inhabitants of Maryland, to punish anyone who attempted to persecute or annoy others on account of their religious beliefs, to instill the principles of the Christian religion and to insure to all the fullest freedom to worship God after the dictates of their own consciences.

The banner of liberty which was then unfurled in the little city of St. Mary's heralded the glad tidings which have developed the glory of our national life.

From its first conception Maryland was meant to be the haven of rest to the persecuted of the earth.

Her very charter was a pledge of religious freedom between a Protestant King and a Roman Catholic lord, and it is well known that Cecilius Calvert founded his colony for the noble purpose of offering peace and security to those who were being oppressed in Great Britain. This new light of religious liberty which was set aflame at the Assembly of 1649 became a beacon which led many wanderers into this promised land and eventually illumined the path across the Atlantic, guiding the persecuted for conscience sake to Maryland as to a haven of refuge. They came from all parts of Great Britain to avail themselves of the immunity from molestation insured to all believers in Jesus Christ.

The Puritans came from Virginia, the Quakers from New England, the Dutch from New Amsterdam, the Scotch, the French Huguenots and many others, until Maryland became known as the "Land of Sanctuary." To have been the pioneer of religious liberty in the world is the greatest honor any government could desire and one which happily always has been accorded to the state which has been first in so many progressive movements in both the spiritual and material world.

The Act of Religious Toleration, which may be read in full in the Assembly Proceedings of Maryland for the year 1649, under the Bill entitled "An Act concerning Religion," begins as follows "For as much as in a well governed and . . . . Commonwealth matters concerning Religion and the honor of God ought in the first place to bee taken into serious consideration etc." After providing for the punishment of any who should Blaspheme against the name of either of the Holy Trinity, the Act continues as follows "And whereas the inforcing of the conscience in matters of Religion hath frequently fallen out to be of dangerous consequence in those Commonwealthes where it hath been practised, And for the more quiett and peaceable government of the Province and the better to preserve mutual Love and amity amongst the Inhabitants thereof, Be it therefore also by the Lo; Proprietary, with the advised and consent of this Assembly Ordeyned and enacted . . . . that noe person or persons whatsoever within this Province, or the Islands, Ports, Harbors, Creekes or havens thereunto belonging, professing to believe in Jesus Christ, shall from henceforth bee in any waies troubled, molested or discountenanced for or in respect of his or her religion, nor in the free exercise thereof within this Province or the Islands thereto belonging, nor compelled to the beliefe or exercise of any other Religion, against his or her consent etc."

The names of those who passed this Act of Religious Toleration, making Maryland the only place in the known world at that time where a man might worship according to his own conscience, should be more honored indeed than those who signed the Declaration of Independence. The names of this noble band are Governor William Stone,

William Stone

Robert Clarke

Thomas Greene

John Pille

Richard Bankes

Walter Pakes

Philip Conner

Richard Broune

Thomas Thornborough

John Ince

William Bretton

Robert Vaughn

Thomas Hatton

John Maunsell

RARE AUTOGRAPHS FROM THE AUTHOR'S COLLECTION OF THOSE WHO PASSED THE ACT ENSURING RELIGIOUS TOLERATION IN MARYLAND APRIL 21, 1649

Thomas Greene, Phillip Conner, John Maunsell, John Pille, Robert Clarke, John Ince, George Manners, Thomas Hatton, William Thorne, Cuthbert Fenwick, William Bretton, Thomas Thornborough, Walter Pakes, Robert Vaughan, Richard Browne, Richard Bankes.

CHAPTER XXIII

THE CURIOUS LAW OF DEODAND

AMONG the many interesting old English laws enforced in the Province of Maryland none is more curious than that known as "deodand," being derived from *Deo dandum*, "a thing that must be offered to God."

This, according to Bouvier, relates to any personal chattel whatever, animate or inanimate, which is the immediate cause of the death of a human creature, "The deodand was forfeited to the King to be distributed in alms by his high almoners for the appeasing of God's wrath." says Coke.

In the year 1637, according to the Provincial Court proceedings an inquest had been taken before the coroner at Mattapient, in St. Marie's county, upon the view of the body of one John Briant, late of Mattapient, planter, deceased, then and there lying dead before him, by the oath of Richard Garnett, John Wyatt, John Halfehide, Edward Fleete, Thomas Franklin, Xpofer Martin, Randall Revell, John Hilliard, Nicholas Harvey, Richard Lusthead, John Robinson and Zachary Mottershead, planters, to the number of twelve jurors, and charged to inquire how the said John Briant came by his death, who say upon their oath that the aforesaid John Briant by the fall of a tree had his bloud bulke broken, and hath two scratches under his chinne on the left side; and so that by means of the fall of the said tree upon him the said John Briant came by his death, and further the jurors aforesaid upon their oath aforesaid say that the tree moved to the death of the said John Briant and therefore find the said tree forfeited to the Lord Proprietary."

A Latin phrase attributed to Braceton has, sayd Bouvier, "been mistranslated so as to give rise to some erroneous statements by some authors as to what are deodands. *Omnia quae ad mortem movent.*" says he although evidently meaning all things which tend to produce death, has been rendered *move* to death, giving rise to the theory that things in motion only are to be forfeited. A difference, however, according to Blackstone, existed as to how much was to be sacrificed. Thus, if a man was to fall from a cart wheel, the cart being stationary, and be killed, the wheel only would be deodand, while if he were run over by the same wheel in motion not only the wheel but the cart and load became deodand, and this even though it belonged to the dead man.

An illustration of this found in the "Council Proceedings of 1681:" "When upon motion of Mr. Robert Carvile this day made to his Lordship and Council in behalf of Mary Ashbury, of Kent Island, widow and relict of Francis Ashbury, late of the same place, deceased, supplicating his Lordship of his grace and favor to remit unto the said widow the boate wherein the said Ashbury was drowned, together with her appurtenances, issued the following ordinance:

By the Proprietary and Council of Maryland, ss:

Ordered that the boate where Francis Ashbury, late of Kent Island (was, as is conceived), accidentally oversett and drowned, with all her sails, rigging and appurtenances, whatsoever, be and remain the proper goods and chattels of Mary, the widow, and relict of the said Francis, her heyres and assigns forever, to her or their owne proper use and behoofe forever, and that the same or any part or parcel thereof (in whose custody soever) be accordingly safcly delivered to the said Mary, or her order, his Ldspp haveing signified his pleasure favorably to relinquish his claim thereunto the said Mary or her heyres, as aforesaid. Dated at St. Marie's the 19th of April, in the season the yeare of the Dominion of the Rt. honble Charles, etc., Annoq Domini 1682. Signed per order,

JOHN LLEWELLIN, Cl. Consil.

To all whom it may concern this.

This law, which sacrificed "the bana," or slayer, must have a very ancient origin and was, no doubt, founded on deep-rooted superstition. As early as the year 1200 the inanimate death-dealer was given up to the authorities of the community in which an accidental death occurred and these officers made their returns to the King.

Not until the year 1846 was the English statute abolishing deodands enacted.

CHAPTER XXIV

THE PALACE OF LORD BALTIMORE

THE Palace of St. John's!

At last we have learned the name of Maryland's first executive mansion at the "Citie of St. Maries." The infomation is printed on the back of a rare Maryland map recently brought from England, which was published in the 1676 edition of "Speeds' Prospect of the Most Famous Parts of the World." The account of Lord Baltimore's province was, however, written in the year 1674, as Cecil County, erected in that year, is shown, and the map could not have been printed earlier. And as Charles Calvert is mentioned as "the Governor," and called the "Son and Heir of the Proprietary," it could not have been written after November, 1675, as he became the proprietary himself at that time on the death of Cæcilius. The further internal evidence in the names of the Gentlemen of His Lordship's Council determine the date of this account of the province, which is both authentic and extremely valuable in the new light thrown upon the early life and government of the Calverts. I am quoting only such parts as are of special interest.

"The original seat and principal City of this Province where the Provincial Courts, the General Assembly, the Secretaries Office, and other publick Offices are held; and where the Seat of Trade is fixt is St. Maries, situate in St. Maries County, on the East-side of St. Georges River.

"Here formerly at the Palace of St. Johns, the Governor Mr. Charles Calvert used to reside; but he now hath a very pleasant and commodious habitation at a place called Mattapony upon the River Patuxent, about eight miles from St. Maries; here is also another fair house where the Chancellor usually resides.

"As for the present Government of Maryland by the English, the Lord Proprietor in the first place is invested, as hath been mentioned, with absolute power and dominion; by whose sole command all things relating to Peace or War are ordered; and in whose name issue forth all publick Instruments, Patents, Warrants, Writs, etc.

"In the enacting of Laws he hath consent and advice of the general Assembly, which is made up of two estates; the first consisting of His Lordship's Privy Council (of which the Chancellor and Secretary alwaies are) and such Lords of Manors as are called by his Lordships special writ, the other of the Deputies of the province, elected by the free voice of the Free-holders of the respective Province for which each Deputy is chosen."

While those of us who have made any systematic study of our early records know that the Calverts were possessed of "royal rights," and that their province was composed of a landed aristocracy, we now learn for the first time that a regal palace was built as the "Seate of His Lordship."

Yet that this was so there is no doubt after reading our records in the light of this lately discovered account of Maryland.

Nor can it be denied that the Proprietary required the feudal service of "fiance" of those who held manors and other lands of him.

In corroboration of the statement on the map, that "here at the Palace of St. Johns" the Governor, Charles Calvert used to reside, we find in the original Calvert papers a letter from Governor Charles Calvert to his father, dated in the year 1664, in which he says: "Mr. White has done some things as to the House and Orchard of St. Johns, which I presume he'll send Yr. Lordship this shipping."

Again in the original Calvert papers, under the date of November 13, 1633, we find Cæcilius Calvert's instructions for settling his first adventurers, addressed to his brother, Leonard Calvert.

After giving him full directions, regarding a permanent settlement, he instructs him "to seate a towne," in which the first choice of lots was to be for a "fit place and competent quantity of grounds for a Forte" and "within or neere unto this, one for 'A convenient house, and a church or chapel adjacent' for the seate of his Lordship, or his Governor or other commissioners, these to be completed only as far as is necessary at present use and not in every part as fine as afterwards they may be."

That these official residences were promptly erected there is no doubt, as the earliest assemblies are known to have met at "the Forte of St. Maries."

On February 11, 1639, certain freemen in St. Mary's County are instructed to "be at Our Secretary's house at St. Johns" and from this time on frequent references are found to the "meeting of the Assembly at St. Johns."

It is interesting to know that we had a veritable "Prince of Maryland," living in a "palace" at St. Mary's, dressing in the ermine robes of state of his rank and in the armor of an English courtier, as shown in his several portraits extant, surrounded by councillors, who were required, by command of the proprietary, to wear some distinguishing mark either in costume or badge. (See Kilty and also original records.)

That Charles Calvert kept his retinue about him none can question who had read his letter to his father in the year 1664, in which he says: "I have 30 to provide victuals for, which does putt me to some care and trouble, besides the expense, which is the least." As Governor Calvert was at that time a widower without children, his niece, Anne Calvert, having charge of his household, it is evident that the other 28 persons were his official and household retainers.

That the Calverts instituted at their capital city a government more feudal in its form and customs than we have realized is now for the first time called to our attention, for, while it has long been known that Maryland was feudal in government, it has been claimed by one of her best local authorities in a review that Lord Baltimore never imposed any tenure by service in Maryland. So emphatic is his statement on this point that it is particularly interesting in view of evidence to the contrary. "If this be the meaning," he says, "I can only say that I see no intimation anywhere that so preposterous an idea ever entered Baltimore's mind, nor can I imagine how he could have carried it out if it had."

Yet our published archives are full of evidences that Lord Baltimore did require feudal service, known as "fiance," or obligation to serve the Lord in his court of justice.

According to the most eminent authorities on feudal service, "the Lord summoned his men to attend, either to serve him with their advice or to take part in the judging of disputes."

From this we turn to our own colonial state papers and find, among many other references which leave no doubt as to the exercise of Lord Baltimore's summoning his men "by writ."

On page 389 of volume I, Maryland Archives, "Thomas Gerrard, his opinion being demanded, as a private man, 'summoned by writt' not one of his Lops (Lordship's) council, but hath formerly been as lord of a manor."

From this it appears that the lords of manors were, therefore, thus summoned to the upper house of the Assembly by the Proprietary, as were the barons of England to Parliament by the king of England. For further proof that the Proprietary "summoned by special writt" those whom he wished to give their feudal "fiance" service we will quote only a few references to show, and that they were "amerced," or fined, for not performing this service when summoned all know who know the Maryland records, and hence the wonder that no one has ever before noted the significance of the fact.

In old Liber M. C. of the Provincial Records, the system is fully proven. On page 155—dated at St. Maries July 28, 1641—is a typical "summons by writt," "Cæcilius, etc., to Thomas Gerard, Lord of the Mannor of Saint Clements, Gent. Greeting: We do hereby authorize and withall will and require you that you repair in person to the House of General Assembly, held at St. Johns by Prorogation on Monday next, there to take and have voice and seat and to give us your advice touching such important affairs of our Province as shall then and there be consulted of, whereof fail not."

A similar one to Giles Brent may be seen on page 136, dated October 12, 1640. Another to Thomas Cornwallis January 18, 1638, and so all through the early records.

On page 90, volume I, Maryland Archives, at an Assembly held at "St. Johns" October 12, 1640, is this confirmatory statement: "Then the house being called all the Gentlemen summoned by special writt, and all the Burgesses that were returned from the several hundreds appeared," etc.

Even the old feudal custom of paying their tribute at a feast day was observed by the Calverts, all grants specifying that the quit rent, whether in silver, gold, tobacco and ear of Indian corn or whatever specified, was "to be paid to us at the two most usual feasts of the year—the Feast of the Annunciation of the Virgin Mary and St. Michael the Archangel—at our citie of St. Maries," etc.

We can imagine the scene at the "Palace of St. John" when all who held lands of his Lordship had repaired to the capital city to pay their tribute and to participate in the "feast" prepared by his Lordship for his "tenants."

This partaking of the feast is known in feudal annals as "dining with the king," as the king furnished the banquet. And so in a lesser degree it was the same in old Maryland.

CHAPTER XXV

SOMERSET COUNTY AND THE PRESBYTERIANS

LET us turn our backs upon the scene of Colonial courtiers and gay cavaliers in drooping plume and velvet doublet at "ye citie of St. Marie's" and wing our way across the "Mother of Waters" into the dim-lit lowlands of the Pocomoke, along its fern-fringed banks, to the scene of the first coming of the Presbyterians on the restful shores of old Somerset. Because ours is a peaceful mission today it must not be forgotten that this quiet shadowy river was the scene of the first naval battle in Maryland, when Lieutenant Raddcliffe Warren commanding the pinnace *Longtail*, manned by thirteen armed men, invaded the Pocomoke river, in response to Captain William Claiborne's orders, only to be pursued by his Lordship's pinnaces, the *St. Helen* and the *St. Margaret*. A lively engagement resulted, and three of the men on the *Longtail*, including its commander, and one of Lord Baltimore's men were killed in the encounter.

After this the country intersected by the many lovely rivers, with their curious Indian names, was left to the tribes which inhabited it until gradually the persecuted Presbyterians from Scotland and Ireland sought the welcoming seclusion of Somerset in preference to the Catholic stronghold on the Western Shore.

There were, however, a few white settlers here previous to the erection of Somerset County in the year 1666—but it was not until the latter half of the century that the charms of this far southern end of the Eastern Shore were fully enjoyed by those who had left the mother country in the interest of religion.

With the coming of Francis Makemie, the young Scotch divine, the scattered members of the faith were gathered together, and the occasional sermons delivered on the various plantations by traveling ministers became things of the past.

At Rehoboth, the plantation of Judge William Stevens, young Makemie preached his first sermon to the Presbyterian flock driven from Ireland and Scotland by the persecutions of a king without any religion of his own. The appropriateness of the Scriptural name "Rehoboth" as the site for a house of worship to those who had been driven to and fro is apparent. In Genesis xxvi, 22, we find: "And he removed from thence and digged another well, and for that they strove not, and he called the name of it Rehoboth, and he said for now the Lord hath made room for us, and we shall be fruitful in the land."

There were four strong Presbyterian churches planted by Francis Makemie in Somerset County, which at the time of his arrival (1680) embraced all the country between the Nanticoke River and the northern line of Accomac County, Virginia, now including the three counties of Somerset, Wicomico and Worcester.

These churches were Rehoboth, Manokin, Snow Hill and Wicomico. The first-named was, as we have seen, the oldest, and near it was the largest settlement on the Pocomoke River. Situated about ten miles from the mouth of the river, it was in the heart of a fine agricultural country.

The Pocomoke River was easy of access from all the lower parts of Somerset County and the Eastern Shore of Virginia, and being deep and navigable for more than thirty miles, naturally became the center of trade and travel. Francis Makemie, who, after his marriage lived in Accomac, kept his sloop, in which he sailed to his several places for conducting religious service.

From Rehoboth to Snow Hill, at the head of the Pocomoke, was a distance of twenty-five miles, but to the missionary no great matter for his occasional visits.

The Manokin Church was established on the river of the same name on which the beautiful town of Princess Anne still flourishes as one of the most interesting social centers in Maryland. The church founded by Makemie stands by the river bank surrounded by venerable trees and the tombs of many of the noble founders of old Somerset. These old brick walls and the surrounding cemetery form an interesting picture in the valley of the Upper Manokin River.

The northern part of Somerset County was the scene of "The Rockawalkin" Church. This country, rich in timber and copious streams, is a veritable garden for the growth of berries, small fruits and vegetables. Here is located Salisbury, the enterprising little Pittsburg of Maryland. The "Rockawalkin" congregation here long since built the Wicomico Presbyterian Church, which is within the town of Salisbury, and the little edifice several miles away is seldom used.

That Francis Makemie and the people with whom he cast his lot were of the higher classes of society and possessed of intellectual culture of no mean order a glimpse of those early days in old Somerset through the early records clearly shows. The immense estates, thousands of acres in extent, the elegant furniture imported from beyond the seas, the smaller luxuries of life, all denote refined and luxurious living, while Makemie's library of 896 volumes, Greek, Latin and Hebrew, besides the English, classical, miscellaneous and theological works, bespeak his higher education. His daughter Anne became the wife of Colonel Robert King, of Kingston, Somerset County, but left no descendants. The Rev. L. P. Bowen, who wrote so feelingly of Makemie's great work, said "there are none left of the blood of Makemie; but the name lives and scatters fragrance and beauty through all the far centuries. . . . There is, however, another child of his which does not wax old or die. It appears as a fertile vine planted by God's hand between the two beautiful bays, sending out its beautiful branches to all points of the compass. The Long Island and New Jersey churches lift the Presbyterian banner and fall into line with Rehoboth. New presbyteries are formed and a synod ere long!"

CHAPTER XXVI

A COLONIAL LENDING LIBRARY

IN OUR recent successful effort to establish traveling libraries in Maryland we have lost sight of the fact that not only is the idea a revival of the movement inaugurated by Dr. Thomas Bray in 1697, but that there still exist in our State several hundreds of these books which composed the first lending library in America. In St. John's College, in Annapolis, there are still preserved 398 out of the original 1095 volumes; at the diocesan library there are 23 of the 45 "belonging to the Library of St. Paul's in Baltimore County," now St. Paul's Protestant Episcopal Church, Baltimore.

In 1691 and 1692 the counties of Maryland were divided into parishes by act of Assembly and churches ordered to be built. In 1695 a petition was forwarded to their Majesties William and Mary "to annex forever the judicial office of commissary, before in the disposal of the Governor, to that which is purely ecclesiastical and at the appointment of the late Bishop of London." Realizing the necessity of having someone in authority to preside over the clergy in the province, a request was sent to the Lord Bishop of London to send over some "experienced, unexceptional clergyman for ye office intended."

The reputation of Rev. Thomas Bray, D. D., vicar of St. Botolph's Church, near Oldgate, England, we are told, "hindered the Bishop from being one moment at a loss whom to choose as the fittest person to model that infant church and establish it on a solid foundation."

In April, 1696, the Bishop offered Dr. Bray the office of Commissary of Maryland. Disregarding his own interest and the great profit which would have arisen from finishing his course of lectures which he had been successfully publishing, he soon determined in his own mind that there might be a greater field of doing good in the plantations than by his labors in England. With this in view he laid before the bishop the conditions— "a library would be the best encouragement to studious and sober men to go into the service, and that as the great inducement to himself to go would be to do the greatest good he could be capable of doing, he did therefore propose to their Lordships that if they thought fit to encourage and assist him in providing parochial libraries for the ministers who should be sent he would then accept the commissary's office in Maryland."

This proposal for parochial libraries being well approved of by the bishops, and due encouragement being promised in the prosecution of the design both by their Lordships and others, he set himself with all possible application wholly to provide missionaries and to furnish them with libraries, with an intent so soon as he should have sent both, to follow himself. That it was no easy matter to raise the necessary funds for his purpose we can judge from his eloquent appeals in his published pamphlets.

To the gentry and clergy of the Kingdom he addresses a proposal for purchasing lending libraries in all the deaneries of England and parochial libraries for Maryland,

Virginia and other foreign plantations. The proposal is as follows:

"*Honorable Sirs:* Amongst the many laudable contrivances for promoting Religion and learning in the world, in which several persons of a Publick spirit have labored more or less in all ages, there seem none to me would be of greater advantages to either, would tend more adapted to the present circumstances of our Parochial Clergy (one-third of whom I am afraid are not enabled by their Preferments to purchase a fourth part of those Books which it is absolutely necessary for every Pastor should peruse, and yet from whom great measures of knowledge are expected in this inquisitive age) than if we could have Lending libraries disposed, one in every Deanery throughout the Kingdom, for the service of those who have occasion to borrow."

"Standing libraries," he continues, "will signifie little in the country where persons must ride some miles to look into a book; but lending libraries, which come home to them without charge, may tolerably well supply the vacancies in their own studies till such times as these Lending may be improved into Parochial Libraries."

To show how closely the ideas of the seventeenth century scholar corresponded with the twentieth century plan of preserving the traveling libraries, we shall give Dr. Bray's own plan as submitted to his contemporaries:

"It being designed that these lending libraries should travel abroad, it may seem that the Books will be in danger to be soon lost by passing through so many hands. However, in order to their being fully secured it may be provided by these following methods: 1. That they be marked upon the cover to what Deanery they belong.

2. They may be locked up in Book presses made on purpose to keep them in. 3. They may be deposited with the Rural Dean, or with the minister or schoolmaster in some market town, if near the center of the Deanery, that so they may with very little trouble be sent for any market day and as easily returned within a limited time. And it may be presumed that any minister or schoolmaster for the use of such a library under his key will be willing to undertake the trouble to lend out the books and receive them in upon occasion. 4. That the limitation of Time for keeping a borrowed Book be determined by the Reverend Subscribers at the Visitation, as a month for a Folio, a Fortnight for a 4mo. and a week for an 8vo, which will have this good effect, that a book will be read over with speed and care, which if one's own might lye in a study without being quickly or very carefully perused, upon presumption that being one's own it may at any time be read, and therefore this, by the way, may be considered as one advantage of lending libraries. 5. That the Borrower having sent a note desiring any Book, his note be filed up, and his name entered in a Book kept in the library for that purpose, what year, month and day he borrowed such a Book, and upon the Return of the book the note be also returned and the name of the Borrower crossed out."

Such were the suggestions from the founder of the first lending libraries in England and America. It is peculiarly interesting to us as Marylanders to know that the first libraries instituted in this country were in our own province, and from here the movement was extended by Dr. Bray to Boston, New York, Albany, Philadelphia and Charleston, S. C.

In this proposal to the gentry and clergy this notable divine writes: "In short, as mere zeal for public service hath excited me to leave no stone unturned to procure parochial libraries in the plantations in which, I thank God, I have had hitherto no mean success, so if with the same labor I can be serviceable in the like design to my dearest Mother, the Church, and my reverend brethren at home I shall think myself sufficiently happy in such an employment; and indeed, as I know not that thing in the world wherein I could take that satisfaction as in this piece of service to our church at home, so, provided this design of lending libraries in England should universally take, whereby without any man's charge, properly speaking, so great an advance will be made toward parochial libraries in the plantations, instead of libraries for Maryland, the bounds of my first design, I shall not only extend my endeavors for the supply of all the English colonies in America therewith, but can most willing be a missionary into every one of those provinces to fix and settle therein when they are obtained, being so fully persuaded of the great benefit of these kind of libraries that I should not think 'em too dear a purchase, even at a hazard of my life, being to both churches and clergy."

Dr. Bray had two book plates made for the books belonging to the lending and parochial libraries by Simon Yelhelin, a young Frenchman who settled in London.

In this collection of Bray books are some marked on the covers as belonging to the Library of Herring Creek, Arundel County; some to the library of K. G. and O. N. S. Parish, in St. Mary's County; others to St. Paul's in Prince George's, Md.

CHAPTER XXVII

COLONIAL CURRENCY

THE Maryland colonists had literally "money to burn," for in the early days tobacco was the only currency of the new country. Lands were bought with it, as well as all commodities. If the tobacco crop failed the planters' hopes of importations of household goods and the Colonial belles' dream of dainty furbelows vanished. In the early wills we find no currency other than tobacco mentioned—"the debts due me in sweet-scented tobacco, so many lbs. neatt in casques" frequently are mentioned and devised. The land records bear testimony that lands bought were paid for with tobacco, 5000 pounds of which would buy a good plantation of 200 acres. Even coffins were bartered for tobacco. In Colonial administration accounts we find that where 100 pounds of tobacco were paid for a coffin, 300 pounds are charged to the account "for baked meats and drink at the funeral."

As the population increased in the colony the value of tobacco naturally depreciated from overproduction, until the need of a currency caused the leading men of the province to appeal to the Lord Proprietary for a fixed and stable money. Cæcilius Calvert thereupon designed coins for his palatinate. On the obverse side of these, several of which are preserved at the Maryland Historical Society, is a bust of himself; on the reverse is the Calvert arms. At a council held at Bushwood, Mr. Slye's house, on Saturday, March 3, was read a letter dated October 12, 1659, at London, from Cæcilius Calvert, addressed to his Lieutenant and council, and directed the secretary touching the mint, as followeth, viz:

"After my hearty commendation, etc., having with great paines and charge procured necessaries for a particular coyne to be used in Maryland, a sample whereof in a piece of a shilling, a sixpence and a Groate I herewith send you, I recommend it to you to promote all you can the dispensing it, and by proclamation to make current within Maryland for all payments upon contracts or causes happening or arising after a day to be by you limited in the said Proclamation, and to procure an act of Assembly for the punishing of such as shall counterfeit the said coyne or otherwise offend in that behalfe."

Just a week before the date of this letter the following order was issued by the King's Council of State, at London, October 4, 1659:

"Upon information given by Richard Pight, clerke of the irons in the mint, that Cecil Lord Baltimore and divers others with him and for him have made and transported great sums of money and doe still go on to make more; ordered, that a warrant be issued forth to the said Richard Pight for the apprehending of the Lord Baltimore and such others as are suspected to be engaged with him in the said offense and for seizing of all such moneys, stamps, tooles and instruments for copying the same as can be met with, and to bring them in safe custody to the Council."

It is evident that Cæcilius Calvert was fully able to vindicate his action, else he would not have forwarded the letter to his lieutenant and Council urging upon them the acceptance of the currency offered them. In the letter referred to he asks for the advice of his Council "touching what you think best to be further done in that matter touching coin, for if encouragement be given by the good success of it this year there will be abundance of adventurers in it the next year."

To his brother, Philip Calvert, he writes under the same date, saying, "It must not be imposed upon the people, but by a lawe there made by their consents in a General Assembly, which, I pray, fail not to signify to the Governor and Council there, together from me, by showing them this letter, signed, your most affectionate brother, Cæcilius C. Baltimore."

In less than two weeks after the reading of these letters in the Council meeting, the memorable revolution headed by Josias Fendall, occurred, and the proclamation of Maryland's freedom was announced from the Council chamber at Bushwood, and with the overthrow of Lord Baltimore's government the question of currency was dropped.

Two years later, when the Calverts had come into their own again, Governor Philip Calvert brought the matter of coinage before the Assembly. It occasioned no little discussion, in which Robert Brooke and Edward Lloyd opposed its passage in the upper house, or Council, on the ground that the Palatinate of Durham had no liberty to coin money; hence the Palatinate of Maryland had none, as it had only the rights and privileges of a bishop of Durham.

The majority, however, carried through the act for the relief and convenience of the colonists, the provisions being that his Lordship be petitioned to set up a mint for the coining of money within the province. That the money coined therein be of as good silver as English sterling and other pieces in proportion; that the offenses of clipping, scaling or counterfeiting, washing, or in any way diminishing such coin be punishable with death and forfeiture of lands and goods to the Lord Proprietary; that his Lordship receive said coin in payment for rents and all amounts due to him. The Proprietary was much gratified with the bill, which was sent to London for his approval, and sent over to the province at once enough coin to meet the needs of the colonists.

In the year 1662 the Assembly passed an act "to put the coin in circulation," requiring "every householder and freeman in the province to take up 10 shillings per poll of the said sums of money proportionately for every such respective family, etc., for three years, etc."

But despite the passing of the law, it is evident that money was neither freely coined nor circulated in the province in early times. One man, writing of the province in 1671, 10 years after the passing of the act to establish a mint, says: "the general way of traffic and commerce there is chiefly by barter or exchange of one commodity for another, yet they want not, besides English and other foreign coins, some of his Lordship's own coins, which at his own charge, he caused to be coined and dispersed throughout the province."

Many historians doubt that a mint was ever established in the province, but Old Mixon in his account of the settlement, published in 1708, tells us that the Lord Proprietary had a mint here to coin money, but it never was much used.

Again he says, "tobacco is their meat, drink, clothing and money; not but that they have both Spanish and English money pretty plenty, which serves only for pocket expenses and not for trade, tobacco being the standard of that, as well with the planters and others as with the merchants." While many acts were passed regulating the currency of the province, payments were made in tobacco as late as 1763 and perhaps later, but in that year gold and silver coin were given their rating in the payments given in lieu of tobacco.

CHAPTER XXVIII

THE DUTCH ON THE DELAWARE

If Maryland had her original territorial rights today Philadelphia would be her metropolis instead of Baltimore.

In the charter granted by King Charles I. to Cæcilius Calvert was included "all that part of the peninsula, or 'chersonese,' lying in the parts of America between the ocean on the east and the bay of Chesapeake on the west, divided from the residue thereof by a right line drawn from the promontory or headland called Watkins Point, situate on the bay aforesaid, near the Wighco on the west unto the main ocean on the east, and between that boundary on the south unto that part of the bay of Delaware on the north which lieth under the fortieth degree of north latitude from the equinoctial, where New England is terminated, and all the tract of that land within the metes underwritten passing from the said bay called Delaware bay in a right line by the degrees aforesaid unto the true meridian of the first fountain of the river Pattowmack; thence verging toward the south, unto the farther bank of the said river, and following the same on the west and south unto a place called Cinquack, situate near the mouth of the said river where it disembogues unto the aforesaid promontory or place called Watkins Point." The area which Maryland is said to have lost includes the whole of Delaware and 20 miles in Pennsylvania including the city of Philadelphia, in addition to half a million acres in Virginia.

It is not our purpose to go into the details of the successful efforts of the Dutch to displace the Swedes from the the Delaware, which resulted in the emigration of not a few of the latter to Maryland.

Our interest centers rather with the Dutch pretensions in relation to Lord Baltimore's rights. Having wrested from the Swedes the land, which they divided into two provinces and called one New Amstel and the other Altoona, the Dutch became uneasy lest the Maryland Proprietary assert his charter rights and deprive them of their ill-gained possessions. In the year 1659, upon the demand of Governor Alricks, of New Amstel for the return of several prisoners who had escaped into Maryland, the question of boundaries arose, and Lord Baltimores' son arriving while the matter was under discussion, ordered that the land between the degrees of his Lordship's grant be reviewed and surveyed, and when ascertained be reduced under his jurisdiction, without the intention of abandoning any part of it. Without waiting for the results of the resurvey, many of the Dutch of New Amstel moved down into Maryland and Virginia.

At a meeting of the Maryland Council, Colonel Nathaniel Utie was commissioned to "repair to the pretended Governor of a people seated on Delaware bay within his Lordship's province, without notice given to his Lordship's lieutenant here, and to require them to depart the province"—and what was more important still, he was instructed "to insinuate unto the people there seated that in case they make their application to his Lordship's Governor here, they shall find good conditions according to the conditions of plantations, granted to all comers into this province, which shall be made good to them, and that they shall have protection in their lives, liberty and estates which they shall bring with them."

A protest was sent by Governors Alricks and Beekman, and by the Council and Schepens, namely, Alexander d'Hinoyosa, John Williamson, John Crato, Hendrick Ripp and signed by the secretary, G. Van Sweringen. This protest accused the Marylanders of luring away the citizens of South River by promises of "protection and much liberty."

Governor Stuyvesant, hearing of Colonel Utie's mission, was not for parleying and at once appointed his "beloved, discreet and faithful Cornelius van Ruyven, secretary, and Captain Martin Krugier" to dispose and regulate all the affairs on South River, making Krugier commander of the military forces there, to protect the settlements from Maryland invasions. Colonel Utie was to be "arrested as spy" and the Lord Baltimore men generally put to flight.

The news, however, that Colonel Utie had departed and was preparing to return to New Amstel with a force of several hundred armed men changed the attitude of the testy Governor of New Amsterdam, who decided to send his ambassadors to the Lord Baltimore in a "friendly and neighborly way."

Consequently on September 30, 1659, Augustine Herman and Resolved Waldren, the two accredited ambassadors of Stuyvesant, started for Maryland under the guidance of several Indians and the protection of an escort of Dutch soldiers.

Augustine Herman, in his journal, gives an account of the dangers and expense of this trip. On October 7 they arrived at Secretary Calvert's house, hence it took eight days to accomplish the distance, which is now covered in a few hours.

The declarations delivered by the Dutch ambassadors to the Maryland Council were received and debated by that august body consisting of Captain William Stone, Dr. Thomas Gerrard, Dr. Luke Barber, Colonel Nathaniel Utie, Colonel Baker Brooke and Edward Lloyd.

These gentlemen ordered that warning should be given to the Dutch to be gone; "that when we are able to beat them out they may not plead ignorance."

A letter to this effect was sent to the States General of the Manhattans.

The directors of the Dutch West India Company, took the matter up, and Captain James Neale, agent for Lord Baltimore in Holland, was instructed by the Proprietary of Maryland to see if his rights on the Delaware were recognized; if not, to protest against the attitude of the Dutch and demand their surrender of the lands they had usurped.

In consequence of these instructions Captain Neale had an audience with the Council of Nineteen of Amsterdam, who claimed their right by possession, etc.

Our space is too limited to enter into the particulars of the prolonged controversy which finally ended in Maryland losing so much of her territory, and in New Amsterdam losing some of her representative men who joined the Lord Baltimore's subjects and became distinguished in his Lordship's service.

CHAPTER XXIX

THE ORIGIN OF LYNCH LAW

THE popular idea that "lynch law" originated in the Southern States and was without any precedent in the English code is a fallacy. Every constable appointed by his Lordship's provincial justices was required in his oath of office to swear that he would "levy hue and cry" and cause refractory criminals to be taken. A glance at the process of this ancient custom will readily convince us that the modern practice of summary execution under the name of "hue and cry" was flourishing in England from earliest times, and was only beginning to be brought under control in the thirteenth century. According to the law, before the time of King Edward I, "when a felony is committed, the hue and cry should be raised." The literal meaning is given by some as "up foot and cry," the proper cry being "Out! out!" "The neighbors should turn out with the bows, arrows and knives, that they are bound to keep, and besides much shouting there will be hornblowing, the 'hue' will be horned from vill to vill." Sir Frederick Polock, of Oxford, and Hon. Frederick W. Maitland, of Cambridge Universities, give the most comprehensive account of this ancient custom. Their exposition of it shows that "if a man is overtaken by hue and cry while he has still about him the signs of his crime he will have short shrift. Should he make any resistance he will be cut down. But even if he submits to capture his fate is already decided. If he was still holding the gory knife or driving away stolen beasts, he was brought before a court (likely enough one hurriedly summoned for the purpose), and without being allowed to say one word in self-defense he would be promptly hanged, beheaded or precipitated from a cliff, if guilty of stealing, the owner of the goods would act as amateur executioner. It is said by the commentator that while the royal judge did not much like it, it did in truth rid England of more malefactors than the King's Court could hand." The origin of this law was in the days when the criminal taken in the act was *ipso facto* an outlaw. He was not entitled to any "law," the proof that he was taken redhanded was sufficient evidence for speedy sentence and execution. It was quite evident that the old feudal law of the hue and cry which was proclaimed in Maryland and Virginia in early Colonial days, and which was brought into the colonies along with the other ancient English customs, is perpetuated in the modern lynch law, which has been often pronounced a purely Southern institution. It is rather a bit of barbaric justice (?) which is a survival of the days when America was unknown, and when the early progenitors of all alike, whether of the North or the South, of the East or the West, "upfooted" and away with the echoing "Out!" Out!" through the forests and glades of old England in hot pursuit of the criminal.

CHAPTER XXX

THE GENTLE HEARTED INDIAN

THE passing of the Indian as a charge of the government to an independent property holder makes peculiarly interesting a glimpse at his original characteristics, when first discovered by the English.

Indeed, the picturesque side of the settlement of Maryland must largely include the Indian, strikingly fantastic against the dark background of the primeval forest. Our clearest view of him is from a word picture drawn by those who saw him as he appeared to the interested and startled gaze of the English settlers.

To the red man, as to all unenlightened minds, mystery meant menace, and it is therefore not surprising that we are told by the adventurers that "at the first loaming of our ship upon the river we found the king of the Paschattoways had drawn together 1500 bowe men."

These dusky warriors, "grotesquely painted with blue from the nose upward, and red downward, in a very ghastly manner, their jet black hair, long and straight, tied up in a knot over the left ear with a string of wampampegge; upon their foreheads a copper fish, armed with long bows and arrows," must have given the adventurers quite as severe a shock as they gave the frightened natives in "their great canoe as big as an island, with as many men as there be trees in the woods."

Here was the true and genuine Indian dear to the heart of the small boy, and as such may he be preserved to the childish imagination along with his dear old Santa Claus, and not ruthlessly despoiled of his warpaint, feathers and arrows by his too practical instructors and presented in "an old plug hat, a modern rifle and any old clothes he can find," as I recently heard the Indian described to one of Thompson Seton's most ardent worshipers! The disillusioning of this imaginative little lad was pathetic, and even if we grown-ups are glad for the redman to go, let the small boy keep his Indian as his forefathers found him—that first night when the woods were lit up with great beacon fires, against which the English could see him in council and on guard.

We are told that "the emperor soon lost his fear and went privately aboard the ship, where he was courteously entertained, and understanding we came in a peaceable manner bade us welcome and gave us leave to sit down in what place of his kingdom we pleased."

While this king was aboard, "all the Indians came to the water side, fearing treason, whereupon two of the king's men that attended him in our shippe were appointed to row on shore to quit them of this feare; but they refusing to go for fear of the popular fury, the interpreters standing on the deck shewed the king to them, that he was in safety, wherewith they were satisfied."—

At last they ventured to come aboard. "It was worth the hearing for those who understood them to hear what admiration at our ship, calling it a canow and wondering where so great a tree grew that made it, conceiving it to be made of one piece, as their canows are." Again we learn that "our great ordinance was a fearful thunder they had never heard before, all the country trembles at them."

The fear of the Indian soon turned to love, and the

Werowance, or king of Yaocomico, in a speech interpreted to the adventurers by Captain Henry Fleete, declared "I doe love the English soe well that if they should kill me, so that they left me with so much breath as to speak unto my people, I would command them not to revenge my death."

From this gentle-hearted Indian chief the newcomers "to avoid all just occasion of offense and collour of wrong, bought for hatchetts, axes, bowes and cloathes a quantitie of some 30 miles of land we call Augusta Carolina."

The Indians of Yaocomico had been much harassed by the "Sasquesa-hanoughs," a mighty bordering nation, who came often into their country to waste and destroy, and "had driven many of the former tribe to leave their country and pass over the Patoemeck to free themselves from peril before we came," which fact the English considered a dispensation of Divine Providence as preparing the way for those who were "to bring His law and Light among the Infidels."

"Is not this a place of wonder," writes an adventurer, "that a nation which a few dayes before was in armes with the rest against us should yield themselves now unto us like lambs, and give us their houses, lands, livings for a trifle? *Digitus Dei est hic;* and surely some great good is entended by God to his nation!"

Thus spoke with the tongue of prophecy one of the men who helped to found this great American people.

Strange as it seems, we are told that these wild men of the forest held a religious belief similar in many particulars to our own.

"First," says our adventurer, "they acknowledge One God of Heaven which they call our God, and cry a thousand shames upon those Christians that so highly offend so good a God. They also believe in the immortality of the soul and that there is a place of joy and another of torment."

Quite as astonishing is the statement that these red men had a tradition of Noah and the flood which destroyed the world for sin.

Again we are told that the Indians also adored corn and fire as two gods very beneficial unto man's nature. In Longfellow's "Hiawatha" we have had transmitted to us the legend of the origin of the maize, or Indian corn. First how Hiawatha prayed for a food for his people other than the fishes and animals of the forest, and because he fasted and prayed—

> Not for greater skill in hunting,
> Not for greater craft in fishing,
> Not for triumphs in the battle
> And renown among the warriors;
> But for profit of the people,
> For advantage of the nations.—

the Master of Life sent "Mondamin," or the Maize, as a new gift to the nations which should be their food forever.

In careful reading of the death, burial and resurrection of "Mondamin" one cannot but be impressed with the symbolic likeness to the Christian belief, and it is not surprising that the Indians having this legend of the corn should worship it as the sustainer of life and "a new gift from the Great Spirit," through whom was their salvation in their time of physical peril.

We have reason to believe that all the interesting customs and legends connected with the corn-huskings, which

ORIGINAL ASSIGNMENT OF "HOMEWOOD" TO CHARLES CARROLL, GRANDFATHER OF CHARLES CARROLL OF CARROLLTON

Found by the Author in the original records of Maryland, and photographed by her for the Executive Exhibit at The Jamestown Exposition

form such a picturesque part of the old plantation life in Maryland, were drawn directly from the Indians during the period when the two races lived in close contact.

The custom of making a circle around the young corn, to keep out the cut-worm and the crow, was an Indian one. The merrymakings of the women over the huskings of the corn, the superstition that the finding of the red ear meant a handsome husband for the lucky maiden, have come down to us in the rural districts of Maryland, and were found by Longfellow to exist in the Land of the Dacotahs among the remnant of the northern tribes; and so we are gradually learning that the Indians have left a stronger impress upon the white race than we supposed, for the traditions which we have long thought to be of negro origin antedate his advent among us.

All of the early Colonial writers unite in describing the native (Indian) as "so noble that you cannot doe them any favour or good turnes, but they return it. There is a small passion among them, but they weigh all with a calme and quiet reason. And to doe this the better in greate affaires they are studdying in a long silence what is best to bee said or done, and then they answer yea or no in two words, and stand constantly to their resolution." To our shame we learn, "they are of great temperance, especially from Hott waters or wine, which they are barely brought to taste, save only whom the English have corrupted with their vices." Their simplicity is shown in the following: "They doe runne unto us with smiling faces when they see us and will fish and hunt for us if wee will; and all this with entercourse of very few words, but wee have hitherto gathered their meaning by singnes."

After learning from this unprejudiced source the true characteristics of the Indians when first neighbors to the English, we cannot but believe that these simplehearted children of nature were driven to cruelty, hatred and revenge by the white men, to whom they so freely had resigned their homes, and with whom they showed every desire to live in peace. Surely of those self-sacrificing and trustful redskins it could not honestly be said that "the only good Indian was a dead Indian."

CHAPTER XXXI

WITCHCRAFT IN MARYLAND

THE fact that there was a belief in witchcraft among the ignorant classes in Colonial Maryland is made evident in the court proceedings in the year 1654, when testimony was taken on June 23 regarding the execution of Mary Lee, a witch, on board a ship bound for Maryland as follows:

"The Deposition of Mr. Henry Corbyn, of London, aged about 25 years. Sworne and examined in the Province of Md. before the Governor and Councell the 23 June, Anno Domini 1654. Saith that at sea upon this Deponent's voyage, hither in the ship called "The Charity of London," Mr. John Bosworth, being Master, and about a fortnight or three weeks before said ship's arrivall in this Province of Maryland, or before a Rumour amongst the Seamen was very frequent that one Mary Lee, then aboard the said Ship, was a witch, the said Seamen confidently affirming the same upon her own deportment, and discourse, and then more earnestly than before Importuned the said Master that a tryall might be had of her, which he the said Master, Mr. Bosworth, refused; but resolved (as he expressed to put her shore upon the Barmudos), but cross winds prevented and the Ship grew daily more Leaky—almost to desperation—and the Chief Seamen often declared their Resolution of leaving her if an opportunity offered itself, which aforesaid Reasons put the Master upon a consultation with Mr. Chipsham and this Deponent, and it was thought fitt, considering our said condition, to Satisfie the Seamen in a way of whether she were a witch or not, and Endeavoured by way of delay to have the Commanders of other ships aboard, but stormy weather prevented, in the Interime two of the seamen apprehended her without order and searched her and found some signall or marke of a witch upon her, and then calling the Master Mr. Chipsham and this Deponent, with others to see it, afterwards made her fast to the Capstall between decks, and in the morning the Signall was Shrunk into her body for the most part, and an examination was thereupon importuned by the Seamen, which this Deponent was desired to take, whereupon she confessed as by her confession appeareth, and upon that the seamen importuned the said Master to put her to Death, which as it seemed he was unwilling to doe, and went into his Cabbinn, but being more vehemently pressed to it he told them they might doe what they would and went into his cabbinn, and sometime before they were about that action he desired this deponent to acquaint them that they should doe no more than what they should justifie, which they said they would doe by laying all their hands in generall to the execution of her.

(Signed) HENRY CORBYN."

Francis Daily also testified to the fact that Mary Lee was hanged as a witch on the ship above mentioned.

It does not appear upon record what punishment was meted out to those who executed the woman.

In October of the same year Richard Manship brings suit in court against Peter Godson for saying his (Manship's) wife was a witch. The testimony is very interesting as reflecting those times:

"Barito Herrings, aged 40 years or thereabouts, sworne, saith that Peter Godson and Richard Manship, meeting on your petitioner's plantation, Richard Manship asked the said Peter Godson whether he would prove his wife a witch. Peter Godson replied, take notice what I say. I came to your home where your wife layed two straws and the woman in a jesting way said: They say I am a witch, if I am a witch, they say I have not the power to skip over these two straws, and bid the said Peter Godson to skip over them, and about a day after the said Godson said he was lame, and thereupon would maintain his, Manship's, wife to be a witch."

Happily, however, the witch was not put to death on such evidence, and after retractions by Peter Godson the case was dismissed.

No doubt it is from this element in Colonial Maryland that the belief in the power of spells and tokens has descended among the ignorant classes. In the rural districts of Maryland accidents to life and limb are still traced to the enmity of someone who has put a "spell" on the unfortunate victim, but, as Kipling says, that is another story, and will be more fully treated under the head of Maryland folklore in a later edition.

It should be particularly gratifying to all Marylanders to know that the belief in witchcraft did not reach the ruling classes, and that no law exist regarding witches, hence Maryland has the proud and comforting satisfaction of never having tainted her soil with the innocent blood of helpless men and women in the name of religion.

CHAPTER XXXII

THE FIRST THEATRE IN AMERICA

IN VIEW of the general interest in theatres in this country it is worthy of notice that in the year 1752 what is claimed to be the first theatre in America was advertising its attractions at Annapolis by consent of the President of the Council. This bill appeared in the Maryland *Gazette* on June 18, 1752:

"By permission of His Honor the President at the new theatre in Annapolis, by the company of Comedians from Virginia on Monday next, being the 22d of this instant, will be performed "The Beggars' Opera;" likewise a farce, called "The Lying Valet;" to begin precisely at 7 o'clock. Tickets to be had at the printing office—Box 10s; pit, 1s 6d. No person to be admitted behind the scenes."

The company, however, did not confine its performances to farces, as "King Richard III," "Cato" and other historical plays were produced.

Whether this was the first theatre in Annapolis or not it is impossible to say, but it is the earliest of which we find any mention. It was not large enough to long accommodate the increasing population at the capital, which, with its growing wealth and fashion, was fast becoming the "social Athens of America."

Eight years later we find another new theatre advertised in the *Gazette* to be opened "by permission of his Excellency the Governor."

The opening night witnessed "The Orphans" and was no doubt largely attended. In the year 1771 Eddis, the King's Surveyor of Customs at Annapolis, wrote to a friend in England: "You well know that I have ever been strongly attached to the rational entertainment resulting from theatrical exhibitions. When I bade farewell to England I little expected that my passion for the drama could have been gratified in any tolerable degree at a distance so remote from the great mart of genius, and I brought with me strong prepossessions in behalf of favourite performers whose merits were fully established by the universal sanction of intelligent judges. My pleasure and surprise were therefore excited in proportion on finding performers in this country equal at least to those who sustain the best of the first character in your most celebrated provincial theatres.

"Our Governor, from a strong conviction that the stage, under proper regulations, may be rendered of general utility and made subservient to the great interests of religion and virtue, patronizes the American Company; and, as their present place of exhibition is on a small scale and inconveniently situated, a subscription by his example has been rapidly completed to erect a new theatre on a commodious, if not elegant, plan. The manager is to deliver tickets for two seasons to the amount of respective subscriptions, and it is imagined that the money which will be received at the doors from non-subscribers will enable him to conduct the business without difficulty, and when the limited number of performances is completed the entire property is to be vested in him. This will be a valuable addition to our catalogue of amusements. The building is already in a state of forwardness and the day of opening is anxiously expected."

In November, 1771, the third and commodious theatre was opened in the Ancient City, and the audiences which crowded it during the season are described as of "a fashionable and brilliant appearance."

Again we are indebted to one of Eddis' personal letters for a description of the new theatre, in which he says the structure is not inelegant, but, "in my opinion, on too narrow a scale for its length: the boxes are commodious and neatly decorated; the pit and gallery are calculated to hold a number of people without incommoding each other; the stage is well adapted for dramatic and pantomimical exhibitions, and several of the scenes reflect great credit on the ability of the painter."

"I have before observed that the performers are considerably above mediocrity, therefore little doubt can be entertained of their preserving the public favor and reaping a plenteous harvest."

The names of the American Company were Mr. and Mrs. Hallam, Mr. and Mrs. Parker, Mr. and Mrs. Osborne, Mr. and Mrs. Burdett, Mrs. Jones, Mrs. Page and Mrs. Malone, Messrs. Jefferson, Dailey, Verling, Spencer, Wall, Morris and Darby.

The names of the Virginian Company of players which have come down to us from the days of the first theatrical performers advertised in 1752 are those of Messrs. Evanson, Herbert, ——— and Kean.

CHAPTER XXXIII

A COLONIAL BUSINESS WOMAN

DINAH NUTHEAD, the first seventeenth century business woman in Maryland, and perhaps in America, received a license from the General Assembly to set up her printing press at Annapolis "to print blanks, bills, bonds, writs, warrants of attorney, letters of administration and other necessary blanks useful for the public offices of this Province." In her petition before the Assembly she had declared her willingness to forfeit her license and her bond and go out of business if she should print anything other than specified.

The Assembly having graciously granted Dinah's humble petition she gave bond for £100 lawful money of England, with Mr. Robert Carville and William Taylard, of St. Mary's County, as her securities, and proceeded to carry on the business which had previously been established by her deceased husband, William Nuthead, public printer for the government.

Curiously enough this energetic and progressive Maryland woman, who was clever enough to conduct this important business could not write her own name.

It is quite evident from this that Dinah had no thought of sticking type with her own fair hands. She merely supplied the money and brains, leaving the mechanical part to her more highly educated employes.

Despite the modern idea that the twentieth century woman is a new species of woman because she has taken a more assertive part in the world's affairs, we find that in the middle of the seventeenth century, while few had the education of text books, the women of that day were endowed with executive ability and a rare natural intelligence, else the keen men of that pioneer period would not almost invariably have appointed their wives—and if unmarried their sisters—as executors of their wills.

Estates were often difficult to settle in Colonial times, false claims to property were frequently set up in the absence of the rightful heirs in England or other foreign parts—a notable instance being the attempt to wrest the property of Mr. Benjamin Gill, of Charles County, from his daughter, Ann Gill Neale, and her husband, Captain James Neale, during their absence from Maryland.

As executors and administrators of estates women had the same legal right to appear in court that they have today, and, whenever it was to their interest to do so, they did not hesitate openly to defend their claims. From this fact the superficial students of those times have drawn the conclusion that the woman with the "power of attorney" vested in her was a lawyer by profession.

Thus this pretty and picturesque Portia of the Maryland provincial bar is despoiled of her gown and mortar board 'neath the X-rays of historic research, and is compelled to take her rightful place with the other bright and intelligent Colonial women who, by their office, appeared in the halls of justice to execute the business committed to them.

There is a unique case on record in which the jury of women was impaneled to give their verdict regarding the guilt of a woman named Judith Catchpoll, who was accused of infanticide.

The trial was held at a General Provincial Court in session at Patuxent, September 22, 1656.

While the jury was called upon to give a verdict only on a certain phase of the case, its decision established Judith's innocence in the eyes of the Council, of whom were present Captain William Fuller, Mr. Richard Preston, Mr. Edward Lloyd, Mr. John Pott and Mr. Michael Brooke.

The names of the women composing the jury were Rose Smith, Mrs. Belcher, Mrs. Chaplain, Mrs. Brooke, Mrs. Battin, Mrs. Canady, Mrs. Bussey, Elizabeth Caxton, Elizabeth Potter and Dorothy Day—the number being 10, two less than the legal male jury.

Evidently women of Colonial Maryland, were quite as brainy as their present-day descendants, since the gentlemen of the Council recognized the fact that the opinion of 10 intelligent women was equal to that of 12 men at any time!

A description of the Maryland girls, written in the year 1660 by one who had spent several years in the colony, says: "They are extreme bashful at the first view, but after a continuance of time hath brought them acquainted, then they become discreetly familiar and are much more talkative than men. All complemental courtships, drest up in critical rarities, are meer strangers to them, plain wit comes nearest their Genius; so that he who intends to court a Maryland girle, must have something more than the tautologies of a long-winded speech to carry on his design, or else he may (for aught I know) fall under the contempt of her own frown and his own windy oration."

From this we can conclude that the old-time Maryland girls were not to be taken in by pretty speeches. They must all have been belles, as some married not only once, but many times, it being no unusual thing to find a Colonial dame who had been four times led to the altar. Four seems, however, to have been the limit, as there is no record so far as known, where anyone promised to obey the fifth time!

CHAPTER XXXIV

NEW LIGHT ON CLAIBORNE'S CLAIM TO KENT ISLAND

At last, after a lapse of two and three quarters centuries, we are to know the truth regarding the Claiborne claim to Kent Island. Not only did he wage a bitter contest for its possession, but whose who have come after him have from time to time written him up as a much-injured saint or written him down as a pirate and rebel, so that the readers of history have had to draw their own conclusions and let the contest of words go on. The transcript of records in the High Court of Admiralty at London recently made by R. T. Marsden, has put us in possession of the testimony brought out during his Majesty's trial of Claiborne for piracy and murder, and in some cross-suits of Cloberry and Clayborne, partners in a trading company. We find from these hitherto unfamiliar records that Claiborne never had the faintest claim to Kent Island. That King Charles issued only a license to trade and make discoveries will be readily seen by the following: "Charles, by the grace of God King of England, Scotland, France and Ireland, Defender of the Faith," etc.

"Whereas our trusty and well-beloved William Clabourne, one of our councell and Secretary of State from our Colony of Virginia, and some other adventurers with him have condescended with our trusty and well-beloved councellor of both kingdoms. Sir William Alexander, our principal secretary for our Kingdoms of Scotland, and others of our lovinge subjects, who have charge over our colonies of New Scotland and New England to keepe a course for interchange of trade amongst them as they shall have occasion. As also to make discoveries for increase of trade in those parts, and because wee do very much approve of all such worthy intentions, and desirous to give good encouragement to these proceedings therein, being for the relief and comfort of those Our Subjects and enlargement of our dominions, these are to license and authorize the said William Cleburne, his associates and company freely and without interruption from time to time to trade and traffic corne, furs or any other commodities whatsoever with their shipps, men, boates, and merchandise in all sea coasts, rivers, creeks, harbors, land and territories in or neare those parts of America for which there is not already a patent granted to others for trade."

We see from this that no right to any land was given to Claiborne or the company he represented. Indeed, so entirely did he monopolize things that history has failed to throw much light upon his partners. From the High Court of Admiralty records, however, we learn that the company consisted of four partners of whom William Cloberry, a wealthy London merchant, was the largest stockholder. He had traded with Canada, and with some others had a patent to trade with Guinea in Africa. Claiborne, who had lived in Virginia for ten years, directed the attention of William Cloberry to the facilities for money-making in America. Consequently a trading company was formed composed of William Cloberry, Maurice Thompson, John Delabarr, Simon Turgus, and William Claiborne, the shares to be six in number, of which William Cloberry held two and each of the others one.

Having secured their license to trade, the ship *Africa* having on board Captain William Claiborne and a cargo of goods valued at £1,318 9s 8d. with twenty men-servants, "one mayde to wash our linen," named Joan Young, some passengers for Virginia and one Henry Pincke to read prayers, who we are told later "breake his legge and was unserviceable," sailed from Dale, England, on the 28th of May, 1631.

Two months later the *Africa* arrived at Kecoughtan, Virginia, where she landed the persons bound for that place, and proceeded to the Isle of Kent.

John Esten Cooke some years ago gave the cause of the Calverts' opposition to Claiborne a romantic turn. He claimed that Sir George Calvert and Thomas Cleburne both loved the Lady Agnes Lowther, daughter of Sir Richard Lowther, of Lowther, and that Thomas Cleburne, of Westmoreland, bore off the prize, leaving a feud of bitter hate and jealousy between the Calvert and the Claiborne blood. It is strongly intimated, therefore, that the young kinsmen of the rival lovers took up the fight and that Lord Baltimore registered a vow that the Claiborne men should not despoil the Calverts of both their loves and their lands!

The records give no suggestion of any such sentimental basis for the Claiborne rebellion, and as the fight was begun by Claiborne it cannot be ascribed to any but its real cause—his desire to own Kent Island whilly-nilly. Early in the year 1635, despite the order from his sovereign sent to Governor Harvey commanding him to recognize Lord Baltimore's right to Kent Island, Claiborne defiantly sent his pinnace, called the *Longtail*, to traffic without license in Maryland waters. This small privateer was captured by Captain Thomas Cornwaleys, one of his Lordship's commissioners.

In retaliation Claiborne issued a special warrant of commission under his hand to Lieutenant Ratcliffe Warren to seize and capture any of the pinnaces or other vessels of the government at St. Mary's. History tells us he fitted out an armed boat, manned with about thirty men from Kent Island, and placed it under Warren's command.

Leonard Calvert was not slow in making ready the pinnaces *St. Helen* and *St. Margaret*, which he placed under the command of Captain Cornwaleys, and the victory of Lord Baltimore's men in the first naval engagement in Maryland waters is well known.

The trial which resulted before the Maryland Assembly brought out the facts that Claiborne fired the first shot, which killed William Ashmore. Cornwaleys' men returned the fire, killing Ratcliffe Warren, John Bellson and William Dawson, when Claiborne surrendered.

In a suit with Lord Baltimore Claiborne makes a strong attempt to prove the right of his trading company to Kent Island under the license granted to him and his partners in 1631 to trade and make discoveries, yet in a later suit, brought by his partners against him for not rendering an account or making any returns to them for their five-sixths part of the stock invested, he coolly ignores his testimony in the former suit and declares that Cloberry and Company had no authority given them to take possession of any of the islands mentioned and neither did he take possession of them by virtue of his Majesty's license to trade.

In view of the wide interest in and the divergent opinions of William Claiborne, of Kent Island, we cannot dismiss this doughty adventurer from our consideration until we have more fully studied him in the light of the High Court of Admiralty Records, which the eminent R. T. Marsden, of the London bar, has recently sent to the Maryland Historical Society, and which now for the first time are given to the public.

In the suit of King Charles I against Claiborne for piracy and murder the prisoner testifies in his own behalf. The trial is in the year 1638, and "the Right Worshipful Sir Henry Marten is the judge of His Majesty's High Courte of the Admiralty," before whom the testimony is given.

In response to the judge's question whether he sent an armed vessel under command of Lieutenant Warren to seize and capture the Lord Baltimore's pinnaces, Claiborne admitted reluctantly that he did send one Lieutenant Ratcliffe Warren in a little boat like a wherry with some men, having, some of them, pieces to defend them from the Indians in Maryland, "but noe other armes, to demand some pinnaces that the Marylanders had taken from him."

Such was the naïvely innocent coloring given to Warren's attack upon the Lord Baltimore's naval forces which resulted so disastrously to Claiborne's commander and the men under him.

In response to the court's question regarding his having induced Lieutenant Warren to believe that he (Claiborne) had a commission to settle the Isle of Kent, the prisoner disclaimed the insinuation and declared that on the contrary the inhabitants of the island, suffering extreme want of corn, came to him complaining that the Marylanders, in opposition to his Majesty's express command, had taken all their pinnaces from them and urged him to give them authority to go to re-demand the boats.

As the suit of the King against Claiborne progresses, questions calculated to embarrass the prisoner seem to be lightly answered and summarily dismissed by the latter, but his answers convict him despite his affected innocence.

From the testimony it develops that Claiborne's commander had captured one of Governor Calvert's pinnaces and conveyed it to the rebellious would-be ruler of Kent before the engagement of their forces in the Pocomoke River, which, as history recounts, resulted in the death of Warren.

When questioned by the judge of the Admiralty Court on this point Claiborne admits that "the said Lieutenant Warren did bringe a boate with some trucking stuffe belonging to Maryland to the Isle of Kent." He adds that he sent the Governor of Maryland "worde that he might fetch the same away."

It is amusing to read this amiable and meekly innocent account of Claiborne's part in the rebellion against Lord Baltimore as given from his own lips.

The side lights thrown on his character by these suits against Claiborne leave his admirers little ground to stand on, for whatever doubts we of the present may have felt regarding the honesty and good faith of Claiborne it is certain that his partners, Cloberry, Morehead and Company, held a very different view, for in their suit against him—the records of which are now for the first time published in extenso—they charge him with having misappropriated the company's capital, of having set fire to their goods, and, finally, to have entered Cloberry's house in London on the pretenses of examining his accounts, "when he, without the said Cloberry's privity or consent, did take and carry away nine several bookes of accounts or thereabouts which concerned or contained the proceedings, passages and occurrences of the said trade, discovery and plantations, or part thereof, together with divers and sundry letters other bookes of accompts, and papers concerning the said trade, etc., which the said Cleborne still keepest and possesseth."

In this suit of his partners against Claiborne they recite that the accused employed the capital of the company in building houses, boats, etc., and in raising crops to the extent of many thousand dollars; that he trafficked with the company's goods in furs and tobacco alone to the amount of £5000.

The partners state that they paid over £700 in freight to the owners of the ship *Africa* on her return to England after delivering the goods to Claiborne in Maryland. The sixth part of all this should have been borne by Claiborne, as the following contract will show, but not only did he fail to pay his part of the legitimate expenses of the company, but for six years he continued to withhold all profits from the partners at London.

The following is the agreement between Claiborne and Cloberry and Company, as set forth by the latter:

"William Cleborne did informe and intimate unto William Cloberry and Company, or some one of them, of a very profitable and beneficial trade that might be had and made in the Bay of Chesapeake in Virginia, and some other rivers, posts and places there, or neare thereto adjoining, as also for Delaware bay, Hudson river, New England and Nova Scotia, for furrs, beaver skins, corne and other commodities.

"That upon the said notice and information given unto the said William Cloberrye and Companie, or some or one of them, by the said Cleborne as aforesaid, the said Cloberrye and Companie did agree and resolve, with the said Clebornne, to settle and did settle and undertake a trade, discoverye and plantation in a joint stocke for those parts forgowinge in accounts of sixthes, viz.: Two-sixthes parts thereof for the account of William Cloberrye, one-sixthe parte for the account of John Delabar one-sixthe part for the account of Marria Thompson, one-sixthe part for the account of Simon Turgis, and one-sixthe parte for the account of the said William Clebornne, and the said Clebornne was to goe and proceed uppon the said discoverye of plantation, and did promise and agree to give just and true accounts of all tradinge, truckeinge, buyeinge, sellinge, barteringe, plantinge, sowinge, increase of cattle and generally all increase and profit whatsoever (that) should any manner of weies arise, grow or acrew by the said plantation should bee for the use and behalfe of the said joint stocke in sixthes, as aforesaid.

"That the said William Clebornne did saye and affirm unto the said William Cloberrye and Company, or some or one of them, that unless hee had a speciall commission from the King's Most Excellent Majestie of Great Britaine, he could not proceed uppon the said discovery, trade or plantation, but should be hindered or opposed in the saied designe by the Governor of Virginia, whoe by his power and authoritie might so doe or to the like effect," etc.

The manuscript then recites that Cloberrye secured the desired royal commission, and that Claiborne took the goods, as stated.

Claiborne acknowledged the agreement as above stated, but claimed that Cloberrye did not secure the commission from the King, and its procurement devolved upon him (Claiborne).

During the suit it is shown that Cloberry and Company sent over several very valuable shiploads of goods, all of which Claiborne sold and appropriated the money to his own uses to the amount of £20,000. The complainants also charged that he traded and sold all tobacco and grain raised by him for the company and engaged in a general merchandise business on the company's capital, buying, selling and trading in the colonies and with England; also, that he used their boats in a freight business of his own and appropriated the company's servants to his own service and benefit, gaining much money thereby. The burden of this suit was that during all the years on Kent Island he sold to persons in Virginia, New England and in London tobacco, corn, furs and divers other goods without the knowledge of the company and never accounting to them therefor.

William Claiborne very promptly sued his accusers for libel for £500 damages for saying he set fire to the company's goods on Kent Island.

Another cause of contention between Claiborne and his partners developed when the former was summoned to England to answer the charge against him. It appears that he requested Cloberry and Company, to send out someone to take charge of their affairs and to examine the accounts. They promptly responded by appointing

Captain George Evelyn to come to Maryland with another cargo of goods and about 16 servants. Evelyn testified that Claiborne only yielded him partial possession of the island and then tried to take it back again, and not only refused to surrender his management but took the new goods and servants.

Claiborne in a cross suit declared that George Evelyn had displaced him and had so mismanaged affairs as practically to ruin the company and damaging him £800. He claimed that Cloberry and Company never sent him any goods after the first shipment, that he used his own means for the company's good and finally had to resign his office in Virginia to the loss of £1000 per annum to look after the company's trading interests!

So intricate and contradictory the various damages and libel suits became, that one would not know how to discriminate between the true and the false had not the events which led up to them been well known in history.

Following the suit against Claiborne, Cloberry and Company sued the Lord Baltimore for £35,000 damages for taking Kent Island and all their goods by Leonard Calvert.

CHAPTER XXXV

ORIGIN OF THE GROUND RENT

THE ground-rent system peculiar to Baltimore, which has prevented much real estate from changing hands, is a survival of the old feudal system under which Maryland was bestowed on the Calverts. When King Charles I granted these territorial lands to Cæcilius, second Lord Baltimore, he exempted him from knight's service, which was an inseparable part of the land tenure in England, and declared Cæcilius and his heirs absolute lords and proprietors of the lands, "saving always the faith and allegiance and sovereign dominion due to us, our heirs and successors," "to hold of us Kings of England as of our Castle of Windsor in the County of Berk in free and common socage by fealty only for all services, and not in capite nor by knight's service."

In feudal days every landholder was bound to go forth to war at his own expense whenever the king required. When this personal attendance, or knight's service, grew irksome, a pecuniary payment was substituted for the military service, and the king hired troops where he chose. This tax was called "scutage." While meant as a relief, it was levied whenever the sovereign felt so inclined, until the "king's pleasure," as it was termed, became intolerable and was one of the many abuses that led up to Magna Charta, one of the provisions of that great charter being that no "scutage" could be imposed upon the people without Parliament had first consented.

The king, in granting the territory of Maryland to the Lords Baltimore, required their fealty to be offered in the form of two Indian arrows paid at Windsor Castle the Tuesday in Easter week each year. This was, perhaps, besides being a survival of the feudal custom, a clever means of not letting these barons across the sea develop into independent sovereigns themselves. By a curious contradiction the people and not the barons become American sovereigns.

Having had the pleasure of handling and copying the receipts for the first year's rent promptly paid to the King, I give the wording of this document:

"Tuesday, XXIII day of April, 1633, in the Ninth yeare of the raigne of ye Soveraigne Lord King Charles.

"Memorand that the day and year above said the right honorable Cecil Lord Baltimore hath tendered and left by the hands of his servant John Langford at and in the Castle of Windsor, in the Countie of Berk, two Indian arrowes for one yeare's rent due to the Kinge's Majestie this present day for a Territory or Continent of land called Maryland, in America, granted by his Majesty under the great Seale of England to the said Lord Baltimore under the yearlie rent aforesaid. In testimonie whereof we have hereunto subscribed the day and year above said.

W. THOMAS,
Keeper of His Majesty's Wardrobe.
JAMES ENELEGH,
GEORGE STARKEY."

This John Langford, the trusted bearer of his Lordship's "fealty" to the king, was the first Surveyor-General of Maryland, to which office he was appointed March 24, 1641. This commission is, so far as known, the only one on record in Maryland which is an appointment to office for life.

Following the precedent set him by his Majesty, Cæcilius Calvert required a yearly rent for all lands granted, which was known as a "quit rent," and constituted a release from the services required under the feudal land tenure. All grants were issued in the name of the Proprietary and were "to be holden of our manor of St. Maries, of Nanticoke, Monacacy," or wherever the land patented happened to be located. These quit rents were payable at "our city of St. Maries at the two most usual feasts of the year, the Annunciation of the Blessed Virgin Mary and St. Michael the Arch-angel." These were irredeemable and became a great burden to the planters, except in those cases where the grants made in recognition of some service or mark of favor required only a mark of fealty, as "a bushel of Indian corn at Christmas, an Indian arrow, or some other merely formal evidence of loyalty."

In the earliest grants, the annual quit rent was 10 bushels of wheat for every 50 acres. Some grants call for 4 shillings in silver or gold and for a fine upon every alienation of the said land or any part or parcel thereof one whole year's rent. The land was at first given to early settlers to encourage immigration without other cost than their own transportation and the annual quit rent. After 1683 no such inducements were given, the province having by that time made its success and influence sufficiently felt to be sought voluntarily for its natural advantages to all who were looking out for opportunities for advancement. In the early years of the colony only British and Irish subjects could take up land under the "Condition of Plantation" issued in 1636. In the year 1648, however, new conditions were published and extended the privilege to those of French, Dutch and Italian descent, within the discretion of the Governor. All through the old archives we find acts for the naturalization, or, as it was called in Colonial days, the "denization of foreigners." Not till the year 1683 could persons of all nationalities own lands in Maryland.

That the quit rents, each small in itself, taken together aggregated an immense income, will be seen in the claim filed by Henry Harford, heir of Frederick Calvert, against the English Crown for his lands confiscated during, or rather, at the close of the American Revolution. Harford stated his loss to be about £450,000. The claim was, however, not fully recognized, the English government allowing him only £90,000 or about one-fifth of his demand.

While the ground-rent system had its root in the quit rent of the Lords Baltimore, it differs in going to a private individual instead of the governing head of the Commonwealth. The common tax, which was made a law in the year 1777, gave no relief to the ground-rent system, for, while it overthrew the lords of the soil, refusing to reimburse the last heir of the line in Maryland on the basis that "the people of Maryland should not occupy the degraded condition of tenants to a superior lord, a foreigner and a British subject," it left the ground rent payable to the land holders.

It seems a strange anachronism that in this practical and unpicturesque twentieth century, in the electric glare of which all mediæval pageantry would seem a ludicrous masquerade, that even a vestige of the feudal system could flourish.

"HOMEWOOD," HOME OF CHARLES CARROLL, SON OF THE SIGNER

Now owned by the Johns Hopkins University. From the Author's Collection

CHAPTER XXXVI

EDUCATION IN THE PROVINCE

A TABLET erected to Governor Francis Nicholson, the liberal-minded patron of the first free school in the province, commemorates the crowning effort of the many preceding and unsuccessful attempts to establish an educational system in Maryland.

Those who have viewed this tablet in its place upon the wall of our great university must dismiss the idea that it perpetuates the first impetus toward the intellectual uplift which has made Maryland world-renowned as the seat of America's greatest institution of learning. Twenty years prior to the erection of King William's School at Annapolis at the meeting of the Assembly on April 13, 1671, an act was passed by the upper house "for the founding and erecting of a school or college within this province for the education of youth in learning and virtue." A few days later, with certain restrictions, it passed the lower house—and thence from sight. Just why this first legislative act for the establishment of a school was not put into force does not appear upon the records, nor is it of special interest to follow the successive discussions of the educational idea until its final endowment and foundation under the patronage of Governor Nicholson.

Of much more interest is the striking fact that what proved to be a part of Maryland afterward was in 1624 designed as the site of the first "university" in America. This bit of unfamiliar history was discovered by Niell in the will of Edward Palmer, in the record office at London, and is of great interest to all Marylanders. Palmer's Island, a picturesque spot in the Susquehanna River, which the tourist may easily see from the train window as he crosses the high bridge which spans the river, was the spot chosen for this Arcadian seat of learning. In his transcript of the original records Niell tells us that Edward Palmer, for whom this island was named, was a distinguished London virtuoso, who on July 3, 1622, received a patent of land from the Virginia Company.

In his will, made November 22, 1624, he leaves all his lands and tenements in Virginia and New England, in the event of all issue failing, "to remaine for the foundinge and maintenance of a universitie and such schools in Virginia (as all below New England was then called), as shall be erected, and shall be called Academia Virginiensis et Oxoniensis, and shall be divided into several streets, or alleyes of twenty foot broade."

Palmer then provides that all those who can thereafter prove their lawful descent from his grandfather, John Palmer, Esq., of Leamington, and from his grandmother, "being sonnes, shall be freely admitted and brought up in such schools as shall be fit for their age and learninge, and shall be removed from time to time as they shall profit in knowledge and understanding."

Being evidently a firm believer that "Satan finds some mischief still for idle hands to do," this seventeenth century dreamer of a twentieth century reality continues:

"And further my will is that the schollers of said universitye for avoyding of Idleness at their houres of recreation shall have two paynters, the one oyle cullors and other for water cullers, which shall be admitted fellowes in the same college to the end and intent that the said schollers shall or may learne the arts of payntinge, and further my will and mind is that two grinders, the one for oyle collors and the other for water collours and also couleers oyle and gumme water shall be provided from tyme to tyme at the charges of the said college, beseeching God to add a blessing to all these intents." It is peculiarly interesting to us to know that the site of this prospective university proved to be a part of Maryland after the settlement. The provision for an art department is unique for that period.

We would believe that Palmer planned with the idea that his dream would not be realized for many generations did we not learn that he was "at many thousand expense in purchasing and preparing Palmer's Island for the object, but was transported to another world, leaving to posterity the monument of his worthy but unfinished institution. It is said that "he had a curious collection of coins and subterranean antiquities which one embezzled."

Unfortunately for the youth of the province, this ideal plan did not materialize, and the sons of the gentry had to be educated either by resident tutors, often in the person of the clergyman, or else go to England or France for their schooling. Many of the indentured apprentices were educated gentlemen, and frequent references are found in the old records relating to the sale of a school teacher, which meant simply that the time for which he had sold his services had not expired.

On the registers of Oxford University many names of youths from the colony of Maryland are enrolled. In early wills fathers provide for the education of their sons "as befits their station," frequently directing that they be sent to England to college.

Thus were family ties cemented by keeping in touch with the mother country, and it is probable that the influential men in the province preferred to send their sons to England because of social as well as intellectual advantages, and hence made no effort to further the early founding of a college at home. After the Revolutionary War, however, the situation being so radically changed, the victorious young Americans were not particularly happy at the English seats of learning, and very soon after Washington College, at Chestertown, became the first important foundation in Maryland.

ST. JOHN'S COLLEGE, ORIGINALLY KING WILLIAM'S SCHOOL

First Free School in America. From the Author's Collection

CHAPTER XXXVII

FIRST FREE SCHOOL IN MARYLAND

HAVING found that the "higher education" was the one first conceived for Maryland, it is peculiarly interesting to investigate the establishment of the free schools in the province.

It has been over 200 years since Colonel Francis Nicholson came from Virginia to succeed Sir Lionel Copley as royal governor of Maryland, after a wise and memorable term of rule over the Old Dominion. There he had lent his influence toward the founding of William and Mary College, for the support of which the inhabitants of Maryland, as well as Virginia, were taxed a penny per hogshead on tobacco exported to England. Here many Maryland lads were sent, in consequence, which largely accounts for the many intermarriages between the early families of "Leah and Rachel," as Maryland and Virginia were termed by John Hammond in his famous pamphlet.

That Governor Nicholson was a stanch believer in the doctrine of "the greatest good to the greatest number" is apparent in his progressive acts regarding the seat of government and the prompt establishment of the free schools in the province.

In one of his first messages to the provincial assembly he requested that "a way be found out for building of a free school, and the maintenance of a schoolmaster and usher and writing master that can cast accounts," which, if it be agreed to, his Excellency would give £50 a year toward the building of the school and £25 a year toward the support of the master.

So favorably was this proposition received by the House of Burgesses that ten days after it was read the matter had been discussed and adopted with a subscription of 45,000 pounds of tobacco raised by the members, who, in their messages to Governor Nicholson, thanking him for his liberal donation, doubted not "that every well-minded person within this province will contribute to the same."

The Assembly went beyond the request of the Governor for the establishment of one free school by decreeing that there should be one on the Eastern Shore and one on the Western, recognizing how completely the dividing arm of the bay separated the two parts of the State.

After debating as to the site of the respective schools, Oxford was chosen for the former and Severn for the latter. A school fund was provided by an export duty on furs and later on beef and bacon and an import duty on liquors, etc.

On October 18, 1694, we find a letter to "their Sacred Majesties King William and Queen Mary, for the erection of free schools" and a letter from the Governor and the Secretary of the Province, Sir Thomas Lawrence, in the name of the Council to the Right Reverend Father in God Henry, Lord Bishop of London (Bishop Henry Compton) in charge of the church in Maryland—and perhaps other colonies.

This letter, which was written after the Protestant Revolution of 1689 had firmly established William of Orange upon the throne of the United Kingdom, breathes the spirit of the age in which it was penned. It reads as follows: "Under so glorious a reign wherein, by God's providence, His true religion has been so miraculously preserved, should we not endeaver to promote it we should hardly deserve the name of good Protestants or good subjects, especially considering how noble an example is set before us by their Majesties' royal foundation now vigorously carried on in Virginia. We have, therefore, in Assembly attempted to make learning a handmaid to devotion and founded free schools in Maryland—to attend their college in that colony.

"We are confident you will favor our like pious designs in this province, where in instructing our youth in the orthodox religion, preserving them from the infection of heterodox tenets and fitting them for the service of the church and state in this uncultivated part of the world, are our cheerful end and aim."

It was not until two years later that the Council forwarded a message to the lower house or Assembly that the Lord Bishop of London had sent over a schoolmaster and it was therefore thought necessary that the school building go forward.

In response to this the Assembly resolved that the trustees of the free school, or the major part of them, should meet together and treat with the workmen and agree upon the building, which was to be estimated on according to the subscriptions donated, which tobacco, as money, was to be collected as need required.

As the schoolmaster arrived before the money was collected for the schoolhouse the lower house proposed that his Excellency shall make him reader in some parish, and that he have half the 40 pounds per poll if the same exceed not 10,000 pounds of tobacco.

The name of the first official schoolmaster was Mr. Andrew Geddes, who enjoyed the patronage of the Lord Bishop of London and because of which the Council proposed that something be paid him out of the money raised for the school fund by the tax on furs, etc. The representatives of the people thought the schoolmaster sufficiently "encouraged" by his appointment as reader of All Saints' Parish, Calvert county, and when the vacancy there was filled it was proposed that Mr. Geddes be "placed out as undermaster to the college school in Virginia, to save a present charge and to gain himself the more experience against the school here is built." That Mr. Geddes accepted the invitation to seek experience and employment in Virginia is evident from the fact that he is not heard of in connection with our school when finally established.

The first corporate school board was organized by act of Assembly, 1696.

"To his most Excellent Majesty and Dread Soverigne" the act is addressed. As it is the first act investing a school board with power to own property and control educational matters, it should be of interest to all who are now in touch with the twentieth-century evolution of the free-school idea of the Colonial days. Therefore I quote largely from the address to the King by the Maryland Assembly of July, 1696, as follows:

"From the sincerity of our humble and loyall hearts we offer to your sacred person our most Dutiful and sincere thanks for your Royal care and protection to us, etc., etc., here in we become your humble suitors to your most sacred Maty to extend your Royall grace and ffavor to us your Maty's subjects of this Province represented in this your Maty's General-Assembly thereof, that it may be enacted and may it be enacted by the King's most excellent Maty by and with the advice, prayer and consent of this present General Assembly, and the Authority of the same, that for the Propagation of the Gospell and the education of the youth of the Province in good letters and manners, that a certain place or places for a free school or schools or place of study of Latin, Greek, writing and the like, consisting of one master, one usher and one writeing master or scribe to a schoole of one hundred scholars more or less, according to the ability of the s'd Free school may be made erected, founded propagated and established under your Royall patronage, and that the Most Reverend Father in God Thomas by Divine providence Lord Archbishop of Canterbury Primate and Metropolitan of all England may be Chancellor of the said schools, and that to perpetuate the memory of your Ma'ty it may be called King William's School and managed by certaine Trustees to be chosen and appointed by your Sacred Majesty (to-wit) as also by the following Trustees nominated and appointed by this General Assembly, (that is to say) by your Ma'ty's said Governor Francis Nicholson Esq., The Hon. Sir Thomas Lawrence Barronett, Colonel George Robotham, Colonel Charles Hutchins, Colonel John Addison of your Matys honorable Council of this Province the Reverend Divine Mr. Peregrine Cony and Mr. John Hewett together with Robert Smith, Kenem Cheseldyn, Henry Coursey, Edward Dorsey, Thomas Ennalls, Thomas Taskers, Francis Jenkins, Willm Dent, Thomas Smith, Edward Boothby, John Thompson and John Bigger, gentlemen, or the greatest part of the successors of them, upon and in a central place of this Province called Ann Arundell Town, upon Seaverne River, and at such other place or places as by the General Assembly of this Province shall be thought convenient and fitting to be supported and maintained in all coming time and that your Maty will for your heirs and successors Grant and give leave to the said Francis Nicholson and Trustees aforesaid or the Major part or longest livers of them, that they may be enabled to take hold and enjoy and that they may be apt and Capable in law for taking holding and enjoying all mannors Lands Tenements, Rents services Rectories, Portions Annuityes Pensions with all other inheritances ffranchises and Possessions whatsoever, spiritual or Temporall, to the value of fifteen hundred pounds sterling and all other goods Chattells moneys and personall Estate whatsoever of the gift of any person whatsoever that is willing to bestow them for the said use or any other gifts grants assignments Legacys or appointment of the same or any of them etc., etc., for the defraying of the charges that shall be laid out in erecting and fitting the Edifices of the said free school or school etc. That as soon as the said free school or schools be erected and founded the said Francis Nicholson and the other Trustees above named shall apply and appropriate to the use and benefit and maintenance out of the Revenue or incomes to the said Trustees for the use aforesaid the sume of one hundred and twenty Pounds sterling per annum, for the salary supporte, and maintenance, of the first mentioned ffree schoolmaster, usher and scribe, and the necessary repairs and improvements of the same etc."

I wonder how much of this appropriation of $600 a year was left for repairs and improvements after paying the "sallarys" of three instructors!

The act goes on to state that for "the uses and purposes aforesaid they, the said Francis Nicholson and the trustees aforesaid, the survivors, or the major part of them, shall be incorporated into a body politique, by the name of Rectors, Governors, Trustees and Visitors of the Free Schools of Maryland, with full power to plead and be impleaded, to sue and to defend and be defended, to answer and be answered in all and every cause, complaint and action, real, personal or mixt, of whatever kind or nature it shall be, whatsoever courts and places of judicature belonging to your Maty, your heirs or successors, or by, from or under your royal grant or authority, etc. And that they the said Governors, visitors and Trustees aforesaid, and their successors, shall forever be 18 men, and not exceeding 20 in the whole, to be elected and constituted in the way and manner hereafter specified, of which one discreet and fit person, that shall be called rector of the said free school and schools, and that from time to time and in all times coming the said rector shall exercise the said office during one year (death and legal disability excepted) and after till some others of the said visitors and governors of the said school and schools shall be duly elected, preferred and sworn to the said office and that from time to time and at all times coming after the said year is expired, or after the death of the said rector, the visitors or governors of the said school or schools, or the greatest part of them, shall have power to elect and nominate another discreet and fit person from amongst themselves to be the rector of the said ffree schools. That the said rector for the time being by and with the advice and consent of three or more of the said governors and visitors, shall and may from time to time punish any disorder, breaches, misdemeanors or offenses of any master, usher or scribe or scholars of any of such free schools against any orders, laws or decrees of the said governors and visitors aforesaid; and if they find cause to alter, displace or turn out any master, usher or scribe of any such schools. And also that the rectors, governors, visitors, etc., of the free schools have one common seale, which they may make use of in whatsoever cause and business belonging to them."

In conclusion the act provides for the "erecting of a ffree school in every county of this province as fast as they should be enabled."

Five years after this act of Assembly the first free school was opened at Annapolis, the center of the social and official life of the colony. We can imagine the lean and underfed master, usher and scribe who taught the young ideas how to shoot in Colonial Maryland.

The fad for things antique happily does not include the matter of "ffree schools;"—Colonial furniture, Colonial silver and Colonial dames are very charming, but let us have twentieth century "ffree schools," with their teachers well paid, as befits the times.

CHAPTER XXXVIII

RENAISSANCE OF ANTIQUES

IF THE moral taught us in the story of "Aladdin's Lamp" had been taken to heart there are many among us who would still be in possession of family treasures of rare value, and would not have been enamored of the "new lamps for old," which resulted in the clearing out of all old-fashioned furniture a quarter of a century ago in the burst of admiration for the newer charms of golden oak. I have heard a woman tell, with tears rolling down her cheeks, of the solid mahogany tester bed of ancient regime in the family, being sold for a dollar to be got rid of, and of the pure Chippendale tables almost given away because of their stiffness, and of the Colonial sofa exchanged for a Morris chair. Ye gods! All too late she realized that in giving the old for the new she had lost the magic charm of the real thing. This woman lacked the appreciation that a Washington dame of Maryland ancestry recently exhibited. Her house, filled with exquisite Colonial furniture, was for sale and an ambitious New York millionaire offered to purchase her furniture with it. She resented his suggestion even, and in recounting it to a friend declared that such as he should never enter exclusive society on "the spindle legs and claw feet of her ancestors!" The revival of interest in family history has naturally fostered a love of hereditary possessions and the restoration to places of honor of things long relegated to the attic. Even the children in certain families have caught the fever, a lad of eight summers having recently been seen to turn up his small nose at the table of modern make in his own playroom, while this same little antiquarian set up a plea that the miniature of his great-grandfather be kept in its old-fashioned frame "because of its quaintness," and, said he, with disdainful mien, "if you put a new gold frame on it people will think the picture a reproduction."

A very funny incident in connection with the clearing out of the cellars and attics of everything old a few years ago was that of giving away of some family portraits.

The owner of these met his cousin on the street one day and said: "By the way, there are some portraits in my cellar you might like to have—one is your grandmother, and perhaps the other your grandfather." The granddaughter was rejoiced, for, like the average woman, she had an appreciation of what it meant to have had grandparents; so she had the portraits cleaned and hung in her hall.

The pleasant surprise had been kept for her mother who knew nothing of the late acquisition until she was led into the hall and told to look at the portrait of her own mother. The old lady, instead of appearing pleased, burst into a fit of uncontrollable laughter, and when she could speak she said, "it is not your grandmother at all—it is the grandmother of your cousin himself." So Cousin Tom had given away his grandmother. The Maryland Indians would have taught him a higher reverence for his progenitors; for when the Nanticokes left the State they carried the bones of their ancestors with them!

But an individual should not be ridiculed for what was the result of the spirit of the times. Following the

1. OLD STAFFORDSHIRE, AND SALT GLAZE "SPORTIVE INNOCENCE," PITCHERS

Shown through the courtesy of Miss Mary V. Dorsey, of Dorchester County

2. HOUSEHOLD IMPLEMENTS OF COLONIAL TIMES

Shown through the courtesy of Miss Mary V. Dorsey, of Dorchester County

Revolutionary War there was a manifest contempt for anything which tended toward caste and coronets. Family history was not preserved, coats of arms were destroyed and even erased from family silver in some cases, and all evidences of pride of lineage frowned down by the American patriots and their descendants, so that not to know one's grandmother was not rare. Things have assumed their normal condition now, and the young American having clasped hands with her English cousins has felt the thrill of kinship, and delights in the knowledge that she is as lineally entitled to the ancient history of England as those who remained the king's subjects. That indifference to family was a development of Revolutionary times is very evident to all who have dipped into the Colonial records and have found the legacies of historic interest which are directed to be kept in the family, such as ancient silver, a coat of arms, gold watches described as "family pieces to be retained," etc. Land was entailed on the eldest son to keep up the family estates, and consequently the family pride.

But if evidences of pride of birth and station are in the early records, stronger still are the proofs of family affection. Deeds of gift of large tracts of land to sons and daughters "for natural love and affection" bring us in touch with the human side of these personages who have become only names to their far-off descendants. It is refreshing to find, like Portia's little candle, these good deeds shining across the centuries to us voicing the devotion and consideration of fathers in those days, when sons were given a start and not expected to wait until the death of their parents to have a home. In those days fathers encouraged their sons to marry early, and with a comfortable plantation this was no difficult matter. Daughters were also made happy and given an added dignity by the gift of a tract of land by a considerate father at the time of marriage. The old way was a good one. The young folks were given a chance and the little home thus begun took deep root in the soil, and many of these are still the basis of family pride to the ninth generation in this country.

CHAPTER XXXIX

PRESTON-ON-THE-PATUXENT

As THE scene of the beginning of the first battle between Englishmen on American soil, the old Preston mansion in Calvert County is the most notable survival of the early Colonial times.

This dwelling was built by Richard Preston, the military commander and Provincial Councilor, in the year 1650, large tracts of land having been granted him by Lord Baltimore, through Governor William Stone, at whose invitation Richard Preston, Edward Lloyd, William Durand and other high Puritan leaders left Virginia on account of religious intolerance there and settled in Maryland.

Born to leadership, we find Mr. Richard Preston in 1652 one of the commissioners appointed by the English Parliament to reduce to submission and to govern the rebellious colony of Maryland, which had shown itself favorable to a royal ruler.

Governor Stone was accordingly deposed and Mr. Richard Preston, Colonel Francis Yardley, Mr. Robert Brooke, Mr. Job Chandler, Captain Edward Windham and Lieutenant Richard Banks assumed control of the province in the name of Oliver Cromwell.

When a few months later Captain Stone repented of his rashness and promised loyalty to the Protectorate he was reinstated as governor, with the former commissioners as members of his council.

The year following in response to an appeal from a hundred or more leading inhabitants of Maryland, the

English Parliament empowered its representatives to remove the seat of government from the center of Lord Baltimore's adherents at "the citie of St. Marie's" to the dwelling house of Mr. Richard Preston, on the north or Calvert side of the Patuxent River. This was accordingly done, and the Preston mansion became the provincial court and the place for the meeting of the Assembly and the repository of the official records, from which time until 1660, when King Charles II came to his own, Preston-on-the-Patuxent was the center of the court life in the colony.

To quell the discontent caused by the removal from the capital city Mr. William Claiborne and Mr. Richard Bennett, Cromwell's Virginia commissioners, came into Maryland and, with headquarters at Preston, issued a proclamation "in the name of his Highness the Lord Protector" commanding obedience by the turbulent inhabitants of the province.

The governor and people became outwardly submissive, but that there was an undercurrent of disloyalty to the Protector is very certain.

Lord Baltimore, who was then in England, being of the King's party, was not inclined to submit meekly to this usurpation of his Palatinate and the setting up of Government House at Preston-on-the-Patuxent in opposition to his own "citie of St. Marie's." Hence, in the autumn of the year 1654 there sailed into the colony the ship *Golden Fortune*, having on board the aristocratic William Eltonhead, bearing a commission from "my Lord Baltimore" to the effect that Governor Stone was forthwith to issue a proclamation denouncing the Puritan government at Preston, to raise a force of his loyal subjects, seize the rebellion records and force the Puritans into subjection.

In response Governor Stone raised a little army of about 200 men, with the purpose of capturing Richard Preston and of overthrowing the Puritan stronghold at Providence near Annapolis. To attack both places simultaneously it was necessary to divide his forces, which Governor Stone did, and one party headed by Josias Fendall (afterward governor) sailed across the Patuxent River and laid siege to Preston.

The gallant "commander of all the forces north of the Patuxent" was away from home; having no suspicion of his Lordship's purpose, he had gone off with his men leaving the house, with its valuable records and stores of ammunition to the keeping of the gentle women of his family. We can imagine their consternation when from their dormer windows these high-bred Colonial dames beheld a party of soldiers wearing Lord Baltimore's uniform making fast their pinnaces at the foot of the box-bordered garden! It is a matter of record that Madame Preston, alone with her children and a goodly number of maid servants, made a vigorous defense against the surly rudeness of the intruders, who demanded the records of the province "in the name of his Lordship," and who ransacked every corner of the house within and without for Richard Preston, "that we might hang him for his rebellion against Lord Baltimore."

Being stouter of heart than of body the Preston women were no match for the red-coated ruffians, who took possession of records and ammunition and made off with them. Thus began the battle which was fought to a finish at Providence—the fight betwixt Cavalier and

Roundhead, begun at the court of Charles I; which led the king to the scaffold, drove his son into exile and hundreds of his subjects to the colonies—and was the first occasion of their crossing swords on American soil.

The victory of the Cavaliers at Preston was shortlived, for at Providence, in the "Battle of the Severn" the Puritans shouting our their battle cry, "In the name of God fall on; God is our strength," made a fierce and victorious struggle declaring they would "rather die like men than live like dogs."

After celebrating their victory by a thanksgiving service the Puritans tried Governor Stone and others for treason against the Commonwealth of England. Stone was finally set free, but Mr. William Eltonhead, bearer of My Lord's commission, lost his head for his loyalty.

After the accession of King Charles II and the restoration of the Lord Baltimore to power in the colony of Maryland, the latter granted to Madame Eltonhead large tracts of land as recompense for her husband's services. She therefore remained in the province along with her friends and kinsfolk, Madame Fenwick of Fenwick Manor, being sister of her martyred liege lord.

When looking at the pictures recently made of Preston-on-the-Patuxent, it must be borne in mind that it was a mansion in its day, and one of the few dwellings built of brick in the colony. This main structure was no doubt originally supplemented by wing additions containing kitchens and servants' quarters, which was the architectural plan of early Colonial houses.

Not until fully a hundred years later was it possible to build and equip mansions such as are now typical of pre-Revolutionary times in Maryland and Virginia.

Shorn of all that lent charm to the once luxurious home of the commander of the Patuxent, by the same despoiler which changes the bloom of youth to the wrinkles and lack-lustre of old age, we have had to turn to the official records of two and a half centuries ago for the facts which throw an atmosphere of rare interest about this decaying old mansion. Surrounded by the 1200 acres granted to Richard Preston in 1650, we have repeopled it with men and women conspicuous in the early and stormy period of provincial life.

Richard Preston himself presents a unique figure in Colonial history. He was always in office under the differing administrations, and must have possessed rare diplomacy in that, at various times, he represented the Lord Baltimore, the Parliament and the people. Indeed, there was no post of honor, civic or military, which he did not fill with tact and ability.

Just when Richard Preston resigned "the carnal sword" for that of the spirit, and doffed the wig and gown of judge for the quiet Quaker garb is not laid down upon the records, although we are told that at "Preston" Thomas Thurstone and Josias Cole, the foreign Quaker preachers, were given refuge and protection before being expelled from the colony.

That he became as strong a power in religion as he had been in diplomacy and statecraft, is evident in a letter of Charles Calvert, dated 1663, addressed to his father, Lord Baltimore, in London, in which he refers to "Richard Preston, the great Quaker" as having sent a "Runlett of Tobacco" for "a token" to his Lordship. To Mr. Samuel Troth, of Philadelphia, the lineal descendant of this "fighting Puritan and peaceful Quaker" we are indebted for the discovery of Preston-on-the-Patuxent and for many sidelights on the character of its Colonial proprietor. Of this ancient survival he says truly that "the old Preston house at Patuxent kindles in imagination many a picture of men and things in Colonial Maryland, as fancy reproduces the historical incidents within its walls.

"The hall of lawmakers and court of justice, with its judges and jurors; the rendezvous of Puritan soldiery, with swords and guns and turmoil, and sudden shift to the solemn, silent worship of a Quaker meeting."

The rooms at Preston are wainscoted and a great iron hook imbedded in the center beam of the ceiling indicates where the lamp hung during the long afternoon sessions of the court in our country's dawn.

Richard Preston was a man of high social position and large wealth, his landed possessions at the time of his death including in addition to Preston-on-the-Patuxent, "Horne's Point" and a tract called "Preston" in Dorchester County, besides the whole of Barren Island, the aggregate amounting to over 4000 acres.

He made frequent trips to England, and his son James was there at the time of his death in the year 1669.

The bequests in Richard Preston's will of land and cattle, of household goods, of "sweet scented tobacco," and money, "of the silver plate already in the house, and that which is to be brought this year out of England," prove conclusively that he enjoyed the luxuries and elegancies of living possible at that time in the colony.

Samuel Preston, Mayor of Philadelphia, prior to 1700, married Rachel Lloyd, daughter of Thomas Lloyd, Deputy Governor under Penn, of the Province of Pennsylvania. From his grandfather, Richard Preston, Samuel inherited

Preston-on-the-Patuxent, which was evidently his birthplace.

The old plantation has long since passed into the hands of strangers, as Samuel Preston died in the Quaker City and left no sons to perpetuate the name. The descendants of Richard Preston, through his daughters and the daughters of Samuel, are numerous, and include many prominent families in Philadelphia and Maryland. One of the Preston daughters married the representative of a titled English family, the other a notable Colonial justice of the provincial court.

It is to the untiring efforts of one who, leaving the beaten track of the professional historian for the neglected byways of unfrequented countrysides, that we are indebted for the discovery of the oldest building extant in Maryland, and perhaps in the United States.

The Society of the Colonial Dames of America would do well to rescue this historic house before it falls into utter decay, in recognition of the defense of the provincial records made by those gentle Puritan dames in the winter of 1655.

CHAPTER XL

COMING OF THE SWEDES

As MANY of our good old Maryland families came from Sweden by way of Delaware, the influences which effected the coming of the Swedes to Seat, on the Delaware, must be of direct interest to Maryland and the history of her people. It was during the reign of Queen Elizabeth, in the picturesque days of Sir Walter Raleigh, Hackluyt and of Drake, that William Usselinx first proposed to the Swedish government a scheme for colonization in America. Usselinx was a man full of the spirit of foreign adventure, imbibed during his residence in Spain, Portugal and the Azores, and himself a native of Antwerp and of a nation distinguished for maritime enterprise.

In the year 1624 he represented to the young and enthusiastic King Gustavus Adolphus the dazzling opportunities for trade in the newly discovered countries beyond the seas. The King was easily convinced of the chance to extend his kingdom without conquest and readily granted to Usselinx a commission to form a trading company. Having been connected with the Dutch West India Company, this enterprising merchant of Stockholm was in a position to describe the beauty of the country and its advantages in point of commerce.

The King recommended the project to the States and an edict was issued at Stockholm July 2, 1626, by royal authority in which people of all ranks were invited to encourage the project and support the company. Gus-

STATUE OF JOHN HANSON, PRESIDENT OF THE UNITED STATES IN CONGRESS ASSEMBLED

Erected by the State of Maryland in the Hall of Fame in the Capitol at Washington, D. C., shown through the courtesy of his great-great-grandson, Mr. Douglas H. Thomas

tavus pledged the royal treasure for its support to the amount of $400,000. Harte says it is not to be described how much all these new schemes delighted the Senators. Companius relates that the plan was supported by the King's mother, by His Highness John Cassimir, Prince Palatine of the Rhine, who had married the King's sister; by the members of his Majesty's Council, by the principal nobles and others in high authority.

Ships and all necessaries were provided, an admiral, vice-admiral, officers and troops, etc. were appointed. All was ready for the expedition when the German war interrupted the project. Harte, however, claims that the little Swedish squadron started, but was captured by the Spanish in the interest of the Germans and Poles.

The death of Gustavus Adolphus ended this first attempt of the Swedes to start a colony in America. The next step toward this much desired end was successfully carried out by Peter Minuit, who had been director-general of the Dutch West India Company and governor of the New Netherlands, who, it is said, quarreled with the people there and returned to Holland. Minuit was succeeded in New Amsterdam by the famous Wouter Van Twiller in 1633.

Oxenstein, the great Prime Minister of the young Queen Christina, the infant daughter of Gustavus Adolphus, bearing in mind the purpose of his Majesty, influenced the Queen, who had ascended the throne, to accept the plans proposed by Peter Minuit for a settlement on the Delaware.

After several years' delay two vessels were equipped and started on their voyage of adventure. These were called the *Key of Calmar* and the *Bird Grip*, the former being an armed ship and the latter a transport. Both were well stored with provisions, with presents for the Indians and with arms and ammunition for defense.

These sailed from Gottenburg, on the west side of Sweden, in the autumn of 1637 and in the spring of 1638 arrived at Point Paradise, afterward named Christina, in honor of the young Queen. The colony thus landed, we are told by earlier historians, was planted without bloodshed and maintained in peace until the end of Peter Minuit's life, in 1641.

In 1640 some adventurers from Maryland and some others, among them the pioneers of Sir Edmund Plowden, settled on Salem Creek, but were finally expelled by the Swedes and Dutch.

Upon the death of Minuit the Swedish government determined to enlarge the sphere of its operations, and when sending out John Printz, the new governor, a high army officer in the service of the Queen, he was put in command of a large party of colonists. Accompanying him was the most formidable armament that had ever entered the Delaware, composed of two ships of war, the *Svan* and *Charitas*, and an armed transport called the *Fame*, having on board arms, ammunition and troops to resist any offensive intrusion of the Dutch.

Many of the colonists who came with Printz later accepted the invitation of the Maryland Proprietary to remove into the peaceful boundaries of Maryland, bringing into our Colonial life a strain of sturdy Swedish blood which left its impress upon the descendants of these men of daring.

CHAPTER XLI

A PROVINCIAL POET'S LINES

IN VIEW of the Baltimore dock improvement and all that it will mean to Maryland in increase of commerce, the lines written by the first poet in the province are peculiarly interesting as showing the foresight of one who wrote in the year 1662.

>Trafique is earth's atlas that supports
>The pay of armies and the height of courts,
>And makes mechanics live that else would die
>Meer starving martyrs in their penury,
>None but the merchant of this thing can boast;
>He, like the bee, comes laden from each coast,
>And to all kingdoms as within a hive
>Stows up those riches that doth make them thrive,
>Be thrifty, Maryland, keep what thou hast in store
>And each year's trafique to thyself get more!

George Alsop, the indentured apprentice to Mr. Thomas Stockett (1658-1662), wrote so enthusiastically of the Province in his "A Character of Maryland" that it has even been suggested that Cæcelius Calvert had employed him to write an account of the new settlement to encourage immigration. There is nothing, however, to prove that the writings of this early scribe were prompted by anything but his own enthusiasm for his adopted home.

Each chapter of his book ends with a panegyric to Maryland, which should be familiar to her citizens. For example:

'Tis said the Gods lower down the chain above
That tyes both Prince and subject up in Love
And if this Fiction of the Gods be true
Few, Maryland, in this can boast but you.
Live ever blest, and let those clouds that do
Eclipse most States, be always Lights to you
And, dwelling so, you may forever be
The only emblem of Tranquility.

Again—

Couldst thou, O earth, live thus obscure, and now
Within an age, sheu forth thy plentious brow
Of rich variety, yielded with fruitful fame
That, trumpet like, doth herald thy name
And tells the world there is a land now found
That all earth's Globe canst parallel its ground.

CHAPTER XLII

THE FIRST STEAMBOAT

WHILE Maryland has been first in so many movements touching the great affairs of both church and state in their national life, it is gratifying that she has not been second in practical inventions which have helped in the material progress of the world.

In the year 1784 James Rumsey, great-grandson of the early Maryland settler on the Bohemia River, applied for a patent for his new invention—the steamboat.

This was before there was a United States constitution and patents were granted by local legislatures.

Although James Rumsey was born in Cecil County, Maryland, he was living in Virginia at this time, and there received the exclusive right of steam navigation on the rivers of that State.

It appears that after serving in the Revolutionary war he was appointed by Washington superintendent of the Potomac Navigation Company, which the latter organized after retiring to private life.

In Rumsey's petition to the Maryland Legislature for a patent in November, 1784, he stated that he had been "several years engaged in perfecting plans for moving boats by steam." That Washington was a believer in the invention of the Maryland genius is evident from the following certificate of indorsement:

"I have seen the model of Mr. Rumsey's boat constructed to work against stream, examined the powers upon which it acts, been the eyewitness to an actual experiment in running water of some rapidity, and give it as my opinion, although I had but little faith before, that he has discovered the art of working boats by mechanism and small manual assistance against rapid currents; that the discovery is of vast importance, may be of the greatest usefulness in our inland navigation and if it succeeds, of which I have no doubt, that the value of it is greatly enhanced by the simplicity of the works, which when seen by and explained to may be executed by the most common mechanic. Given under my hand at the town of Bath, county of Berkeley, in the State of Virginia, this 7th of September, 1784, Geroge Washington."

After receiving the desired patent from the Legislature of Maryland Rumsey removed to Philadelphia, where he won the interest and friendship of Benjamin Franklin, a fellow-scientist. The Rumseian Society was there formed, with Franklin as president. It will be seen by this that the greatest intellects of that day appreciated the clever inventor, who had been dubbed Crazy Rumsey in a less appreciative community.

Although James Rumsey was of a wealthy Maryland family, he spent his patrimony in his experiments, and being of a mechanical turn had his own forge and workshop in which to work out his ideas.

The Rumseian Society, which was perhaps the first scientific association in America, sent Rumsey to London to build a boat on the Thames River. It was not long before the British government gave him a patent for his invention, proving conclusively that he had no predecessor there. The boiler of Rumsey's first steamboat was a potash kettle, with the lid bolted and soldered down.

Before his untimely death in London he succeeded in launching a steamboat of 100 tons burden. In addition to this he made marked improvements in steam engines, and to him is due the adoption of the cylindrical boiler.

It is generally believed by those familiar with Rumsey's career that Robert Fulton, with whom he was associated in London, gained many of his ideas from our Maryland genius. Fitch and Rumsey had a memorable controversy over the priority of the invention of the steamboat, but the verdict is believed to have been in favor of the latter.

While James Rumsey died just as he was about to demonstrate his ideas in a lecture on his model before the Society of Arts, in London, the scientists of both continents recognized the worth of his invention, and as late as 1839 the Congress of the United States voted to his only surviving child a gold medal commemorative of his father's invention. An interesting bit of unfamiliar history of the steamboat was brought to light some years ago by Hon. John H. B. Latrobe, who showed conclusively that Nicholas Roosevelt, of New York, received a patent from Congress in 1814 for "a boat or vessel with two wheels over the sides." This was the first patent for propelling steamboats by the use of vertical wheels over the sides of vessels. Rumsey's invention included a vertical pump operated by steam in the middle of his boat, that drew in water at the stem and expelled it at the stern through a horizontal trunk in the bottom.

An effort is being made to erect a monument to Rumsey by the people of West Virginia. They have reserved a site on a cliff overlooking the landing from which Rumsey started the boat one winter morning so long ago. An appropriation was asked of the West Virginia Legislature at its last session. One who wrote in the interest of the Rumsey monument at that time said with point: "How Fulton was the recipient of Rumsey's work, which he carried on to complete success is well known to history. But as Columbus should have given his name to the new-discovered world instead of Americus, his follower, so Rumsey should have had the first honors in the great invention that changed the face of the world, and the Potomac, not the Hudson, should be honored as its birthplace."

CHAPTER XLIII

OLD SOUTH RIVER CLUB

THE old South River Club, known to be the first organization of the kind in America, is one of the most interesting survivals of Colonial Maryland. The date of its beginning is unknown, because of the destruction by fire of the first clubhouse and the earliest records. That it was in existence long before 1742, in which year the present clubhouse was built, is evident from the resolution adopted on February 11 of that year, which directed that a committee be appointed "to collect the names of the members that have ever belonged to this society to the best of their memories, inasmuch as the present list appears very defective." In the year 1746, on July 13, the Maryland *Gazette* calls it the "ancient South River Club." Hence the members have good reason for believing that it was organized soon after the inauguration of "The Everlasting Club" in England which Addison tells us began during the civil wars and was interrupted during the great fire (1666), but resumed after three weeks and continued to flourish.

The club movement in England was at its height during the time of Addison and Steele, when the former said, "All matters of importance were concerted in a club."

It is not surprising, therefore, that the Colonial gentry of Maryland should emulate their English kinsfolk and institute for social purposes a duplicate of the London coffee clubs. Whether or not the first clubhouse was in

London town, history sayeth not. The records tell only of the purchase of the site of the present building from "John Gassaway's father," the son confirming the deed in the year 1740. Hence it is reasonable to suppose that the earlier clubhouse was on the same site.

It is interesting to note that Mr. Louis Dorsey Gassaway, a lineal descendant of the first owner of the club site and an important member in the early recorded list, should have been the leading spirit in the recent movement to infuse new interest in the ancient club. It happened that the old records of the South River Club came to Mr. Gassaway's attention quite accidentally but at once aroused his active interest, and writing to the four surviving members in the hope of a reunion, Mr. Gassaway was rewarded by enthusiastic responses. This was in the year 1895, when the membership was composed of Judge Alexander B. Hagner, of Washington; Mr. William Donaldson Steuart, of Baltimore; Mr. Harry H. Brogden, of Washington, and Mr. Richard Parran Sellman, of South River.

Judge Hagner requested the privilege of serving the dinner on that memorable occasion, and asked that Mr. Gassaway invite a number of gentlemen to participate who would be eligible to membership in the South River Club.

This was a red-letter day in the history of the organization. The loving cup presented by Judge Hagner was passed around, and all drank to the memories of their ancient forebears who, in the early days, would meet for interchange of news and views and sociability. While the discussion of both religion and politics was strictly forbidden, yet the club recognized political events; for in the minutes of July 24, 1746, we find: "Last Thursday was observed as a day of rejoicing by this society on account of the glorious victory of H. R. H. the Duke of Cumberland over the rebels by drinking of Loyall healths, firing of cannon and great demonstration of Loyalty was shown on that happy occasion by numbers of gentlemen then present. Also a handsome dinner was found by Mr. John Brewer, one of the present members, at the expense of the society. Also served Mr. Thomas Caton his second time, according to rule. At a previous meeting Rev. Mr. William Brodgen and Mr. John Monat were appointed by the club "to waite on his Excellency to desire his company that day."

In the little old clubhouse, which stands in the shadow of several great oak trees, which, like giant sentinels, have guarded it from wind and weather, there still remain in service several interesting heirlooms. These include the old punchbowl from which the Royal Governor drank the health and victory of the Duke of Cumberland, the lemon squeezer, large enough to serve for a veritable Brobdignagian, the punch ladle, mixing stick, rush-bottom chairs, green-bordered English platters and an old brazier. Not least interesting are some brass quoits presented by a visitor from Philadelphia in the year 1742 and still used on club days. The rules in an old frame are in the keeping of the present recorder, Mr. L. Dorsey Gassaway, and read as follows:

Resolved, That the following rules be observed by each member belonging to the society meeting at a house in Capt. Thomas Gassaway's old field known by the name of "the South River Clubhouse":

1. That there be a chairman chosen by a majority of voices annually the first club day after New Year's Day.

2. That the person so chosen shall speak the mind of the society upon any default of a member or members or to strangers.

3. That every chairman shall find a sufficient book to make all entries in that may be thought proper by the society.

4. That no entry shall be made in said book but what shall be agreeable to a majority of the society and which shall be made within the clubhouse, read and approved.

5. That no person be admitted a member of this society without signifying his intentions to some member of the society the club day preceding his election, and if any member or members should be absent the steward of the day shall make known to them such applicant, and he can then on the succeeding club day be admitted by the unanimous voice of the members present, and which shall be determined by ballot.

6. That no member shall invite his friend or friends into club unless he is the steward of the day; and if such steward invites his friend or friends he shall reduce their names to writing and the same shall be handed round to the members previous to dining.

7. That if any stranger or strangers invited shall after leaving the club make known or disclose any part of the conversation in the course of the afternoon, tending to the prejudice of any member or members, he can never thereafter be admitted either as a friend or a member of the society.

8. That the society meet every first Thursday in the month and no oftener, except in the month of July, when the meeting will be on the fourth day annually, unless

CONTEE SILVER BOWL, HALL MARK 1727, ENGRAVED WITH CONTEE ARMS

Owned by Mr. Douglas H. Thomas, shown through his courtesy

when it falls on a Sunday, and then it shall be on the day following.

9. That each member take his turn, according to a list drawn in the chairman's book.

10. That the steward that appears not in person or by his proxy at the usual place of meeting, provided with two and a half gallons of spirit with ingredients of toddy, by 1 o'clock, and a sufficient dinner, with clean pipes and tobacco, shall serve the following club day for such default.

11. That each steward at the close of his stewardship shall secure the house, take care of the bowls, glasses, etc; and he shall send the keys and book to the succeeding steward at least eight days previous to the time of serving and in default thereof he shall serve in his stead.

12. That each member annually on the first club day of the new year pay into the hands of the treasurer such sum of money toward defraying the necessary charges of the club as may be thought necessary by the society.

13. That there be a treasuer appointed to collect and receive all moneys paid in by the members, and that he shall keep a book of the same and render a fair account annually on the first club day of the new year of all expenditures by order of the society.

14. That there be no liquor mixed after 6 o'clock in summer and 4 o'clock in winter, and that there be no swearing, ill-language or any kind of gaming in the said society.

15. That there be a recorder appointed, who shall transcribe annually all the entries from the chairman's book into the record book belonging to the society.

16. Should any misunderstanding or difference happen between any of the members in the club, every member

belonging to the society shall be in duty bound to endeavor to bring about a reconciliation.

17. That these rules be put in a frame and hung up in some conspicuous place in the clubhouse, and if required by any member to be read by the chairman, if present, if not, by the steward of the day, every club day.

18. That no resignation of any member of this society shall be received here without first paying all arrearages due thereto.

These rules are those that have always governed the South River Club, with such slight changes as the time of meeting, the Fourth of July, having been introduced after independence was declared.

The membership is now limited to 25, and there is always a waiting list. Governor Warfield was elected in 1902 a member of this famous old club, in which his ancestors were prominent members.

The entire membership from 1742 until the present includes the following. Some of the first named were enrolled prior to 1742, but no date is extant as to their time of election: Robert Saunders, Thomas Stockett, James Monat, John Gassaway, Samuel Jacobs, Benjamin Stockett, John Howard, Samuel Burgess, Samuel Day, Robert Harding, Thomas Sparrow, Rev. William Brogden, Captain Joseph Cowman, John Watkins, William Chapman, Turner Wooten, James Dick, Samuel Chambers, Dr. Samuel Preston Moore, William Chapman, Jr., Captain Anthony Beck, James Nicholson, John Brewer, Captain Christopher Grendall, Zachariah Maccubbin, James Hall, Darby Lux, Henry Gassaway, Jonathan Sellman, Charles Steward and Richard Moore, prior to 1742.

In 1742 to 1904—Captain John Dixon, Thomas Caton,

Joseph Brewer, John Ijams, William Reynolds, Stephen West, Jr., John Watkins, Captain John White, Rev. Archibald Spencer, Henry Woodward, Thomas Gassaway, Captain John Dare, Joseph Cowman, Samuel Chapman, Captain William Strachan, Richard Burgess, Joseph Brewer, Lewis Stockett, Samuel Watkins, Captain Thomas Gassaway, Andrew Wilkie, Colonel Richard Harwood, Jr., Thomas Stockett, Captain Thos. Harwood, Stephen Watkins, Dr. Thomas Noble Stockett, Dr. James Thompson, Rezin Hammond, Thomas Harwood, Jr., Richard Watkins, Captain Thomas Watkins, Dr. Thomas Gantt, Henry Jones, William Harwood, William Saunders, Dr. William Murray, John L. Brogden, William Sellman, Robert John Smith, Edward Sefton, Nicholas Watkins, of Stephen, Ferdinando Battee, Dr. Robert Welsh, Rev. Mason Locke Weems, Major Jonathan Sellman, Mr. Samuel Maccubbin, Colonel Richard Harwood, David Stewart, Benjamin Watkins, Samuel Watkins, Captain Joseph Watkins, Dr. Robert Welsh, John Bard, Caleb Stewart, Thomas Prudy, William Stewart, James Macculloh, Benjamin Welsh, Edward Lee, Solomon Sparrow, Jr., Major Thomas Harwood, Major William Brogden, Joseph Cowman, Robert Welsh, Osborn S. Harwood, William Elliott, Richard Stewart, James Noble Stockett, John Gassaway (1806), William Sanders, Ferdinando Battee, Captain John B. Weems, Joseph Harwood, John Watkins, Samuel Harrison, Dr. John S. Stockett, Benjamin Harwood, Thomas Snowden, Richard Sellman, Dr. Willian Brogden, John Stevens Sellman, Major John Mercer, Virgil Moxey, Thomas Snowden, Major O. S. Harwood, Richard C. Hardesty, John T. Hodges, Ramsey Waters, Colonel Robert W. Kent, Dr. Benjamin Watkins, Thomas Welsh, James H. Harwood,

Alfred Sellman, James Harper, W. H. Woodfield, Edward Clagett, David McC. Brogden, Joseph E. Cowman, Dr. Richard Harwood, James B. Smith, Thomas Hodges, John Mercer, Captain Isaac Mayo, Thomas S. Iglehart, Charles C. Stewart, George Gale, William O'Hara, Dr. John H. Sellman, R. S. Mercer, John C. Rogers, Franklin Deale, James Kent, George D. Clayton, Dr. William N. Pendall, Colonel G. W. Hughes, Dr. Thomas Mercer, Henry Latrobe, Hamilton Hall, Charles S. Contee, N. H. Shipley, Dr. Augustus G. W. Owens, Judge Alexander B. Hagner (1852), W. R. S. Gittings, Frank H. Stockett, Dr. Howard M. Duvall, Nicholas H. Green, William D. Stewart, William Mayo, James Boyle.

In October, 1874, the club adjourned to December 1 (Tuesday), when the dinner failing to be served, it did not meet again until July 4, 1895, the date of the reunion of the four living members and the election of new ones. All who have been enrolled since and on that date are Messrs. John Wirt Randall, Frank H. Stockett, Jr., Daniel R. Randall, Dr. D. Murray Cheston, L. Dorsey Gassaway, Nevitt Steele, Thomson M. King, Beale Worthington, Blanchard Randall (1895), General George H. Steuart, Dr. James D. Iglehart, Mr. Robert Murray Cheston, Messrs. Wyatt W. Randall, Richard B. Sellman, James M. Monroe, Nicholas Harwood Green, Dr. J. W. F. Best, Messrs. Benjamin Watkins, Joseph Noble Stockett, Laurence Bailliere, Benjamin N. Wright, John T. Parrott, Franklin Weems, Prof. William Wirt Fay, Messrs. Thomas S. Iglehart, Richard W. Iglehart, Thomas A. Duckett, Samuel Brooke, George R. Gaither, Jr., Paul Iglehart, William Meade Hollyday, Frank Stockett Sellman, Governor Edwin Warfield, Dr. Richard S. Hill.

CHAPTER XLIV

LOSING THE FLITCH OF BACON

IN THE original manuscript records of the Provincial Court of Maryland one frequently happens on a reference to "losing the bacon" in suits which bring to light matrimonial disagreements. This Colonial maxim or bit of folklore is particularly interesting as indicating the locality from which many of our early settlers came. In Staffordshire Sir Philip de Somerville, who must have been a skeptic regarding matrimonial felicity, instituted the curious custom of hanging a flitch of bacon in his hall at Whichenovre ready arrayed at all times in the year but in Lent, to be given to every man or woman married, a day and a year after their marriage, in the following form: "Whensoever that anyone such before named will come to inquire for the bacon in their person they shall come to the bailiff or to the porter of the lordship of Whichenovre and shall say to them in the manner as ensueth: 'Bailiff or porter, I do you to know that I am come for myself to demand one bacon flyke hanging in the hall of the Lord of Whichenovre after the form thereto belonging.' After this a day is assigned by the porter upon the applicant's promise to return with twain of his neighbors. In the meantime the porter or bailiff and two of the freeholders of the lordship of Whichenovre go to the Manor of Rudlow, belonging to Robert Knightleye, commanding him to be ready at the time appointed at prime of day with his carriage—that is to say, a horse and saddle—a sack and a pryke, for to convey the said bacon and corn a journey out of the county of Strafford at his costage.

"Then the bailiff shall, with the said freeholders, summon all the tenants of the manor to be ready on the day appointed at Whichenovre for to do and perform the services which they owe the bacon.

"And at the day assigned all such as owe services to the bacon shall be ready at the gate of the Manor of Whichenovre, from the sun rising to noon, attending and waiting for the coming of him who fetcheth the bacon, and when he is come there shall be chaplets delivered to him and his fellows and to all those who desire to do services due to the bacon. And they shall lead the demandment with trumps and tabors and other manner of minstrelsy to the hall door, where he shall find the Lord of Whichenovre or his steward, ready to deliver the bacon.

"And he that demandeth the bacon shall kneel upon his knee, and shall hold his right hand upon a book, which book shall be laid upon the bacon and corn, and shall make the following oath:

"'Hearye, Sir Philip de Somerville, Lord of Whichenovre, mayntener and giver of this bacon, that I, A, sithe I wedded B, my wife, and sithe I had hyr in my kepyng by a year and a day after our marriage, I would not have changed for none other, farer ne fowler, richer ne pourer, ne for none other descended of greater lynage at noo tyme, and if the sayd B were sole I would take her to be my wife before all wymen in the world of what condiciones soever they be, good or evylle, as help me God and His seytes and this flesh and all fleshes.'"

After making this oath and his neighbors have testified

to the truthfulness of his words the man who thus wins the bacon is escorted from the Manor of Whichenovre with trumpets and taborets and all the homage paid a conquering hero!

According to the old register kept at Whichenovre, the first to demand the bacon as a reward for a year and day of married life without a cross word, was Aubrey de Falstaff, son of Sir John Falstaff, knight, with dame Maude, his wife, he having bribed twain of his father's companions to swear falsely in his behoof, whereby he gained the flitch, but he and his said wife falling immediately into a dispute how the said bacon should be dressed it was by order of the judges taken from him and hung up again in the hall.

The next one, Alison, the wife of Stephen Freckle, brought her said husband along with her and set forth the good condition and behavior of her consort, adding withal that she doubted not but he was ready to attest the like of his wife, whereupon he, the said Stephen, shaking his head she turned short upon him and gave him a box on the ear. Three others applied, but each proved unworthy. After this, the old record says, many years passed over before any demandment appeared at Whichenovre Hall, insomuch that one would have thought that the whole country were turned Jews, so little was their affection for the flitch of bacon. Later the sentence pronounced against one Gervase Poacher is "that he might have had bacon with his eggs if he had not hitheto scolded his wife when they were overboiled."

But two couples won the bacon during the whole first century. The first, we are told, was a sea captain and his wife, who since the day of their marriage had not seen each other until the day they claimed the flitch of bacon. The other was an honest pair in the neighborhood. The husband is described as "a man of plain good sense and a peaceable temper; the woman was dumb!"

CHAPTER XLV

THE KING'S REBELS

MANY errors, which crept into earlier historical writings with regard to so-called convict settlers, have caused a most erroneous impression in ignorant quarters respecting the status of the real founders of the province.

Happily the nearer we get to the truth of Maryland's settlement the more we find to arouse our pride in the men who in those trying early days proved themselves to be men of character and ability.

There is no romance so fascinating as the true history of early Maryland under the Lords Baltimore. First the "gentlemen of very good fashion," with the sturdy artisan class to make them comfortable; later other "adventurers" who came to seek their fortunes—or to add to those already enjoyed; the indentured apprentices and redemptioners, either entering a voluntary "time of service" for their passage over and the promise of fifty acres of land, or those who had been captured by "crimps" in London and basely sold against their wills into a term of servitude.

The romances, the heartbreaks and the strange experiences are all bound up in the fading old parchments in the record offices.

Then came the persecuted from other lands and other colonies into Maryland—such as the Puritans and Quakers. Then after the battle of Bothwell Bridge came the first of the Scots banished because of their loyalty to their religious belief. These were the Covenanters persecuted by King Charles II.

With the accession of James II affairs grew worse in Scotland, and persecution stalked abroad.

We can see in our mind's eye Margaret MacLaughlin and Margaret Wilson, one feeble with age, the other radiant with youth and her rare Scotch beauty, tied to stakes on the Solway shore, with the tide creeping, creeping, inch by inch, until it enveloped them, martyrs to their faith. Then came the Jacobite uprising, and after the defeat at Preston, there was death, torture and banishment for the rebels. And in the year 1716 we find two shiploads of these political prisoners arriving in Maryland to be sold into seven years' servitude. These men were sons of women like those who faced the creeping tide of Solway rather than forsake their principles.

The King tried to break their spirit by adding martyrdom to banishment. He knew the pride of his Highland clans, and he let them live to suffer humiliation.

But let none who descended from these King's prisoners feel that their servitude was a disgrace. It should be rather looked upon as the halo of their martyrdom!

What more glorious than the courage to rebel against the oppression and cruelty of such a tyrant! The proclamation issued by Governor John Hart in the year 1716 is as follows: "Whereas his most sacred Majesty (George I), out of his abundant clemency has caused eighty of the rebels (most of them Scotsmen, lately taken at Preston, in Lancashire), to be transported from Great Britain into this province in the ship *Friendship*, of Belfast, Michael Mankin commander, and signified to me his royall pleasure by one of his principall secretaries of state

GENERAL OTHO HOLLAND WILLIAMS
From Peale Portrait at Maryland Historical Society. From the Author's Collection

that the said rebells to the number aforesaid should be sold to the assigns of the merchants, who shall purchase them for the full term of seven years and no lesser time. And that I should cause the said rebells to enter into indentures to performe such service or otherwise grant the respective purchasers proper certificates to be recorded the better to enable them to detain them, lest they should at any time attempt to make their escape not being bound. It appearing to be his Majesty's pleasure, the aforesaid rebells should continue in this province for and during the whole term and space of seven years aforesaid.

"And whereas the said rebells, notwithstanding his Majesty's clemency and pleasure signified as aforesaid, have obstinately refused to enter into such indentures; that the greatest part of them already have been sold, and the rest will in all probability be disposed of with such proper certificates as by his Majesty directed in order to enable to retake any such who may at any time hereafter attempt to make their escape."

After notifying the sheriffs, constables, magistrates, officers and the inhabitants of the province to apprehend any such fugitives "who may attempt to go out of this province to some other plantation or province where they may not be known, and consequently have the greater opportunity to return to Great Brittain in order to pursue their wicked and rebellious practices and designs against his Majesty's and the Protestant succession, I do hereby, with the advice of his Lordship's councill, command the aforesaid officers, etc., to use their utmost endeavors to prevent the same by all possible diligence, etc." This proclamation in full was ordered to be published at "courthouses, churches, chapels and other most publick and frequented places in their respective counties and by fixing attested copies thereof at all such places whereof they are not to fail at their perills. Given at the city of Annapolis, under the Great Seale, this 28th day of August in the 3rd year of the reign of our Sovereign Lord George, of Great Britain, France and Ireland, Defender of the Faith, etc., Anno Domini 1716.

    (Signed) JOHN HART,
         JOHN BEARD, Cl. Council."

The names of the men banished and sold under the King's orders are of the proudest in all Scotland and of the most powerful of her clans, hence King George's fear of their influence should they return to Great Britain until he was more firmly seated on the throne.

In the British Museum there is preserved an original letter sent by one of these fearless rebels to his father after he had been sold in Maryland. In this he says: "The people here speak as they do in Inverness." This gateway to the Highlands was inhabited by the English, Fort William being there named in honor of William, Prince of Orange, after his accession to the throne.

It is a source, indeed, of surprise that no patriotic society has yet been organized to perpetuate exclusively the names of these Scotch exiles. Their tartans, their war cries, their pipe clan music and their badges—these are heritages worth preserving along with the record of their martyrdom.

CHAPTER XLVI

THE SCOTCH EXILES

THE pathetic appeal of Allestra MacGregor recalls the enormity of the punishment meted out to the Scotch rebels when banished beyond the seas by the victorious sovereign.

The Highlanders had an attachment to their native land which amounted to a passion, and hence death was preferable to banishment. Therefore when MacGregor prayed the King to be allowed banishment he had reached a state of heroism which was ready to sacrifice self that his "innocent bairnes" might pass to liberty.

While, however, his plea was unheeded, others were sent to America after each great victory during the civil wars in the seventeenth and eighteenth centuries. Keltie says it is generally believed that this strong feeling of love of country has come from the powerful effect which the eternal objects of nature seen in the wildest and most fantastic forms and features are calculated to impress upon the imagination. But while the Scotch exile remembered and loved every craig and loch of his native heath it was "home sweet home" for which he pined. In the year 1716 and 1717 many of the leaders in the Scotch uprisings were, after being taken prisoners of war, banished to Maryland, and so fearful was the King of their power that he prohibited, as we have seen, any of them from returning within seven years. But despite Governor Hart's proclamation, issued at the King's command, warning all persons against helping them to return to Great Britain, some did succeed in getting back to Scotland and were exempted in the King's act of grace. Most of these sturdy clansman, however, remained and settled in large number in Prince George's County and called their home "New Scotland;" and let us hope it was a happier one. The names of those who fought against the King at Preston and were banished to Maryland were: John Pitter, James Nethery, Dugall Macqueen, Alexander Smith, Abraham Lowe, Henry Wilson, Alexander Gorden, John Hay, William Seimn, Alexander Spalding, Leonard Robinson, John Blondell, John Sinclair, William Grant, Thomas Spark, James Webster, William Cumin, Allen Machen, John Robertson, Farq. Macgilvary, David Mills, Patrick Cooper, Jeremiah Dunbarr, John Degedy, William McBean, Thomas Lowey, John Glaney, William Macgilvary, Alexander Nave, James Hindry, William Mabbery, James Small, James White, John Macbayn, Robert Henderson, Thomas Potts, George Thompson, John Ramsey, Alexander Reind, Thomas Forbus, William Davidson, James Mitchell, James Lowe, James Derholme, James Allein, James White, Thomas Donoldson, James Hill, David Stewart, Henry Lunsdale, Arch. Macdonall, alias Kennedy; Charles Donalson, William Mare, Hector Macqueen, John Maclean, John MacIntire, William Onam, Alexander Macqueen, Alexander Macdugall, David Macqueen, John Macdonald, John Poss, Robert Stobbs, Finley Cameron, John Mertison, Alexander Swinger, William MacGilvray, Patrick Hunter, Henry Farchaser, Alexander Mortimer, James Robertson, Thomas Butter, Andrew Davidson, Thomas Smith, Thomas MacNabb, James Shaw, Donald Robertson, Andrew Daw, John Couchan, Henry Murray. These were sent over as

King's rebels in the ship *Friendship*, of Belfast, August 20, 1716. On the 18th of October a second shipload was sent to Maryland, and included William Macferson, Thomas Shaw, Miles Beggs, John Macgregier, Daniel Steward, Duncan Ferguson, John Mackewan, David Graham, William Johnson, James Mallone, George Neulson, John Chambers, James Sinclare, Alexander Orrach, James Crampson, John Stewart, Pott. Smith, George Hodgson, Malcolm Malcolm, James MacIntosh, John Cameron, David Lauder, Francis Macbean, William Simpson, John Kennery, James Bowe, Laughlin McIntosh, Alexander MacIntosh, William Furguson, James Dixon, Richard Withington, Thomas Berry, James Maclearn, Rowland Robertson, Ninian Brown, Daniel Kennedy, Patrick Mackey, Angus Macdermott, James MacIntosh, Hugh Macdugall, John Maccollum, William Shaw, Hugh MacIntire, Finloe MacIntire, Richard Brick, James Shaw, Daniel Grant, Hugh White, James Rutherford, Thomas Hume, James Renton, Alexander Macgiffin, Humphrey Sword, James Sumervill, John Shaftal. These names, copied by Scharf from the London Public Record office, are only those sent as prisoners of war after the defeat of Mar and Derwentwater's rising, 1715-16. No official list of those sent after 1651-52 has been brought to light, although it is known from references in the history of the various uprisings in the seventeenth century that prisoners taken by the victors were sent beyond the seas. Some records fix definitely the name and lineage of individuals who were banished.

CHAPTER XLVII

THE FOUNTAIN PEN IN THE TIME OF CHARLES II

THE quill pen and inkhorn have long been thought to be the most elegant accessories of a Colonial gentleman's writing desk known in the period of the Stuart kings. There is now, however, reason to believe that many a courtier in drooping plume and velvet doublet carried a fountain pen tucked away in some hidden pocket behind his lace ruffles, for in the criminal records of the English local courts the writer recently found an entry, dated "December 17, Charles II," stating that several persons broke into the house of one George Agard (in England) and stole among other things, "three silver fountain pens, worth 15 shillings."

The fact that there were three of these pens in one household is evidence that they were not rarities and were in common use at that day in England. It is not improbable that some of these very useful and convenient articles came in the *Ark* with the first adventurers. That they were in use in Maryland early in the next century and fully 100 years before the modern invention of the fountain pen of the nineteenth century, is certain, for in the year 1734 Robert Morris, the elder, has entered upon his private ledger, "one fountain pen" among the expenses of Robert Morris the younger, who was at the time under the care of Mr. Robert Greenway, in Philadelphia, where he was being educated.

The curious thing is not so much to find that the fountain pen was a commonplace article in the seventeenth century, but to note its disuse and its revival as a new invention not more than 100 years later. Robert Morris, Jr., was a lad of about fourteen years of age when his father allowed him a fountain pen to use at school. There is no record to enlighten us as to its form, neither are we told what the "fountain" consisted of in the English pens stolen of five shillings value each. Certain it is, however, that after that time, the quill pen was the only one known for a long period. It is possible that the English silver fountain pen was one of the articles of luxury which the colonists could do without and would not import after the troubles began with the mother country, and after the final separation the quill pen of home manufacture was used perhaps in the same spirit that homespun was worn by the women who scorned the Stamp Act.

It is, however, exceedingly interesting to find that what we have considered a very up-to-date invention of the strenuous days is in reality nothing more than a revival of the Colonial period.

CHAPTER XLVIII

EARLY DIVORCE LAW

IN VIEW of the recent prominence given to the question of divorce as the result of the action of the Episcopal Convention at Boston, it is pleasing to find that there was no divorce court in early Maryland, where evidently the old-fashioned way was to marry for better or worse. The home life was fuller in the early days, and every woman's mission was to be queen of her household and the father generally was content to be the revered head of his kingdom, where many little pattering feet ran to do his bidding and many sweet, young, flower-like faces wreathed his daily board as for a festal feast. These were the days on which the ideal of the home life is based. The sanctity of the marriage vow was inviolable in early Maryland. Knowing this to be true, it was more than surprising—it was shocking—to hear a son of a Colonial family recently assert that the reason why there were no very early marriage licenses in the county court houses, is because people were not as a rule married in Colonial times. Indeed, this youth was apparently as pleased with his discovery as a new convert to Darwinism is when he first claims his monkey origin!

However, as Maryland was settled by a Christian people of a civilization which produced a Shakespeare, we need not give other proofs of the marriage vow, but will rather cite the most notable case on record regarding the impossibility of obtaining a divorce in the Palatinate of Lord Baltimore. It appears on record that one Robert Holt was married to one Christiana Bonnefield by the Rev. William Wilkinson in the year 1658, and in the trial that ensued it transpired that Robert Holt had a wife still living, from whom the Rev. Mr. Wilkinson had released him from all claim of marriage by drawing and signing a paper to that effect upon his wife's refusal to be reconciled. The result of the rector's action fully confirms the sacredness of the marriage vow at that date in Maryland. Robert Holt was indicted for bigamy and Rev. William Wilkinson as an accessory. The indictment against Holt is for marrying Christiana Bonnefield during the lifetime of his "lawful wife;" that of Rev. Mr. Wilkinson "for feloniously joining the parties after he had divorced ye said Robert Holt."

The impossibility of a legal divorce in the province is confirmed by the investigations of the late George Lachlan Davis, who, referring to Rev. William Wilkinson's guilt, says the Bishop of London had no power under the English law to dissolve the bond. The Parliament was without any practical or real jurisdiction over the case, and the Provisional Assembly never granted a divorce *a vinculo* for any cause whatever; and the English Church having no higher representative or depositary of her authority in the province than the clergyman indicted.

CHAPTER XLIX

QUAKERS NOT PERSECUTED IN MARYLAND

IN LOOKING backward upon her early history, there is nothing which should excite more gratification in Maryland today than the knowledge that there were no persecutions of any moment for conscience sake in provincial Maryland. In tracing our lineage to Colonial governors or councilmen, to members of the Assembly or of the provincial courts, we find none of their hands stained with the innocent blood of those who worshipped God in a manner different from their own. And while for a brief term a law banishing Quakers from Maryland was in force in the province, it soon was repealed and Maryland became the haven of rest to the persecuted from other colonies.

As we recall the fact that this new religion was first brought across the seas by two gentle-hearted women, Mary Fisher and Ann Austin, we are more than glad that the annals of our State have preserved no harrowing tales of cruelty in connection with these early Friends. These first two missionaries arrived in Boston in the year 1656 and, according to Sewall, after much harsh treatment and persecution were compelled to return to England. In the same year Elizabeth Harris evidently visited Maryland, as Bowden quotes a letter to her from Robert Clarkson, dated "From Severn, the 14th of the eleventh month, 1657," and underneath is written, "this is in Virginia." The references to Herring Creek, Roade River, South

River, Kent, etc., prove that Clarkson used the word "Virginia" in the sense that others sometimes did, meaning any place south of New England. In an early record I found recently a reference to "a place in Virginia called Maryland."

In the year 1657–58 Josiah Cole and Thomas Thurston arrived in Virginia, and being joined by Thomas Chapman, came on foot to Maryland. These are said to have been the earliest Quakers in Maryland. Here they began their missionary work, and so evidently successful were they that on July 8, 1658, "upon information that Thos. Thurston and Josiah Cole refused to subscribe the engagement by the articles of March 24 last, a warrant was issued to the sheriffs to bring them before the Council."

The "engagement" referred to was a promise to submit to the authority of the Lord Baltimore, and applied to all residents of the province and was substituted for the oath of allegiance.

One week later Josiah Cole was found guilty "of seducing the people and dissuading them from taking the engagement." He was therefore ordered by the Governor and Council "to be taken in custody and kept without bail or main prize."

Later, in 1658, an order was passed as follows: "Where as it is too well knowne in this province that there have bin several vagabonds and idle persons known by the name of Quakers that have presumed to come into this province as were dissuading the people from complying with the military discipline in this time of danger, as also giving testimony, being jurors, in causes depending between party and party or bearing any office in the province, the justices of the peace are ordered to apprehend and cause them to be whipped from constable to constable until they should reach the bounds of the province." So far as known to the writer there is no record of any Quaker having actually been whipped.

In 1661 John Everett was called to answer his contempt in "running from his colors when prest to goe to Susquehanna Fort." He pleaded that he could not bear arms for conscience sake. He was then ordered to be "kept in chaynes and bake his own bread" until the next provincial court.

In the year 1658 William Burgess and Thomas Mears, who had been appointed to the offices of commissioners or justices of the peace, refused to take the necessary oath "pretending it was in no case lawful to swear."

It is evident that not many years elapsed before the sentiment against Quakers in Maryland changed very radically, and the Friends themselves overcame their aversion to office-holding, for many of the most important military and civil posts were, before 1700, filled by Quakers. Among these office-holding Friends may be mentioned William Burgess, Samuel Chew, Richard Preston, William Richardson and others of West River.

In the year 1697 the sheriff of Anne Arundell County, in making his report on the different dissenters from the Church of England in the county, says: "The Quakers have one timber-work meeting house built at West River upon land formerly owned by Mr. Francis Hooker, where they keep their yearly meetings, which is at Whitsuntide. Also a quarterly meeting at the house of Samuel Chew. Also a monthly meeting at Herring Creek meeting house standing on land purchased of Samuel Chew, also a weekly meeting at the same house. Also monthly and weekly meetings at the house of William Richardson, Sr., on West River. A weekly and monthly meeting at the house of Annie Lumboldt, near the head of South River. Also a monthly meeting at the house of John Belt.

"So far as I have the account from Mr. Richardson, I can understand of no preachers they have in this county, but Mr. Richardson and Samuel Galloway's wife." George Fox, the founder of Quakerism, came to Maryland in the year 1672 and was present at the first general meeting. In October of the same year Fox attended the general meeting for all Friends at Treadhaven, the Eastern Shore stronghold of the Quakers, where the name of John Edmondson, Wenlock Christison and others are prominently identified.

It is pleasant to find that in the year 1688 the Lord Baltimore felt so kindly toward the Quakers that he issued a proclamation dispensing with oaths in testamentary cases. This gracious act on the part of the Proprietary was gratefully acknowledged in an address from the Friends' quarterly meeting at Herring Creek.

As early as the year 1682 the yearly meetings had become of great interest in the province, and it is a matter of record in the journal of John Richardson, published in London in the year 1700, that during William Penn's visit to Maryland in 1682 he accompanied the Lord and Lady Baltimore to the yearly meeting at Treadhaven; but "it was late when they arrived and the lady was much disappointed, as the spirit of the Lord had departed from the meeting."

An admirable custom of the early Friends was to look after the welfare of "the widows and orphans."

In the year 1679 "the Widow Ford hath referred herself to our Man's meeting for advice and assistance in the matter relating to her outward estate." That this young widow was fully capable, however, of looking after her own welfare is evident from an agreement which she made with Edward Pinder, the Colonial justice. In the year above mentioned, Sarah Ford, widow, leases to Edward Pinder land in Dorchester County, called Widow's Lott, on condition that "he provide and allow for her three children, Samuel, Josias and Rebecca Ford, lodging and washing, housing, apparel, meat and drink, for and during the term of seven whole years from date, and in consideration that he will teach, or cause to be taught, her said children, to read and write according and so far as their capacitys will attain within the time and term aforesaid." It is not surprising that Edward Pinder wisely married the widow and thus canceled his lease.

There is no character which stands out more clearly in the history of the Quakers in Maryland than that of Wenlock Christison, whose persecutions and sufferings in Boston and Plymouth were harrowing in the extreme. It is pleasant to think that after being starved, beaten, robbed and sentenced to death, this fearless martyr found in Talbot County, Maryland, a peaceful home, a wife, children, loving friends and freedom to spread his message of peace.

It is a striking fact that many of the representative families of Maryland became Friends, and their descendants today are among the best element, not only in this State, but in every other one in which they made the loftiness of their character felt.

COMMUNION SILVER PRESENTED TO ST. ANNE'S CHURCH, ANNAPOLIS, BY KING WILLIAM III, ENGRAVED WITH THE ROYAL ARMS AND CYPHER

CHAPTER L

EARLY PARISHES

IN ENGLAND we find that Honorius, the fifth Archbishop of Canterbury, about the year 636, was the first to ordain parishes that he might assign to every priest his particular flock. Before this the bishop and whole clergy of the diocese were as one body, living upon their endowments bestowed on the bishopric and their treasure that came from the sundry places of devotion, whither some one or other of them, at the bishop's appointment, was sent to preach the word and minister the sacrament, every clerk having his dividend for his maintenance.

From these facts it is evident that the Protestant Episcopal Church in Maryland began its life in the way of the primitive English Saxon Church, as for the first half century the individual Episcopal churches in the province paid their tithes to the Lord Bishop of London. Of these there were a goodly number, the old Poplar Hill Church having been built as early as 1642, with a rector as early as 1650.

It was not, however, until after the Protestant revolution and the accession of William and Mary that the Maryland Assembly passed "an act for the service of Almighty God and the establishment of the Protestant religion in this province." By this act the counties were divided into parishes and churches ordered to be built, "such parishes as have already churches and chapels built in them excepted." Thus the Church of England became the established church of Maryland.

The province was divided into thirty parishes, of which seventeen were on the Western Shore and thirteen on the Eastern, St. Mary's, in which there had been at least one Protestant Episcopal Church since 1642, was divided into two parishes, "King William and Mary" and "King and Queen." Anne Arundel was given four—St. Margaret's, Westminster, St. Anne's, St. James and All Hallow's; Baltimore County into St. Paul's, St. George's and St. John's; Charles into Port Tobacco, Durham, William and Mary, Piscataway or St. John's. Kent was given the two parishes of Kent Island and St. Paul; Talbot County, St. Peter's, St. Paul's and St. Michael's; Somerset, Stepney, Coventry, Somerset and Snow Hill; Dorchester into Dorchester and Great Choptank parishes.

It is evident from the act of 1697 that some persons who made gifts of land for the building of churches did not do so in legal form, and their heirs were not equally liberal minded. This was "an act for confirming titles of land given to the use of the churches and several chapels of ease within this province." It empowered the commissioners of the respective counties and vestrys of the parishes to take up certain parcels of land for the use of the same. All gifts or grants were to be recorded in the county courts and a copy filed in the High Court of Chancery.

Among the various good provisions for the parishes upon the establishment of the Protestant Church was that which decreed that a "Register" be appointed to make due entry of vestry proceedings, births, marriages and burials and provide books accordingly under penalty. In the year 1696 the Council upon investigation found that this regulation had been universally disregarded, none having returned the prescribed lists, and a fine was consequently imposed.

It is to such neglect on the part of the early vestries that so little is to be known from the church records. That the established church had a struggling existence in many parishes the records of those times make evident.

Church-going was encouraged in the province, and a unique act was passed exempting persons from arrest while attending divine service. After the establishment of the Protestant Church in Maryland the absence of a bishop or commissary left an organization without a head, for under the peculiar royal rights and privileges of the Lords Baltimore the Bishop of London, who was the nominal head of the Episcopal Church in Maryland, had really no authority to remove the incumbent who had been appointed to "the living" by the Proprietary. To this life tenure on a parish is ascribed many abuses which grew up among the early clergy. With no spiritual head to fear, and with an independence furnished by the per poll tax, a rectory with glebe lands attached and few services, the life led by many of the young divines was more fitted to the fox-hunting squire than to a member of the cloth. In view of this, it is remarkable that a whole century elapsed between the establishing of the Episcopal Church in Maryland and the election of the first Bishop, one whose life was a benediction to the church, and whose ancestral motto, "The acceptable grace of God," was the watchword of his character.

CHAPTER LI

DIVERSITY IN SPELLING COLONIAL NAMES

The uninitiated "seeker after truth" in family history through the Colonial records would soon be discouraged if he discarded all names which were spelled contrary to the modern mode. The diversity in the spelling of surnames as they appear in the official records has long been one of the most interesting phases of the absorbing study which includes the names, origin, lives and homes of the makers of Maryland.

Some names entirely lost their original form at the hands of the recording clerks in the early province, and this peculiar state of affairs made it necessary for men of landed possessions to adopt the incorrect spelling of their names to preserve their identity as the persons to whom such lands were patented. There being no rule for proper names, they were spelled phonetically in many cases and according to the way the special clerk in whose office they were recorded happened to think they were spelled. Therefore, the tracing of family lineages would be a hopeless and disappointing pursuit did not experience prove that there were as many ways to spell some names in early Maryland as there were clerks in the offices. The name of Smith, Smyth or Smythe often stood for the same persons, as did Maignard for Maynard, etc., and William De Courcy first appears on the early records as William Coursey, and so his descendants might have continued to be written had not an early one of the Maryland De Courcy men given the proper spelling of his name to his sons, with instructions to so sign themselves forever after. The early Darcys were written Darcy, Dorsey, Dossey, Dawsey—the double "s" no doubt indicating the soft English pronunciation that prevailed in the province settled principally by men of that nationality; and while in one branch of that family the name appears as Dossey in the records, and even signed to the wills of several, the name was, however, written out with the "r" in mentioning the children as heirs.

We find the name Hammond spelled Hamon and even Hamor. One of the most striking examples of the diversity of spelling in a single name is that of the French Huguenot Benojs Brasseuir, who came into Maryland from Virginia in 1658 and was naturalized in 1662. After this the spelling of his name and that of his descendants has varied as follows: Brasseuir, Brasseur, Brashieur, Brushier, Brasshear and Brashears.

There are many other names that could be cited to show with what variations a given name appeared in early records, and how impossible it would be to locate an individual if only the spelling of the name were taken as a guide to the identity of a family. It is quite likely that serious complications occurred in olden times in transferring land or proving the title to it. A very amusing situation arose only a few years ago when a man who desired to join one of the patriotic societies had a struggle with his conscience about swearing to his own identity. We will say that he was christened "John Henry S——," but not liking the name he reversed it and from his youth wrote himself as "Henry John S——." The preamble to the application read: "I, Henry John S——, of the city of Baltimore," etc. "But," said this man of tender conscience, "can I subscribe myself under oath when I am really John Henry S——?" "Yes," replied his friend, "are you not Henry John S——, of the firm of brokers?" There was a clincher. He certainly was that man, and he was as surely by rite of baptism the other. It was a case of the old woman and the little dog who was to determine for her "If I be I."

After long wrestling with his conscience and the persuasive arguments of his friends he at last swore that he was the man he was supposed to be—i. e., Henry John S——. He certainly had no idea of making such trouble for himself when changing the relative position of his names. Neither, we are sure, would our ancestors have permitted the carelessness of clerks to have destroyed their identity in so many cases had they dreamed of the weary hunt they were laying up for their twentieth century descendants.

CHAPTER LII

A COLONIAL SANITARIUM

IN THIS day of public hospitals and free sanitariums we are apt to flatter ourselves that these institutions for the benefit of suffering humanity are evidences of a modern virtue and one of which our forebears knew nothing. It is, therefore, surprising to find in the year 1698 the provincial Assembly empowering a body of trustees to purchase land upon which to erect a hospital for the benefit of the sick poor. It appears that the province had been heavily afflicted with an epidemic of illness, mostly likely the old-fashioned chills and fever, known now as malaria.

In April of the year mentioned, Captain John Dent, living in Charles County, but owning certain lands in St. Mary's, wrote to the Assembly a letter evidently calling attention to the "healing fountains" which had been discovered on his estate in the latter county, and probably offering to sell to the government.

The Assembly declared the communication to be "an idle letter not worth answering," and laid the matter on the table. It seems, however, that the people in the vicinity of the "cool springs" drank renewed health to themselves in their sparkling waters during the ensuing summer so that the fame of the miraculous cures penetrated as far north as New York. At an October meeting of the Council, Governor Francis Nicholson speaks of "the printed news lately received from New York," which "delivers several representations relating to the coole springs in St. Mary's County" and proposes that "if the house doe consent to have some small tenement built there in the nature of an hospital, he will give £25 sterling toward the building thereof." Here we find the patron of the free schools in Maryland, the pioneer subscriber to the first free hospital in the province or State, and then, as now, it took but the earnest endeavor of one man to turn the sentiment of the Assembly, for we find the same men who had treated Captain Dent's letter with indifference now following the Governor's lead and throwing their influence to the desired end.

On the 20th day of October, 1698, the following act was passed, having first been framed by the Governor and his Council and submitted to the Lower House:

"Whereas, by the favor of Almighty God, there hath been of late a discovery made of fountains of healing waters called the Cool Springs, in St. Mary's County, whose healing quality has been experienced by many impotent and diseased persons to their great help and comfort and for so great blessing, benefit and gifts of Almighty God may not be neglected, but a right use thereof made, it is most fitting and convenient that a particular care should first be had of all poor impotent persons as repaire thither for care and for the purpose or other such charitable or pious uses a small Tract or parcell of land, near adjoining, may be purchased thereon to build and erect houses for the entertainment of said poor, and fuell for fireing and other such necessarys for their reliefe, the Delegates of this present Generall Assembly therefore pray it may be enacted, by the King's Most Excellent Majesty, by and with the advice and consent of this present General Assembly and the authority of the same; that the persons hereafter named may and are hereby appointed trustees for and on behalfe of His Majesty's Province of Maryland to buy and purchase in the name of our Sovereign Lord the King, his heires or successors, for pious and charitable uses 50 acres of land adjoining to and in which the said fountains shall be included."

The trustees named were Colonel John Courts, Thomas Brooke, Esq., Captain James Keech, Captain Jacob Moreland, of St. Mary's County, and Captain Philip Hoskins, Captain John Bayne and Mr. Benjamin Hall, of Charles County, or any three of them.

CHAPTER LIII

ESTABLISHMENT OF THE LAND OFFICE

During the life of Cæcilius Calvert, second Lord Baltimore and first Proprietary of Maryland, he kept a sharp lookout for the distribution of lands, and all grants of manors and patents of lands, according to the conditions of plantations, were issued in his name by his representative in the province; in which formality, however, the Surveyor-General and Secretary of the Province also had their parts to play. Cæcilius during the forty-odd years of his reign by proxy over his little kingdom beyond the seas, kept a firm hand upon his rents and his dues, and from time to time issued instructions to his representatives regarding his land affairs. For many years before his father's death Charles Calvert, the third Lord Baltimore, as Governor of the province, had control of the Maryland estates, but it was not until five years after his father's death that Charles inaugurated a separate land office and appointed a register—Mr. John Llewellyn. This was in the year 1680.

The commission issued to this first custodian of the land records reads as follows: "Charles, Absolute Lord and Proprietary of the Province of Maryland and Avalon, Lord Baron of Baltimore, etc., to all persons to whom these presents shall come greeting in our Lord and God everlasting: Know ye that we, reposing special trust and confidence in the great care, truth, fidelity and circumspection of John Lewellin, of the county of St. Maries, within this our said Province of Maryland, and for divers other good causes and considerations us there unto moving, have ordained, constituted and appointed as by these presents we doe hereby ordaine, constitute and appoint the said John Lewellin to be clerk and register of our land office within this our said province for all matters relating to land specially and particularly now lately erected and appointed, hereby authorizing and empowering the said John Lewellin as register to take into his care and charge all and singular the records, transcripts, books, papers and memorandums whatsoever to the same belonging or in anywise appertaining; giving also hereby full power and authority to our said clerk, or register, to take the probate of all rights for land due to any person or persons inhabiting, residing or trading in this province, according to the conditions of plantations by our deceased father Cæcilius, etc., of noble memory, published and set forth and remaining upon record within our said office, as shall from time to time and at all times hereafter be brought and tendered to him for that purpose, and upon due proof thereof made to issue out and signe warrants, and upon return of the certificates thereof to draw patents for the same as is usuall, keeping a true and perfect record of what shall by him be done and perpetuated by vertue thereof in execution of his said office, and in all things to act, doe and perform as to the said place and office may or of right ought to be done, according to condicons of our deceased father Cæcilius, etc., as aforesaid, or such other conditions as shall by us from time to time and at all times hereafter be set forth and published within this our said province, and, according to such further orders, instructions and directions as he shall from time to time receive from us or our leiutenant-general or other chief governor for the time being. Provided alwaies that noe special warrant, warrant of re-survey or other special matter whatsoever relating to land as aforesaid shall be issued out, but by speciall order from us or our lieutenant-general or other chief governor as aforesaid, anything to the contrary before mentioned notwithstanding. To Have and to Hold the said place and office of clerk and register of our land office to the said John Lewellin for and during our pleasure. Given under our hand and lesser seale at armes the 19th day of April, in the fifth year of our Dominion, etc., Anno Domino 1680."

Four years after this, Lord Baltimore, who is preparing for a trip to England, "moves the advice of his council concerning some instructions to be left with a particular council his Lordship designed to constitute in his absence, to hear and determine all matters of land and acts of grace and favor therein."

Calvert next issued a commission to the four gentlemen, whom he constituted "our especiall and select council for us and in our name to heare and determine all matters relating to lands, etc. These were Colonel Henry Darnall, Colonel William Digges, Major Nicholas Sewall and Mr. John Darnall, esquire."

The commission to these "Trusty and well-beloved Councillors" was issued at Mattapony Sewall the 5th day of May, 1684.

The Lord Baltimore having been summoned to London on matters of vital interest to himself, took ship for England in the year above mentioned. Here trouble assailed him from many directions, and his final misfortune

John Coode

Nicholas Greenberry

Nehemiah Blakiston

William Burgess

Henry Sewall

William Digges

Henry Darnall

Richard Bennett

John Hammond

Francis Nicholson

Augustin Herman

Edmund Andross

Nathaniel Utie

RARE AUTOGRAPHS FROM THE AUTHOR'S COLLECTION OF SOME HIGH COLONIAL OFFICIALS IN THE SEVENTEENTH CENTURY OF ANCESTRAL INTEREST

in having his orders delayed in proclaimimg William and Mary's accession led to his losing his power in Maryland at the instigation of the association for the "defense of the Protestant religion"—formed in 1689 and headed by John Coode. As a result, Lord Baltimore was deposed, and in the year 1692 the King sent out a royal governor, Sir Lionel Copley, and appointed a council, and even officers in minor places.

Sir Thomas Lawrence, secretary of the province for King William, claimed the right of controlling the land affairs—such as issuing warrants and collecting fees.

The Lord Baltimore submitted to the loss of his power, but fought for his rights in the soil—and his agent refused to issue patents without the same fees were paid to him.

It is interesting to know that a dispute occurred over the custody of the land records; the agent demanded them to be left in his personal possession, the Assembly declaring that they should remain in the secretary's office "for the inspection of the people who were interested in them."

CHAPTER LIV

THE FIRST LABOR-SAVING INVENTION IN MARYLAND

THE first labor-saving invention in Maryland was the water mill set up adjoining the town of St. Mary's for the grinding of the corn in less than six months after the settlement. The old way of crushing the grain between stones or by the use of the pestle and mortar were the only ones known to the natives, but with the white man came the easier methods of civilization. That Lord Baltimore took great pride in this evidence of enterprise is gathered from his comments regarding its erection, concluding: "And thus, without boasting, it may be said that this colony hath arrived to more in six months than Virginia did in as many years."

Later, with the coming of numerous Dutch from New Amsterdam the Holland windmill was introduced in such parts of the colony as had no streams of water with sufficient force to turn the mills. In Dorchester County, where the long stretches of lowlands were particularly adapted to the windmills, this early and crude though satisfactory importation still performs its original mission of grinding the corn of the farmers, despite the modern steam gristmills in the county town.

Surprising as it may seem to twentieth century readers, specimens of the original pestle and mortar used for crushing and pounding the grain have recently been found in Dorchester; also a handmill such as that described in the Scriptures in the reference to "two women grinding at the mill." This is formed by two large stones, an upper and nether. In the upper one a stick with two handles rests in a socket in the stone. Two women do the turning.

These mills are still in use in the homes of some old colored folk and are valuable as survivals of our primitive civilization. The water mills in the colony did not increase in the ratio of the corn crop, and we find in the year 1699 an act for the encouragement of such persons as will undertake to build water mills, etc., was passed by the General Assembly, to the effect that "daily experience sheweth that the want of water mills is true cause that husbandry in tilling the ground and for sowing of wheat and barley is but coldly prosecuted, though the advantage thereby in raising the stock of neat cattle be great, etc.

"Be it enacted by the King's Most Excellent Majesty and with the consent of the present General Assembly and the authority of the same, that any person after the publication hereof that shall desire to sett up a water mill upon any land next adjoining any Run of water within the Province, not being the proper possessor or freeholds of such person, nor leased to them. . . . . that twenty acres of such land lying at such Run—ten acres on each side—should be granted to such persons by the purchase of a writ out of his Majesty's Court of Chancery."

In other words, any person desiring to put up and run a water mill for the convenience of the public was given the right to enter on and have granted to him twenty acres of another man's estate, "with free egress and regress," and the privilege of cutting such timber as was necessary to build said mill.

The toll for grinding was also regulated by the Assembly at this time, to the effect that no master or miller should demand or receive for grinding above one-sixth part of every bushel of Indian corn and one-eighth part of every bushel of wheat, upon penalty of 1000 pounds of tobacco to the uses of his Majesty.

To those who associate the wild animals of Mr. Seton's acquaintance with the regions of the Far West, it will be surprising to learn, perhaps, that the English found buffaloes, elks, lions, bears, wolves and deer "in great store" in Maryland, also foxes, beavers, otters and many other sorts of beasts.

They had to import from Virginia and from England their sheep, hogs, cattle and horses. That there was no dearth of flesh, fish and fowl in Maryland and her waters in the beginning of her history we can readily believe when reading the enthusiastic descriptions given by those who first feasted on them.

The wild turkeys are mentioned as plentiful and as weighing fifty pounds and upward. Partridges then filled the meadows and woodlands. In addition to these delicacies were enumerated "swans, cranes, geese, herons, duck, teal, widgeon, brants and pigeons and other sorts whereof are none in England."

Of the fish that inhabit the waters of Maryland, Lord Baltimore says they are "whales, sturgeons, very large and good, in great abundance. There are grampus, porpuses, mullets, trouts, soules, place, mackerall, perch, crabs, oysters, cockles and mussels, but, above all, the fish that have no English names are the best." These must have been our shad, taylor and rock.

No mention is made of the now world-famous diamondback terrapin, which was so commonly used in Colonial days that it has become a dainty beyond the enjoyment of all but the rich, who now pay fancy prices for the dish which the indentured apprentices refused to eat as a steady diet.

It is not certain to what extent we are indebted to the red man for many secrets in the art of healing, but certainly the settlers acknowledge that "the country affords many excellent things for physick and surgery, the perfect use of which the English cannot yet learn from the natives. They have a root which is an excellent preservative against poison, called by the English snake root. Other roots and herbs they have wherewith they cure all manner of wounds; also saxafas, gummes and balsum." An instance of the Indian's skill in healing is given in which a settler who was suffering with toothache received quick relief by holding in his mouth a piece of a tree root given him for the purpose by an Indian.

In the letters of an indentured apprentice, written to relatives in London some years later, and after the colony was firmly seated and established as a trading point, we learn that between November and January "there arrive in this province shipping to the number of 20 sail and upward, all merchantmen, laden with Commodities to trafique and dispose of, trucking with the Planter for silks, Hollands, serges and with other necessary goods, prized at such and such rates as shall be judged on is fair and legal, for tobacco at so much the pound and advantage on both sides considered—the Planter for his work—the Merchant for adventuring himself and his commodity into so far a country."

We are told by this writer that "the Ketches and Barkes

from New England arrive in September, and bring mostly Wicker Chairs, tin candle sticks, Medeira Wines, salt and sugars." The light thrown on the characteristics of the early Maryland planters by this witty and picturesque Colonial writer is too valuable to pass unnoted.

"Sir," he says to his friend in London, "if you send any adventure to this Province, let me beg to give you this advice in it: That the Factor (or agent) you imploy be a man of brain, otherwise the Planter will go near to make a skimming dish of his skull. I know your genius can interpret my meaning. The people of this place," he continues, "whether the saltness of the ocean gave them any alteration when they first went over, or their continual dwelling under the remote clyme where they now inhabit I know not, are a more acute people in general in matters of trade and commerce than in any other place of the world—to be short he that undertakes merchants' imployment for Maryland must have more Knave than fool in him."

"COOKE'S POINT," ESTATE OF EBENEZER COOKE,
MARYLAND'S POET LAUREATE NOW
"THE MOORS"

CHAPTER LV

A POET LAUREATE IN COLONIAL MARYLAND

WHETHER or not the bay leaves were ever really twined about his brow, history sayeth not, but that Ebenezer Cooke, Gentleman, Deputy Receiver General to the Right Honorable Charles, fifth Lord Baltimore, signed himself as "Laureate" in his elegy on the death of Hon. Nicholas Lowe, Esq., relative to his Lordship, this extant publication bears witness. The elegy was published in the year 1728.

This talented colonist had come to Maryland before 1708, and returned to London with his father, a wealthy captain of a vessel which made frequent trips to the Province.

In his earliest poem, "The Sot-weed Factor, or a voyage to Maryland," which he terms "a Satyr in Burlesque Verse," he signs himself—Eben. Cooke—Gent.

This was published at London by B. Bragg, at "The Raven" in Pater Noster Row, 1708.

He probably returned to Maryland after his father's death in 1717 and became a prominent official.

The fact that Ebenezer Cooke was a real person, and not a nom de plume as those who edited the reprints of his poems supposed, was discovered by the author, by the finding of his father's will, recorded among the Land Records of Dorchester County, Maryland. The preservation of this interesting and important document was due to the fact that it was entered among the deeds, and not the wills of the County, as the Register of Wills office was burned, with all its records, in the year 1853.

The land mentioned as "Cooke's Point" in the will of Captain Andrew Cooke, still bears his name and tradition preserves the fact that he was buried on his estate, the part including the grave yard having long since been carried away by the lapping of the waves of the Great Choptank River (Indian Blue Water), thus the erstwhile mariner went out to sea alone, long after his last voyage on his staunchly built merchant vessel.

Ebenezer Cooke continued to live in Cecil County, Maryland, and on March 20, 1720, received a commission as Deputy Receiver General, under Henry Lowe, Esq. See Baltimore County Land Records, Liber T. R., No. D. S., folio 237, April 6, 1721.

The will proving the identity of Maryland's Poet Laureate is recorded in Old Liber 8, folio 46, Clerk's Office, Cambridge, Maryland, and is dated December 31, 1711, probated November 17, 1717, and is here given in full:

"I, Andrew Cook of the Parish of St. Giles in the Field, in the County of Middlesex, Gent., doe make this my last will and Testament as followeth—

"Imp. I give to my son Ebenezer Cooke and Anne Cooke my daughter all my Right and Title of and to two houses in the possession of —— paner in Plumtree Street known by the name of Cherry Tree, and the other house in the possession of Wm. Hawster Butcher in St. Giles afs. share and share alike.

"Imp. I give all my lands called 'Cooke's Point' lying at the mouth of Great Choptank River, lying in Dorchester Co., in Maryland to them share and share alike and make them joint Executor and Executrix of this my last will and test—in witness whereof I have here unto set my hand and seale the 31st day of December, 1711." This will was also probated in London.

In the year 1730 "E. C. Gent" appeared as the author of "The Sotweed Redivivus, or The Planter's Looking Glass, in Burlesque Verse" which was printed at Annapolis by William Parks "for the Author."

Two years before this Parks had printed R. Lewis' translation of "Muscipula—The Mousetrap, or the Battle of the Cambrians and the Mice," by Edward Holdsworth, the Latin Poet and Classical Scholar, the first edition of which had appeared in London in the year 1709. See "The Dictionary of National Biography," page 123.

CHAPTER LVI

LIFE ON COLONIAL PLANTATIONS

WITH the exception of the capital city, which was the center of official and commercial life, towns did not flourish in early Maryland.

The English settlers, true to the habits and traditions of the mother country, preferred to live in the heart of large landed possessions, which gave them both the power and seclusion so dear to the Briton.

These estates, or plantations, were the centers of the social life in the early days, when there was no lack of servants, since every outgoing ship laden with its crop of sweet-scented tobacco bound for England returned with consignments of not only comforts and luxuries for the planters, but also with adventurous young immigrants, who became apprentices to the landholders for a term of five years in payment of their passage over.

The planters were eager to buy the time of these young fellows, who were in many instances of good blood and education, but without means.

The romance of the conditions which naturally arose on the estates has been grasped by the modern novelist with good effect, and the unfortunate relation between these well-born youths in a state of temporary servitude has been strongly pictured. These free-will indentured servants were called "redemptioners." These entered service voluntarily to get a foothold in the new country which was attracting men of all stations who wished to better their fortunes. The law required that at the end of his term of indenture each man should have given him "one new hat, one new suit of kersey or broadcloth, a white linen shift, a pair of French fall shoes, stockings, two hoes, one axe, one gun of twenty shillings value, not above four feet in the barrel nor under three and a half feet."

We find many cases of men of wealth bringing into the province their young kinsmen, nephews, cousins and friends, for everyone of whom they received fifty acres of land. Chancery proceedings and many old wills prove that in such cases the indentured servant received from his wealthy kinsman the fifty acres, when after a few years' service he is given his freedom.

As we look back on that period we can appreciate why men of pride and wealth subjected these young fellows to a term of apprenticeship, which was, without doubt, done for the purpose of keeping control of them in a strange community and to keep them out of mischief, perhaps, through idleness. At any rate, these transported young men usually profited by their time of service and were able to start on little farms of their own after they had learned to cultivate the soil.

The fact of his having served another for a term of years did not retard his success in the province, nor did it in any way effect his social standing if the redemptioner was a young man of family and character. Indeed, there are not a few of our best families who number among their forebears distinguished Colonial officials who served a term of indenture to some affluent planter.

Next there were the indentured servants who were, without their consent, sent over from London by the "crimping" officers, as well as those who were induced to come by alluring promises of wealth and an easy life. Both of these classes were without their consent sold to the planters at the wharves upon the arrivals of the ships from England. The pathetic and unjust sufferings of these have been set forth in several novels of Colonial times, and tomes could be written of their miseries if one could really know all that it meant to them to be shipped to a strange land beyond the seas without a word of farewell to friends and sold into positive slavery for a term of years.

CHAPTER LVII

MARYLAND—THE PROMISED LAND TO THE PERSECUTED

DURING the entire seventeenth century the crowned heads of Europe seemed more concerned with the religious beliefs of their subjects and less interested in the salvation of their own souls than ever was known perhaps in the world's history.

In England, Scotland, Ireland, France, Germany and Holland the rulers pursued to the bitter end those who dared to differ from them in their beliefs of how to worship God.

No sooner had King James I of England united the three kingdoms of England, Scotland and Ireland than each division of the British Empire hoped that its own religion might flourish.

But Scottish James, dubbed by Burleigh, "the wisest fool in Europe," conformed to the Established Church of England and decreed that all his subjects should do likewise.

Catholics were treated with especial cruelty, and all priests were deported from England in the year 1604.

While the king was trying how knavish he could be to his subjects his bishops and high churchmen were formulating doctrines which, according to Hallam, were more dangerous to liberty than all that had gone before. We find, according to this authority, that the canons of 1616 prescribed passive obedience in all cases to the established monarch.

"Civil power is God's ordinance," is the second canon's doctrine.

Again we find the declaration that "the king is above law by his absolute power, and may disregard his coronation oath. He may break all laws inasmuch as they were not made to bind him, but to benefit the people; and to fetter the king is to injure the people." It is little wonder, therefore, that the monarch should accept this excess of power and openly assert in the star chamber: "It is atheism and blasphemy to dispute what God can do; good Christians content themselves with His will as revealed in His work. So it is presumption and high contempt in a subject to dispute what a king can do, or say that a king cannot do this and cannot do that."

George Calvert, principal secretary to King James I, must have felt a genuine contempt for the assumption of divine attributes by this vain egotist, and it was no doubt his nearness to the royal person and the close knowledge of his life in relation to his subjects which turned his attention to colonization and the freedom of conscience. The persecuted of France, the banished Huguenots, the condemned Catholics of England and Ireland, the Puritans of England, were all looking with wistful eyes toward a haven of rest from oppression. All they needed was a Moses to lead them into the promised land, and George Calvert pointed the way in which his son led the first settlers across the unknown seas to the land of plenty and religious freedom.

It may be well to recall the fact that Sir George Calvert first received a grant for the southern part of Newfoundland, which he called "Avalon," and which he had to abandon on account of the severity of the climate.

CHAPTER LVIII

OLD TOWNS OF THE EASTERN SHORE

A TRIP to the old Eastern Shore, the scene of much of the aristocratic life of the early settlement, appeals to all of the old blood.

Hence it was the most natural thing in the world to find one's self landing at Chestertown late one evening, when the only thing to be distinctly seen was the old Custom House, the white walls of which appeared a gray ghost of the days when Chestertown was a port of entry and the Custom House was the scene of a very different nature than its present isolation.

Here was all life and animation as the officials, the lords of the manor and the gentlemen planters crowded the wharf to catch the first news from England brought by the incoming ships.

The young macaronis, in lace ruffles, drooping plumes and other masculine frippery of the period of the Restoration, lolled about the old Custom House, watching the ships unloading their precious cargoes, including the latest importations of London fashions.

Much of the superb silver, fine mahogany furniture and rare books imported in those far-off days still add beauty and elegance to the homes of the living descendants of the early Kent families. Nor must we forget the patriotism displayed at this same port of entry, when the audacious little ship Geddes arrived with a consignment of tea, which was promptly served to the finny tribe by the indignant sons of Kent.

There is a charming touch of quaintness about this old town, with its homes of Colonial architecture, overlooking sloping gardens in the rear, past which the Chester River flows, lapping at their base. Suggestive as are the old homes of the Ringgolds and the Hynsons, the Wickses, Perkins and Chambers, the Masseys and the Wilmers, the Williamsons and the many other early aristocrats of Kent, the earlier memories of the Isle of Kent dimly outlined in the distance will clamor for attention, and we see in our mind's eye the arrival of Claiborne in his ship, the *Africa*, in the interest of Cloberry and Company, who had been granted license to trade.

The fights and heartaches between Claiborne and the Calverts upon the arrival of Leonard several years later, are still very real upon the records. We yearn to go over the site of Fort Kent Manor, the home of Giles Brent and the scene of Ingle's raid. Here Mistress Margaret Brent would come to visit her brother, the lord of the manor, sailing across the bay from the manor of St. Gabriels, in St. Mary's County, where she was paid fealty as lady of the manor.

But time pressed and Kent Isle was left to its memories. Passing from the habitat of the Ringgolds, of Eastern Neck Manor, those merchant princes of Colonial days, whose ships bore rich cargoes both to and from England, and whose wives were chosen only from the highest in the land, we crossed the Chester River early one morning behind two brisk trotters and sped along between the hedgerows of Queen Anne's highways, through the land of the De Courseys, the Thomases and all the other of the country gentry.

Formed by a portion of Kent and a slice of Talbot, Queen Anne's County includes the early families of both,

MACKUBIN FAMILY SILVER
Owned by the Misses Walton of Annapolis, great-great-granddaughters of Mrs. James Mackubin, the beautiful partner of General Washington at the ball given to him in the Old State House December 23, 1783

and we find the sons of each paid little heed to imaginary boundaries when seeking the hand of their ladyloves.

After a day in the county we turned our faces toward the more ancient seat of Talbot County, which also has produced many makers of Maryland history, among whom the Lloyds of Wye still have a typical representative in Colonel Edward Lloyd; the Tilghmans of the Hermitage, of whom Colonel Oswald Tilghman is the distinguished head; Goldsboroughs of Myrtle Grove, of Hon. Robert Goldsborough descent, and others too numerous to mention. It would seem unmindful indeed to pass through the habitat of Colonel Tench Tilghman without halting long enough to recall that gallant aide-de-camp to General Washington who rode in hot haste from Yorktown to Philadelphia to carry the triumphant news of Cornwallis' surrender.

In strong contrast to the warriors, the councilors and statesmen in Talbot, is the memory of the Tred Haven meetings in this home of the Quakers, as well as of the cock-fighting and fox-hunting squires. Here the great William Penn himself attended a yearly meeting in 1681, accompanied by the Lord and Lady Baltimore and their retinue. This was the Lady Jane Baltimore, whose brother, Colonel Vincent Lowe, was high sheriff of Talbot County and possessor of about 15,000 acres in Talbot and Queen Anne's Counties. Hence we may readily believe that the beautiful Lady Baltimore combined social as well as religious pleasures in her visit to Tred Haven.

The records here, even after long acquaintance, under recently improved conditions, were so interesting that an extra day was cheerfully given to them, when loath enough we turned our backs upon this "Land of Legendary Lore" and faced toward the county which in the year 1666 was erected and named by Lord Baltimore in honor of "our deare sister, the Lady Mary Somerset."

Cosmopolitan in its early days, with its population composed of stanch Presbyterians from Scotland and Ireland; Quakers and Church of England people from Virginia, French Huguenots and many English gentlemen, Somerset was full of variety and interest always.

Almost without exception her settlers belonged to the gentry, and not a few to titled families. One man of high degree devises in his will, among other property, his house "over against the palace of the Archbishop of Canterbury in the city of Canterbury, England."

In Somerset as in all the other counties visited, an observation of more than passing interest, is the fact that the names which appear first on the records nearly three centuries ago are still making their impress in the counties today. Hence it was no matter of surprise to hear the names of two Jackson brothers spoken of for high office in the land where the Jackson name is among the first on the Colonial records, nor that a Miles is still to the front where the Miles name has never been behind.

In the county offices it was the same experience of history repeating itself. For as we find the Lord Baltimore commissioning "Edmond Beauchampe Clark and Keeper of the Records 1666" in this year of Our Lord, 1904, his descendant, O. T. Beachchampe, is filling the same office. The names of other old families are perpetuated in the deputies Mr. Hall and Mr. Stewart, while the register of wills, Mr. Thomas Dixon, and Mr. Sidney Waller, his deputy, are following in the steps of a long line of ancestors in being prominently identified with county history.

This association of old county names with the public offices is not peculiar to Somerset, however, for up the shore we had found Mr. F. G. Wrightson, clerk of the Talbot court, a representative of a distinguished Colonial name, while in his deputy, Colonel Henry C. Hollyday, of St. Aubins, was the worthy descendant of the Hollydays of Readburne, and in the register's office Mr. Morgan, the deputy, also a descendant of the old Eastern Shore gentry. In Queen Anne's and Kent old family names were still in office—Mr. Robert W. Thomas, register of wills, in Queen Anne's, and Mr. William Roberts, his deputy. In Kent the good old Dixon family is represented by Mr. James Dixon, clerk of the court.

And Mr. James E. Norris, register of wills, and his deputy, Mr. Ford, round out the list of old county names in office. But this excursus has taken us away from the delightful old country town of Princess Anne, which has been such a modest miss that her praises have never been sufficiently sung. No spot more typical of the early aristocracy can be found in Maryland.

Princess Anne Street, with its stately oaks and extensive lawns surrounding the exclusive-looking old mansions certainly has no rival in the State, while Prince George's Street is only a degree less attractive.

The old-fashioned garden adjoining the Gale mansion, while perhaps not more than of a century's growth, is, with its low box-bordered flower beds, tall crepe myrtles and lilies, its vine-clad arbors, giving charming perspective glimpses of brilliant flower beds, suggestive of the days of Madam Elizabeth Gale, a Colonial lady who, like Madam Henrietta Maria Lloyd, was a notable personage of her time.

Spreading its hospitable wings across the entire width of Prince George's Street, stands the Teackle mansion, whose high English walls and gatekeeper's lodge are still remembered by the present generation. As the scene of "The Entailed Hat" it is interesting, but even more so for the true history of the family whose mansion it once was.

The whole atmosphere of old Somerset is pulsating with historic associations, and while having to leave this charming old country, whose patroness was in the beginning the Lady Mary Somerset, there is a feeling of keen satisfaction that the old families are still to the front, with William H. Jackson in Congress, with ex-Senator E. Stanley Toadvin, land commissioner, with Judge Charles F. Holland and Henry Page on the bench—all the scions of Somerset's best blood—contemporary in the early days with the Revells and Coulbournes, the Riders and Stevenses, Walkers and Covingtons, Horseys and Henrys, Kings and Waterses, Dashiells, Woolfords and Winders, Somers and Wilsons.

CHAPTER LIX

GIVING NAMES TO LANDS

One of the most distinctively English customs instituted by the Lord Baltimore in his Palatinate of Maryland was the granting and patenting of land under definite names. These names were then entered upon the Rent Rolls and the owner was always easily identified by his possessions, and nothing is more interesting than to follow the family history through the descent of their estates, which invariably had names as hereditarily their own as those borne by the heirs to estates in old England.

It was but natural, therefore, that the feudal custom should be instituted in the new province by the young Proprietary, Cæcilius Calvert, who was lord of the soil and drew from all of his subjects the quit-rent or knight's fee as did the kings of England. It is evident that the patentee was allowed to choose the name under which his lands were enrolled, as not a few were made to perpetuate the family estates in Great Britain, either maternal or paternal. This was particularly the case in the naming of manors, as Bromley, one of Dr. Thomas Gerrard's estates; Sotterly, the home of the Platers; Chilham Castle, of the Diggs; Wollaston Manor, of the Neales, and others. Robert Brooke perpetuated the maternal home, Battle, in England, in his possessions along the Patuxent, where we find Battle Town and Battle Creek, adjacent to De La Brooke Manor. Many others gave their own names to their estates, as did Robert Brooke. We find this in the case of the Carrolls, of Carrollsborough, Carrollton, etc., the Tyldens, of Great Tylden's Manor; the Prestons, of Preston, etc.

Many of the names chosen give evidence of marked lack of sentiment for the homes left behind them, and equally little originality in the selection of interesting names for their own newly acquired lands. An occasional evidence of Irish wit is recognized in the patent of a tract, while characteristics of the land-hungry Englishmen were loudly proclaimed in naming a tract of land "Would Have Had More." One less grasping evinced his contentment with "Beyond Far Enough."

A well known young colonist, who must have had difficulties over his land rights in England, named his new possessions in Maryland "Ye End of Controversie."

We find the Welsh settlers giving to the names of their estates those of the mountains and rivers of their native lands—Plimhimmon, Wye, and others. The banished Scotch lessened their grief for their "ain countrie" by establishing themselves in the heart of another Dundee, Dumblane, Edinborough, Fifeshire and Ringan. One lordly Englishman was content with no less an estate than Windsor Castle itself, while a more modest and less ambitious settler eased his land hunger with "Luke's Plaster." The "Land of Valleys" suggests the poetic appreciation of the owner of this estate, situated among the Linganore hills. Indeed, the old rent rolls are full of both interesting and absurd names.

Of course not all of these comprised dwelling plantations, and hence the owner was not designated as of such, except in the official records. For the home some more hospitable title would be chosen, for instance, than "Gates Close" or "Knave Keep Out."

There is a charm and dignity about the names of many of these old estates, which are peculiarly attractive and which fix the identity of the families in which they have descended.

CHAPTER LX

PROPRIETARIES AND THEIR REPRESENTATIVES

In giving the following list of the governors, deputy governors and parliamentary commissioners in Colonial Maryland, the author has given the year in any portion of which any of the men named were in power, simply to fix approximately the date of service without giving exact term of office, or date of commissions, 1634–1776.

Proprietaries of Maryland

Cæcilius Calvert, 1632; Charles Calvert, 1675; Benedict Leonard Calvert, 1715; Charles Calvert, 1715; Frederick Calvert, 1751; Henry Harford, 1771–1776.

Governors Commissioned by Proprietary or King

Leonard Calvert, 1634–1647; William Stone, 1648–52–54; Josias Fendall, 1656–57–58–60.

Charles Calvert, 1661–1675; Cæcilius Calvert, (Infant) 1676; Thomas Notley, 1676; Benedict Leonard Calvert, 1684–1688; William Joseph, 1688–1689; John Coode, 1689.

Royal Governors

Sir Lionel Copley, 1691–1693; Sir Edmund Andros, 1692–99; Sir Francis Nicholson, 1692–1694; Nathaniel Blakiston, 1698–9; John Seymour, 1704–1709; Captain John Hart, 1714–1715.

Governors

Captain Charles Calvert, 1720; Benedict Leonard Calvert, 1727; Samuel Ogle, 1731; Charles Calvert, 1732; Samuel Ogle, 1733; Thomas Bladen, 1742; Samuel Ogle, 1746–7; Benjamin Tasker, 1752; Horatio Sharpe, 1753; Captain Robert Eden, 1769–1776.

Deputy Governors

John Lewger, 1638; Captain Thomas Cornwalleys, 1638–41; Captain Giles Brent, 1643–44; William Brainthwayt, 1644; Captain Edward Hill, 1646; Thomas Green, 1647–49; Thomas Hatton, 1650; Luke Barber, 1657–58; Philip Calvert, 1669–1676; William Calvert, 1669–1676; Jerome White, 1669–1676; Baker Brooke, 1669–1676; Jesse Wharton, 1676; Thomas Notley, 1676–79; Vincent Lowe, Henry Darnell, William Digges, William Burgess, Nicholas Sewell, Edward Pye, Clement Hill, Henry Coursey, Henry Lowe, 1684–88, commissioned as a Council by Charles 3d Lord Baltimore to govern for his infant son, Benedict Leonard Calvert; Sir Thomas Lawrence, 1693; Colonel Nicholas Greenberry, 1693–94; Thomas Tench, 1702; Edward Lloyd, 1709; Richard Lee, 1774, and June and July, 1776.

"July 24, 1660. Commissioned by Cæcilius Calvert, to be Deputy Governors in the event of the death of Governor Philip Calvert, who was commissioned Governor on the same date, James Neale, Robert Clarke, Baker Brooke, Edward Lloyd, Henry Coursey, Captain William Evans."

(Since the above commission as deputy governor has not been included in the distinctions of the above named six gentlemen in the Society of Colonial Wars, or of the Colonial Dames of America, the author now publishes them for the first time, from an original manuscript—No. 205, Calvert papers, Vault of the Maryland Historical Society, of Baltimore.)

Parliamentary Commissioners to Govern Maryland under Oliver Cromwell, Lord High Protector of England, etc., July, 1654–March, 1657.

Richard Bennett, Edmund Curtis, William Claiborne, William Stone, Captain William Fuller, Richard Preston, William Durand, Edward Lloyd, John Smith, Leonard Strong, John Lawson, John Hatch, Richard Wells, Richard Ewen, Sampson Waring, William Parker, William Parrott, Captain Robert Sly, Thomas Meeres, Thomas Marsh, Woodman Stockley, Michael Brooke, Robert Pott, John Potts, Philip Morgan, William Ewens, Thomas Thomas, Philip Thomas, Samuel Withers, Richard Woolman.

Richard Ingle.

Nehemiah Blakistone—appointed by John Coode.

CHAPTER LXI

LORDS OF THE MANOR IN COLONIAL MARYLAND, WITH THEIR ORIGINAL LAND SURVEYS TAKEN FROM LORD BALTIMORE'S RENT ROLLS

Leonard Calvert—First governor of Maryland, Lord of St. Michael's Manor, 1500 acres, in St. Mary's County, surveyed August 13, 1641. Also Lord of Trinity Manor, in St. Mary's County, surveyed August 13, 1641.

Abell Snow—Lord of Snow Hill Manor, 6000 acres, in St. Mary's County, surveyed February 23, 1639.

Captain William Hawley—Lord of St. Jerome's Manor, 2100 acres, in St. Mary's County, surveyed January 15, 1648.

Cuthbert Fenwick—Lord of St. Inigoe's Manor, 2100 acres, in St. Mary's County, surveyed July 28, 1641. Also Fenwick Manor, 2000 acres, in St. Mary's County, surveyed April 24, 1651.

Thomas Weston—Lord of Westbury Manor, 1200 acres, in St. Mary's County, surveyed January 10, 1642.

Philip Calvert, Esq.—Lord of Wolselly Manor, 1900 acres, in St. Mary's County, surveyed August 18, 1664.

Thomas Gerrard—Lord of St. Clements Manor, 11,400 acres, in St. Mary's County, surveyed 1639, and resurveyed in 1678 for Justinian Gerrard.

Thomas Gerrard was also Lord of Basford Manor, 1500 acres, in St. Mary's County, surveyed March 27, 1651.

Richard Gardiner—Lord of St. Richard's Manor, 1000 acres, in St. Mary's County, surveyed December 6, 1640.

Nicholas Harvey—Lord of St. Joseph's Manor, 1000 acres, in St. Mary's County, surveyed December, 1642.

Robert Brooke—Lord of De La Brooke Manor, 4000 acres, in St. Mary's County, surveyed July 28, 1650.

Thomas Cornwallis—Lord of Cornwallis Cross Manor, 2000 acres, in St. Mary's County, surveyed 1639. Also Lord of St. Elizabeth's Manor, 2000 acres, in St. Mary's County, surveyed 1639. Also Lord of Resurrection Manor, 4000 acres, in St. Mary's County, surveyed March 24, 1650.

Giles Brent—Lord of Kent Fort Manor, on Kent Island, surveyed September 10, 1640.

Richard Thompson—Lord of Thompson's Manor, 1430 acres, on Kent Island, surveyed November 6, 1640.

Thomas Fisher—Lord of Godhead Manor, 2000 acres, in Queen Anne's County, surveyed September 19, 1685.

Nicholas Sewall—Lord of Sewall's Manor, 4000 acres, in Queen Anne's County, surveyed April 29, 1684.

Thomas Adams—Lord of Prior's Manor, 1000 acres, on Kent Island, surveyed March 5, 1640.

George Evelyn—Lord of Evelynton Manor, in St. Mary's County, surveyed and granted 1638.

Thomas Godlington—Lord of Godlington Manor, 1000 acres, in Kent County, surveyed September 15, 1659.

Samuel Penfax—Lord of Stephen Heath Manor, 1000 acres, in Kent County, surveyed September 16, 1659.

Major Peter Sayer—Lord of Warfell Manor, 1000 acres, in Cecil County, surveyed October 10, 1683.

John Pate—Lord of St. John's Manor, 3000 acres, in Cecil County, surveyed October 10, 1683.

Samuel Chew—Lord of Chew's Resolution Manor, 1073 acres, in Baltimore County.

SIDE-LIGHTS ON MARYLAND HISTORY

Charles Carroll—Lord of Doughoregan Manor, 10,000 acres, in Baltimore County, surveyed May 2, 1707.

Lord Baltimore—Lord of His Lordship's Manor, 12,634 acres, in Anne Arundell County.

Augustine Herman—Lord of Bohemia Manor, 16,439 acres, in Cecil County, composed of several surveys and grants as follows:

	Acres
June 3, 1660	4,000
November 14, 1678	1,339
October 8, 1681	6,000
October 28, 1681	1,000
September 27, 1683	4,000
Total	16,439

Thomas Matthews—Lord of St. Thomas Manor, 4080 acres, in Charles County, surveyed October 25, 1649.

Captain James Neale—Lord of Wollaston Manor, 2000 acres, in Charles County, surveyed October 29, 1642.

Nicholas Causeen—Lord of Eltonhead Manor, 5000 acres, in Calvert County, surveyed May 24, 1662.

John Abbington—Lord of Abbington Manor, 1000 acres, in Calvert County, surveyed September 7, 1653.

Thomas Allanson—Lord of Christian Temple Manor, 1000 acres, in Calvert County, surveyed April 13, 1659.

Josias Fendall—Lord of Cool Spring Manor, 1050 acres, in Prince George's County, surveyed May 27, 1657; also Great Oak Manor, 2000 acres, in Kent County, surveyed August 5, 1659.

Thomas Reynolds—Lord of Parrott's Manor, 1097 acres, in Prince George's County, surveyed June 18, 1703.

Edward Carter—Lord of Worton Manor, 2300 acres, in Kent County, patented 1658.

Jerome White—Lord of Portland Manor, 2722 acres, in Anne Arundell County, surveyed December 6, 1667.

Richard Tilghman—Lord of Canterbury Manor, 1000 acres, in Talbot County, surveyed August 25, 1659.

Captain Robert Morris—Lord of Ratcliffe Manor, 800 acres, in Talbot County, surveyed August 25, 1659.

John Harris—Lord of Grafton Manor, 1000 acres, in Talbot County, surveyed August 20, 1659.

Richard Chandler—Lord of Stratford Manor, Kent County, surveyed September 15, 1659.

Richard Keene—Lord of St. Richard's Manor, 1000 acres, Calvert County, 1641.

Governor Thomas Greene—Lord of Bobing Manor (Poplar Island).

William Digges—Lord of Warburton Manor, Prince George's County.

Thomas Sprigg—Lord of Northampton Manor, Prince George's County.

John Douglass—Lord of Blithwood Manor, Charles County.

Henry Darnall—Lord of Portland Manor, Anne Arundell County.

Richards Snowden—Lord of Snowden's Manor, Prince George's County.

William Nicholson—Lord of Nicholson's Manor, Baltimore County.

Thomas Clagett—Lord of Godlington Manor, Kent County.

George Talbot—Lord of Susquehanna Manor, Cecil Connty.

Luke Barbier—Lord of Barberton Manor, Charles County.

(The above list does not include all who were Lord Manors in Colonial Maryland, as the author is making frequent finds through original investigations.)

CHAPTER LXII

MARYLAND COLONIAL MILITIA

MARYLAND Company in the Expedition against Canada, 1746.

Original muster roll found by the author, in the Public Record office, London, who secured this certified copy, which is now published for the first time.

"Mustered then one of the Companys of Foot Raised in the Province of Maryland for an expedition against Canada commanded by His Excellency the Honourable George Clinton, Captain General and Commander-in-Chieff of the Province of New York, &c, &c, &c. One Captain, One Lieutenant, One Ensign, Four Sergeants, Four Corporals, Two Drum's and Ninety Four Private men (His muster being from the time Officers enter'd into his Majesty's Service and the several days of the men's Enlistments as above specified and Ending the Twenty Fourth day of June (Inclusive) One Thousand Seven Hundred and Forty Six.

DUD. CROFTS,
CORNELIUS BROOKSBY,
JOHN FRAZIER.

This is to Certify that One Captain, One Lieutenant, One Ensign, Four Sergeants, Four Corporals, Two Drum's and Ninety Four Private Men (The Officers from the time they entered into His Majesty's Service and the Several days of the men's Enlistments) were Effective in my

Company to the twenty-fourth day of June (Inclusive) One Thousand Seven Hundred and Forty Six.

DUD. CROFTS.

"The Situation of the Forces on the Present Expedition being such at the time this Muster ought to have been Taken has Render'd it impossible to follow the usual forms Directed by Act of Parliament and Articles of Warr, and the Roll (Pursuant to an Order from his Excellency the Honourable George Clinton, Captain and General Commander-in-Chieff of the Province of New York) being Prepared and Returned to me as on the other side, I have (in order not to obstruct the good of his Majesty's service) Signed the same, leaving the said Roll to be rectifyed in the Office according to the Returns Sent home from time to time of the effectives by the Commander-in-Chieff.

CADR. COLDEN, Junr. Com."

When entered the service 1746	Officers
June 1st	Dudley Crofts (Esqr.), Captain.
June 1st	Corns. Brooksby, Lieut.
June 1st	Jno. Frazier, Ensign
	Sergeants
June 6th	Sam'l Wood
June 7th	Israel Henly
June 9th	Elijah Stansbury
June 10th	Henry Holliday

	Corporals	
June 7th	Law. Atkinson	
June 7th	Jno. Cornish	
June 10th	Wm. Barefoot	
June 12th	Wm. Dodd	
	Drums	
June 9th	Mich'l Green	
June 6th	Thos. Bridgen	
	Men	No. of men
June 13th	Peter Albert	
June 13th	James Adams	
June 9th	Thos. Archer	
June 9th	Edm'd Barnaby	
June 12th	Thos. Barker	
June 13th	Edw'd Bushnell	
June 13th	Matt'w Beck	
June 14th	Samuel Burnham	
June 16th	David Barry	
June 18th	James Bell	
June 9th	Thos. Clickett	10
June 12th	Thos. Cook	
June 13th	Jo. Creak	
June 19th	James Cooper	
June 6th	Alex. Drummond	
June 7th	Jno. Eisley	
June 13th	James English	
June 7th	Richard Fairweather	
June 10th	Anto. Fenance	
June 13th	James Frazier	

June 14th	Matt Franks	20
June 18th	Jno. Fossett	
June 19th	Joshua Farguson	
June 6th	Jno. Green	
June 10th	David Gibson	
June 12th	Jno. Gassutt	
June 14th	Jno. Greenland	
June 19th	Wm. Glover	
June 6th	Law Heyburn	
June 6th	Thos. Hill	
June 10th	James Hailes	30
June 13th	Thos. Harlow	
June 18th	Thos. Hamerton	
June 19th	Wm. Hopkins	
June 7th	Thos. Insull	
June 10th	Rob. Jones	
June 14th	And'w Jumphry	
June 16th	Thos. Kelly	
June 10th	Rob't Lane	
June 12th	Jno. Lackey	
June 14th	David Lawson	40
June 14th	Jo. Lancaster	
June 16th	Rob't Leake	
June 6th	Chris. Mew	
June 7th	Jno. McCarty	
June 7th	Chris. Major	
June 9th	Alex. McCarty	
June 9th	Dan'l McKinly	
June 10th	Edw'd McCormack	
June 10th	Wm. Manion	
June 10th	Phitt. McQueen	50
June 13th	Jno. Maplis	

June 14th	Alex. McLoad	
June 14th	Roger McElloud	
June 6th	Rob. Norton	
June 12th	Joshua Nicholson	
June 14th	Jno. Newman	
June 16th	William Norris	
June 7th	Wm. Penymore	
June 12th	James Peck	
June 16th	Jacob Pindall	60
June 16th	Thomas Pindall	
June 6th	Wm. Rose	
June 10th	And'w Robinson	
June 12th	Robt. Rogers	
June 16th	Jno. Rogers	
June 6th	Nich's Sherlock	
June 7th	Edw'd Simmonds	
June 9th	James Shore	
June 9th	Ashby Sutton	
June 10th	James Stedman	70
June 12th	Rob't Sherrin	
June 12th	Peter Lee	
June 13th	Eman'l Smith	
June 14th	Wm. Stinson	
June 14th	Thos. Stevens	
June 21st	Henry Smith	
June 7th	Edm'd Thos. Tucker	
June 19th	Fran's True	
June 18th	Jno. Tapper	80
June 18th	Thos. Tool	
June 16th	James Trent	
June 18th	Jo. Thompson	
June 16th	Jno. Terrill	

June 6th	James Willis	
June 9th	Thos. Weasey	
June 19th	Geo. Williams	
June 21st	Jo. Woodland	
June 19th	Edm'd Wicks	
June 6th	Rob. Young	90
June 24th	Jno. Yeoman	
June 24th	James Yeates	
June 24th	Thos. Youngblood	
June 24th	Geo. Zealand	

I certify that the foregoing is a true and authentic copy.
J. F. HANDCOCK,
Assist. Keeper of the Public Records.
15th. August, 1908.

OFFICERS OF THE COLONIAL MILITIA IN MARYLAND

Taken from the original muster rolls preserved among the Manuscript Records of Maryland, from 1732 to 1748-9 (State Papers deposited at Md. Hist. Soc.).

The rolls are evidently not complete, as several counties are not represented at all, and others have only brief lists of names—but all the officers that were preserved are here published.

NOTE.—Where the asterisk is used the name of the county was missing from the original muster roll, and is supplied by the author from her knowledge of the men mentioned, and the counties in which they were located.

St. Mary's County

"An account of the number of Militia in St. Mary's County in Pursuance of an Instruction from the Board of

Trade to his Excellency the Governor of the Province under the command of Coll. George Plater.

The following are the officers of Troops of Horse:

1st Troope—Justinian Jordan (Dead) Lieut. Coll.
Thomas Aisquith, Major.
George Aisquith, Captain.
Joseph Hopewell, Lieutenant.
John Morris, Cornet.
Charles King, Quartermaster.
Hugh Hopewell, Clk.

2nd Troope—Justinian Jordan, Captain.
Thomas Shanks, Lieutenant.
James Miller, Cornet.
Samuel Briscoe, Quartermaster.
Jeremiah Jordan, Clk.

3rd Troope—Stephen Chilton, Captain.
Robert Hemmet, Lieutenant.
John Stanfield, Cornet.
McKelvie Hemmet, Clk.

4th Troope—Thomas Greenfield, Captain.
Mevell Lock, Lieutenant.
John Burrows, Cornet.
John Cartwright, Clk.

Following are the officers of the Foot soldiers (St. Mary's).
George Clark, Lieut. Coll.
Abraham Barnes, Major.

1st Company—John Bond, Captain.
Theodorus Jordon, Lieutenant.

Peregrine Bond, Clk.
Ensign, ————.

2nd Company—Kenelyn Truman Greenfield, Captain.
Lieutenant, ————.
William Harrison, Ensign.
Samuel Southern, Clk.
Sergeant & Corporal, ————.

3rd Company—James Briscoe, Captain.
Edward Able, Ensign.
James Thomas, Clk.

4th Company—Richard Ward Key, Captain.
James Wilson, Lieutenant.
John Taney, Ensign.
John Booker, Clk.

5th Company—Robert Chelsey, Captain.
Isaac Doyn, Lieutenant.
John Dossey, Ensign.
John Newton, Clk.

Charles County

A list of the Militia in Charles County, in the Province of Maryland, Anno 1748, (viz):

Under Command of:
    Captain Arthur Lee, 73 horse.
    Captain Allen Davis, 73 horse.
    Captain William Hanson, 78 horse.
    Captain William Theobold, 108 foot.
    Captain Richard Harrison, 182 foot.
    Captain John Thomas, 82 foot.

Captain Barton Warren, 102 foot.
Captain Samuel Cheever, 90 foot.
Captain Francis Ward, 136 foot.
Captain Jn. Stodert in Pr. George County, but now assessed to Charles County by a late Act of Assembly, 61 foot.
985 men in all.

In obedience to an order from the Governor and Council of the Province bearing date of the 21 December 1748, requiring an aud. from the several colonels of the number of men enlisted in the Militia of their respective counties, I humbly certify that the above is a Just acco. of the number of men enlisted in the Militia of Charles County according to the lists given to me by the Respective Captains above mentioned. Given under my hand this 18th day of February 1748.

GEORGE DENT.

Calvert County

Upper Hundred of the Clifts.

A lyst of the Militia under the command of Captain Sutton Isaacks—Mr. Joe Wilson, Lieutenant; Mr. William Allnutt, Ensign. Sergeants—William Lyle, Hillery Wilson, Sabret Lyle.

A list of the officers in the Company of Foot Commanded by Captain Edward Gant in Calvert County:

Edward Griffis and Absalom Stallings, Sergeants.
John Norfolke, Henry Harrison, John Stone, and Newman Harvey, Corporals.
George Wyley, Clerk.

A list of Officers in the Militia Company of foot in Calvert County, under the command of Captain Robert Sollers, October 15th, 1748 at St. Leonards Town:

>Cleaverly Dare, Lieutenant.
>Benjamin Ellt, Ensign.
>Gideon Turner, Sergeant of St. Leonards Creek Hundred; James Kirshaw and Samuel Dare, Sergeants, of Lower Hundred of the Clifts.
>Richard Day, Sergeant of Eltonhead Hundred.

Prince George's County

A list of Captain Thomas Sappington's Company furnished by himself in Prince George's County, November 15th, 1749:

>James Crow, Lieutenant.
>Benjamin West, Ensign.
>Sergeants were as follows: Benoi Fowler, John Davis, Jeremiah Fowler, Wever Barns.
>Corporals, James Odell, Basil Williams, William Ijams, Richard Lansdle.

A list of officers of Captain Tobias Belt's Company in Prince George's County in 1748:

>Richard Harwood, Lieutenant.
>Nehemiah Belt, Jr., Ensign.
>Basil Waring and Samuel Richards, Sergeants.
>Corporals, Isaac Lansdale, John Perry, Samuel Clark, Nathan Wells.
>Boruch Williams, Clk.

A list of officers of Captain George Beall's troop of Horse in *(Prince George's County) in the year 1748:

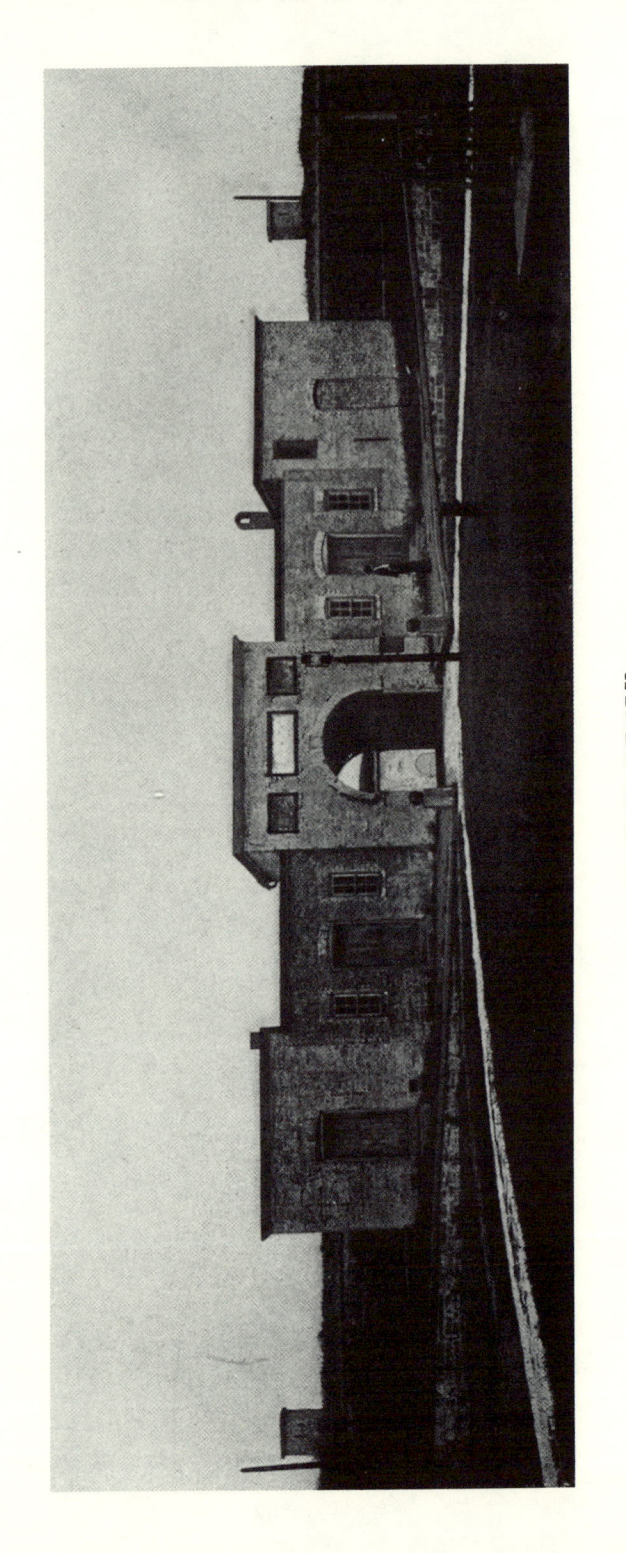

FORT McHENRY

The defense of which inspired Key to write "The Star Spangled Banner"

William Beall, Lieutenant.
William Davis, Cornet.
Groves Tomlinson, Quartermaster.
Corporals, Alexander Beall, Josiah Bedel, Charles Harding, Walter Evans.
Samuel Beall, Clerk.

Captain James Wilson Commanded a Company of Militia in Prince George's County in 1748-9 numbering 69 men and officers. Following were the officers:

John Lawson, Lieutenant. (Said there was no Ensign.)
Sergeants were: Hezekiah Magruder, William Read, Mackall Skinner.
The Corporals: Levin Wales, Thomas Baden.
Alexander Magruder, Clk.

Captain Wilson made out the report in his own hand, February 20, 1748-9 and signed

J. WILSON.

Roll of Foot Militia in the County aforesaid, under the Command of Captain Samuel Magruder in 1749:

James Magruder, Lieut.
Marine Duvall, Ensign.
Mark Webb, John Goodman, Benjamin Brookes and James Gibson, Sergeants.
Thomas Finch, James Magruder (Son of Ninian), Henry Brookes and Jeremiah Magruder, Corporals.
Lingan Wilson, Clk.

*(*Somerset County*)

A list of officers in the Company of Militia Commanded by Captain Nathaniel Waller, who furnished the list

March 15, 1748-9. The list was furnished to the Honorable Colonel Robert King, of Somerset County. Following are the names of the officers:

John Polk, Lieutenant.
David Hall, Ensign.
Nathaniel Waller, Allen Gray and Matthew Oliphant.
Christopher Piper, Clk.

*A list of Officers in the Militia Company in Somerset County commanded by Captain Day Scott in 1748:

Samuel McCloster, Ensign.
Daniel Walter, Sergeant.
Arthur Hickman, Sergeant.
Sidney Brown, Corporal.
Obediah Reed, Corporal.
William Dashiell, Clk.

*A list of Officers in the Militia Company in Somerset County under the command of Captain John Williams:

William Turpin, Lieutenant.
Thomas Dixon, Cornet.
Thomas Beauchamp, Quartermaster.
Kirk Gunby, Whittey Turpin and Marcey Beauchamp, Corporals.
Marcy Fountain, Clearke, signed this Roll March 1st, 1748-9.

*A list of officers and men belonging to the troop under the command of Captain Thomas Gillis:

Thomas Gillis, Captain.
Charles Ballard, Lieutenant.
David Polk, Cornet.
Clement Dashiell, Quartermaster.

William Winder, Corporal.
Francis Allen, Corporal.
Louther Dashiell, Clarke.

*A list of Captain John Handy's Troope.

William Nelson, Lieutenant.
Douty Collier, Cornet.
Robert Collier, Junior Quartermaster.
William Gillis, Junior Corporal.
Joseph Nicholson, Corporal.
James Dashiell, Corporal.
Henry Dashiell, Clarke.
March 20th, 1749.

*A list of Officers of Captain William Jones' Company of Militia in Somerset County:

Panter Laws, Lieutenant.
Daniel Jones, Ensign.
John Addames (Adams) and George Jones, Sergeants.
Thomas Jones, Clerk.
Isaac Noble, Corporal.
Joseph Ellis, Corporal.
William Roberson, Corporal.

*A list of a Troope under the Command of Captain John Waters:

Mr. James Polk, Lieut.
Edward Waters, Quartermaster; Wm. Fleming; Aaron Tilman, Corporals; Whittington King, Clarke.

A list of Captain Wm. McClamy's Company, March 24, 1749:

John Turpin, Lieutenant.
Sollomon Tull, Ensign.
James Furnis, Serjant,
John Maddox, Serjant.
Jacob Aires, Serjant.
Samuel Tull, Corporal.
Isaac Holland, Corporal.
Randall Mitchell, Corporal.
Jesse King, Clk.

*A list of the Troop under the command of Captain Joseph Mitchell:

John Selby, Left Tennant.
Peter Clayvell, Cornet.
William Walton, Quartermaster.
William Brittingham, John Richardson, John Johnson, John Teague, Corporals.
Daniel Selby, Clarke.

Dorchester County

A list of the Severil Troops of Horse and Company of foot belonging to the Militia of Dorchester County.

Captain Francis Haywards' Company, officers and soldiers.

Capt. Thomas Travers,	Ditto &c.
Capt. Henry Ennalls,	" "
Capt. Turner Browne,	" "
Capt. James Woolford,	" "
Capt. Peter Taylor,	" "
Capt. John Hodson's	" "

Capt. Henry Travers' Troop.

Capt. John E. Eccleston's   Troop
Capt. Henry Hooper's   "
Capt. James Insley's   "
Capt. Roger Hooper's   "
Capt. William Grantham's   "
Capt. John Brown's   "
Capt. Levin Hicks'   "
Capt. Thomas McKeele's   "
Capt. Charles Dickinson's   "
Capt. Thomas Wing's   "
Capt. John Robson's Company.

Talbot County

There is a partial Roll of officers and Men in a Militia Company in Talbot County from which the name of the Captain is absent. The officers given follow:

Tristram Thomas, Lieutenant.
Phillimon Hambleton, Cornet.
John Padison, Quartermaster.
William Alexander, Thomas Hay, Robert Spencer, David Robinson, Jacob Lockerman, Samuel Hopkins, Thomas Jenkins, William Harris, and Impy Dawson, Corporals.

A list of officers in the Militia Company in Talbot County under the command of Captain Robert Goldsborough in 1748:

Woolman Gibson, Lieutenant.
Then follow as "Officers" (Rank not stated):
Richard Bruff, Samuel Kinnemont, David Fitspatrick, William Garey, Wm. Brown Vickers, James Virgen, James Stainer, Thomas Mason, Robert Hall, and Ephraim Start.

Then the following:
"A true copy taken off the Muster Roll per me.
WM. THUNDERGEN,

Clarke, January 27th, 1748-9.
"11 officers, 152 soldiers, 163 Totell."

Captain Thomas Porter commanded another Militia Company in Talbot County. No other officers of the Company given.

Captain Haddoway (no given name stated) commanded another company of Militia in Talbot County. No other officers stated.

Cecil County

There is an old list stained by damp and time, worm-eaten and ragged, addressed to his Excellency Samuel Ogle, Governor of Maryland, containing the names of militia officers and men in Cecil County in the year 1740.

Captain John Baldwin's Company officers were:

George Veazey, Lieutenant.
Thomas Davies, Cornette.
John Lusby, Quartermaster.
William Beaston and John Pennington, Corporals.

A foot company commanded by Captain Edward Jackson had the following officers:

Robert Story, Lieutenant.
Henry Jackson, Ensign.
Neall Carmichall and William Ewing, Sergeants; Thomas Miller, John Read, Tobias Lane and Christopher Tuchstone, Corporals.

Officers of the Militia Company in Cecil County Commanded by Captain Thomas Johnson (deceased):

>Nicholas Hyland, Lieutenant.
>James Alexander, Cornet.
>Edward Johnson, Quartermaster.
>John Hemsley, William Barry and Robert Holey, Corporals.

Officers of foot under command of Captain John Veazey in the Cecil County Militia:

>John Pennington, Lieutenant.
>Thomas Ward, Ensign.
>Valentine Silcock, Michael Ruly, and Benjamin Childs, Sergeants; Edward Morgan, John Roberts, Jr., Joshua Meakines, James Prince and William Morgan, Corporals.

Officers of the Company of foot in Cecil County commanded by Captain Zebulon Hollingsworth:

>Edward Barey, Lieutenant; refuses to serve.
>Moses Alexander, Ensign.
>William Currer, George Briestow, and Walter Sharp, Sergeants.
>Jacobus Paulson, Simon Palmson, Jr., John Phillips and James Phillips, Corporals.

Officers in the Company of Militia in Cecil County commanded by Captain William Rumsey:

>William Knight, Lieutenant.
>Benjamin Slyter, Cornett.
>John Holland, Peter Bushnells, Andrew Zelipow, and William Price, Corporals.

Officers in the Company of Militia in Cecil County Commanded by Peter Bayard:

James Bayard, Lieutenant.
Samuel Bayard, Ensign.
Jeremiah Larkins, Thomas Reynolds, Jacob Harper, Robert Patton, Sergeants.
Nicholas Wood, Richard Reynolds, Jacob Hann, John Woods, John Latham, Steven Julian, Samuel McClery, and John Oglesby, Corporals.

The Report was signed, Jno. Ward, in a bold hand.

Queen Anne's County

May it please your Excellency:

In obedience to your Excellency's Commands relating to the Militia of Queen Anne's County I humbly beg to inform you that there are in the said County four Companys of foot soldiers and one troop of Horse.

The Troop commanded by myself, James Earle Junr, Captain; Lieutenant Solomon Clayton; Cornet ———. The first Company of foot commanded by Lieutenant Ernault Hawkins; William Elliott, Lieutenant; James Hutchins, Ensign. The second Company of foot commanded by Major William Turbitt; Lieutenant, vacant; William Meredith declines to serve. The third Company of foot commanded by Captain Edward Wright; Lieutenant, vacant; Ensign, vacant. The fourth Company of foot commanded by Captain Andrew Price; William Jump, Lieutenant; Ensign, vacant.

And upon advising with the field officers I humbly propose William Hemsley to be Lieutenant, and William Coursey Ensign of Major Turbutt's Company, John Collings, Lieutenant; and Nathaniel Cleave, Ensign to Captain Edward Wright's Company, and Thomas Rowe to be Ensign to Captain Andrew Price's Company, etc. June 30th, 1732.

R. TILGHMAN.

I humbly beg leave farther to inform your Excellency that Queen Anne's Co. is capable to raise another Company of Foot soldiers, which would be an ease to the inhabitants upon the upper part of Chester and Choptank, who are now obliged to come a great way to attend Musters, and recommend Augustine Thompson to be Captain. James Goned, Lieutenant; and James Brown Ensign of such Company, all of which is humbly submitted by

R. TILGHMAN.

June 30, 1732.

Worcester County

A list of officers in the Militia Company of Worcester County commanded by Captain Adam Spence:

William Nelson, Lieutenant.
John Scarborough, Clarke.
William Willett, Joseph Bishop, Thomas Willett, Stephen Hall, and Robert Nelson, Sergeants.

*A list of Officers of the Militia Company of Captain John Evans in Worcester County:

Ebenezer Evans, Lieutenant.
Daniel Tingle, Ensign.
William S. Hill, Quartermaster.
Zadock Purnell, Clk.

A list of the officers of the Militia Company in Worcester County commanded by Captain Joseph Miller, March 28th, 1749:

Perry Morgan, Lieutenant.
John Evans, Cornet.
William Howard, Quartermaster.
Hugh Tingle, George Howard, Thomas Colengs and Ambrose White, Corporals.
Matthew Wise, Clk.

*Officers of Captain Joshua Sturgis' Company of Militia in Worcester County. Cornelius Bevans, Left Tenant.

Solomon Townsend, Samuel Taylor and William Taylor, Sergeants.
Elijah Laws, Clerk.

A list of the officers of the Company of Militia in Worcester County, Commanded by Captain William Lane:

Moses Mills, Lieutenant.
Smyth Mills, Ensign.
Robert Stevenson, Serjeant.
John Molton, Serjeant.
Solomon Webb, Serjeant.
Nathaniel Mills, Serjeant.
Elisha Jones, Clk. and Serjeant.

CHAPTER LXIII

NAMES OF ONE THOUSAND EARLY SETTLERS IN MARYLAND WITH THEIR EARLIEST LAND SURVEYS, AS RECORDED IN LORD BALTIMORE'S RENT ROLLS FOR THE VARIOUS COUNTIES

St. Mary's County

"*The Sisters Freehold*"—70½ acres, surveyed October 7, 1639, for Margaret & Mary Brent.

"*The White House*"—63 acres, surveyed October 9, 1639, for Giles Brent.

"*St. Ann's*"—55 acres, surveyed October 15, 1639, for Thomas Green.

"*Lewis Neck*"—30 acres, surveyed December 4, 1640, for William Lewis.

"*Gerrarde Freehold*"—243 acres, surveyed April 21, 1640, for Thomas Gerrard.

"*St. Johns Freehold*"—200 acres, surveyed February 18, 1640, for John Lewger.

"*Pope's Freehold*"—100 acres, surveyed February 26, 1639, for Nathaniel Pope.

"*Snow Hill Mannour*"—6000 acres, surveyed February 23, 1639, for Abell Snow.

"*St. Peter's Key*"—50 acres, surveyed July 15, 1640, for John Harris.

"*Corbet*"—100 acres, surveyed October 22, 1640, for Hutton Corbet.

"*St. Ann's*"—1000 acres, surveyed September 18, 1640, for John Lewger.

400 acres, surveyed July 27, 1641, for Cuthbert Fenwick.

"*Skrettons*"—650 acres, surveyed March 1, 1649, for Barnaby Jackson.

"*Clocker's Marsh*"—100 acres, surveyed April 21, 1651, for Daniel Clocker.

"*Pountney Marsh*"—200 acres, surveyed September 17, 1651, for Henry Pountney.

"*Bolton's Freehold*"—200 acres, surveyed April 5, 1651, for Francis Brookes.

"*Hunting Creek*"—250 acres, surveyed March 15, 1654, for Thomas Hatton.

"*Nuthall*"—200 acres, surveyed July 28, 1654, for Thomas Cornwallis.

"*Innis Choyce*"—100 acres, surveyed October 21, 1659, for Thomas Innis.

"*Hawks Nest*"—350 acres, surveyed August 18, 1661, for Barnaby Jackson.

"*St. Peters*"—150 acres, surveyed October 7, 1664, for Philip Calvert, Esq.

"*Whitewell*"—100 acres, surveyed October 10, 1664, for Philip Calvert, Esq.

"*Come-A-Way*"—100 acres, surveyed May 26, 1664, for Thomas Courtney.

"*Vineyard*"—100 acres, surveyed May 9, 1665, for Jerome White.

"*Brick Hill*"—200 acres, surveyed May 9, 1665, for Jerome White.

"*Cole Harbour*"—150 acres, surveyed September 26, 1664, for Edward Horn.

"*Hunting Quarter*"—150 acres, surveyed March 5, 1664, for William Boarman.

"*Hampstead*"—200 acres, surveyed May 6, 1665, for William Hempstead.

"*Blewston Run*"—150 acres, surveyed October 25, 1665, for Daniel Jenifer.

"*Burwastcott*"—50 acres, surveyed May 5, 1665, for George Day.

"*Stratford*"—100 acres, surveyed May 2, 1666, for Thomas Harpin.

"*Clark's Freehold*"—50 acres, surveyed July 2, 1641, for Robert Clark.

"*Rithing*"—100 acres, surveyed May 2, 1666, for Thomas Wynne.

"*Denby*"—250 acres, surveyed May 2, 1666, for Thomas Wynne.

"*Fosberry Plain*"—430 acres, surveyed August 19, 1664, for John Gittine.

"*Smith's Town House*"—63 acres, surveyed September 25, 1666, for William Smith.

"*Crokenfield*"—100 acres, surveyed June 6, 1667, for William Cate.

"*Edenburgh*"—100 acres, surveyed March 10, 1667, for Peter Key.

"*Vansweringen's Point*"—50 acres, survey, August 18, 1667, for Garrett Vansweringen.

"*Halfhead's Folly*"—200 acres, surveyed July 24, 1664, for John Halfhead.

"*Loughbourough*"—150 acres, surveyed August 1, 1673, for Henry Exon.

"*Miles Meadow*"—150 acres, surveyed March 13, 1664, for Francis Miles.

"*Wills Swamp*"—150 acres, surveyed March 6, 1674, for William Sergison.

"*Galloway*" or "*Betty's Folly*"—50 acres, surveyed May 6, 1675, for Richard Chilman.

"*Oxford*"—209 acres, surveyed May 3, 1675, for Robert Ellys.

"*Halfes*"—400 acres, surveyed April 30, 1675, for Henry Darnall and Thomas Courtney.

"*Paris*"—150 acres, surveyed September 17, 1675, for Charles de la Roch.

"*Kirby's Fortune*"—106 acres (no time given for survey), for William Kirby.

"*Towles Discovery*"—100 acres, surveyed October 26, 1680, for Roger Towle.

"*Wheatley's Chance*"—272 acres, surveyed 1680, for John Wheatley.

"*Netherbury*"—200 acres, surveyed November 27, 1680, for Andrew Abington.

"*Poplar Point*"—100 acres, surveyed November 9, 1680, for Thomas Batson.

"*Dunsmore Meath*"—40 acres, surveyed June 22, 1681, for Abraham Read.

"*Poplar Hill*"—63 acres, surveyed April 8, 1682, for Anthony Evans.

"*Aisquith's Folly*"—100 acres, surveyed January 28, 1681, for William Aisquith.

"*Maiden's Lott*"—100 acres, surveyed April 5, 1682, for Winifride Horn.

"*The Grove*"—50 acres, surveyed 1682, for Thomas Price.

"*Cornwallis Cross*"—2000 acres, surveyed September 19, 1639, for Thomas Cornwallis; he also had "*St. Elizabeth's,*" 2000 acres, surveyed September 9, 1639.

GENERAL JOHN EAGER HOWARD

After Peale Portrait in the Maryland Historical Society. From the Author's Collection

"*Westbury Mannour*"—1200 acres, surveyed January 10, 1642, for Thomas Weston.

"*West St. Mary's Mannour*"—2000 acres, surveyed September 20, 1640, for Thomas Cornwallis.

"*Wolselly Mannour*"—1900 acres, surveyed August 18, 1664, for Philip Calvert, Esq.

"*Dryden*"—334 acres, surveyed May 12, 1676, for Kenelm Cheseldyn.

"*St. Leonard's*"—2400 acres, surveyed April 30, 1675, for his Lordship.

"*Basford Mannor*"—1500 acres, surveyed March 27, 1651, for Thomas Gerrard.

"*St. Clements Mannour*"—11,400 acres, resurveyed June 13, 1678, for Justinian Gerrard. This Mannour was originally granted about 1639 to Dr. Thomas Gerrard.

"*St. Richard's Mannour*"—1000 acres, surveyed December 6, 1640, for Richard Garret.

"*St. Joseph's Mannour*"—1000 acres, surveyed December 2, 1642, for Nicholas Harvey.

"*Rich Neck*"—2000 acres, surveyed March 8, 1648, for William Eltonhead.

"*De La Brooke Mannour*"—2000 acres, surveyed July 28, 1650, for Robert Brooke.

"*Resurrection Mannour*"—4000 acres, surveyed March 24, 1650, for Thomas Cornwallis.

"*Fenwick Mannour*"—2000 acres, surveyed April 24, 1651, for Cuthbert Fenwick.

"*Trent Neck*"—600 acres, surveyed May 25, 1657, for Thomas Truman.

"*The Farm*"—500 acres, surveyed August 28, 1666, for Mary Bateman.

"*Punk Neck*"—100 acres, surveyed September 20, 1666, for Thomas Turner.

"*St. John's*"—1480 acres, surveyed August 28, 1668, for Luke Gardiner.

"*Long Lookt for Come at Last*"—250 acres, surveyed August 1, 1679, for Thomas Truman.

Kent County

"*Wharton Mannour*"—2300 acres, surveyed August 16, 1658, for Henry Muse and patented by Colonel Edward Carter.

"*Packerton of Salters Load*"—Surveyed August 16, 1658, for Edward Packer.

"*Cornwallis' Choice*"—1000 acres, surveyed August 16, 1658, for Captain Thomas Cornwallis.

"*Great Oak Mannour*"—2000 acres, surveyed August 15, 1658, for Josias Fendall.

"*Skidmore*"—550 acres, surveyed August 2, 1659, for Edward Skidmore.

"*Buck Neck*"—550 acres, surveyed August 11, 1666, for Joseph Hopkins.

"*Fair Lee*"—1900 acres, surveyed May 18, 1674, for James Browning.

"*Spring Hill*"—150 acres, surveyed April 13, 1667, for Robert Niefe.

"*Stiles Addition*"—550 acres, surveyed April 15, 1667, for Nathan Stiles.

"*Denbigh*"—700 acres, surveyed April 25, 1671, for Robert Wilson.

"*Howell's Addition*"—300 acres, surveyed April 2, 1669, for Thomas Howell.

"*Falmouth*"—200 acres, surveyed December 26, 1671, for William Salisbury.

"*Pearch Meadow*"—300 acres, surveyed May 17, 1672, for Richard Hill.

"*Eastern Neck*"—200 acres, surveyed October 24, 1692, for Cæsar Prince and John Powell.

"*Martin's Nest*"—80 acres, surveyed June 10, 1674, for Thomas Martin.

"*Coney Warren*"—1000 acres, surveyed September 22, 1674, for Vincent Elliott.

"*Hareford*"—200 acres, surveyed November, 1680, for Richard Hopewell.

"*St. Antonio*"—500 acres, surveyed October 16, 1681, for Ebenezer Blackston.

"*Probus*"—150 acres, surveyed October 19, 1681, for John Wicks.

"*Poplar Farm*"—400 acres, surveyed June 10, 1682, for Elias King.

"*Howard's Gift*"—300 acres, surveyed June 12, 1682, for William Scott.

"*Pope's Forest*"—300 acres, surveyed July 4, 1687, for Mathew Pope.

"*Galloway's Chance*"—200 acres, surveyed April 9, 1684, for William Galloway.

"*Staples Choice*"—200 acres, surveyed August 9, 1684, for Henry Staples.

"*Miller's Satisfaction*"—78 acres, surveyed September 4, 1694, for Michael Miller.

"*Carvill's Prevention*"—26 acres, surveyed July 25, 1694, for John Carvill.

"*Carola*"—150 acres, surveyed October 30, 1694, for Charles James.

"*Crouch's Addition*"—70 acres, surveyed September 28, 1694, for John Crouch.

"*Tolchester*"—520 acres, resurveyed March 12, 1673, for William Tolson.

"*Ashly Green*"—200 acres, surveyed May 20, 1696, for William Elmes.

"*Heath's Longlands*"—150 acres, surveyed July 5, 1700, for James Heath.

"*Redriff*"—100 acres, surveyed August 20, 1700, for John Tweeg.

"*Beckworth*"—100 acres, surveyed October 14, 1680, for Edward Beck.

"*Covent Garden*"—500 acres, surveyed September 25, 1683, for Michael Miller.

"*The Hermitage*"—300 acres, surveyed June 18, 1686, for Matthew Pope and Sutton Queny.

"*Wyhill Down*"—100 acres, surveyed June 4, 1686, for John Willis.

"*Hollman's Town*"—200 acres, surveyed August 3, 1658, for William Hollman.

"*Stone Town*"—500 acres, surveyed August 4, 1658, for Richard Stone.

"*Utisley*"—300 acres, surveyed August 4, 1658, for Nathaniel Utye, Esq.

"*Yapp*"—500 acres, surveyed September 3, 1659, for William Yapp.

"*Verina*"—1000 acres, surveyed August 21, 1658, for Captain Thomas Cornwallis. Possessed by Daniel Pierce, William Freeman, Samuel Bostic, James Wilson, William Smith and John Wilson.

"*Fish Hall*"—225 acres, surveyed May 16, 1664, for William Fisher.

"*The Folly*"—400 acres, surveyed January 23, 1664, for Richard Bennett, Esq.

"*Draycott*"—275 acres, surveyed May 16, 1664, for Henry Jones.

"*Drayton*"—1200 acres, resurveyed June 14, 1677, for Charles James.

"*Morton*"—600 acres, surveyed October 9, 1666, for Richard Leak.

"*Hen's Roost*"—200 acres, surveyed October 9, 1666, for Thomas Prior.

"*Fair Promise*"—600 acres, surveyed May 3, 1667, for Godfrey Bailey.

"*Larkin's Addition*"—800 acres, surveyed March 2, 1668, for John Larkin.

"*Fareall*"—200 acres, surveyed March 3, 1668, for John George.

"*Tiballs*"—550 acres, surveyed June 7, 1668, for Philip Heleger.

"*Indian Range*"—250 acres, surveyed August 7, 1669, for Jarvis Morgan.

"*Stanley's Hope*"—550 acres, surveyed June 5, 1669, for William Stanley.

"*Buckingham*"—1300 acres, surveyed May 17, 1668, for Henrietta Maria and Susanna Maria Bennett.

"*Wright's Rest*"—200 acres, surveyed October 26, 1672, for Thomas Wright.

"*Down Dale*"—150 acres, surveyed May 9, 1694, for Thomas Dale.

"*Godfrey's Point*"—150 acres, surveyed July 30, 1678, for William Pierce.

"*Blay's Addition*"—450 acres, surveyed February 1, 1678, for Edward Blay.

"*Chance*"—250 acres, surveyed December 18, 1678, for Richard Thornton.

"*Duck Pye*"—100 acres, surveyed February 7, 1678, for William Pierce.

"*Suffolk*"—742 acres, surveyed March 3, 1681, for James Stavely.

"*Warner's Adventure*"—200 acres, surveyed May 9, 1682, for George Warner.

"*Hopeful Unity*"—150 acres, surveyed May 12, 1680, for Charles James, James Frisby, John Howell, George Warner, Joseph Hopkins, William Pierce, Richard Pullen, Ebenezer Blackiston, Joseph Grundy, Edward Blay, Robert Sanders and John James.

"*Camells Worthmore*"—1150 acres, surveyed June 17, 1682, for William Marr and Thomas Collins.

"*Adventure*"—510 acres, surveyed June 1, 1683, for Bryan O'Maly.

"*Coffin*"—170 acres, surveyed July 17, 1680, for Edward Jones.

"*Levell Ridge*"—1000 acres, surveyed August 17, 1683, for James Murphy.

"*Winfield*"—500 acres, surveyed September 15, 1683, for Thomas Impey.

"*The Levell*"—500 acres, surveyed September 18, 1683, for Perigrine Brown.

"*Chance*"—50 acres, surveyed June 11, 1686, for James Courcey.

"*Lamb's Meadows*"—215 acres, surveyed November 2, 1694, for Pierce Lamb.

"*First Part Free Gift*"—2000 acres, surveyed September 10, 1694, for Captain Richard Smith.

SIDE-LIGHTS ON MARYLAND HISTORY 297

"*Providence*"—159 acres, surveyed September 26, 1700, for John Briscoe.

"*Boston*"—40 acres, surveyed November 20, 1700, for William Haywood.

"*Lincoln Inn Fields*"—400 acres, surveyed June 11, 1696, for Jonothan Lincoln.

"*Forest Dean*"—600 acres, surveyed February 20, 1704, for William Harris.

"*Heath's Range*"—1350 acres, surveyed August 31, 1704, for James Heath.

"*Godlington Mannour*"—1000 acres, surveyed September 15, 1659, for Thomas Godlington.

"*Walnut Neck*"—100 acres, surveyed August 21, 1665, for Andrew Skinner.

"*The Fork*"—300 acres, surveyed July 8, 1667, for Henry Hawkins.

"*Comegys Choice*"—350 acres, surveyed November 20, 1668, for Cornelius Comegys.

"*Maiden Lott*"—600 acres, surveyed August 20, 1666, for Sarah Conner.

"*Bradfield*"—300 acres, surveyed September 29, 1658, for Thomas Broadnox.

"*Sutton*"—400 acres, surveyed June 8, 1680, for Humphrey Davenport.

"*Ridgley*"—300 acres, surveyed January 24, 1664, for Henry Ridgley.

"*Town Relief*"—800 acres, surveyed June 30, 1680, for William Rawles.

"*Kegerton*"—1000 acres, surveyed September 21, 1659, for Robert Keger.

"*Tulley's Fancy*"—600 acres, surveyed February 26, 1670, for John Tully.

"*Boulston*"—500 acres, surveyed July 6, 1672, for John Bowles.

"*Prickle-Pear*"—200 acres, surveyed August 20, 1675, for Thomas Norris.

"*Batchelor's Hope*"—290 acres, surveyed August 22, 1686, for John Davis.

"*The Chance*"—200 acres, surveyed June 20, 1680, for Nicholas Painter.

"*Reurden*"—300 acres, surveyed September 29, 1658, for Robert Vaughan.

"*Hansford*"—100 acres, surveyed July 6, 1672, for Hans Hanson.

"*Pentridge*"—1000 acres, surveyed June 26, 1670, for William Hemsley.

"*High Park*"—600 acres, surveyed September 28, 1665, for Deliverance Lovely.

"*Stephen Heath Mannour*"—1000 acres, surveyed September 16, 1659, for Samuel Spenser.

"*Whitfield*"—1000 acres, surveyed August 7, 1668, for William Coursey.

"*Hinchingham*"—2200 acres, surveyed July 19, 1659, for Thomas Hynson.

"*Greenbranch*"—200 acres, surveyed January 10, 1670, for John and James Ringgold.

"*Middlespring*—400 acres, surveyed, March 6, 1663, for John and James Ringgold.

"*Stradford Mannour*"—Surveyed September 15, 1659, for Richard Chandler.

"*Langford's Neck*"—1500 acres, surveyed September 20, 1658, for John Langford.

"*Trumpington*"—400 acres, surveyed September 22, 1658, for Thomas South.

"*Church Warden Neck*"—400 acres, surveyed January 24, 1664, for Henry Woolchurch.

"*Woodland Neck*"—400 acres, surveyed July 18, 1667, for Philemon Lloyd.

"*Queen Carlton*"—400 acres, surveyed June 13, 1677, for Samuel Tovey.

"*Boxley*"—300 acres, surveyed April 13, 1667, for John Scott.

"*Webley*"—400 acres, surveyed December 3, 1672, for Edward Webb.

Willmer's Farm"—500 acres, surveyed May 20, 1680, for Simon Wilmer.

"*Tilghman & Foxley Grove*"—1000 acres, surveyed February 15, 1675, for Mary Tilghman.

"*Tilghman's Farm*"—900 acres, surveyed September 24, 1668, for Richard Tilghman.

"*Batchelor's Resolution*"—1000 acres, surveyed January 24, 1664, for Mathew Mason.

"*Plain Dealing*"—250 acres, surveyed October 18, 1683, for John Parsons.

"*Hopewell*"—300 acres, surveyed July 6, 1682, for Richard and Joseph Hopewell.

"*Partnership*"—3000 acres, surveyed August 15, 1684, for John Lewellin.

"*Middlebranch*"—200 acres, surveyed August 2, 1686, for William Dean.

"*Worth's Folly*"—1036 acres, resurveyed August 19, 1687, for John Worth.

"*Chance*"—500 acres, surveyed September 20, 1683, for James Sedgwick.

"*Denton*"—380 acres, surveyed July 3, 1677, for George Holland.

"*Cumberland*"—600 acres, surveyed October 18, 1683, for William Dixon.

"*Well Meaning*"—830 acres, surveyed June 8, 1683, for John Salter and John Parsons.

"*The Remain of My Lord's Gracious Grant*"—5000 acres, surveyed January 11, 1696, for Richard Smith.

"*Partnership*"—970 acres, surveyed March 8, 1704, for Samuel Wallace.

"*Lowe's Bennett*"—1400 acres, surveyed August 10, 1707, for Colonel Henry Lowe.

Calvert County

"*Parker's Clifts*"—600 acres, surveyed October 27, 1651, for William Parker.

"*Device*"—150 acres, surveyed November 23, 1659, for Thomas Davis.

"*Selby's Clifts*"—200 acres, surveyed October 27, 1651, for Edward Selby.

"*Meares*"—400 acres, surveyed October 27, 1651, for Thomas Meares.

"*Angelica*"—600 acres, surveyed October 27, 1651, for Leonard Strong.

"*Jamott*"—300 acres, surveyed October 27, 1651, for William James.

"*Beakle*"—500 acres, surveyed October 5, 1651, for Phill Thomas.

"*Plum Point*"—400 acres, surveyed October 5, 1651, for Edward Castor and Truman Bennett.

"*Upper Bennett*"—1150 acres, surveyed October 25, 1651, for Richard Bennett.

"*Major's Choice*"—500 acres, surveyed June 24, 1664, for Thomas Marsh.

"*Sterling's Nest*"—550 acres, surveyed October 20, 1663, for Thomas Stirling.

"*St. James*"—1138 acres surveyed August 8, 1666, for Arthur Thompson.

"*Swinfens Rest*"—1000 acres, surveyed November 20, 1666, for Francis Swinfens.

"*Alexander's Hope*"—200 acres, surveyed February 2, 1666, for Alexander Magruder.

"*Clare's Hundred*"—100 acres, surveyed July 9, 1663, for Mark Clare.

"*Brooke's Neck*"—150 acres, surveyed August 3, 1666, for Major Thomas Brooke.

"*Troublesome*"—150 acres, surveyed June 24, 1678, for William Kemp.

"*Robinson's Rest*"—1150 acres, surveyed February 2, 1663, for Henry Robinson.

"*Leitchworth's Chance*"—1100 acres, surveyed April 30, 1663, for Thomas Leitchworth.

"*Good Luck*"—300 acres, surveyed August 4, 1679, for John Cobreth.

"*Cornhill*"—350 acres, surveyed May 4, 1663, for Francis Billingsley.

"*Ball's Chance*"—100 acres, surveyed November 2, 1694, for Benjamin Ball.

"*The Neglect*"—125 acres, surveyed February 18, 1678, for Richard Johns.

"*Illingsworth's Fortune*"—365 acres, surveyed July 20, 1666, for William Illingsworth.

"*Lordship's Favour*"—1108 acres, surveyed May, 1663, for Charles Calvert, Esq.

"*Agreement*"—300 acres, surveyed December 1, 1663, for James Shacklady and Richard Hammond.

"*Whittle's Rest*"—250 acres, surveyed May 4, 1663, for George Whittle.

"*Preston's Clifts*" or "*Charles Gift*"—1000 acres, surveyed May 5, 1652, for Richard Preston.

"*Hodgkins Gift*"—200 acres, surveyed May 10, 1652, for John Hodgkins.

"*Hooper's Clifts*"—1000 acres, surveyed May 26, 1652, for Henry Hooper.

"*Miles End*"—400 acres, surveyed May 3, 1663, for Tobias Miles.

"*Mills Runn*"—150 acres, surveyed May 2, 1663, for Nicholas Carr.

"*Middlesex*"—100 acres, surveyed May 21, 1663, for Ambrose Biggs.

"*Rockey Neck*"—100 acres, surveyed January 24, 1667, for John Pardoe.

"*Mount Misery*" or "*Break Neck*"—212 acres, surveyed April 12, 1661, for Richard Gaines.

"*Prevent Danger*"—250 acres, surveyed April 26, 1681, for Francis Mauldin.

"*Morgan's Fresh*"—400 acres, surveyed May 26, 1652, for Phill Morgan.

"*Warbleston*"—300 acres, surveyed February 28, 1659, for Richard Keen.

"*Rocky Point*"—360 acres, surveyed January 25, 1682, for John Edmonson.

"*Gary's Chance*"—600 acres, surveyed February 2, 1664, for John Gary.

"*Norwood*"—200 acres, surveyed October 27, 1651, for John Norwood.

"*The Angle*"—100 acres, surveyed August 10, 1664, for Gabriel Goulden.

"*Sharp's Outlet*"—200 acres, surveyed February 26, 1664, for Peter Sharp.

"*Devill's Wood Yard*"—150 acres, surveyed August 5, 1669, for Ambrose Biggs.

"*Rattlesnake Hill*"—200 acres, surveyed May 8, 1674, for Richard Johns.

"*Gunsby*"—200 acres, surveyed October 2, 1691, for Thomas Todd.

"*Point Patience*"—360 acres, surveyed August 6, 1661, for John Ashcomb.

"*Nutt's Clifts*"—128 acres, surveyed February 17, 1667, for John Nutt.

"*Eltonhead Mannour*"—5000 acres, surveyed May 24, 1662, for Edward Eltonhead.

"*Cleggate's Design*"—376 acres, surveyed November 3, 1682, for Thomas Clegate.

"*Desart*"—1048 acres, surveyed October 25, 1682, for Benjamin Lawrence, Nathaniel and Samuel Ashcomb.

"*Stiles Lott*"—150 acres, surveyed July 28th, 1651, for Nathaniel Stiles.

"*Coal's Clifts*"—200 acres, surveyed October 27, 1651, for Thomas Coal.

"*Dear Bought*"—200 acres, surveyed August 11, 1651, for Thomas Thomas.

"*Red Clift*"—300 acres, surveyed May 26, 1662.

"*Cold Harbour*"—400 acres, surveyed July 15, 1652, for Matthew Stone.

"*Cage*"—250 acres, surveyed July 29, 1652, for William Parrot.

"*Brooke Place*"—2100 acres, surveyed for Robert Brooke, October 13, 1650.

"*Goldson's Inheritance*"—150 acres, surveyed June 27, 1678, for Daniel Goldson.

"*Harwood*"—150 acres, surveyed October 6, 1651, for Phill Harwood.

"*Smith's Purchase*"—408 acres, surveyed June 26, 1696, for Richard Smith.

"*Short Come Off*"—22 acres, surveyed July 25, 1694, for James Duke.

"*Joseph Place*"—200 acres, surveyed November 24, 1682, for Joseph Edlowe.

"*Punch*"—150 acres, surveyed February 3, 1681, for Thomas Cosden.

"*Burk's Chance*"—200 acres, surveyed September 11, 1663, for William Burk.

"*Magruder*"—500 acres, surveyed January 17, 1652, for Richard Harris.

"*Godsgrace*"—200 acres, surveyed April 20, 1663, for John Bagby.

"*Coursey*"—195 acres, surveyed April 21, 1653, for Henry Coursey.

"*Brumal*"—500 acres, surveyed July 22, 1656, for William Brumal.

"*Stoakley*"—700 acres, surveyed August 5, 1659, for Woodman Stoakley.

"*The Orchard*"—750 acres, surveyed May 5, 1663, for Edward Keen.

"*Abbington Mannour*"—1000 acres, surveyed September 17, 1663, for John Abbington.

"*Archer's Hays*"—300 acres, surveyed February 9, 1664, for Peter Archer.

"*Turner's Place*"—300 acres, surveyed August 4, 1664, for Robert Turner.

"*Land's Land*"—238 acres, surveyed before 1670, for John Athee.

"*Hardesty's Choice*"—550 acres, surveyed May 19, 1663, for George Hardesty.

"*Ringan*"—200 acres, surveyed March 19, 1667, for Ninian Beall.

"*Brooke's Partition*"—1000 acres, surveyed before 1674 for Baker Brooke.

"*Lingan's Purchase*"—503 acres, resurveyed June 22, 1697, for George Lingan.

"*Parran's Park*"—300 acres, surveyed March 20, 1706, for Alexander Parran.

Prince George's County

"*Brooke's Court*"—2000 acres, surveyed November 21, 1650, for Robert Brooke, Esq.

"*Taylorton*"—800 acres, surveyed October 19, 1653, for Robert Taylor.

"*Brookbridge*"—1000 acres, surveyed April 16, 1664, for Robert Brooke, Esq.

"*Westphalia*"—500 acres, surveyed February 16, 1670, for Robert Wells.

"*Addition to Keverton Hedge*"—498 acres, surveyed June 19, 1695, for Ninian Beall.

"*Leith*"—500 acres, surveyed February 22, 1681, for James More.

"*Brookes Reserve*"—1100 acres, surveyed June 15, 1680, for Rodger Brooke.

"*The Horse Race*"—300 acres, surveyed, March 6, 1681, for James Moore.

"*The Vale of Benjamin*"—1030 acres, surveyed October 29, 1670, for Benjamin Wells.

"*The Exchange*"—229 acres, surveyed September 14, 1694, for Colonel Darnell.

"*Bowdel's Choice*"—750 acres, surveyed July 2, 1670, for Thomas Bowdel.

"*Cool Spring Mannour*"—1050 acres, surveyed May 27, 1657, for Josias Fendall.

"*Brazenthorpe Hall*"—460 acres, surveyed July 19, 1670, for Edward Isaac.

"*Howerton Range*"—400 acres, surveyed May 17, 1670, for John Howerton.

"*Larkin's Forest*"—400 acres, surveyed July 13, 1694, for Thomas Larkin.

"*Holliday's Choice*"—500 acres, surveyed August 2, 1689, for Thomas Holliday (Hollyday).

"*Ryly's Range*"—800 acres, surveyed February 19, 1694, for Hugh Ryly.

"*Forrest*"—712 acres, surveyed November 12, 1694, for Colonel Henry Darnall.

"*Jericoe*"—700 acres, surveyed July 10, 1696, for Samuel Walters.

"*Essenton*"—1300 acres, surveyed November 25, 1669, for Demetrious Cartwright.

"*Enfield Chance*"—1600 acres, surveyed October 4, 1681, for John Sewell.

"*Cotton*"—500 acres, surveyed October 4, 1681, for Robert Carvill.

"*Dunkel*"—340 acres, surveyed February 23, 1681, for John Scott.

"*Beare Bacon*"—600 acres, surveyed June 24, 1703, for Mark Richardson.

GOVERNOR THOMAS JOHNSON AND FAMILY

By Charles Wilson Peale. Original at the Maryland Historical Society. From the Author's Collection

"*Bear Garden*"—137 acres, surveyed June 17, 1703, for Thomas Sprigg.

"*Parrott's Mannour*"—1097 acres, surveyed June 18, for Gabriel Parrott.

"*Foxe's Denn*"—1000 acres, surveyed October 3, 1702, for Thomas Reynolds.

"*The Three Sisters*"—1050 acres, surveyed January, 1683, for Thomas Hillary.

"*Stinson's Choice*"—618 acres, surveyed February 20, 1684, for John Stinson.

"*Chartsey*"—1000 acres, surveyed August 15, 1671, for Thomas Carleton.

"*Woodcock's Range*"—500 acres, surveyed May 10, 1689, for James Brown.

"*Chew's Meadows*"—100 acres, surveyed February 4, 1695, for Joseph Chew.

"*The Partnership*"—1500 acres, surveyed November 9, 1680, for Major Nicholas Sewall.

"*Carroll's Forrest*"—500 acres, surveyed May 3, 1689, for Charles Carroll. (This was the Emmigrant Carroll.)

"*Dann*"—3697 acres, surveyed September 16, 1694, for Thomas Brooke.

"*Brightwell's Hunting Quarter*"—1086 acres, surveyed August 29, 1695, for Richard Brightwell.

"*Whitehaven*"—759 acres, surveyed April 9, 1689, for William Hutchinson.

"*Friendship*"—1571 acres, surveyed October 16, 1694, for William Dent.

"*Bristoll*"—1670 acres, surveyed August 9, 1675, for John Sanders.

"*New Castle*"—250 acres, surveyed August 9, 1675, for John Lawson.

"*Friendship*"—1400 acres, surveyed June 14, 1675, for Clement Hill and Richard Gardiner.

"*Wheeler's Purchase*"—500 acres, surveyed July 10, 1663, for John Wheeler.

"*Markett Overton*"—1200 acres, surveyed August 8, 1662, for Zachariah Wade.

"*Apple Door*"—607 acres, surveyed March 27, 1688, for Robert Middleton.

Charles County

"*Wooleston Manour*"—2000 acres, surveyed October 29, 1642, for Captain James Neale, Gentleman.

"*Gills Land*"—1220 acres, surveyed October 15, 1646, for Benjamin Gill.

"*Hatch*"—250 acres, surveyed October 2, 1650, for John Hatch.

"*Smootly*"—400 acres, surveyed January 25, 1652, for William Smoot.

"*Marsh*"—200 acres, surveyed May 29, 1658, for John Courts.

"*West Hatton*"—500 acres, surveyed June 22, 1663, for Thomas Hatton.

"*Harrison's Venture*"—50 acres, surveyed April 14, 1671, for Richard Harrison.

"*Mitchell's Platt*"—300 acres, surveyed August 19, 1658, for Thomas Mitchell.

"*Smith*"—100 acres, surveyed October 25, 1649, for Richard Smith.

"*Asher*"—450 acres, surveyed September 25, 1649, for Thomas Petit.

"*Harris*"—300 acres, surveyed May 15, 1651, for Thomas Harris.

"*Stump Dale*"—450 acres, resurveyed May 14, 1651, for Thomas Batchellor.

"*Robbins*"—550 acres, surveyed June 10, 1651, for Robert Robbins.

"*Burford*"—400 acres, surveyed November 30, 1652, for Mathias Bryan.

"*Burough Hall*"—500 acres, surveyed February 4, 1666, for Robert Henly.

"*Blithewoode*"—100 acres, surveyed May 10, 1667, for John Douglass.

"*Promise*"—140 acres, surveyed November 9, 1673, for John Dent.

"*Essex*"—75 acres, surveyed March 7, 1677, for William Lee.

"*Dover*"—300 acres, surveyed February 21, 1670, for Elizabeth Young.

"*Burnhams Beginning*"—85 acres, surveyed for William Burnham, May 23, 1672.

"*Batts Dale*"—80 acres, surveyed for Thomas Warfield, March 15, 1682.

"*Bakers Rest*"—400 acres, surveyed October 1, 1673, for Thomas Baker.

"*Marshall*"—500 acres, surveyed March 21, 1651, for William Marshall.

"*Walker*"—300 acres, surveyed May 21, 1658, for James Walker.

"*Burlaines Hill*"—300 acres, surveyed August 24th, 1654, for Richard True.

"*Huckelberry Swamp*"—300 acres, surveyed October 10, 1664, for John Nevill.

"*Chestnut Point*"—200 acres, surveyed January 14, 1664, for Edward Swan.

"*Lawrence Spring*"—100 acres, surveyed February 23, 1665, for John Clark.

"*Nevitt's Desire*"—200 acres, surveyed for John Nevitt, July 10, 1665.

"*Russell*"—75 acres, surveyed for Christopher Russell, May 15, 1658.

"*Batchellor's Hope*"—492 acres, surveyed October 15, 1649, for Richard Bennett.

"*Warren's Discovery*"—280 acres, surveyed for Humphrey Warren, July 31, 1683.

"*Putney*"—115 acres, surveyed for Randell Brandt, September 12, 1683.

"*Littleworth*"—189 acres, surveyed for William Thompson, March 18, 1683.

"*Williams Folly*"—265 acres, surveyed for John Williams, March 22, 1688.

"*St. Patricks or Spring Plains*"—350 acres, surveyed December 11, 1663, for John Cane.

"*Simpson's Delight*"—300 acres, surveyed October 24, 1663, for Alexander Simpson.

"*St. Thomas' Mannour*"—4080 acres, surveyed October 25, 1649, for Thomas Matthews.

"*Causeens Mannour*"—1000 acres, surveyed October 15, 1649, for Nicholas Causeen.

"*Goose Creek*"—900 acres, resurveyed March 1, 1675, for Richard Chandler.

"*Jarbo*"—200 acres, surveyed April 14, 1653, for John Jarbo.

"*St. Matthews*"—1000 acres, surveyed October 10, 1663, for Thomas Matthews.

"*Greens Inheritance*"—2400 acres, surveyed October 1, 1666, for Leonard, Robert and Francis Green.

"*Bryerwood*"—650 acres, surveyed November 10, 1665, for Gerard Fowke.

"*Wassell*"—200 acres, surveyed May 14, 1670, for John Robinson.

"*St. Edmundsbury*"—100 acres, surveyed February 23, 1617, for Edmund Taylor.

"*Kerrigderry*"—100 acres, surveyed May 7, 1672, for Owen Jones.

"*Durham*"—400 acres, surveyed September 7, 1674, for Eleanore Beane.

"*Love*"—100 acres, resurveyed March 31, 1682, for John Lemare.

"*Mattenlys Hope*"—300 acres, surveyed May 19, 1666, for Thomas Mattenly (now spelled Mattingly).

"*Friendship*"—2000 acres, surveyed June 13, 1672, for Bennett Hoskins.

"*Hull*"—600 acres, surveyed May 18, 1675, for Stephen Cawood.

"*Moore*"—500 acres, surveyed 1662, for Henry Moore.

"*Come by Chance*"—100 acres, surveyed September 20, 1666, for Jacob Peterson.

"*Mobberly*"—90 acres, surveyed January 4, 1675, for Ralph Shaw.

"*Eltham*"—75 acres, surveyed June 10, 1681, for James Smallwood.

"*Haberdoventure*"—150 acres, surveyed March 16, 1682, for Thomas Bearfoot.

"*Partnership*"—700 acres, surveyed May 22, 1660, for Daniel Johnson.

"*Barton's Woodyard*"—100 acres, surveyed June 22, 1663, for William Barton.

"*Barkers Rest*"—150 acres, surveyed May 16, 1666, for John Barker.

"*Harges*"—200 acres, surveyed September 24, 1669, for William and Thomas Hargess.

"*Battens Dale*"—1000 acres, surveyed September 7, 1662, for William Batten.

"*The Birds Nest*"—300 acres, surveyed September 25, 1661, for Thomas Burdit.

"*Verlinda*"—300 acres, surveyed June 17, 1663, for Mrs. Verlinda Stone.

"*Ashbrooks Rest*"—150 acres, surveyed August 19, 1664, for Thomas Ashbrook.

"*Inglethorpe*"—100 acres, surveyed June 15, 1664, for John Ward.

"*Randall's Addition*"—200 acres, surveyed June 12, 1667, for Richard Randall.

"*Maryland Point*"—600 acres, surveyed August 17, 1654, for John Tomkinson.

"*Woodberry Harbour*"—300 acres, surveyed September 27, 1667, for James Lee.

"*Wentworth's Rest*"—100 acres, surveyed June 14, 1669, for Thomas Wentworth.

"*Toner Hill*"—250 acres, surveyed September 29, 1670, for William Marloe.

"*Watson's Purchase*"—300 acres, surveyed May 9, 1659, for Andrew Watson.

"*Cow Spring*"—400 acres, surveyed February 9, 1661, for Daniel Gordon.

"*Christian Temple Mannour*"—1000 acres, surveyed April, 1659, for Thomas Allanson.

"*Mackeys Park*"—200 acres, surveyed August 4, 1668, for James Mackey.

"*Montagues Addition*"—100 acres, surveyed June 11, 1669, for Stephen Montague.

"*Howland*"—334 acres, surveyed December 24, 1700, for Richard and Mary Nelson.

"*Strife*"—235 acres, surveyed January 20, 1699, for Benjamin Hall.

"*Lapworth*"—516 acres, surveyed August 16, 1669, for Thomas Slye.

"*Lambey*"—450 acres, surveyed January 31, 1664, for Thomas Lamax.

"*Brathwood*"—800 acres, surveyed June 12, 1665, for John Compton.

"*Morris*"—700 acres, surveyed May 17, 1665, for Richard Morris.

"*Sarum*"—1000 acres, surveyed November 12, 1680, for Joseph Pile.

"*Barbadois*"—1000 acres, surveyed September 24, 1673, for Elizabeth Wharton.

"*Mudds Rest*"—200 acres, surveyed July 12, 1686, for Thomas Mudd.

Somerset County

"*Coleburn*"—650 acres, surveyed August 18, 1663, for William Coleburn.

"*Dixon's Choice*"—550 acres, surveyed August 19, 1663, for Ambrose Dixon.

"*Williamston*"—300 acres, surveyed September 4, 1663, for Thomas Williams.

"*Waters River*"—1280 acres, surveyed September 5, 1663, for William Waters.

"*Straights*"—600 acres, surveyed September 4, 1663, for George Johnson.

"*Boston Town*"—350 acres, surveyed August 20, 1663, for Henry Boston.

"*Cheap Price*"—500 acres, surveyed September 4, 1663, for Thomas Price.

"*William's Conquest*"—300 acres, surveyed September 4, 1663, for Michael Williams.

"*Yorkshire Island*"—100 acres, surveyed June 2, 1664, for William Wilkinson.

"*Boyce's Branch*"—300 acres, surveyed April 9, 1664, for William Boyce.

"*Hall's Choice*"—300 acres, surveyed June 6, 1665, for Charles Hall.

"*Watkin's Point*"—150 acres, surveyed February 20, 1664, for John Horsey.

"*Emmesox*"—300 acres, surveyed February 10, 1663, for Benjamin Summers.

"*Make Peace*"—150 acres, surveyed February 9, 1663, for John Roach.

"*Johnson's Lott*"—200 acres, surveyed February 12, 1663, for John Johnson.

"*Hartford Broad Oake*"—400 acres, surveyed October 26, 1666, for Robert Cattlin.

"*The Desert*"—400 acres, surveyed March 10, 1665, for Stephen Horsey.

"*Contention*"—300 acres, resurveyed February 1 (no year given, but early), for Edward Dickinson.

"*Maddox Hope*"—100 acres, surveyed January 14, 1666, for Lazarus Maddox.

"*Salisbury*"—200 acres, surveyed April 3, 1667, for John Rhodeson.

"*Armstrong's Purchase*"—200 acres, surveyed April 3, 1667, for Matthew Armstrong.

"*London's Gift*"—50 acres, surveyed January 3, 1667, for William Furnace.

"*Johnson's First Choice*"—Surveyed June 2, 1667, for William Stevens.

"*Teags Down*"—16 acres, surveyed September 6, 1667, for Ambrose London.

"*Discovery*"—150 acres, surveyed May 2, 1668, for William Cheesman.

"*Jones' Island*"—100 acres, surveyed March 19, 1669, for Leonard Jones.

"*Kirk's Purchase*"—200 acres, surveyed May 29, 1669, for John Kirk.

"*Hill's Folly*"—150 acres, surveyed August 18, 1672, for John Hill.

"*Long Acre*"—100 acres, surveyed October 9, 1673, for Alexander Draper.

"*Boston*"—300 acres, surveyed September 16, 1676, and assigned to Thomas Cottingham.

"*Bear Neck*"—350 acres, surveyed September 9, 1676, and assigned to Robert Dukes.

"*Price's Vineyard*"—200 acres, surveyed January 25, 1676, for James Price.

"*Little Usk*"—100 acres, surveyed July 4, 1677, and assigned to William Jenkins.

"*Chestnut Ridge*"—100 acres, surveyed July 4, 1677, and assigned to Cornelius Ward.

"*Vulcan's Vineyard*"—200 acres, surveyed March 10, 1677, for Thomas Cottingham.

"*Daniel's Den*"—100 acres, surveyed March 3, 1674, for Daniel Denahoe.

"*Wood Strut*"—300 acres, surveyed November 3, 1677, for John Emmett.

"*Double Purchase*"—3000 acres, resurveyed November 19, 1679, for Randolph Revell.

"*Martin's Hope*"—100 acres, surveyed 1679, for William Green.

"*The Exchange*"—200 acres, surveyed July 24, 1679, and assigned to John Rockson.

"*Merchant's Treasure*"—150 acres, surveyed June 9, 1679, for Stephen Costin.

"*Brickle Hoe*"—300 acres, surveyed August 23, 1679, for John White.

"*Hopewell*"—100 acres, surveyed June 26, 1679, for for John Garrett.

"*Pomfrett*"—1400 acres, surveyed June 13, 1679, for William Coleburn (Colebourne).

"*Mitchell's Lott*"—400 acres, surveyed 1679—and assigned to Randall Michell.

"*Long's Lott*"—100 acres, surveyed April 26, 1680, and assigned to Samuel Long.

"*Galloway*"—150 acres, surveyed April 20, 1680, for John Kirk.

"*Long Hedge*"—250 acres, surveyed February 25, 1679, for John Carter.

"*Ragland*"—150 acres, surveyed May 15, 1683, and assigned William Scott.

"*Rest*"—150 acres, surveyed January 7, 1683, for Joseph Gray.

"*Rehoboth*"—1000 acres, surveyed July 18, 1665, for William Stevens (Colonel).

"*Mannings Resolution*"—800 acres, surveyed October 16, 1662, for Thomas Manning.

"*Hackland*"—1100 acres, surveyed October 18, 1662, for John Vankak.

"*Bozman's Choice*"—300 acres, surveyed March 2, 1663, for William Bozman.

"*Marcomb's Lott*"—400 acres, surveyed March 7, 1663, for John Marcomb.

"*Sweetwood*"—300 acres, surveyed February 12, 1663, for John Elzey.

"*Covington's Vineyard*"—300 acres, surveyed March 1, 1663, for Nehemiah Covington.

"*Wallers Adventure*"—300 acres, surveyed November 1, 1666, for John Waller.

"*The Second Choice*"—200 acres, surveyed February 14, 1666, for Henry Hayman.

"*David's Destiny*"—350 acres, surveyed May 21, 1668, for David Williamson.

"*Noble Quarter*"—1000 acres, surveyed September 8, 1663, for John Taylor.

"*Rice Land*"—1000 acres, surveyed September 8, 1663, for Nicholas Rice.

"*The Dispence*"—1000 acres, surveyed December 8, 1663, for David Spence.

"*Kellum's Folly*"—550 acres, surveyed June 6, 1665, for Robert Ingram.

"*Bennett's Adventure*"—2500 acres, surveyed June 7, 1665, for Richard Bennett, Esq.

"*Walley's Chance*"—300 acres, surveyed June 9, 1665, for Thomas Walley.

"*Taunton Dean*"—300 acres, surveyed June 7, 1665, for William Thorne.

"*The Hazard*"—400 acres, surveyed November 2, 1664, for William Thomas.

"*Kikotan Choice*"—300 acres, surveyed April 2, 1664, for John Winder.

"*What You Please*"—300 acres, surveyed December 1, 1668, for William Keen.

"*Evershamp*"—500 acres, surveyed March 16, 1673, for Thomas Hollbrook and John Holland.

"*Hoggs Down*"—450 acres, surveyed July 10, 1679, for Edward Southern.

"*Brereton's Chance*"—300 acres, surveyed November 10, 1675, for William Brereton (now Brewington).

"*Munsley*"—354 acres, surveyed June 26, 1694, for William Elgate.

"*Little Belean*"—1200 acres, surveyed January 31, 1677, for Robert Ridgley.

"*High Suffolk*"—1450 acres, surveyed October 10, 1677, for Captain John Walker.

"*Pemberton's Goodwill*"—700 acres, surveyed September 3, 1682, for John Winder.

"*Samuel's Adventure*"—1000 acres, surveyed June 7, 1665, for Colonel Samuel Smith.

"*Colebrook*"—550 acres, surveyed October 20, 1662, for William Cole.

"*Harmon*"—350 acres, surveyed February 8, 1682, for John Parker.

"*Fountain's Lott*"—300 acres, March 12, 1663, for Nicholas Fountain.

"*David's Choice*"—600 acres, surveyed March 14, 1663, for James Davis.

"*Nelson's Choice*"—300 acres, surveyed March 22, 1663, for John Nelson.

"*Glanvill's Lott*"—500 acres, surveyed March 11, 1663, for William Glanvill.

SIDE-LIGHTS ON MARYLAND HISTORY 319

"*Almondington*"—1000 acres, surveyed November 10, 1663, for John Elzy.

"*The First Choice*"—210 acres, surveyed September 23, 1663, for Richard Ackworth.

"*Nutters Delight*"—150 acres, surveyed September 23, 1665, for Christopher Nutter.

"*Woolford's Chance*"—300 acres, surveyed November 22, 1667, for Roger Woolford.

"*Bridges Lott*"—1100 acres, surveyed 1673 for Joseph Bridges.

"*Woolfordsland*"—700 acres, surveyed November 11, 1672, for Roger Woolford.

"*Beckford*"—500 acres, surveyed November 24, 1679, and assigned to Edmond Howard.

"*White Oke*"—250 acres, surveyed July 30, 1683, for Henry Miles.

"*Owen G'andore*"—300 acres, surveyed March 1, 1663, for Germon Gillett.

"*Blake's Hope*"—Surveyed March 9, 1663, for Joel Blake.

"*Chuckatuck*"—1000 acres, surveyed October 28, 1665, for Robert Pitts.

"*More Clack*"—500 acres, surveyed November 4, 1668, and assigned James Henderson.

"*Leverton*"—220 acres, surveyed February 4, 1674, for John Bozman.

"*Bear Point*"—500 acres, surveyed July 10, 1679, and assigned Stephen Costin.

"*The Late Discovery*"—600 acres, surveyed November 22, 1679, for John Robins.

"*Warwick*"—400 acres, surveyed June 20, 1679, and assigned Roland Bevan.

"*Salem*"—350 acres, surveyed December 20, 1680, for Samuel Cooper.

"*Middlesex*"—450 acres, surveyed April 28, 1680, for William Harris.

"*Cowley*"—800 acres, surveyed March 15, 1680, and assigned to Mark Manlove.

"*Stanley's*"—1350 acres, surveyed July 24, 1663, for Hugh Stanley.

"*Shaftsbury*"—700 acres, surveyed October 1, 1681, for Edward Hammond.

"*Turnstile*"—300 acres, surveyed July 19, 1679, and assigned John Brown.

"*Bedford*"—500 acres, surveyed April 4, 1680, and assigned James Wetherly.

"*Spring Hill*"—1000 acres, surveyed March 3, 1680, and assigned Francis Jenkins.

"*Darby*"—350 acres, surveyed March 3, 1680, and assigned Thomas Wilson.

"*Pharsalia*"—2400 acres, surveyed June 25, 1675, for Southby Littleton.

"*Purnell's Lott*"—500 acres, surveyed about 1675, for John Purnell.

"*Ingleteage*"—1550 acres, surveyed October 13, 1675, for John Robins.

"*The Lock*"—250 acres, surveyed December 16, 1680, for Mathew Scarborough.

"*Bantry*"—1400 acres, surveyed April 18, 1674, for Daniel Selby.

"*Mount Ephraim*"—2000 acres, surveyed previous to 1660, for Robert Richardson.

"*Parramours Double Purchase*"—1500 acres, surveyed previous to 1660, for John Parramour.

WIFE AND DAUGHTER OF JUDGE SAMUEL CHASE
By Charles Wilson Peale. From original at Maryland Historical Society. From the Author's Collection

"*Durhams Hope*"—2300 acres, patented, December 24, 1675, to Henry Bishop.

"*Assateague Field*"—1000 acres, surveyed November 12, 1675, for Edward Wall.

"*Fair Haven*"—450 acres, surveyed July 2, 1677, for William Nock.

"*Fairfield*"—800 acres, surveyed November 21, 1676, for Thomas Purnell.

"*Winchester*"—800 acres, surveyed December 12, 1678, for George Hamblin.

"*Genzar*"—2200 acres, resurveyed November 4, 1678, and assigned Edward Wall.

"*Hilliard's Discovery*"—150 acres, surveyed August 6, 1679, and assigned Walter Powell.

"*Wiltshire*"—500 acres, surveyed June 13, 1675, for John Glass.

"*Rochester*"—2900 acres, surveyed February 10, 1682, for John Godden.

"*Choice*"—1200 acres, surveyed November 5, 1685, for John Osborn.

"*Denwoods Den*"—300 acres, surveyed December 16, 1681, and assigned to Levin Denwood.

"*Cox's Discovery*"—745 acres, surveyed May 15, 1688, for Edward Day.

"*Coventry*"—450 acres, surveyed May 31, 1689, for Hugh Porter.

"*Friends Endeavor*"—2700 acres, surveyed October 3, 1689, for William Joseph.

"*Summerfields*"—400 acres, surveyed April 1, 1688, for William Whittington.

"*Partners Desire*"—375 acres, surveyed October 10, 1679, for Richard and John Waters.

"*Doe Better*"—2000 acres, surveyed July 1, 1669, for Thomas Gillis.

"*Suffolk*"—1000 acres, surveyed June 11, 1679, for William Morris.

"*Killglan*"—1000 acres, surveyed April 29, 1699, for Ephraim Wilson.

"*Assateague*"—500 acres, surveyed October 8, 1706, for Captain John Franklyn.

"*Shields Folly*"—1300 acres, surveyed September 20th, 1700, for Thomas and James Dashield.

"*Danbury*"—300 acres, surveyed February 4, 1672, for Samuel Jackson.

Anne Arundel County

"*Carter*"—600 acres, surveyed October 28, 1651, for Captain Edward Carter.

"*Bennetts Island*"—275 acres, surveyed October 28, 1651, for Richard Bennett, Esq.

"*Town Land*"—200 acres, surveyed October 29, 1651, for William Ayers.

"*Gordon*"—300 acres, surveyed November 18, 1659, for Alexander Gordon.

"*Ram Gott Swamp*"—600 acres, surveyed November 18, 1659, for Richard Cotton.

"*Paget*"—250 acres, surveyed November 18, 1659, for William Paget.

"*Kequotan Choice*"—300 acres, surveyed May 5, 1663, for Stephen Benson.

"*Benjamin's Choice*"—280 acres, surveyed July 7, 1663, for Richard Well.

"*Jerico*"—200 acres, surveyed July 3, 1663, for William Crosby.

"*Burrage*"—500 acres, surveyed March 20, 1662, for John Burrage.

"*Dan*"—490 acres, surveyed July 3, 1663, for Robert Paca.

"*Dinah Ford's Beaver Dam*"—400 acres, surveyed November 27, 1662, for Thomas Ford.

"*Wells*"—600 acres, surveyed November 22, 1659, for Richard Wells.

"*Maidstone*"—350 acres, surveyed August 3, 1663, for William Hunt.

"*Pascall's Chance*"—Surveyed December 6, 1662, for George Pascall.

"*Birkhead's Parcell*"—600 acres, surveyed February 10, 1661, for Christopher Birkhead.

"*Greenwood*"—150 acres, surveyed July 12, 1663, for Armiger Greenwood.

"*Morely*"—300 acres, surveyed July 7, 1663, for Joseph Morely.

"*Trent*"—450 acres, surveyed July 17, 1663, for Joseph Marley.

"*His Lordship's Mannour*"—12,634 acres, surveyed in 1663.

"*Broughton Ashly*"—950 acres, surveyed January 5, 1663, for Francis Holland.

"*Davistone*"—240 acres, surveyed October 20, 1701, for Thomas Davis.

"*Portland Mannour*"—2722 acres, surveyed December 6, 1667—2000 acres for Jerome White, Esq., and 500 acres for Edward Talbott—remainder granted to Colonel Henry Darnell.

"*Pascall's Purchase*"—300 acres, surveyed October 24, 1651, for Edward Selby.

"*Sanetley*"—450 acres, surveyed August 3, 1663, for Samuel Chew.

"*Bersheba*"—100 acres, surveyed July 5, 1663, for John Wilson.

"*Smith's Delight*"—300 acres, surveyed March 2, 1664, for Nathan Smith.

"*Daborn's Inheritance*"—250 acres, surveyed August 27, 1668, for Thomas Daborn.

"*Papa Ridge*"—155 acres, surveyed July 13, 1673, for Edward Parish.

"*Mavorn Hills*"—50 acres, surveyed March 12, 1678, for William Tuckbury.

"*Gover's Venture*"—295 acres, surveyed August 31, 1678, for Robert Gover.

"*Devoir's Range*"—220 acres, surveyed August 24, 1675, for Richard Devoir.

"*Gullock's Folly*"—85 acres, surveyed September 11, 1678, for Thomas Gullock.

"*Emerton's Addition*"—200 acres, surveyed June 17, 1679, for Humphrey Emerton.

"*Conant's Chance*"—25 acres, surveyed January 2, 1679, for Robert Conant.

"*Knighton's Purchase*"—197 acres, surveyed January 3, 1679, for Thomas Knighton.

"*Purnell's Angle*"—140 acres, surveyed February 24, 1679, for Thomas Purnell.

"*Range*"—211 acres, surveyed July 2, 1684, for George Burgess.

"*Harrison's Enlargement to Gramarrs Chance*"—425 acres, surveyed 1699, for Richard Harrison.

"*Heath's Landing*"—138 acres, surveyed March 1, 1705, for James Heath.

"*Marsh's Seat*"—150 acres, surveyed October 24, 1651, for Thomas Marsh.

"*Woolman*"—100 acres, surveyed November 26, 1651, for Robert Harwood.

"*Sparrow's Rest*"—590 acres, surveyed September 22, 1652, for Thomas Sparrow.

"*Northwest River*"—260 acres, surveyed November 1, 1652, for John Brown, Christopher Rowles and John Moseby.

"*Brownton*"—660 acres, for John Brown and John Clark.

"*Great Bonnerton*"—100 acres, surveyed November 11, 1659, for James Bonner.

"*Watkins*"—600 acres, surveyed October 21, 1652, for Roger Gross.

"*Cumberton*"—600 acres, surveyed November 12, 1659, for John Cumber.

"*Hooker's Purchase*"—300 acres, surveyed March 7, 1661, for Thomas Hooker.

"*Taylor's Chance*"—300 acres, surveyed March 3, 1661, for Thomas Taylor.

"*Barren Neck*"—150 acres, surveyed June 16th, 1663, for Richard Ewen.

"*Waterton*"—120 acres, surveyed November 28, 1662, for Nicholas Waterman.

"*Talbott's Ridge*"—300 acres, surveyed November 30, 1662, for Richard Talbott.

"*Galloway*"—250 acres, surveyed December 4, 1662, for Richard Galloway.

"*Watkins's Hope*"—300 acres, surveyed July 8, 1663, for John Watkins.

"*Ewen Upon 'Ewenton'*"—400 acres, surveyed November 1, 1665, for Charles Calvert, Esq.

"*Barwell's Choice*"—100 acres, surveyed November 11, 1665, for John Barwell.

"*Norman's Damms or Mill Haven*"—Surveyed June 13, 1668, for John Norman.

"*Goldsbury's Choice*" (Goldsborough)—surveyed May 13, 1672, for Robert Goldsbury (Goldsborough).

"*Pratt's Neck*"—100 acres, surveyed May 13, 1672, for Thomas Pratt.

"*Beverdam Branch*"—307 acres, surveyed May 7, 1674, for Robert Franklyn.

"*Francis and Robert*"—300 acres, surveyed August 17, 1678, for Francis Butler.

"*Lockwood's Addition*"—100 acres, surveyed July 25, 1675, for Robert Lockwood.

"*Hooker's Chance*"—154 acres, surveyed July 16, 1678, for Thomas Hooker.

"*Puddington's First*"—300 acres, surveyed January 6, 1651, for George Puddington.

"*Burgess*"—300 acres, surveyed January 21, 1651, for William Burgess.

"*Larkiston*"—300 acres, surveyed October 21, 1652, for Ellis Brown.

"*Wrighton*"—100 acres, surveyed November 26, 1651, for Walter Mansfield.

"*Coxby*"—100 acres, surveyed December 6, 1658, for Edward Cox.

"*Scorton*"—800 acres, surveyed 1658, for George Wastill.

"*Lavall*"—100 acres, surveyed August 28, 1650, for Marien Devall (Mareen Duvall).

"*Bessonton*"—350 acres, surveyed November 3, 1659, for Thomas Besson.

"*Brewerton*"—400 acres, surveyed November 3, 1659, for John Brewer.

"*Townhill*"—400 acres, surveyed November 8, 1659, for Edward Townhill.

"*Cheney's Resolution*"—700 acres, surveyed 1661, for Richard Cheney.

"*Beard's Habitation*"—1260 acres, surveyed January 4, 1661, for Richard Beard.

"*Freeman's Fancy*"—300 acres, surveyed February 20, 1661, for John Freeman.

"*Covel's Folly*"—500 acres, surveyed February 16, 1661, for Ann Covel.

"*Plumton*"—280 acres, surveyed February 23, 1661, for George Walker.

"*Larkin's Hill*"—450 acres, surveyed March 3, 1661, for John Larkin.

"*Abington*"—875 acres, surveyed January 26, 1663, for Robert Proctor and John Gater.

"*Middle Plantation*"—600 acres, surveyed May 23, 1664, for Mareen Duvall.

"*Shaw's Folly*"—260 acres, surveyed 1665, for John Shaw.

"*Arnold Gray*"—300 acres, surveyed January 26, 1668, for Richard Arnold and John Gray.

"*Obligation*"—663 acres, surveyed July 19, 1669, for Thomas Stockett.

"*Champ's Adventure*"—300 acres, surveyed June 1, 1669, for John Champ.

"*Rowdown*"—800 acres, surveyed July 26, 1669, for George Yate.

"*Jones Lott*"—350 acres, surveyed November 1, 1669, for William Jones.

"*Godwell*"—805 acres, resurveyed September 9, 1678, for George and William Parker, father and son.

"*Roper Gray*"—480 acres, surveyed August 4, 1681, for William Roper.

"*Equality*"—140 acres, surveyed January 30, 1684, for James Sanders.

"*Robin Hood Forest*"—1976 acres, surveyed June 5, 1686, for Richard Snowden.

"*Duvall's Delight*"—1000 acres, surveyed October 9, 1694, for John Duvall.

"*Littleton*"—280 acres, surveyed June 22, 1703, for John Summers.

"*Howard*"—650 acres, surveyed July 3, 1650, for Mathew Howard.

"*Crouchfield*"—150 acres, surveyed 1650, for William Crouch.

"*Todd*"—100 acres, surveyed July 8, 1651, for Thomas Todd.

"*Acton*"—100 acres, surveyed November 15, 1651, for Richard Acton.

"*Porter's Hills*"—200 acres, surveyed November 20, 1651, for Peter Porter.

"*Baldwin's Neck*"—260 acres, surveyed January 7, 1661, for John Baldwin.

"*Richardson's Folly*"—200 acres, surveyed January 19, 1661, for Lawrence Richardson.

"*Wardridge*"—600 acres, surveyed February 20, 1661, for James Warner.

"*Wyatt's Ridge*"—450 acres, surveyed 1662, for Nicholas Wyatt.

"*Howard's Heirship*"—420 acres, surveyed January 26, 1662, for Cornelius Howard.

"*Howard's Hope*"—100 acres, surveyed January 26, 1662, for Samuel Howard.

"*Howard's Interest*"—Surveyed January 28, 1662, for John Howard.

"*Hockley in the Hole*"—400 acres, surveyed January 27, 1663, for Edward Dorsey (Major Edward Dorsey).

"*Mountain Neck*"—190 acres, surveyed August 8, 1664, for Thomas Hammond.

"*Bruton*"—150 acres, surveyed January 3, 1664, for John Bruton.

"*Orphans Inheritance*"—200 acres, surveyed May 21, 1666, for Elizabeth Sisson.

"*Lancaster's Plains*"—180 acres, surveyed August 28, 1674, for John Hudson.

"*Widow's Addition*"—130 acres, surveyed January 10, 1678, for Elizabeth Read.

"*Cordwell*"—300 acres, surveyed September 4, 1682, for John Marriott.

"*The Range*"—384 acres, surveyed July 4, 1684, for Thomas Lightfoot.

"*Warfield's Forest*"—182 acres, surveyed June 7, 1673, for Richard Warfield; also "*Warfield's Plains*," 300 acres, surveyed March 30, 1681; also "*Brandy*," 300 acres, surveyed September 29, 1681; also "*Warfield's Range*," 1080 acres, surveyed 1694, for Richard and John Warfield—1862 acres in all.

"*Ridgely's Forest*"—264 acres, surveyed June 3, 1686, for Henry Ridgely.

"*Sheppard's Chanse*"—240 acres, surveyed June 12, 1686, for Nicholas Sheppard.

"*Dryer's Inheritance*"—254 acres, surveyed February 25, 1695, for Samuel Dryer.

"*Owen's Range*"—162 acres, surveyed February 15, 1688, for Richard Owen.

"*Young's Range*"—162 acres, surveyed March 15, 1704, for John Young.

"*Pen Loyd or Swan Neck*"—570 acres, surveyed 1650, for Edward Lloyd.

"*Hawkins*"—600 acres, surveyed September 27, 1652, for Ralph Hawkins.

"*Homewood's Lott*"—210 acres, surveyed February 13, 1650, for James Homewood.

"*Maidston*"—250 acres, surveyed September 22, 1659, for Elizabeth Strong.

"*Durand's Place*"—100 acres, surveyed February 14, 1662, for Alice Durand.

"*Addition*"—400 acres, surveyed July 3, 1668, for James Connaway.

"*Sewell's Increase*"—500 acres, surveyed May 25, 1680, for Henry Sewell.

"*Eagleston's Range*"—206 acres, surveyed May 25, 1680, for Bernard Eagleston.

"*Greenberry's Forest*"—Surveyed for Nicholas Greenberry, June 15, 1680.

"*Lewis's Addition*"—325 acres, surveyed September 20, 1678, for Henry Lewis.

"*Huckelberry Forest*"—1611 acres, surveyed June 6, 1687, for Thomas Richardson.

"*Altogether*"—1200 acres, surveyed May 10, 1719, for Thomas Worthington.

"WHITEHALL," HOME OF GOVERNOR HORATIO SHARP
Built about 1760. From the Author's Collection

"*Hammond's Gift*"—1000 acres, surveyed June 7, 1723, for Charles Hammond.

Baltimore County

"*Spesutie*"—2300 acres (an island), surveyed July 25, 1660, for Col. Nathaniel Utie.

"*Carter's Rest*"—400 acres, surveyed July 25, 1661, for Edward Carter.

"*Benjamin's Choice*"—400 acres, surveyed May 11, 1678, for Colonel George Wells.

"*Addicon*"—200 acres, surveyed 1695, for John Miles.

"*Sprie's Inheritance*"—640 acres, surveyed February 12, 1668, for Oliver Sprie.

"*Goldsmith's Hall*"—800 acres, surveyed July 15, 1658, for Samuel Goldsmith.

"*Planter's Delight*"—600 acres, surveyed July 15, 1658, for Harekins and Thomas Goldsmith.

"*Poplar Neck*"—1000 acres, surveyed for Mark Richardson, September 20, 1683.

"*Timber Proof*"—200 acres, surveyed 1672, for George Wells.

"*Persimon Point*"—400 acres, surveyed August 1, 1659, for James Rigby.

"*Langley's Habitation*"—300 acres, surveyed August 30, 1659, for Thomas Overton.

"*Cranberry Hall*"—1547 acres, surveyed October 14, 1604, for John Hall.

"*Gibson's Ridge*"—500 acres, surveyed September 19, 1683, for Miles Gibson.

"*North Yarmouth*"—200 acres, surveyed September 4, 1683, for James Howgate.

"*The Addition*"—400 acres, surveyed October 24, 1668, for Walter Tucker.

"*The Grove*"—250 acres, surveyed January 3, 1671, for John Tarkinton.

"*Delph*"—600 acres, surveyed April 14, 1669, for Francis Stockett.

"*Hunting Neck*"—300 acres, surveyed April 25, 1668, for Thomas Cole and William Hollis.

"*Palmer's Forest*"—500 acres, surveyed June 23, 1675, for William Palmer.

"*Goodman's Adventure*"—250 acres, surveyed May 13, 1678, for Edward Goodman.

"*Turkey Hill*"—200 acres, surveyed June 29, 1672, for John James.

"*Wilson's Range*"—100 acres, surveyed November 18, 1686, for John Wilson.

"*Pork Point*"—100 acres, surveyed April 14, 1667, for James Phillips.

"*Upper Ring*"—100 acres, surveyed August 14, 1659, for Thomas Sampson.

"*Crab Hill*"—100 acres, surveyed March 23, 1665, for John Lee.

"*Martin's Rest*"—196 acres, surveyed July 15, 1688, for Lodwick Martin.

"*Holland's Lott*"—400 acres, surveyed August 15, 1678, for George Holland.

"*Friendship*"—1000 acres, surveyed June 15, 1679, for Robert Lockwood.

"*Mould's Success*"—Surveyed June 10, 1681, for John Mould.

"*Vincent's Castle*"—500 acres, surveyed July 13, 1683, for Vincent Lowe.

"*Mount Yoe*"—400 acres, surveyed January 9, 1683, for John Yoe.

"*Parker's Chance*"—550 acres, surveyed June 15, 1683, for George Parker.

"*Elford's Field*"—500 acres, surveyed June 10, 1684, for William Blankinson.

"*Langley's Forest*"—356 acres, surveyed March 10, 1683, for Robert Langley.

"*Abbott's Forrest*"—1000 acres, surveyed June 10, 1684, for George Abbott.

"*Friendship*"—600 acres, surveyed May 10, 1684, for William Harris.

"*The Land of Promise*"—2000 acres, surveyed May 14, 1684, for Colonel Thomas Taylor.

"*Andrew's Conquest*"—780 acres, surveyed September 10, 1683, for Andrew Mattson.

"*Benjamin's Choice*"—254 acres, surveyed September 25, 1683, for Thomas Hedge.

"*Expectation*"—350 acres, surveyed September 25, 1683, for Peter Ellis.

"*Bell's Camp*"—1000 acres, surveyed September 22, 1683, for Ninion Bell (Beall).

"*Bushwood*"—150 acres, surveyed August 15, 1659, for Abraham Holdman.

"*Warrington*"—650 acres, surveyed February 9, 1664, for Nathaniel Shields.

"*Ranger's Lodge*"—500 acres, surveyed June 15, 1682, for David Jones.

"*Planters Paradise*"—829 acres, surveyed November 29, 1679, for William Cornwallis.

"*Scott's Close*"—100 acres, surveyed March 25, 1703, for John Ewins.

"*Campbell's Adventure*"—349 acres, surveyed August 31, 1704, for John Campbell.

"*Cheapside*"—500 acres, surveyed September 15, 1703, for Thomas Preston.

"*Cecils Adventure*"—491 acres, surveyed October 24, 1704, for Joshua Cecil.

"*Billberry Hall*"—190 acres, surveyed October 12, 1703, for John Brice.

"*Charles Bounty*"—1000 acres, surveyed October 25, 1704, for James Bowles.

"*Refuge*"—239 acres, surveyed November 17, 1705, for Luke Ravan.

"*Expectation*"—406 acres, surveyed August 8, 1705, for Thomas Boston.

"*Quinn*"—500 acres, surveyed April 13, 1705, for Thomas Macnemarra.

"*Collingborn*"—200 acres, surveyed June 6, 1669, for Henry Howard.

"*Pools Island*"—200 acres, surveyed July 27, 1659, for Captain Robert Morris.

"*The Lyon*"—300 acres, surveyed November 19, 1664, for Captain Thomas Harwood.

"*Anderson's Lott*"—400 acres, surveyed October 15, 1685, for John Anderson.

"*Edward's Lott*"—300 acres, surveyed July 9, 1686, for William York.

"*Groom's Chance*"—300 acres, surveyed April 28, 1687, for Moses Groom.

"*Ranger's Range*"—200 acres, surveyed May 18, 1687, for Charles Ranger.

"*Dandy Hill*"—353 acres, surveyed April 10, 1695, for George Burgess.

"*Bear Neck*"—500 acres, surveyed October 10, 1694, for Walter Smith.

"*France's Freedom*"—1000 acres, surveyed September 27, 1683, for Samuel Young.

"*Scott's Grove*"—500 acres, surveyed November 6, 1695, for Daniel Scott.

"*Chivy Chase*"—400 acres, surveyed July 26, 1695, for John Thomas.

"*Brown's Discovery*"—500 acres, surveyed February 24, 1701, for Thomas Tench, Esq.

"*The Agreement*"—500 acres, surveyed January 20, 1686, for Thomas Thurston.

"*Friends Discovery*"—500 acres, surveyed August 21, 1704, for Richard Colgate.

"*Paca's Delight*"—257 acres, surveyed June 14, 1703, for Aquila Paca.

"*Good Hope*"—200 acres, surveyed September 19, 1683, for James Banister.

"*The Garden of Eden*"—150 acres, surveyed January 18, 1685, for Adam Burchell.

"*Daniel's Lott*"—454 acres, surveyed June 16, 1688, for Daniel Peverell.

"*Concord*"—500 acres, surveyed January 20, 1686, for William Ayleward.

"*Aha-at-a-Venture*"—200 acres, surveyed May 7, 1687, for John Hathaway.

"*Fanny's Inheritance*"—893 acres, surveyed January 12, 1695, for Edward Boothby.

"*Convent Garden*"—450 acres, surveyed June 3, 1667, for William Osbourn.

"*Musketo Proof*"—250 acres, surveyed December 22, 1672, for James Ives.

"*Altrop*"—500 acres, surveyed December 29, 1664, for Thomas Griffith.

"*Ann's Lott*"—500 acres, surveyed June 8, 1683, for Miles Gibson.

"*Forest of Bucks*"—200 acres, surveyed August 25, 1699, for Robert Love.

"*Miles Forest*"—252 acres, surveyed August 24, 1699, for John Miles.

"*The Range*"—240 acres, surveyed 1685, for Henry Constable.

"*Owen's Adventure*"—450 acres, surveyed October 10, 1694, for Captain Richard Owen.

"*Roberts Choice*"—153 acres, surveyed March 27, 1668, for Thomas Roberts.

"*Goose Harbour*"—200 acres, surveyed 1679, for Rowland Thornbury.

"*Curtiss Neck*"—200 acres, surveyed April 2, 1662, for Paul Kinsey.

"*Homewood Range*"—300 acres, surveyed July 5, 1670, for John Homewood.

"*Young's Lott*"—300 acres, surveyed April 14, 1699, for Aaron Rawlins.

"*Triangle*"—300 acres, surveyed August 24, 1699, for Dutton Lane.

"*Robin's Camp*"—100 acres, surveyed September 8, 1699, for Robert Rogers.

"*Denton*"—190 acres, surveyed June 24, 1669, for Thomas Todd.

"*Powell*"—300 acres, surveyed July 28, 1659, for Thomas Powell.

"*Ely O'Carroll*"—1000 acres, surveyed January 13, 1695, for Charles Carroll.

"*Howard's Square*"—150 acres, surveyed February 1, 1698, for Joshua Howard.

"*Kindness*"—234 acres, surveyed March 20, 1688, for John Richardson.

"*Wincowpen Neck*"—833 acres, surveyed 1701, for Richard and Benjamin Warfield.

"*Venison Park*"—800 acres, surveyed December 28, 1701, for John, Charles and Frank Warfield.

"*Hookers Range*"—500 acres, surveyed February 4, 1701, for Thomas Hooker.

"*White Wine and Claret*"—1400 acres, surveyed April 26, 1702, for Captain John Dorsey.

"*Litterlouma*"—400 acres, surveyed January 25, 1695, for Charles Carroll.

"*Athel*"—617 acres, surveyed November 12, 1694, for James Murray.

"*Cockey's Trust*"—300 acres, surveyed April 8, 1696, for William Cockey.

"*Adam the First*"—500 acres, surveyed April 8, 1687, for Adam Shipley.

"*East Humphreys*"—300 acres, surveyed October 1, 1679, for Mary Humphreys.

"*Willin*"—398 acres, surveyed September 5, 1679, for Charles Gorsuch.

"*The Batchelor's Hope*"—550 acres, surveyed February 7, 1664, for Edward Gill and Rich Merryday.

"*Dixon's Neck*"—450 acres, surveyed June 7, 1667, for John Dixon.

"*Brothers Expectation*"—250 acres, surveyed October 30, 1695, for George Hollingsworth.

"*Oulton's Garrison*"—340 acres, surveyed May 13, 1696, for Captain John Oulton.

"*Cromwell's Range*"—200 acres, surveyed October 19, 1695, for Richard Cromwell.

"*Timberneck*"—300 acres, surveyed March 21, 1665, for Richard Ball.

"*Come by Chance*"—282 acres, surveyed November 24, 1694, for John Richardson.

"*Friends Discovery*"—1000 acres, surveyed June 12, 1694, for Job Evans.

"*Parishes Range*"—2000 acres, surveyed October 5, 1678, for Edward Parish.

"*Holland's Choice*"—580 acres, surveyed August 11, 1677, for Arthur Holland.

"*Body's Adventure*"—700 acres, surveyed September 14, 1676, for Captain John Body.

"*Andover*"—1640 acres, surveyed September 12, 1677, for Nicholas Painter.

"*Pierce's Encouragement*"—1000 acres, surveyed October 11, 1677, for John Pierce.

"*Floyds Adventure*"—320 acres, surveyed January 4, 1695, for James Floyd.

"*Wilmot's Range*"—200 acres, surveyed November 20, 1672, for John Wilmot.

"*Talbot's Vineyard*"—1021 acres, surveyed April 16, 1689, for Edward Talbot.

"*North Point*"—330 acres, surveyed April 8, 1664, for Ralph Williams.

"*Old Roade*"—1150 acres, surveyed November 20, 1652, for Thomas Thomas and William Batten.

"*Long Reach*"—448 acres, surveyed March 12, 1694, for Edward Dorsey.

"*Chews Resolution Mannour*"—1073 acres, surveyed April 15, 1684, for Samuel Chew.

"*Moors Morning Choice*"—1368 acres, surveyed May 5, 1689, for Dr. Mordy Moor.

"*Maidens Choice*"—218 acres, surveyed November 30, 1694, for Mary Richardson.

"*Midsummer Hill*"—201 acres, surveyed July 18, 1689, for John Bevins.

"*Back Lingan*"—450 acres, surveyed November 6, 1682, for George Lingan.

"*The Valley of Jehosophat*"—2500 acres, surveyed September 27, 1683, for Captain Richard Smith.

"*Claxson's Hope*"—600 acres, surveyed September 28, 1683, for Robert Claxon.

"*Blethyn-a-Cambria*"—5000 acres, surveyed for William Bladen, April 18, 1705.

"*Brooms Bloom*"—100 acres, surveyed August 5, 1684, for John Broom.

"*Doughoregan*"—10,000 acres, surveyed May 2, 1707, for Charles Carroll, Esq.

Cecil County

"*Wheeler's Point*"—250 acres, surveyed August 3, 1658, for John Wheeler.

"*Marklefield*"—100 acres, surveyed August 3, 1658, for Marcus Siverson.

"*Clementshill*"—50 acres, surveyed August 3, 1658, for Clement Michaellson.

"*Petersfield*"—200 acres, surveyed August 3, 1658, for Peter Jacobson.

"*Burly's Journey*"—500 acres, surveyed August 2, 1658, for Robert Burly.

"*Spry's Hill*"—600 acres, surveyed August 21, 1658, for Oliver Spry.

"*Grove*"—1000 acres, surveyed August 23, 1658, for Philip Calvert, Esq.

"*Hackley*"—800 acres, surveyed August 21, 1658, for Stephen Hack.

"*The World's End*"—500 acres, surveyed April 27, 1665, for Francis Child.

"*None So Good in Finland*"—350 acres, surveyed May 20, 1664, for Bartlett Hinderson.

"*Frisby's Addition*"—300 acres, surveyed August 22, 1665, for James Frisby.

"*Middleneck*"—600 acres, surveyed August 7, 1669, for Jarvis Morgan.

"*Pain's Lott*"—480 acres, surveyed June 7, 1671, for Thomas Pain.

"*Money Worth*"—150 acres, surveyed January 9, 1671, for Robert Money.

"*Daley's Desire*"—500 acres, surveyed July 10, 1673, for Bryan Daley.

"*Sylvan's Folly*"—100 acres, surveyed October 1, 1680, for Henry Pennington.

"*Neighbor's Grudge*"—175 acres, surveyed December 14, 1681, for William Ward.

"*Frisby's Meadows*"—1000 acres, surveyed November 30, 1682, for James Frisby.

"*Mesopotamia*"—340 acres, surveyed April 22, 1684, for Edward Jones.

"*Coaster's Refreshment*"—1600 acres, surveyed July 14, 1683, for Colonel William Diggs.

"*Cedar Branch Neck*"—841 acres, surveyed November 19, 1700, for Matthew Smith.

OLD ST. PAUL'S CHURCH, BALTIMORE
From rare engraving

"*Clemerson*"—400 acres, surveyed July 21, 1662, for Andrew Clemerson.

"*Hay Down*"—300 acres, surveyed March 5, 1664, for Henry Downes.

"*True Game*"—150 acres, surveyed April 14, 1665, for Anne Morgan.

"*Corrobough*"—300 acres, surveyed April 12, 1665, for Daniel Mackey.

"*Uppermost*"—500 acres, surveyed April 29, 1665, for Richard Booker.

"*Hazel Branch*"—300 acres, surveyed August 24, 1666, for Thomas Wamsley.

"*Poplar Neck*"—1400 acres, surveyed August 24, 1666, for William Fisher.

"*Kings Aim*"—500 acres, surveyed November 29, 1679, for Thomas Rumley.

"*Clifton*"—883 acres, surveyed March 22, 1660, for John Browning.

"*Sarah's Jointure*"—600 acres, surveyed September 13, 1682, for Richard Peacock.

"*Bohemia Mannour*"—6000 acres, surveyed October 8, 1681, for Augustine Herman; also "*Little Bohemia*," adjoining 1000 acres, surveyed October 28, 1681; also "*Misfortune*," adjoining 1339 acres, surveyed November 14, 1678; also "*Bohemia Sisters*," 4100 acres, surveyed September 27, 1683, and also 4000 acres not named, surveyed June 3, 1660, which makes Bohemia Mannour over 16,000 acres.

"*Danby*"—500 acres, surveyed September 13, 1682, for George Spencer.

"*Piccadilly*"—1000 acres, surveyed May 25, 1683, for Robert Jones.

"*Wheeler's Purchase*"—100 acres, surveyed October 1, 1680, for Anna Wheeler.

"*Worfell Mannour*"—1000 acres, surveyed October 10, 1683, for Major Peter Sayer.

"*Perry Point*"—800 acres, surveyed July 20, 1658, for John Bateman.

"*Turkey Point*"—1000 acres, surveyed August 21, 1658, for Richard Wright.

"*Brereton*"—500 acres, surveyed September 9, 1659, for William Brereton.

"*Thomson's Town*"—500 acres, surveyed September 10, 1659, for George Thompson.

"*Collettstown*"—700 acres, surveyed September 15, 1659, for Richard Collett.

"*Mount Ararat*"—150 acres, surveyed August 4, 1664, for Thomas Griffith.

"*Convenient*"—400 acres, surveyed August 18, 1664, for George Goldsmith.

"*St. John's Mannour*"—3000 acres, surveyed August 4, 1664, for John Pate.

"*Ricroft's Chance*"—300 acres, surveyed September 22, 1678, for John Bullen.

"*Knowlwood*"—1000 acres, surveyed September 2, 1672, for Richard Edmonds.

"*The Glasshouse*"—500 acres, surveyed February 20, 1675, for Richard Gray.

"*Gotham Bush*"—100 acres, surveyed April 10, 1678, for Robert Willen.

"*Anchor and Hope*"—500 acres, surveyed March 25, 1679, for Daniel Carnall.

"*Johnson's Adventure*"—300 acres, surveyed July 22, 1678, for John Johnson.

"*Kildare*"—700 acres, surveyed January 22, 1680, for George Talbott, Esq.; also "*Ormond*," 600 acres, surveyed January 22, 1680; also "*Balle Connell*," 2000 acres, surveyed January 24, 1680.

"*New Munster*"—6000 acres, surveyed July 16, 1683, for Edmund O'Dwyer.

"*High Lands*"—2305 acres, resurveyed October 8, 1684, for John Highland.

"*Lower Tryumph*"—500 acres, resurveyed July 29, 1684, for William Dare.

"*Symms Forrest*"—400 acres, surveyed November 14, 1685, for Marmduke Symms.

"*Netherlands*"—1100 acres, surveyed 1687, for Colonel George Talbott.

"*Levell*"—900 acres, surveyed March 3, 1687, for Casparus Herman.

"*Tuscararo Plains*"—961 acres, surveyed April 25, 1695, for Nicholas Sporne.

"*Daniel's Denn*"—400 acres, surveyed February 28, 1668, for Daniel Sullivan.

"*Morton*"—1000 acres, surveyed September 13, 1659, for Philip Calvert, Esq.

"*Mount Quigley*"—300 acres, surveyed September 22, 1686, for Charles Quigley.

Talbot County

"*Salter's Marsh*"—100 acres, surveyed October 13, 1658, for John Salter.

"*Grange*"—150 acres, surveyed October 15, 1658, for William Granger.

"*Morgan St. Michaell*"—300 acres, surveyed October 13, 1658, for Henry Morgan.

"*Wade's Point*"—400 acres, surveyed October 19, 1658, fur Zachary Wade.

"*Hatton*"—500 acres, surveyed October 19, 1658, for William Hatton.

"*Scott's Close*"—200 acres, surveyed November 5, 1658, for James Scott.

"*Linton*"—600 acres, surveyed November 5, 1658, for Edward Lloyd.

"*Harbour Rouse*"—100 acres, surveyed July 26, 1659, for Anthony Griffin.

"*Pickburn*"—200 acres, surveyed July 26, 1659, for Nicholas Pickard.

"*Hemersby*"—400 acres, surveyed July 26, 1659, for Thomas Emerson.

"*Williston*"—224 acres, surveyed July 28, 1659, for William Champ.

"*Kirkham*"—350 acres, surveyed July 28, 1659, for Martin Kirk.

"*Martingham*"—200 acres, surveyed July 28, 1659, for William Hambleton.

"*Mile End*"—400 acres, surveyed July 28, 1659, for Thomas Miles.

"*Choptank Island*"—1200 acres, surveyed August 11, 1659, for Seth Foster.

"*Cudlington*"—400 acres, surveyed August 11, 1659, for Cuthbert Phelps.

"*Hir-Dir Lloyd*"—3050 acres, surveyed August 11, 1659, for Edward Lloyd, Esq.

"*Readly*"—800 acres, surveyed August 11, 1659, for Thomas Read.

"*Plimhimmon*"—600 acres, surveyed August 15, 1659, for Henry Morgan.

"*Anderton*"—600 acres, surveyed August 15, 1659, for John Anderton.

"*Ottwell*"—500 acres, surveyed August 15, 1659, for William Taylor.

"*Turner's Point*"—400 acres, surveyed August 16, 1659, for William Turner.

"*Grafton Mannour*"—1000 acres, surveyed August 20, 1659, for John Harris.

"*Summerton*"—200 acres, surveyed August 20, 1659. for Thomas Seymour.

"*Marshy Point*"—700 acres, surveyed August 23, 1659, for James Adams.

"*Canterbury Mannour*"—1000 acres, surveyed August 23, 1659, for Richard Tilghman.

"*Eastwood*"—300 acres, surveyed August 24, 1659, for Robert Jones.

"*Tilghman's Fortune*"—1000 acres, surveyed August 24, 1659, for Samuel Tilghman.

"*Ratcliff Mannour*"—800 acres, surveyed August 25, 1659, for Captain Robert Morris.

"*Woolsey or Chancellor Point*"—1000 acres, surveyed August 25, 1659, for Philip Calvert, Esq.

"*Todd-Upon-Dirwan*"—400 acres, surveyed August 30, 1659, for Thomas Todd.

"*Hopkins Point*"—800 acres, surveyed August 25, 1659, for Robert Hopkins.

"*Huntington*"—300 acres, patented to Andrew Skinner June 18, 1663.

"*Jennings Hope*"—1000 acres, surveyed January 31, 1660, for Richard Jennings.

"*Job's Content*"—1000 acres, surveyed January 31, 1660, for Job Nutt.

"*Meersgate*"—300 acres, surveyed June 24, 1659, for William Hemsley.

"*Exchange*"—200 acres, surveyed May 16, 1663, for Thomas Manning.

"*Sutton's Grange*"—600 acres, surveyed October 19, 1662, for Henry Catlin.

"*Bullen's Chance*"—350 acres, surveyed April 7, 1662, for Robert Bullen.

"*Cottingham*"—900 acres, surveyed July 22, 1662, for William Shaw.

"*Ashby*"—800 acres, surveyed July 20, 1663, for Roger Gross.

"*New Scotland*"—700 acres, surveyed March 12, 1662.

"*Dundee*"—400 acres, resurveyed October 12, 1675, for John Kinnemount.

"*The Mile Spring*"—600 acres, surveyed November 16, 1663, for Henry Woolchurch.

"*Dover*"—800 acres, surveyed November 18, 1663, for Daniel Jenifer.

"*Eldridge Point*"—100 acres, surveyed November 28, 1663, for William Eldridge.

"*Weeping Spring*"—200 acres, surveyed October 13, 1663, for Francis Armstrong.

"*Nominy*"—1100 acres, surveyed November 16, 1663, for John Smith, William Robinson and George Watts.

"*Rich Neck*"—300 acres, surveyed March 12, 1662, for John Alley and Nicholas Barkley.

"*Plain Dealing*"—200 acres, surveyed December 5, 1663, for Joseph Winslow.

"*Patrick's Choice*"—200 acres, surveyed March 30, 1663, for Patrick Mullican.

"*Mitcham Hall*"—300 acres, surveyed August 25, 1663, for Henry Mitchell.

"*Beaver Neck*"—600 acres, surveyed November 17, 1663, for Ralph Williams.

"*White Phillips*"—300 acres, surveyed November 25, 1663 for Thomas Phillips.

"*Edmondson's Fresh Run*"—400 acres, surveyed July 17, 1664, for John Edmondson.

"*Widow's Choice*"—640 acres, surveyed April 16, 1664, for Elizabeth Brewer.

"*Chance Ridge*"—150 acres, surveyed February 7, 1663, for William Moore.

"*Hookland*"—100 acres, surveyed April 27, 1664, for Henry Wharton.

"*Lamberton*"—150 acres, surveyed April 26, 1664, for Josias Lambert.

"*Bone Hill*"—250 acres, surveyed April 26, 1664, for Robert Curtis.

"*Hampton*"—550 acres, surveyed April 28, 1664, for Thomas Hammond.

"*Blessland*"—590 acres, surveyed April 29, 1664, for Thomas Vaughan.

"*Jadwin's Choice*"—300 acres, surveyed March 25, 1665, for John Jadwin.

"*Pitts Chance*"—400 acres, surveyed June 24, 1665, for John Pitt.

"*Whettstone*"—300 acres, surveyed June 25, 1665, for Thomas Whetstone.

"*Chestnut Bay*"—1000 acres, surveyed July 1, 1665, for Peter Sharp.

"*Noble's Chance*"—300 acres, surveyed July 12, 1665, for Robert Noble.

"*Turkey Neck Illingsworth*"—500 acres, surveyed March 20, 1663, for William Illingsworth.

"*Long Neck*"—200 acres, surveyed March 12, 1664, for Ralph Elston.

"*The Addition*"—400 acres, surveyed June 28, 1665, for Philemon Lloyd.

"*Jamaica*"—250 acres, surveyed May 18, 1666, for John Richardson.

"*Hull's Neck*"—400 acres, surveyed April 24, 1666, for Edward Hull.

"*Rumley Marsh*"—300 acres, surveyed September 18, 1666, for Edward Roe.

"*Chance*"—100 acres, surveyed March 12, 1666, for Arthur Emory.

"*Poplar Hill*"—200 acres, surveyed July 10, 1667, for Henry Hawkins.

"*Rest Content*"—100 acres, surveyed August 26, ——, for William Godwin.

"*Waterton*"—660 acres, surveyed June 1, 1668, for William Shirt.

"*Harwood's Lyon*"—600 acres, surveyed September 28, 1666, for Philip Stevenson.

"*Cabbin Creek*"—500 acres, surveyed October 9, 1672, for John Morgan.

"*Normanton*"—800 acres, surveyed December 8, 1673, for George Cowley.

"*Frankford's St. Michael*"—616 acres, surveyed December 15, 1673, for Thomas Lacy.

"*Timothy's Lott*"—300 acres, surveyed July 17, 1676, for Timothy Goodridge.

"*Troth's Fortune*"—400 acres, surveyed August 15, 1676, for William Troth.

"*Swampstick*"—100 acres, surveyed May 13, 1673, for Thomas Martin.

"*Fishburn's Neglect*"—130 acres, surveyed February 4, 1677, for John Whittington.

"*Poplar Neck*"—400 acres, surveyed August 5, 1680, for William Berry.

"*Sommerly*"—300 acres, surveyed June 15, 1679, for James Barber.

"*Buckby*"—400 acres, surveyed June 24, 1679, for John Wootters.

"*Buckingham*"—300 acres, surveyed June 23, 1679, for George Robins.

"*Lambeth*"—200 acres, surveyed February 20, 1679, for Henry Costin.

"*Coventry*"—300 acres, surveyed February 22, 1679, for John Newman.

"*Dixon's Lott*"—100 acres, surveyed May 26, 1681, for William Dixon.

"*Anketill*"—500 acres, surveyed May 23, 1681, for Frances Anketill.

"*Dudley's Choice*"—200 acres, surveyed July 29, 1681, for Richard Dudley.

"*The Parsonage Addition*"—100 acres, surveyed August 10, 1681, for Rev. James Clayland.

"*Joseph's Lott*"—100 acres, surveyed September 17, 1681, for Joseph Withgott.

"*Security*"—200 acres, surveyed April 17, 1687, for William Combs.

"*Scarborough*"—1400 acres, surveyed June 6, 1672, for William Corwin.

"*Lord's Gift*"—450 acres, surveyed May 20, 1682, for Thomas Hutchinson.

"*Cook's Hope*"—1000 acres, surveyed August 23, 1659, for Miles Cook.

"*Walker's Tooth*"—147 acres, surveyed July 19, 1694, for Daniel Walker.

"*Huntington*"—510 acres, surveyed December 28, 1694, for Michael Russell.

"*Henrietta Maria's Purchase*"—412 acres, surveyed May 5, 1696, for Henrietta Maria Lloyd.

"*Shridlay's Fortune*"—391 acres, surveyed August 28, 1694, for Robert Grundy.

"*Come Whitton*"—200 acres, surveyed January 4, 1694, for William Dickinson.

"*Lowe's Rambles*"—1440 acres, surveyed May 28, 1696, for Nicholas Lowe.

"*Hemsley's Arcadia*"—1030 acres, surveyed December 12, 1688, for William Hemsley.

"*Bloomsbury*"—200 acres, surveyed February 28, 1686, for George Hurlock.

"*Champenham*"—450 acres, surveyed September 20, 1695, for Robert Bishop.

"*Sherwood's Neck*"—268 acres, surveyed October 8, 1713, for Philip Sherwood.

"*Sayer's Forrest*"—2250 acres, patented to Major Peter Sayer.

"*Caerdiffe*"—100 acres, surveyed June 6, 1666; "*Cuba*," 150 acres, surveyed June 6, 1670; "*Willenbrough*," 200 acres, surveyed June 9, 1671; "*Hatfield Edition*," 250 acres, surveyed March 11, 1672; "*Jamaica*," 50 acres, surveyed March 11, 1672, for John Richardson in Talbot County.

Dorchester County

"*Bentley*"—300 acres, surveyed July 7, 1659, for Richard Bentley.

"*Chaplin's Holme*"—300 acres, surveyed July 1, 1659, for William Chaplin.

"*Hogepoint Neck*"—100 acres, surveyed April 16, 1662, for Michael Brooks.

"*Jordan's Point*"—1000 acres, surveyed April 28, 1662, for Thomas Jordan.

"*Preston*"—500 acres, surveyed December 29, 1662, for Richard Preston.

"*Sharp's Point*"—200 acres, surveyed December 29, 1662, for Peter Sharp.

"*Cedar Point*"—200 acres, surveyed December 10, 1662, for John Gary.

"*Eaton's Point*"—100 acres, surveyed June 16, 1663, for James Eaton.

"*Huntington*"—100 acres, surveyed March 4, 1663, for John Edmonson.

"*Humphreys Fortune*"—200 acres, surveyed May 20, 1663, for Robert Humphreys.

"*Clifton*"—200 acres, surveyed August 20, 1663, for William Dorrington.

"*Armstrong's Folly*"—400 acres, surveyed December 22, 1663, for Francis Armstrong.

"*Barren Island*"—700 acres, surveyed 1664, for Richard Preston.

"*Smith's Delight*"—1000 acres, surveyed April, 1664, for William Smith.

"*Goodridge Choice*"—1000 acres, surveyed March 12, 1664, for Timothy Goodridge.

"*Stewards Place*"—350 acres, patented August 15, 1665, for John Steward.

"*Cold Spring*"—200 acres, surveyed April 16, 1664, for Robert Harwood.

"*John's Garden*"—300 acres, surveyed May 4, 1664, for Robert Dixon.

"*Skillington's Right*"—300 acres, surveyed March 4, 1663, for Thomas Skillington.

"*Richardson's Purchase*"—500 acres, surveyed 1663, for George Richardson.

"*Phillipsburg*"—2000 acres, surveyed March 25, 1670, for Philip Calvert.

"*Traverse Lott*"—300 acres, surveyed January 17, 1669, for William Traverse.

"*Billingsleys Chance*"—300 acres, surveyed January 18, 1669, for Thomas Billingsley.

"*Darley*"—500 acres, surveyed February 25, 1669, for John Eason.

"*Weston*"—300 acres, surveyed April 22, 1670, for Howell Powell.

"*Hackaday*"—600 acres, surveyed April 22, 1670, for John Pitt.

"*Coney Warren*"—250 acres, surveyed February, 1669, for Henry Trippe.

"*Hopkins Lott*"—150 acres, surveyed January 20, 1669, for William Hopkins.

"*Brambles Desire*"—100 acres, surveyed March 29, 1670, for Thomas Bramble.

"*Skinner's Choice*"—250 acres, surveyed March 31, 1670, for Thomas Skinner.

"*Taylor's Chance*"—500 acres, surveyed about 1670, for Henry Beckwith.

"*Doncaster*"—700 acres, surveyed January 5, 1670, for Richard Holland.

"*Hartford*"—550 acres, surveyed September 30, 1670, for William Jones.

"*Thompson's Island*"—500 acres, surveyed August 23, 1672, for George Thompson.

"*Northampton*"—100 acres, surveyed May 18, 1672, for Richard Kendall.

"*Stapleford's Desire*"—200 acres, surveyed March 14, 1672, for Raymond Stapleford.

"*Moors Choice*"—300 acres, surveyed March 26, 1671, for Daniel Moor.

"*Rehoboth*"—2350 acres, surveyed March 31, 1673, for John Lee.

"*Wandsworth*"—400 acres, surveyed April 22, 1673, for Charles Hutchins.

"*Windsor*"—350 acres, surveyed October 16, 1673, for Robert Collier.

"*Bartholmews Neck*"—1855 acres, surveyed September 9, 1673, for Bartholomew Ennalls.

"*John's Desire*"—100 acres, surveyed May 8, 1672, for John Mackeel.

"*Timber Neck*"—100 acres, surveyed November 14, 1673, for Edmond Brannock.

"*Bradley's Lott*"—100 acres, surveyed September 3, 1674, for Henry Bradley.

"*John's Delight*"—200 acres, surveyed September 3, 1674, for John Tench.

"*Dawson's Chance*"—300 acres, surveyed February 16, 1673, for Anthony Dawson.

"*The Grove*"—150 acres, surveyed January 10, 1671, for Thomas Pattison.

"*Canterbury*"—225 acres, surveyed May 15, 1674, for William Ford.

"*Bath*"—1010 acres, surveyed August 14, 1675, for Thomas Taylor.

"*Coquericus Fields*"—600 acres, surveyed June 16, 1673, for Thomas Phillips.

"*Rawlins Range*"—200 acres, surveyed June 8, 1671, for John Rawlins.

"*Curtesy*"—500 acres, surveyed March 31, 1673, for John White.

"*Robson's Lott*"—300 acres, surveyed January 14, 1679, for William Robson.

"*Holbourn*"—1000 acres, surveyed August 28, 1679, for Walter Dickenson.

"*Antonine*"—800 acres, surveyed August 13, 1659, for Anthony Le Compt.

"*Richardson's Gift*"—1150 acres, surveyed November 23, 1663, for George Richardson.

"*Lynns Park*"—2000 acres, surveyed August 9, 1688, for Philip Lyne.

"*Taylor's Promise*"—1000 acres, surveyed December 20, 1688, for Jacob Lookerman.

"*Retaliation*"—940 acres, surveyed September 5, 1700, for Hugh Eccleston.

"*Bettys Delight*"—500 acres, surveyed June 29, 1685, for John Woodward.

"*Beaver Neck*"—485 acres, surveyed September 22, 1696, for Francis Howard.

"*Maiden Forest*"—500 acres, surveyed October 29, 1684, for Mary Bateman.

"*Hicks Fields*"—430 acres, surveyed December 5, 1701, for Thomas Hicks.

"*Weston*"—1606 acres, surveyed January 20, 1713, for John Ryder.

"*Dossey's Chance*"—230 acres, surveyed April 29, 1682, for William Dossey.

"*The End of Controversy*"—200 acres, surveyed May 26, 1669, for Robert Harwood—183 acres possessed by William Darcey.

"*Fishing Point*"—200 acres, surveyed April 22, 1664, for William Smith.

"*John's Point*"—200 acres, surveyed November 24, 1665, for John Hodson.

"*Edmondson's Reserve*"—1050 acres, surveyed August 21, 1665, for John Edmondson.

"*Hog Island*"—300 acres, surveyed March 10, 1665, for Thomas Powell.

"*Alexander's Place*"—650 acres, surveyed April 13, 1664, for Henry Ozburn.

"*Deale's Right*"—100 acres, surveyed May 24, 1666, for David Deale.

"*Keen's Neck*"—250 acres, surveyed May 30, 1668, for Richard Keen.

"*Hooper's Lott*"—350 acres, surveyed September 15, 1669, for Henry Hooper.

"*Town Neck*"—650 acres, surveyed January 21, 1669, for Richard Hooper.

"*Richardson's Choice*"—532 acres, surveyed November 12, 1679; "*Willenborough*," 982 acres, surveyed November 14, 1678; "*Hunting Fields*," 500 acres, surveyed July 5, 1662; "*Goodrich's Choice*," 300 acres, surveyed ————; "*Edmondson's Orchard*," 200 acres, surveyed 4th May, 1664, for John Richardson in Dorchester County.

"*Richardson's Clifts*"—1150 acres, surveyed November 23, 1663; "*Richardson's Purchase*," 500 acres for George Richardson in Dorchester County.

CHAPTER LXIV

THE SONS OF LIBERTY

The Sons of Liberty, the first of all patriotic societies founded in American, is particularly interesting to us because of the connection of Governor Warfield's name with the initiative act toward independence in Maryland. The passage of the Stamp Act resulted in the organization of the Sons of Liberty in New York City, with local societies in every colony and a representative in London by name of Nicholas Ray.

Colonel Barre, a member of the English Parliament, made a strong speech advocating the freedom of the colonies, in which he designated their inhabitants as "these sons of liberty." The name struck the popular fancy and was at once adopted by the Whig party in America.

In a letter dated Philadelphia, February 15, 1766, Colonel William Bradford, addressing the New York Sons of Liberty, says: "Our Body in this city is not declared numerous, as unfortunate dissensions in Provincial politics keep us rather a divided people. But when the Grand Cause calls on us you may be assured we shall universally stand forth and appear what we really are—Sons of Liberty—in Philadelphia."

A week after the date of this letter, on February 24, according to the report at that time, "a considerable number of the principal Gentlemen of Baltimore County met at the Market House in Baltimore Town and formed themselves into a society for the maintenance of order and

Protection of American Liberty, by the name of the Sons of Liberty, and resolved to meet at Annapolis on Friday last to oblige the several officers there to open their respective offices and proceed to Business as usual without stamped paper. And that the Society and application might be still the more respectable, the Sons of Liberty in Baltimore gave the most speedy notice to Gentlemen of the neighboring Counties to form themselves into the like Societies and co-operate with them in this so laudable work.

"Saturday Last a much greater number of the Sons of Liberty than could be expected from the shortness of the notice met by adjournment at the Court House in Annapolis. Those of Baltimore and Anne Arundel Counties were present personally, and those of Kent were represented by their Deputy; and after hearing different proposals and Debating thereon with great Decency, Coolness and order, *Resolved*, To make a written application to the Chief Justice of the Provincial Court, the Secretary and Commissary-General and Judge of his Lordship's Land Office to open their respective offices and proceed as usual in the execution of their duties on the 31st of March instant, or sooner, if a majority of the Supreme Courts of the Northern Governments should proceed in Business before that time. And therein to propose 'That if the above officers proceed agreeable to the Request that then an Indemnification be signed by the Sons of Liberty and as many others as could be induced thereto, and that the respective officers be requested to give an Answer in writing under their hands to that Proposition.' A committee having been ordered to deliver the Requisition of the Sons of Liberty to the above mentioned Gentlemen, afterwards returned and reported the verbal answer of the Chief Justice of the Provincial Court and Doctor Steuart, one of the Judges of the Land Office, and communicated the written Answer of the Secretary to this effect, That if the Clerk of the Provincial Court would receive his Directions to act as the Judges should in their Judicial Capacity at the next court order him as their Minister; but before the meeting of the Provincial Court he could not undertake to give Directions to the Clerk to issue Process, Whatever the Determination of the Majority of the Northern Colonies might be whose Courts might sit before ours.

"The Commissary-General not being in town, the Committee could not deliver the Requisition to him. The Verbal Answers were of the Chief Justice, and that of one of the Judges of the Land Office were then taken under consideration, and in Consequence of the order of the Sons of Liberty the Committee again waited on those Gentlemen, and having informed them 'That their Refusal to give their Answers in writing to the Proposition aforesaid was deemed a great indignity offered to the Sons of Liberty, and that their Answers in writing were instantly expected.' They received and reported the following Answers:

"Gentleman—In answer to your application of this day, my connections and circumstances speak my attachment to the liberty of the subjects here. The carrying on Business at the adjourned Provincial Court will, as to myself, depend on the opinion I have yet to form. I shall meet my brethren on the Day to which the court is adjourned, and be governed by those Reasons and Principles which ought to actuate every man who sits in stations similar to that which is filled by your Humble Servant.

"March 1, 1766. "JOHN BRICE."

"A proposition being this Day given in to me, requesting that Business should be done in the Land office of this Province as usual, to which I answered, that the Land office was open and the Records thereof subject to the Perusal of all persons who have occasion to make searches; and that copies of the Records, authenticated by the Register, should be made out to any person so applying, paying the usual fees; and as I apprehend the sale of the Lord Proprietary's Lands are matters of Private concern, respecting his own interest, he may grant warrants, or refuse to grant them as he shall think Proper. Given under my hand at Annapolis this first day of March, 1766.
"GEORGE STEUART."

"To the Sons of Liberty of Baltimore, Anne Arundel and Kent Counties.

"After reading of which answers it was ordered that

copies of the proceedings be transmitted to the several counties and their Sons of Liberty invited to enter into the like associations, and a number, not less than 12 from each county, are requested to attend at Annapolis on the 31st instant to see the event of, or repeat, if necessary, the applications already made."

We know that Dr. Charles Alexander Warfield, a prominent member of the Whig Club, was the daring leader of the Sons of Liberty in Anne Arundel County, and while most of the names have been suppressed, a few have been gleaned from stray sources. Among those who were Baltimore Sons of Liberty are the following: Aaron Levington, S. Hollingsworth, John McLane, Caleb Hall, Michael Allen, John Dever, Isaac Grist, David Shields, William Lux, George Wells, George Lindenberger, David Rusk, Richard Moale, William Baker, Hercules Courtney, William Wilson, R. Adair, Daniel Bowley, William Aisquith, E. Winters, George Leverly, William Spear, Archibald Buchanan, James Cox, Erasmus Uhler, Gerard Hopkins, William Clemm, John Sterrett, Benjamin Griffith, Melchoir Keener, James Sterrett, William Lyon, George Patton, George Duvall, James Calhoun and Cyprian Wells.

"PEGGY STEWART HOUSE," HOME OF ANTHONY STEWART, ANNAPOLIS, MD.

CHAPTER LXV

THE BURNING OF THE "PEGGY STEWART"

THE time has come when Maryland must write her own history, for it is evident that the same spirit which asserts that Maryland had no Colonial aristocracy has ignored that she had any part in the molding of our national history.

The masquerading Boston tea party has well nigh extinguished Maryland's glorious bonfire off Windmill Point on October 19, 1774.

New England historians claim that opposition to the measures of the British Ministry began there.

The student of Maryland history knows that the burning of the *Peggy Stewart* was the culmination of Maryland's opposition to England's oppression, which had been fought since the year 1638, when the Assembly declared it would pass only laws of its own making.

Again in 1758-60 the Maryland Assembly positively declined to make an appropriation for the support of the King's army after the capture of Fort Duquesne, unless a proportionate share of the tax was laid on the lands and revenues of the Proprietary. This demand in equity had a just basis in the fact that "he who had most at stake, who conferred no personal benefit whatever on the colony, neither led its troops nor guided its councils, did not even as its feudal head resist on its behalf all attempts at aggression in Parliament, but merely drew from it his opulent revenues, should bear a reasonable share of the common burden, and this was so apparent that they were resolved to insist upon it." Maryland was thus the first American colony to resist the encroachments of power, to offer a bold front to the "omnipotence of Parliament and to insist that legislation should be on principles of equity and justice, as well as precedent and prerogative."

Governor Sharpe, finding the Assembly inflexible in its determination not to yield, prorogued it on the 17th of April until the 6th of July following. In his speech he said, among other things: "After you have explicitly resolved to admit of no propositions to provide for his Majesty's service upon any other plan, etc., etc., I have no glimmering hope, however expressive of zeal your professions have been." Five times the House had refused to pass any but the bill of its own drawing. Maryland in resisting her royal governor and the dictates of Parliament entered upon the pathway to final independence.

That Maryland has always been ready to exhibit the spirit of friendship to the North was shown in the handsome contribution of £2004 sent to Boston after the great fire of 1760. And when, a little later, the port of Boston was closed as a result of the "tea party," Maryland protested against this act of Parliament and sent assistance to the relief of that city.

In view of the recent admission of some Maryland college students lately that they knew "nothing of *Peggy Stewart* or who or what she was," it will be pardonable for the "Side-Lights" to illumine this page of Maryland history and to claim for our patriotic forbears all the recognition due them.

The treaty signed at Paris on February 10, 1763, ended the fight for supremacy between England and France and caused Great Britain to take first rank among the powers of Europe. While her large territorial accessions gained through her military prowess greatly increased her influence, her treasury was depleted, and in the consciousness of her strength she determined to make the colonies which had so nobly served her, giving their lives and wealth to her service in the French and Indian wars, refill her coffers at the expense of their own progress.

The colonists had therefore hardly ceased their rejoicing over the prospect of freedom from pillage and murder by the Indians, before the lords of the King's treasury—Grenville, North and Hunter—at a meeting in Downing Street, London, September 22, 1763, planned a new and crushing burden for the American colonies to shoulder.

At this meeting a minute was adopted directing the secretary, Charles Jenkinson, to write to the commissioners of the stamp duties, to prepare a draft of a bill to be presented to Parliament for extending the stamp duties to the colonies. In obedience to this order, the famous Stamp Act was prepared and submitted to Parliament. It is known that the perpetrators of the bill, expecting it to meet with opposition, withheld it a year "out of tenderness to the colonies." History claims that "Bute thought up the scheme, Jenkinson elaborated it, Grenville demanded it, North supported it and England accepted it," but, what is more to the point—America rejected it.

Maryland was particularly vehement in her opposition to the Stamp Act, the actual passage of which was thus announced in the Annapolis *Gazette*, May 17, 1764:

"Friday evening last, between 9 and 10 o'clock, we had a very smart thundergust, which struck a house in one part of our town and a tree in another. But we were more thunderstruck last Monday on the arrival of Captain Joseph Richardson in the ship *Pitt* in six weeks from the Downs, with a certain account of the Stamp Act being absolutely passed."

It was a year before a stamp distributor was appointed in Maryland, but upon his arrival from London he met with such a warm reception that he had to flee to New York. The stamped paper was not allowed to be landed in the absence of the legal agent, and as his house had been demolished and himself burnt in effigy, the cause of resentment remained on shipboard. The opposition and excitement caused by this infringement upon their liberty resulted in the open revolt of the people and a demand that the court at Annapolis should repudiate it. This was accordingly done, and the Stamp Act rendered forever null and void in Maryland. The act reads as follows: "It is by the court here ordered that the clerk of this court from henceforth issue all manner of process, file all pleadings, give copies and transact all business whatsoever in his office for which application shall be made to him by any inhabitant of this province as usual without stamped paper." The repeal of the Stamp Act, July, 1766, through the influence of William Pitt, the Right Honorable Earl of Chatham, who advocated its repeal so warmly as to forever win the love of Americans, caused great rejoicing throughout the colonies, and at Annapolis toasts were drunk to the King, cannon fired and general rejoicing reigned.

In the year 1766 the House of Delegates decreed that a marble statue of Chatham be erected in Annapolis, as a lasting testimony of the gratitude of the freemen of Maryland. Maryland's resistance to taxation was not only founded upon the principle of no taxation without repre-

MRS. ANTHONY STEWART, MOTHER OF PEGGY STEWART

Shown through the courtesy of Mr. J. Charles Brogden

sentation, but upon her charter rights from King Charles I, in which he emphatically declares that "we, our heirs and successors shall at no time hereafter set or make, or cause to be set, any imposition, custom or taxation, rate or contribution whatsoever in or upon the dwellers and inhabitants of the aforesaid province for their lands, tenements, goods or chattels within the said province, or to be laden and unladen within any ports or harbors of said province."

"This was the Marylander's birthright as it was of no other colonist, and he would not forego it. Resolutions drawn up in the Assembly were based absolutely upon their chartered rights, closing with the resolution, "that it is the unanimous opinion of this House that the representatives of the freemen of this province in their legislative capacity, together with the other part of the Legislature, have the sole right to lay taxes and impositions on the inhabitants of this province or their property and effects, and that the laying, imposing, levying or collecting any tax on or from the inhabitants of Maryland under color of any other authority is unconstitutional and a direct violation of the rights of the freemen of this province."

Having so declared themselves, the members of the Assembly took "a short recess of a few weeks."

Passing over the nine intervening years, in which a spirit of unrest agitated the hearts and minds of Marylanders, we come to the morning of October 14, 1774, when, according to the Custom-House entry, the brig *Peggy Stewart* arrived at Annapolis. We find that "the *Peggy Stewart* was square stern, of 50 tons burden and manned by six men. She was built in Maryland in the year 1771 and registered at Patuxent April 13, 1773."

Her owners were Messrs. Anthony Stewart, William James, and Joseph Williams. Her master was Richard Jackson.

The cargo on the date above mentioned consisted of "17 cockets of European East India goods" and fifty-three servants from London, from which port she sailed July 23, 1774.

Under the innocent entry of the "17 cockets of East India goods," the owners of the "detestable weed" hoped to smuggle that tea into the province. This was not to be, even though "Tom Williams, who was in England, had it put up in blankets" and put it on the ship without the captain's knowledge.

In a letter of John Galloway to his father, Samuel Galloway, of Tulip Hill, Anne Arundel County, published in the *Pennsylvania Historical Magazine*, a full and particularly interesting account of the *Peggy Stewart* affair is given. In this he says:

"*Honored Sir*—I am now set down to give you an account as well as in my power of yesterday's transactions of the committee of the county and the mob assembled at Annapolis, relative to the 17 chests of tea imported by Thomas Williams and Company and the *Peggy Stewart*.

"It seems by Captain Jackson's, commander of the brig, affidavit, he refused Kelly, Lot and Company to bring any tea to America in his vessel, and that Mr. Thomas Williams, who was then in London, without his knowledge put 17 chests on board, and that he did not discover it till at sea.

"When he arrived at Annapolis, Mr. Anthony Stewart ordered him to enter his vessel and all his cargo except the Tea, but the custom-house officer would not admit him to a partial entry.

"Mr. Stewart having not considered the matter well and to save his vessel from being libeled went himself and entered the whole cargo and paid the duty on the Tea.

"In Thursday's paper there was an advertisement for a meeting of the county as yesterday, but on Friday evening, when it came to be known that the Tea was entered and might, if the owners thought proper, be landed—the committee of Annapolis met, and also on Monday following and the results of their meeting was that the Tea should be burnt, but they deferred doing it till the County Committee had a meeting, which was on yesterday.

"After the Gentlemen of the County Committee had met and determined what should be done they called the inhabitants together to Mr. Jacques' porch and Mr. T. Hammond, as one of the Committee, stood forth and made a speech to the people (to be sure it was the most shocking one I ever heard) and read the concessions that Messrs. Stewart and Williams were to make publickly to the people, for the infringements they had made on the Liberty of the People. After this was over Mr. Charles B. Carroll desired to know the sense of the gentlemen in regard to what was to be done with the Tea, and it was the unanimous opinion of all present that it should be burnt.

"The committee then ordered the Tea from on board the brigg, but some of the mob called out that it should not come on shore, that the vessel should also share the same fate. Matters now began to run very high and the people to get warm, some of the gentlemen from Elk Ridge and Baltimore Town insisted on burning the vessel. Mr. Carroll then went and consulted Mr. Dick, who immediately consented to the destroying of the vessel. Mr. Dick was fearful that if they did not give up the vessel that it would be attended with worse consequences to Mr. Stewart, as the mob had threatened to lay violent hands on him. Mr. Carroll then declared to the people that Tea and vessell should both be burnt. Mr. Quyn then stood forth and said it was not the sense of the majority of the people that the vessel should be destroyed and made a motion, which was seconded, that there should be a vote on the question.

"We had a vote on it and a majority of seven-eighths of the people, still the few that was for destroying the Brigg, was clamorous and insinuated that if it was not done they would prejudice Mr. Stewart more than if the vessell was burnt.

"The committee then, with the consent of Mr. Dick, declared that the vessell and Tea should be burnt. Then Doctor Warfield (a youth that practiced under Doctor Thompson at the Ridge for some time) made a motion that the gentlemen should make their concessions on their knees, there was a vote on it in favor of the gentlemen, they then came and read their concessions to the Publick and then Mr. Stewart went on board of his vessell and set fire to her with his own hands, and she was burning when I left.

"[Signed]   JOHN GALLOWAY."

This is the nearest we have ever got to this thrilling incident in Maryland, which remains unchronicled in the various United States histories, and the encyclopedia of United States history, of which the editor was a John Hopkins man.

The account of the affair, which appeared in the *Maryland Gazette* on October 20, 1774, is familiar to all, but

ANTHONY STEWART, OWNER OF THE BRIG THE PEGGY STEWART

Shown through the courtesy of Mr. J. Charles Brogden

the letter above quoted comes under the head of unfamiliar records, as does also one from Mr. Thomas Ringgold, of Chestertown, the son-in-law of Mr. Samuel Galloway, who concludes his account with this comment—"from the whole of Mr. Stewart's conduct I have no doubt but he has premeditated the exploit to endear himself to the ministry, and I am glad the people have shown so much spirit."

The concessions publicly made by the owner of the vessel and tea were as follows:

"We, James Williams, Joseph Williams and Anthony Stewart, do severally acknowledge that we have committed a most daring insult and act of the most pernicious tendency to the liberties of America; we, the said Williamses, in importing the tea, and said Stewart in paying the duty thereon, and thereby deservedly incurred the displeasure of the people now convened and all others interested in the preservation of the constitutional rights and liberties of North America, do ask pardon for the same, and we solemnly declare for the future that we never will infringe any resolution formed by the people for the salvation of their rights, nor will we do any act that may be injurious to the liberties of the people; and to show our desire of living in amity with the friends to America we do request this meeting, or as many choose to attend, to be present at any place where the people shall appoint, and we will there commit to the flames, or otherwise destroy, as the people may choose, the detestable article which has been the cause of this our misconduct.

ANTHONY STEWART,
JOSEPH WILLIAMS,
JAMES WILLIAMS."

After which Mr. Stewart and Messrs. James and Joseph Williams, owners of the tea, went on board the vessel, with her sails and colors flying and voluntarily set fire to the tea, and in a few hours the whole cargo, together with the vessel, was consumed in the presence of a great number of spectators."

The "old Mr. Dick" referred to in John Galloway's letter, who showed such anxiety about Anthony Stewart's personal safety, was the father of Mrs. Anthony Stewart, who at the time of the thrilling incident was ill, which no doubt accounts for her father's solicitude. Peggy Stewart, for whom the brig was named, was a small girl in pinafores at the date of its destruction.

Anthony Stewart, in July, 1783, was in New York and was one of fifty-one persons who petitioned for grants of land in Nova Scotia. It is not surprising that this son of James Stewart, one of his Majesty's attorneys in his Courts of Exchequer in Scotland, should prefer to hold his allegiance to the crown to which his father was so closely allied.

CHAPTER LXVI

MARYLAND'S DECLARATION OF INDEPENDENCE

IN THE stirring events which led up to the Declaration of Independence and to the final signing of the Articles of Confederation, Maryland filled a conspicuous and important place.

It has been said that Maryland was slow in voting for independence, but her emphatic resistance of all attempts toward an infringement of her rights and liberties are direct contradictions to any suggestion of a want of patriotism. In open day her Sons of Liberty had burned the *Peggy Stewart* and put the tax collector to flight more than two years before the Declaration of Independence. As a result of Governor Eden's proclamation regarding fees he was practically run out of the province, although conducted to his outbound ship with all the dignity due his office and the high esteem in which he was personally held by the men who were resenting England's tyranny. A year before the final break the Convention of Maryland subscribed to the Declaration of the Association of Freemen, and public meetings were held in the counties and resolutions adopted and representative citizens named as committees of correspondence and observation to carry the resolutions of the convention into effect.

The Proclamation of the Freemen of Maryland, which was signed July 26, 1775, reads as follows:

"The long premeditated and now avowed design of the British Government to raise revenue from the property of the colonies without their consent, on the gift, grant and disposition of the Commons of Great Britain; the arbitrary and vindictive statutes passed under color of punishing a riot, to subdue by military force and by famine the Massachusetts Bay; the unlimited power assumed by Parliament to alter the charter of that Province and the constitution of all the colonies, thereby destroying the essential securities of the lives, liberties and properties of the colonists; the commencement of hostilities by the Ministerial forces, and the cruel prosecution of the war against the people of Massachusetts Bay, followed by General Gage's proclamation declaring almost the whole of the inhabitants of the United Colonies, by name or description, rebels and traitors, are sufficient cause to arm a free people in defense of their liberty and to justify resistance, no longer dictated by prudence merely, but by necessity, and leave no alternative but base submission or manly opposition to uncontrollable tyranny. The Congress chose the latter, and for the express purpose of securing and defending the United Colonies and preserving them in safety against all attempts to carry the above mentioned acts into execution by force of arms.

"*Resolved*, That the said colonies be put into a state of defense, and now support, at the joint expense, an army to restrain the further violence and repel the future attacks of a disappointed and exasperated enemy.

"We, therefore, inhabitants of the Province of Maryland, firmly persuaded that it is necessary and justifiable to repel force by force, do approve of the opposition by arms to the British troops employed to enforce obedience to the late acts and statutes of the British Parliament for raising revenue in America, and altering and changing the

SAMUEL CHASE, SIGNER OF THE DECLARATION OF
INDEPENDENCE

*After Peale Portrait in the State House, Annapolis, Maryland.
From the Author's Collection*

Charter and Constitution of Massachusetts Bay, and for destroying the essential securities for the lives, liberties and properties of the subjects in the United Colonies. And we do unite and associate as one land, and firmly and solemnly engage and pledge ourselves to each other and to America that we will to the utmost of our power promote and support the present opposition, carrying on as well by arms as by the Contimental Association restraining our commerce.

"And as in these times of public danger and until a reconciliation with Great Britain on constitutional principles is affected (an event we most ardently wish may soon take place) the energy of government may be greatly impaired, so that even zeal unrestrained may be productive of anarchy and confusion, we do in like manner unite, associate and solemnly engage in maintenance of good order and the public peace, to support the civil power in the due execution of the laws so far as may be consistent with the present plan of opposition, and to defend with our utmost power all persons from every species of outrage to themselves or their property, and to prevent any punishment from being inflicted on any offenders other than such as shall be adjudged by the civil magistrate, the Continental Congress, our Convention, Council of Safety or Committee of Observation.

Signed by: Mat. Tilghman, John Reeder, Jr., Richard Barnes, Jno. Jordan, Jn. V. Thomas, W. Smallwood, Danl. Jenifer, R. Hooe, J. H. Stone, Will Harrison, S. Hanson of Saml., Jno. Dent, Edwd. Gantt, Samuel Chew, Edwd. Reynolds, Benj. Marshall, Josias Beall, Robt. Tyler, Thos. Contee, Joseph Sim, Turbutt Wright, Ja. Tilghman of Annapolis, Th. Wright, Ja. Hollyday, R. T. Earle.

Sol. Wright, Jas. Lloyd Chamberlaine, Ni. Thomas, Edw. Lloyd, Peregrine Tilghman, Wm. Hindman, R. Tilghman, Jun., Jams ——?, —— Balye, Benj. Hall, John Contee, W. Bowie, O. Sprigg, Jos. Beall, Thos. Gantt, Jr., Walter Bowie, David Craufurd, Stephen West, Tho. Sim Lee, —— Rogers, Samuel Chase, Ths. Johnson Junr, Brice John Worthington, Rezin Hammond, J. Hall, William Paca, Matthias Hammond, Chas. Crowley, Charles Carroll of Carrollton, Ephraim Howard, (A. A. Co.), Robert Goldsborough, Henry Hooper, James Murray, Thos. Ennalls, Nath. Potter, Will. Richardson, Richd. Mason, Joshua Clarke, Peter Adams, John Stevens, Wm. Hooper, Henry Dickinson, Wm. Waters, Wm. Molleston, George Dashiell, John Stewart, John Waters, Gustavus Scott, H. Griffith, W. Sprigg Wootton, Rich. Brooke, John Hanson, Jr., Joseph Chapline, Thos. Cramphin, Jr., Upton Sheridan, Benj. Nicholson, Wm. Buchanan, Jo. H'y Chase, John Cratock, Thomas Harrison, Darby Lux, John Moale, Robert Alexander, Thomas Ridgely, son of Wm., Saml. Handy, Zadock Purnell, Wm. Morris, Thos. Stone, Benj. Edw. Hall, Thos. Mond, Richd. Dallam, Ignatius Wheeler, Jr., Wm. Webb, John Veazey, Jr., Jno. D. Thompson, John Cox, Peter Lawson, Nat. Ramsey, William Turner, Chas. Rumsey, Wm. Ringgold, Jr., Thos. Smith, Jos. Earle, Th. B. Hands, Thos. Ringgold, J. Nicholson, Jr.

Public meetings were held in every county, and resolutions adopted and prominent citizens named as committees of correspondence and observation to carry the resolutions of the convention into effect.

In the same month Eddis, in a letter written from Maryland to friends in England, speaking of the state of affairs here declares: "Government is now almost totally annihilated and power transferred to the multitude. Speeches become dangerous, letters are intercepted, confidence betrayed, and every measure evidently tends to the most fatal extremities; the sword is drawn, and without some providential change of measures the blood of thousands will be shed in this unnatural contest. The inhabitants of this province are incorporated under military regulations and apply the greater part of their time to the different branches of discipline. In Annapolis there are two completed companies, in Baltimore seven and in every district of this province the majority of the people are actually under arms; almost every hat is decorated with a cockade, and the churlish drum and fife are the only music of the times."

It is with a feeling of State pride that we recall that Maryland proposed the Continental Congress, selected Philadelphia as its place of meeting, fixed the time as September (1774) and chose the first delegates. These were William Paca, Robert Goldsborough, Samuel Chase, Matthew Tilghman and Thomas Johnson.

The letter to the Virginia Committee of Correspondence proposing this great Congress was in part as follows:

"To save America from destruction it is our most fervent wish and sanguine hope that your colony has the same disposition and spirit, and that by a general Congress such a plan may be struck out as may effectually accomplish the grand object in view. We are also directed to propose that the general Congress be held at the city of Philadelphia the 20th of September next. The limits of our province and the number of its inhabitants compared with yours afforded an opportunity of collecting our general sense before the sentiments of your colony could be regularly ascertained, and therefore as this province had the first opportunity it has taken the liberty of making the first proposition."

In connection with Maryland's part in the national Declaration of Independence it may not be generally remembered that William Paca, John Rogers and Thomas Stone cast the vote of Maryland on the momentous Fourth of July, 1776, when the Declaration of Independence was formally adopted. This document was not signed, according to the journal of Congress, until nearly a month later.

On the 19th of July a resolution was adopted that the declaration passed on the 4th be fairly engrossed on parchment, with the title and style of "The Unanimous Declaration of the Thirteen United States of America," and that the same, when engrossed, be signed by every member of Congress. From this we learn that there were other members of Congress from Maryland whose names are entitled to be enrolled with those who happened to be present when the document was signed, as the great declaration states that it was "unanimous."

The names of those who actually signed from Maryland were William Paca, Thomas Stone, Samuel Chase and Charles Carroll of Carrollton. But two of these signers were present when it was voted for and adopted July 4, 1776. These were William Paca and Thomas Stone. John Rogers, who cast his vote in the great Congress, was not present on the 2nd of August, when the engrossed copy was presented for the signatures of all present.

Certainly the man who had the courage to vote for the passage of this revolutionary measure should have his name recognized and perpetuated with equal honor as the signers. Other men who were members of the Congress in session at the time of the signing, but whose absence from the meeting in some service of their country were Matthew Tilghman, Thomas Johnson, Jr., and Robert Alexander. Maryland owes some recognition to John Rogers, and the above-named members of the Congress who voted for or signed the great Declaration. The following names of those who signed the Declaration of the Association of Freemen in Somerset and Worcester Counties have never been published, and may be of interest to their descendants. Colonel Charles Challie Long, the distinguished explorer, found the original document, which he has had photographed and presented to the Historical Society. The paper is almost illegible in places, and a few names are irreparably lost.

Those deciphered are as follows: Benton Harris, Joseph Mitchell, T. S. Bishop, Robert Done, H. G. Johnson, Joseph Dashiell, Samuel Handy, Peter Chaille, William Morris, John Done, Josiah Mitchell, John Purnell Robins, N. (Nehemiah) Holland, —— Handy, —— Purnell, —— Purnell, —— Purnell (first names illegible), John Selby, Zodak Purnell, John Postly, John Bowie, Thomas Purnell, William Wise, William Morrill, William Selby, Jr., John Neilie, I. Spence Townsend, N. Marvin, Major Tongood, Levin Handy, Peter White, Levin Blake, John Warren, Peter Hall, James Davis, Samuel Summers, James Jackson, George Downes, Mitchell Downes, John ——, Daniel Farsett, Samuel Wise, John C. Andy, James Quinton, Samuel Truitt, William Gasham, George Roberson, Zadoch Hinman, John Green, Moses Gothery, P. Selby Webster, Webster Smith, James Ayeres.

CHAPTER LXVII

THE RIDE OF LIEUTENANT-COLONEL TENCH TILGHMAN

READ by the author, in the old Senate Chamber, Annapolis, upon the occasion of the unveiling of a bronze tablet to Tench Tilghman, by the Baltimore Chapter D. A. R. Society, June 7, 1906:

The ride of Lieutenant-Colonel Tench Tilghman from Yorktown to the Continental Congress bearing the official news of the surrender of Lord Cornwallis, is a subject worthy of a great painter or of a still greater poet.

But the patriotic women of the Baltimore Chapter Daughters of the American Revolution are willing to wait no longer for these geniuses to arise, but have today immortalized in enduring bronze that gallant ride which "meteor-like through the darkened night of suspense and anxiety left a trail of glory behind it as it proclaimed Victory, Peace and Liberty to the Nation."

Lieutenant-Colonel Tench Tilghman's report of it to General Washington is before us, and with the modesty which was one of his chief charms he gives only the bare facts. His letter to Washington, dated at Philadelphia, October 27, 1781, is as follows:

"Sir: On arriving at the place early Wednesday morning although I lost one whole night's run by the stupidity of the skipper who got over on Tangier shoals, and was a whole day crossing in a calm. The wind left us entirely on Sunday evening thirty miles below Annapolis.

LIEUTENANT-COLONEL TENCH TILGHMAN

Washington's Aide who carried the news of the Surrender at Yorktown. Miniature by Peale

'I found that a letter from Count de Grasse to Governor Lee, dated October 18th, had gone forward to Congress in which the Count informed the Governor that Cornwallis had surrendered.

'This made me the more anxious to reach Philadelphia as I knew that both Congress and the public would be uneasy at not receiving dispatches from you. I was not wrong in my conjecture, for some really began to doubt the matter.

"The fatigue of the journey brought back my intermittent fever with which I have been confined almost ever since I came to town. I will set out for Chestertown as soon as I am well enough. I beg you to be assured that I am with utmost sincerity,

Your Excellency's, etc.,

Tench Tilghman."

Longfellow has made famous the Ride of Paul Revere and there is scarcely a child from Boston to Galveston who does not know that stanza:

> A hurry of hoofs in a village street,
> A shape in the moonlight, a bulk in the dark—
> And beneath from the pebbles in passing a spark
> Struck out by a steed flying fearless and fleet.
> That was all! And yet through the gloom and the light
> The fate of a Nation was riding that night,
> And that spark struck out by that steed in his flight
> Kindled the land into flame with its heat.

But the ride of our gallant young Marylander has been perpetuated in neither song nor story, except by one lesser poet, and for the first time in the history of Maryland, have her representative citizens met to enshrine the memory of that long and perilous ride of Washington's aide-de-camp, who with throbbing feverish temples spent four days carrying the good news which proclaimed us a nation!

"We have heard of his delay on the water, but of the hundred miles ride from Rock Hall he has given no details.

"Having heard at Annapolis that word of the surrender had gone unofficially before him, we can imagine his impetuous haste, as he sprung to the saddle and striking spurs, sped through the familiar highways of old Kent, stopping only when his jaded horse made a change of mount necessary.

"Riding up to a quiet farmhouse it is said he would rap lustily with his riding whip on the door, and shout to the startled inmates, 'Cornwallis is taken, a fresh horse for the Congress.' Consternation being quickly turned to delirious joy, the best hunter in the stables was brought for his use, and up and away Tench Tilghman rode, carrying cheer every mile of the journey, to the mothers and sweethearts of the army at Yorktown.

"It was midnight, says Lossing, when he entered the city. Thomas McKean was the President of the Continental Congress and resided in High Street near Second. Tilghman knocked at his door so vehemently that a watchman was disposed to arrest him as a disturber of the peace. McKean arose, and presently the glad tidings were made known. The watchmen throughout the city proclaimed the hour 'All is well and Cornwallis is taken.'

"In a minute, says Bradley T. Johnson, the whole city was wild. Lights flashed in every window—men, women and children poured into the streets. The State House bell rang out its peal, Liberty throughout all the land to all the inhabitants thereof, and the American nation was born unto the world." Howard Pyle in his verses says:

> And so, as the dawn of that day grew bright
> Was the dawn that followed the dreary night
> Of trouble and woe and gloom and fear
> That broke at last to a morning clear,
> Brought by Tilghman over away
> From Yorktown and Gloucester, far below
> To the South, one hundred and twenty-five years ago.

"But the messenger, spent and consumed with fever, having performed his honored mission faithfully, had no part in the festivities and rejoicing as we have seen, being invalided by the exposure and fatigue of his journey.

"It is particularly fitting that in this Maryland Hall of Fame, the glory of which is its association with Washington, that the first tablet erected should be in memory of this loved aide of the great Commander who chose Lieutenant-Colonel Tench Tilghman, our Maryland hero, for this distinguished service. And it is a matter of pride to us all that he was a son of old Maryland. His distinguished descendants will tell us of how Washington loved and honored him, and it remains for me to remind you that we are honoring Lieutenant-Colonel Tench Tilghman today as the bearer of glad tidings to the nation.

"The tidings, but for which we would have neither name nor country as a people. Maryland should be proud of her part in the peace of the nation. Her illustrious son carried the glorious news of victorious peace:—

"Washington here laid down his sword as an emblem of peace:—

"Here the ratification of the Peace Treaty was signed:

"A glorious record.

"We have the divine authority for saying: 'Beautiful upon the mountain are the feet of them that bringeth glad tidings of peace.'

"Lieutenant-Colonel Tench Tilghman—The Baltimore Chapter Daughters of the American Revolution, bearing in mind the hearts of the women you gladdened in your weary but triumphant ride from Yorktown to the Continental Congress, with loving and patriotic hearts, dedicate this tablet to your memory!"

THE STATE HOUSE ANNAPOLIS, MARYLAND—BUILT 1772

CHAPTER LXVIII

WHERE WASHINGTON RESIGNED HIS COMMISSION

THE events which make the old Senate Chamber at Annapolis a veritable memorial hall were of more than local importance—they were national—and in restoring it to its original form Governor Warfield has not only preserved a spot that should be dear to all Marylanders whose forebears sat in the legislative bodies which molded our State history, but has emphasized the fact that the old Senate Chamber at Annapolis is not second even in interest to Independence Hall, for while the Declaration was signed at Philadelphia, the final act—the ratifying of the Treaty of Peace, a victorious peace with Great Britain, the triumph and ensealing of American Independence—took place in Maryland's Senate Chamber on January 14, 1784.

As this fact has never been emphasized in the histories of the United States, it is well that Maryland should make known her claims to national interest.

It was in the spring of 1783 that the General Assembly of Maryland passed resolutions inviting "the honorable Congress" to make the city of Annapolis its permanent place of residence as more central than any other city or town in the Federal States, and equally convenient to the Delegates to travel there by land or water. The resolutions also included the offer of the "State House and Public Circle to the honorable Congress for their use" and "the buildings and grounds in said city appropriated for the residence of the Governor of this State for the habitation of their President."

The sum of £30,000 specie was also appropriated to the erection of thirteen dwelling houses and other buildings for the residences of the delegates of each of the thirteen Confederate States. These resolutions were presented to Congress by Mr. James McHenry and Mr. Daniel Carroll, and the invitation to remove to Annapolis temporarily was accepted by that distinguished body.

The first official business which was brought before the Congress in the old Senate Chamber at Annapolis was the definite treaty of peace between Great Britain and the United States, signed at Paris on the 3d of September, 1783, and a few months later ratified at Annapolis. Here again it was, on the 23d of December, 1783, that our American hero resigned his commission as commander-in-chief of the victorious army, Congress then being in session in our ancient city to act upon the most momentous events in our national life.

The fact that Washington resigned his command of the American army in Maryland was particularly appropriate, since it was his Maryland friend, Thomas Johnson, who had in Congress on July 15, 1775, nominated Colonel George Washington, of Virginia, to be commander-in-chief of the Continental forces.

There was much ceremony and exchange of formalities upon the resignation of his commission between Congress and General Washington, and the great ball given in his honor by the Assembly in the State House is still talked of by the descendants of the gallant men and lovely women whose presence lent brilliance to the occasion.

Here, in the autumn of 1786, assembled the Convention of Six States to consider measures for maintaining harmonious trade relations between the States, which was the forerunner of the Constitutional Convention of 1787.

That Maryland has not been indifferent to the historic importance of the events which have transpired within these old walls is evident from the several fine paintings which perpetuate them, and which still hang in their rightful places. The most notable of these represents Washington resigning his commission and was painted by order of the General Assembly in 1859.

There are life-size portraits of our four Maryland signers of the Declaration of Independence—Carroll, Chase, Paca and Stone. A Gilbert Stuart of Washington and a portrait of General John Eager Howard are also on the walls. The full-length allegorical portrait of William Pitt (Earl Chatham), which hangs in the ante-chamber of the Senate, was presented to Maryland by Charles Wilson Peale in 1794. This represents Pitt in the dress of a Roman Senator lighting the fire on the altar of liberty and commemorates his brilliant advocacy of the struggling colonies before the English Parliament.

The influence of a chief executive (Governor Edwin Warfield), with a fine appreciation of things historic, has already been widely felt in the stimulus to State pride in Maryland. During his brief administration a State flag has been adopted; the official seal of Cæcilius Calvert correctly emblazoned in a window of the State House; a Public Records Commission appointed and the cornerstone laid for the preservation of the historic relics of Maryland in the restoration of the old Senate Chamber.

Let us hope that the good work will go on until not only the stranger within our gates, but the youth of Maryland may, in visiting Annapolis, find many much-needed object lessons of our State's claims to both local and national historic interest.

CHAPTER LXIX

THE SOCIETY OF THE CINCINNATI IN MARYLAND

The Maryland Society of the Order of the Cincinnati which meets every year at Annapolis claims our interest in the origin of this most venerable patriotic society, founded by the men who performed the services which constitute the eligibility of their descendants to membership. The formation of the State societies was but the widening of the circle which started among the comrades in arms in the cantonments on the banks of the Hudson in May, 1783. The Revolutionary War was over, America was free from the thralldom of Great Britain, and the men who had given the best years of their lives in the struggle for independence were now to go back to their ordinary vocations of life and to resume their places as private citizens.

But after offering up their lives, their wealth and their time to secure their country's independence, these men were not willing to break ranks without pledging their future zeal in upholding the principles for which they had bled. The country was free, but its government was chaotic, and therefore it seems particularly appropriate that the officers of the great American Army should before separating pledge themselves to unite in "an incessant attention to preserve inviolate those exalted rights and liberties of human nature for which they have fought and bled and without which the high rank of a rational being is a curse instead of a blessing."

It was on the 13th of May, 1783, that the convention of Continental officers met and organized themselves into the Society of the Cincinnati. Major-General Baron von Steuben presided over the convention, and some have given him the credit of having originated the idea; but the fact that General Henry Knox had in a conversation with Adams and Lee expressed a wish to transmit to his descendants some badge as proof of his having defended their liberties, inclines us to believe that it sprang from the American heart and was not a desire for decorations either, despite John Adams' piercing comments upon what he termed a "French blessing."

A paper dated West Point, April 15, 1783, written by General Knox, still preserved, is designated "a rough draft of a society to be formed by the American officers and to be called the Cincinnati."

It was at the headquarters of Baron von Steuben at Newburg-on-the-Hudson that this society was formed, among other things to perpetuate the attachments formed during the long period of hardships and privations. Their plan assumed a hereditary form to endure as long as they should endure, or any of their male posterity.

The constitution then adopted and which is still maintained reads in part as follows:

"It having pleased the Supreme Governor of the Universe in the disposition of human affairs to cause the separation of the colonies of North America from the domination of Great Britain and after a bloody conflict of eight years to establish them free, independent and sovereign States, connected by alliances founded on reciprocal advantages with some of the great princes and powers of the earth.

GENERAL WILLIAM SMALLWOOD

After portrait by Peale in the State House, Annapolis. From the Author's Collection

"To perpetuate, therefore, as well the remembrance of this vast event as the mutual friendships which have been formed under the pressure of common danger, and in many instances cemented by the blood of the parties, the officers of the American army do hereby, in most solemn manner, associate, constitute and combine themselves into one society of friends, to endure as long as they shall endure, or any of their eldest male posterity, and in failure thereof the collateral branches who may be judged worthy of becoming supporters and members.

"The officers of the American army having generally been taken from the citizens of America, possess high veneration for the character of that illustrious Roman, Lucius Quintus Cincinnatus. And being resolved to follow his example by returning to their citizenship, they think they may, with propriety, denominate themselves 'the Society of the Cincinnati.'"

They then declared it their purpose, besides upholding the exalted rights and liberties for which they had bled, "an unalterable determination to promote and cherish between the respective States that union and national honor so essentially necessary to their happiness and the future dignity of the American empire, and to render permanent the cordial affection subsisting among the officers.

"This spirit will dictate brotherly kindness in all things and particularly extend to the most substantial acts of beneficence according to the ability of the society toward those officers and their families who, unfortunately, may be under the necessity of receiving it."

The following provision was also entered: "Being deeply impressed with a sense of the generous assistance this country has received from France, and desirous of perpetuating the friendships which had been formed and so happily subsisted between the officers of the allied forces in the prosecution of the war, Counts d'Estaing, De Grasse, Rochambeau and those who served in the French auxiliary or co-operating armies with the rank of colonel, or superior rank, and those who served as commanding officers in the French Navy on the American coast should be admitted members.

All commissioned officers of the American army who had served at least three years of the war and been honorably discharged, and all commissioned officers who had been rendered supernumerary and honorably discharged in any one of the several reductions of the army, irrespective of length of service, and all commissioned officers who were actually in service at the definite peace and until disbandment were entitled to become original members.

The first general officers of the Society of the Cincinnati were: General George Washington, Commander-in-chief, president-general; Major-General Horatio Gates, of Virginia, vice-president-general; Major-General Henry Knox, of Massachusetts, secretary-general; Brigadier-General Otho Holland Williams, of Maryland, assistant secretary-general; Major-General Alexander MacDougall, of New York, treasurer-general.

For convenience of the members State societies were organized, and, as we have seen, the Maryland one was formed on November 21, 1783.

The meeting was called by General Smallwood at the Mann House, in Annapolis, and the following officers were present: Brigadier-General Otho H. Williams, Colonel Nathaniel Ramsay, Lieutenant-Colonel John Eccleston, Major Henry Hardman, John Davidson, Willaim

*UNFAMILIAR PORTRAIT OF GEORGE WASHINGTON,
DATED 1772*

*Claimed to be Peale's first portrait of Washington. Owned by an
Eastern Shore family—photographed by the Author. Never
before shown. From the Author's Collection.*

Brown, Richard Dorsey, Henry E. Gaither, William D. Beall, Jacob Price, Edward Oldham, Jonathan Morris, John Kilty, Perry Benson, William Lamar, Benjamin Price, William Bruce, Edward Dyer, Edward Spurrier, Samuel McPherson, George Hamilton, Francis Reveley, Christopher Richmond, William Reily, Lloyd Beall, Michael Boyd, James Bruff, Adamson Tannehill, Philip Reed, Thomas Mason, John Hamilton, James Smith, John Gassaway.

Lieutenants Nicholas Ricketts, Isaac Rawlings, John J. Jacobs, Samuel B. Beall, William Pendergast, Thomas Rowse, Basil Burgess, Arthur Harris, Henry Clements, John T. Lowe, Malakiah Bonham, Henry N. Chapman, Benjamin Fickle, Mark McPherson, John Dow Cary, Samuel Hanson, John Brevitt, Thomas Boyd, Henry Baldwin, Thomas Price, Jr., Thomas A. Dryson, Samuel Edminston, William Smoot, Hezekiah Foard, Isaac Hanson, Thomas Beatty, John Sears. Officers of the staff— Physician to the army, James Craik; regimental surgeons, William Kilty and Ezekiel Haynie; surgeons' mates, John L. Elbert and Gerard Wood. The first officers elected for the Maryland Society of the Cincinnati were Major-General Smallwood, president; Brigadier-General Mordecai Gist, vice-president; Brigadier-General Otho Holland Williams, secretary; Colonel Nathaniel Ramsay, treasurer; Lieutenant-Colonel John Eccleston, assistant treasurer.

While many words of disapproval came from men high in standing and influence, they were in every case men who had not served their country on the battlefields of the Revolution. Samuel Adams, in a letter to Elbridge Gerry in 1784, when the society had its first general meeting in Independence Hall, Philadelphia, wrote: "I confess I do not barely dislike the order. With you I think it dangerous and look upon it with the eye of jealousy. When the pride of family possesses the minds of men it is threatening the community in proportion to the good they have done, ... This is as rapid a stride toward a hereditary military nobility as ever was made in so short a time."

John Adams, John Jay, Benjamin Franklin, Thomas Jefferson and others equally important bitterly opposed the new military order. But Washington, clear-sighted and just, gave it the indelible stamp of his approval, and on October 29, 1783, wrote to Count Rochambeau as follows:

"The officers of the American Army, in order to perpetuate that mutual friendship which they contracted in the hour of common danger and distress, and for the purposes which are mentioned in the instrument of their association, have united together in a society of friends under the name of the Cincinnati and, having honored me with the office of president, it becomes a very agreeable part of my duty to inform you that the society has done itself the honor to consider you and the generals and officers of the army which you commanded in America as members of the society."

The French nation received this message in the proper spirit, and the King, recognizing it as a new tie assuring the duration of the reciprocal friendship begun when France sent her army to the assistance of the American colonies, granted the officers the privilege of wearing the insignia at the court, which was not accorded to any other foreign order excepting that of the Golden Fleece.

The officers of the French navy, who had served in the Revolutionary War presented to General Washington as a mark of their esteem the Cincinnati Eagle in diamonds, which has been transmitted to each president-general in turn.

It is especially significant to find that the Tammany Society, or Columbian Order, was founded in the year 1789 in opposition to the Society of the Cincinnati. It is truly said in the register of this society that "It is a striking commentary on the trustworthiness of political prophecy that, while the Order of the Cincinnati has been of little weight in the history of the country and is now entirely without political influence, its old rival, with its membership of thousands and its arbitrary though nominally democratic methods, has gone on increasing in power and prestige until it has grown into the most formidable and possibly the most dangerous political organization in the Union."

The Society of the Cincinnati has kept strictly to the purpose for which its founders organized it. Founded upon patriotism by the patriots who had bled for their country's freedom, it has been perpetuated by their descendants, who have cherished the cause no less than the names of the Revolutionary officers. There are many other men eligible to membership in the Maryland Society who have not kept in touch with their hereditary claims.

CHAPTER LXX

UNSUNG HEROES OF THE REVOLUTION

As we dwell with pride and reverence upon the memory of Washington and upon the noble army which he so gallantly led on to victory, the unsung wing of the American forces should not be entirely forgotten. These we will call the fathers and mothers of the Revolution, who belong to that class of heroes of whom it is said, "They also serve who only stand and wait."

Let us see what this part of the army did worthy of recognition. The fathers of the Revolution were those who saw their sturdy sons march off to the scene of action, bidding them godspeed, while they, beyond the age of enlistment, stayed behind to guard the home in which was left the mother and the younger children. These were the men who attended to the food supplies for the army, who raised the crops and then defended them from the marauding parties of the British.

In the year 1781 many complaints were sent the governor about the parties of Englishmen who harassed the inhabitants along the rivers and creeks of the Eastern Shore of Maryland. These men were attempting to destroy or capture the means of subsistence of the American army, and were supplying the enemy with the same. As early as 1777 wheat, corn and flour were becoming higher in price because the army had so many of the young planters in the ranks.

All through the Journal of Correspondence we find the Council ordering the British vessels searched for provisions. The men who remained at home had no easy task to defend the home, and with the aid of a few slaves raise the crops with which to feed the army, for not only were the horses and young men gone, but insufficient arms and ammunition were provided the home defenders.

On these old men and on the women the Revolutionary War laid a heavy burden. The enthusiasm of patriotism, the sound of martial music and the clash of battle buoyed up the spirit of the young heroes whose memories we are keeping green.

But those who had the duller, more prosaic and less arduous duty of serving by waiting in the isolated country homes are entitled to our loving remembrance, too.

Many of these unsung heroes died in defense of their homes, and the event has been unchronicled save in the hearts of their descendants through family oral history. And the mothers of the Revolution—did not they lay their all on the war's red altar, and, like the Spartan mothers of old, nobly send out their brave young lads to victory or to death, admonishing them to come with their flag, or enshrouded in it?

We can imagine these mothers of the Revolution helping to make ready the old flintlock muskets which were to put to rout the British redcoats. And how these mothers spun and wove the cloth and fashioned comfortable garments and home-knit socks and mits to clothe not only their own sons but the motherless part of the army as well.

The insignia of the Society of the Daughters of the American Revolution is a spinning wheel, to which a skein is attached, and surrounded by thirteen stars, each the symbol of one of the thirteen States.

To our minds it conjures up a picture of a lonely fireside, on one side of which sits a mother of one or more sons away with the army. Her wheel does not whirr and sing to the love tunes of the days of Priscilla and John Alden, but the whirr is the whirr of the British grapeshot, and the music the tramp of marching feet. Who can guess the love and terror spun into those garments of Revolutionary days by the desolate firesides!

The Sons of the American Revolution, on their insignia, show the figure of a soldier, in whose right hand is a musket, while the left rests on a plow handle—typifying the many private citizens who left their vocations to fight for their country's freedom, after which they returned to the plow or anything it typified.

Now be it remembered the young men who shouldered the musket left the plows—they could not attend to both—but the old men who stayed behind never resigned the plow when called on to strike a blow for the home.

And so, to perpetuate the memory of the fathers of the Revolution, we should have the figure of an old farmer with his musket swung across his shoulders by a strap, as with both hands he pushed the plow to raise the grain to feed the Revolutionary heroes.

These were the unsung vanguard of the American Army; the patient, busy mother by her lonely hearthstone; the brave old, hard-working father, upon whom the heat and burden of the day fell in the absence of his stalwart sons. These were the forces behind the Revolutionary guns!

CHAPTER LXXI

THE VALUE OF FAMILY TRADITIONS

THE question of the value of family traditions is one which is constantly presented to the professional genealogist, and certainly it is one worthy the careful attention of every student of family history.

Not a few persons have the same attitude of mind toward family traditions that they hold toward the validity of the Scriptures, and take the stand that all are right or none at all.

Modern higher criticism has taught us many things on this point and has shown us that because we do not believe that the whale swallowed Jonah we are not shut out from a saving faith in the love of God. Just so with family traditions. Through years of experience we have learned that nearly all of these family traditions have the kernel of truth in them. Even the old joke of the three brothers who came to this country, which is so well known to us all, has been proven oftener true than mythical, and while all families of the same name in Maryland, or elsewhere, do not invariably spring from the same original stock, we have found that in the majority of cases in Colonial Maryland, at least, several brothers did come into the province. The reason for this was that families were large in England and as the oldest son inherited the estates, there was little hope for the younger brothers at home.

The offers of land in the colonies were not to be resisted by these land-hungry young Englishmen, and hence we find various patents from the Lords Proprietary of Maryland to three brothers, together or separately.

In not a few instances a sister came to be a home-maker for her brothers—but she soon appears as the wife of some other girl's brother. The records disclose evidences of as many as five brothers settling in Maryland, while the tradition of the three is practically substantiated.

When does tradition become history? is a question recently put to the writer. Generally speaking, among civilized races not until it is officially recorded. Among barbarians the history of the tribes is transmitted orally from father to son. With these children of nature there is not only no way, but no need, of other proof than the word of the patriarch of the family. But with the white man all is different. Civilization brings ambition and the spirit of rivalry in its train, and one's imagination may take flights if not kept down with the weight of proof. Hence family tradition is generally discredited, and particularly if it deals with a title or disports its subject in a coat of arms.

Happily, however, careful research is bringing to light many pleasant and valuable confirmations of family traditions. There are, however, many sources of historic and genealogical lore hidden away in the attics of the old homes of Maryland, which no doubt would, if carefully examined, prove the truth of other so-called legends, and solve many genealogical riddles given up by the professionals. These sources of private information would prove invaluable as a whole, but they must be gleaned piecemeal; and let us hope the good work of delving into the family land papers, old wills, letters and diaries will begin at once in Maryland. It is interesting work for the long afternoons and evenings in the country.

So many accidents have occurred—houses have been burned, papers carelessly or wantonly destroyed, some worm-eaten; others, if you will but believe it, devoured by hungry pets left by small boys in the attic of a Colonial mansion! These were little foxes, and, while this is an exceptional case, there are other little foxes which are destroying much valuable data—those of indifference, carelessness and ignorance.

In some families the aged grandmother or grandfather is still living, and, as reminiscences are the delight of the old, much of value could be learned from these links between the two centuries, if we of the present generation would patiently encourage them to tell of their forebears and contemporaries. Statements affirmed by our aged parents or grandparents as to the name and service of their fathers or grandfathers leave the realm of tradition and thus become matters of record.

Many of us have lost sight of this fact in our zeal to find broken links, the public record of which cannot be found, but which is a point not really open to question. For example, in the unsettled condition of affairs in Revolutionary times many marriages were not recorded, or, if recorded, the licenses issued were destroyed. The old grandmother knows the names of her grandparents as well as we know hers—and her sworn statement to a question in court would establish heirship to property. It must be accepted as truth in the family history record.

There are Catholic families in this State which have suffered under the stigma of the bar sinister because a certain early marriage record was missing—at the period when the Catholic priest dare not perform the rites of his office under penalty of death. That love maketh a way we all know, and neither the hand of the law nor prison bars can keep those who would marry apart.

Hence, while death awaited a public performance of the marriage ceremony in Colonial Maryland at the period mentioned, there is very conclusive evidence that certain marriages were performed between Catholics of high position and the record not made public. Continued digging among the old records, unearthing of unfamiliar family papers hidden in the old horse-hair trunks in the attics, and perhaps the finding of other buried manuscript treasure, such as the Calvert papers, will in time prove many things yet in question, just as truly as will the excavations of the archæologists prove, through the inscriptions of the tablets unearthed, the validity of the Scriptures; for as Dr. Haupt once said in his appeal for the American Archæological School at Assos, "If men would keep silent, then stones would speak."

CHAPTER LXXII

"MARYLAND, MY MARYLAND"

IF IT is true that more depends upon the songs of a country than upon its laws, then Maryland can never cease to honor the name of Nicholson, for not only is the name of Judge Joseph Hopper Nicholson forever to be associated with the publishing of "The Star-Spangled Banner" and the choosing of the tune which sent Key's song ringing through the city at the opportune moment, but that of his granddaughter, Rebecca Lloyd Nicholson (Mrs. Edward Shippen), should have the recognition of having had Randall's stirring song, "Maryland, My Maryland," published at a time when brave men dared not risk the results of standing sponsor for what has been termed "the 'Marseillaise' of the South." Believing that the history can best be told by the one who was so vitally interesested, I have the following unpublished account of what is certainly a charming incident in the history of our late war:

The facts regarding the setting to music and publishing of the song "Maryland, My Maryland."

"It was early in the month of July, 1861, that a party of young girls known as "the Monument Street girls" met one morning, as was their habit, at the residence of Mr. James Carroll, 105 West Monument Street (now 225 West Monument Street), to sew on garments for the use of the Confederate soldiers. Mrs. Winn, the daughter of Mr. James Carroll, resided there also, with her three daughters, Misses Achsah, Ida and Mary Winn, and here gathered daily their young friends, all of whom were united in sympathy with the South. Many of the young brothers and friends of these girls were shortly to leave their homes to enlist in the Southern cause. Mrs. William Henry Norris, the mother of Mr. Samuel and James Lyon and Mr. Owen Norris, of Baltimore, was a near neighbor and frequently joined Mrs. Winn and these girls in their work. Mr. H. Rozier Dulany, of Baltimore, one of the handsome beaux of the day (a son of Mr. Grafton Dulany, a noted lawyer of the same city), was deeply interested in gathering news of the South, and likewise came daily to bring whatever news of interest he had collected to these Southern sympathizers; and on this particular morning he came in very much pleased with some verses that had been given to him by someone on Baltimore Street, and he proceeded at once to read them, and my pen is inadequate to describe the enthusiastic reception given by all present to the reading of these verses. Mr. Dulany himself proposed they should be set to music, and with one accord everyone agreed with him. A Yale book of songs which was lying on the piano near by was immediately searched for a tune to which these verses could be sung. One after another was tried. Finally Mr. Dulany exclaimed: "This one will suit," selecting one called "Lauriger Horatius" (the German "Tannenbaum, O Tannenbaum"), and then while one of these girls sitting at the piano played this tune Mr. Dulany sang it, all present joining in singing the verses he had read to it, but at the close of the first verse it was found that two more words were needed to make it fit perfectly. After a moment's pause Mr. Dulany exclaimed, "I have it! Let us add 'My Maryland,' " and then and there this was done, and

Mr. Randall's verses were then found to fit exactly the tune of "Lauriger Horatius," to which tune it is still sung, and these enthusiastic young people proceeded to sing it with a will. After quiet was somewhat restored someone suggested that it should be published as a song, and Mr. Dulany was asked if he would not have it published. But these were the days when mothers even had to look for their babies, who wore red sashes and shoulder knots with their white dresses, at police stations, and Southern sympathizers were too often taken off to prison at Fort McHenry nearby, so Mr. Dulany replied to this eager throng: "Oh, thank you, no; I do not care to be put in prison. Fort McHenry is too near." To his utter astonishment, I think, came from every girl's voice there the unexpected taunt, "You are a coward." But he felt, notwithstanding this, that he was among his friends, and so he only repeated: "I am sorry, but Fort McHenry is too near, and I am afraid to have it published;" whereupon one of these young girls impulsively exclaimed: "I am not afraid. My father is a Union man, and if they put me in prison he will get me out." This remark met with warm approval from all present, and Mrs. Norris said: "If you will have it published, do it at once. I will copy the verses for you if you will copy off the music." And this young girl agreed at once to do so and take them to the publishers. She then took the Yale book of songs to her own home, a few doors from Mr. James Carroll's residence, where she had some books in which she copied music, and taking a leaf, she wrote off in a very short time the music and returned with it. Mrs. Norris had copied the verses, adding the two words "My Maryland" after each verse, and that same morning in July, 1861, this young girl herself took the music and the verses to the publishers, Miller and Beacham, who kept a music store on North Charles Street, west side, below Fayette Street. Mr. Miller, whom she knew, came forward, and she explained her errand and asked if he would publish it for her. If so, she would give him the copyright. He said at once that he would publish it, much to her delight, and then asked what he should do about stating who set it to music and had it published. Remembering how much Mr. Dulany had objected to publishing it, she said, "Oh, use any letters but 'R and D,' hence her own initials were left out, and Mr. Miller selected "C and E" as being far away from "R and D." Thus Messrs. Miller and Beacham published this now well-known song in July, 1861, at the request of this young girl, Miss Rebecca Lloyd Nicholson, and they sent her six copies, with their compliments, one of which she has still in her possession, together with another copy, which was a proof sheet. Ever afterward this firm sent her copies of the different Southern songs, with their compliments, until they were arrested for publishing the same. Thus this song was sung many times in the summer of 1861 with those very "Maryland boys" headed by Captain Willie Murray before they left their homes to join the Southern cause.

CHAPTER LXXIII

THE MURAL PAINTINGS IN BALTIMORE COURT HOUSE

Not Historically Correct

IN ACCEPTING the mural painting having for its subject the burning of the *Peggy Stewart*, the mayor of Baltimore laid stress upon the educational value of this and other mural paintings, which are intended to instruct the youth and perpetuate the history of our State on the walls of her municipal buildings. This being the declared object of these paintings, their teachings should be so clear that he who runs may read. Therefore in the sole interest of historical accuracy, and as an earnest student of Maryland history, I take the liberty of giving my *dicta* on both of these superbly executed mural decorations.

The pity is that our gifted son of Maryland should not have studied the details as to the ages of the persons represented and appropriateness of costume.

The anachronisms of "The Burning of the *Peggy Stewart*" are, however, few in comparison with the painting on the opposite wall.

No one can deny the fine conception of the picture nor criticise its execution, but in certain details the artist has failed. For example, in the foreground of the group before the Stewart house he has painted a young lady of strikingly Scotch type, whom he states is meant for Margaret (or Peggy) Stewart, the daughter of Mr. Stewart, for whom the vessel was named. In reality Peggy Stewart was a girl of seven years of age, her mother, Jean Dick, and Mr. Jas. Stewart having been married on March 15, 1764—only ten years at the date of the burning. On page 147 of All Hallows' parish register we find that Margaret Stewart, daughter of the above, was born August 18, 1767. The unappropriateness of her costume for the time and place is an anachronism which will strike any observer. Certainly in the pre-Revolutionary period even, when highbred dames are supposed by many to sit all day in rich brocades, we cannot believe that any young lady would be arrayed in ball costume with court train, etc., in the afternoon, and particularly as it is a matter of record that her mother was lying ill at the time. Therefore the representation of Peggy Stewart is entirely without foundation. As the dates of Mr. Stewart's marriage and of his children's ages are matters of record, there is no excuse for an artist to paint historic pictures with such glaring errors of detail.

As the two principal figures of the middle panel were stated to be portraits of the men they represent, the one of Dr. Charles Alexander Warfield has the emaciated face of an old man, while his portrait, still extant, shows him to have been unusually full-faced and was certainly in the flush of early manhood.

But while we regret that this mural painting just misses the great value of perfection of historic detail, its defects are not the vital ones which make the true Marylander gaze with wonder at the Puritan group across the rotunda. What possible lesson can that decoration impart to our Maryland youth or to the stranger within our gates? The painting is said to represent the landing of the first settlers, who came in the *Ark* and the *Dove,* and again it has been declared to be Leonard Calvert's treaty with the Indians.

That the mural decoration represents neither event is beyond question. We have, accessible to all students of Maryland history, the original account of the arrival of the *Ark* and the *Dove*, sent back to Cæcilius Calvert, second Lord Baltimore, by his brother, Leonard Calvert, and who vouches for its accuracy in a personal letter to the Proprietary. This original manuscript, which was sent to England on the return trip of the *Ark*, gives a picture which is luminous with incident, most significant of which is the planting of the cross by Leonard Calvert and his cavaliers. The time has past when any narrow prejudice against the Catholics should be allowed to pervert the true history of the seating of the colony. Those of us who are Protestants do not think of Leonard Calvert's act as that of a Catholic, but rather that he planted the cross as the symbol of Christianity, and as Maryland became the place of religious liberty and "the Land of Sanctuary," nothing can ever blot out or obscure the first graphic incident of the landing of our cavaliers.

In the mural painting there are three Puritan figures and near to the shore two big ships. A woman, a child and a man—what do they represent? I have tried in vain to surmise. The picture is positively absurd as illustrative of the settlement of Maryland and should be wiped off the canvas or sold to Boston, where it would find its proper setting. As to the peace treaty with the Piscataways it will not do.

The contemporary accounts tell us that Leonard Calvert "left the ship at St. Clements Island, and, taking the pinnace *Dove* and one other bought in Virginia, he sailed up the river to Patowmeck Towne, where the Werowance being a child, Archihau, his uncle, governed him and his country for him." This Indian chief gave them "good welcome." The treaty was not made with the chieftain, however, only an exchange of civilities and a discussion of religious beliefs being recorded as the subject of the interview.

From hence the Governor went to Piscataway, about twenty leagues higher up, where he found many Indians assembled, and here he met with one Captain Henry Fleete, an Englishman, who had lived many years among the Indians and by that means spoke the country language well. Him (our Governor) sent ashore to invite the Werowance to a parley, who thereupon came with him aboard privately, where he was courteously entertained and after some parley being demanded by the Governor whether he would be content that he and his people should find a place convenient for him. While this Werowance was aboard many of his people came to the water side, fearing that he might be surprised, whereupon the Werowance commanded two Indians to go ashore to quiet them of their fear. And we are also told that he showed himself upon the deck of the Governor's pinnace and told his people that he was in safety."

"At Yoacomaca Governor Calvert went to shore with the Werowance there and acquainted him with his coming thither, to which he made little answer, but entertained the Governor and his company in his house, etc."

"There the Governor decided to seat his first colony, and to make his entry peaceably and safely he thought fit to present the Werowance and the wives of the towne with some English cloth, hones and knives, which they accepted very kindly."

We can therefore see that the present canvas does not portray the visit of Leonard Calvert to either Indian chief, two being at Indian towns, and the treaty with "the emperor of all the pettie Indian kings" being on board the Governor's pinnace *Dove*.

With the anachronisms of this canvas I can only say that the helmets of the Governor's escort are not impossible, the moccasins of the chief are improbable, but the peaked hat and broad, flat collar of the Puritan man and the austere garb of the woman and child have no place in the company of cavaliers who stepped with adventurous foot from off the *Ark* and the *Dove*.

The first panel should in the interest of historic truth show the planting of the cross rough-hewn from a tree, with the large company of settlers present, and the *Ark* and the *Dove* off the shore.

The Indian panel should be more correct in detail, and portray Colonial instead of twentieth century Indians; it is more suggestive of Penn's treaty with the Indians than with Leonard Calvert's informal, friendly visits to them. A picturesque incident in the settlement of Maryland was the first military parade attending the ceremony of carrying the colors on shore, which was done with all the pomp possible to the time and place. The "murderers, or cannon," had been landed, and a contemporary account tells us that after a court of guard and storehouse had been erected "the Governor thought fit to bring the colors on shore, which was attended by all the gentlemen and the rest of the servants-in-arms, who received the colors with a volley of shot, which was answered by the ordnance from the ships." This would have been an interesting scene to portray.

It is such a pity for Maryland to miss her opportunity to perpetuate the true history of her settlement, than which none is more interesting! Not only should a mistake be corrected at once, for the sake of the present generation, but because if left to stand it will be copied and perpetuated, as in the case of the official seal of Maryland.

Because the artist who drew it copied it from the incorrect seal on Bacon's Laws, the official seal, which by an act of the Legislature was meant to be the facsimile of the one sent over in 1648 by Cæcilius Calvert, the pennants fly the reverse way and will continue to fly in the face of the lawmakers until the seal is legally broken and a correct one is executed. Let us hope that the Municipal Art Society, with its noble purposes, will appoint a committee to pass upon the historical accuracy of the works of art, while in outline, so that their efforts and those of the artist will not be in vain.

CHAPTER LXXIV

AN INACCURATE LIST OF THE ARK AND DOVE ADVENTURERS

As SPECIAL Executive Historian, commissioned by Governor Warfield to represent the Executive Department of the State of Maryland in the historic work at the Jamestown Exposition, 1907, the author placed in "The Executive Exhibit" the first collection ever made of those who came in the *Ark* and the *Dove*, gleaned by her from original manuscript archives of Maryland, unassisted by anyone, and without the aid of indexes, the early warrants being then unindexed. This collection attracted much attention at Jamestown, and has been a point of interest in the State House at Annapolis ever since the close of "The Tercentenary."

In the interest of historical accuracy, the author, before allowing these volumes to go to press, carefully revised her original list and discarded all names of settlers who were entered as coming in the year 1634, after realizing that those who came in the first adventure really arrived in the year 1633, and as the New Year at that time began on March 25, the landing was on the first day of 1634—thus proving that, as both Father White and Leonard Calvert gave March 3d as the date of arriving in the Potomac, the colonists were in Maryland three weeks before 1633 expired.

This revised list, limiting the first adventurers to those recorded as coming in the year 1633, is now in the Executive Exhibits at Annapolis.

The author, in view of these facts, finds it necessary, in

the interest of history, to call attention to the many errors in the list published by "The *Ark* and *Dove* Society" on June 5, 1910, in which, in addition to the present writer's original list, are included between forty and fifty names not entitled to be in the list of adventurers in the *Ark* and *Dove*.

The following analysis, with the official proofs, fully establish the fact that not one of these new names published by the Society were in reality additions to the list originally made and exhibited by the author.

In the Society's list the four following names are given as separate men: "Althcum John," "Altem John," "Alcome John," "Altome John." By referring to "Liber 1, fols. 27, 37, 166, 19" and "A. B. H. fols. 65-66, 31"—it will be seen that there is but one and the same man indicated. Two Ralph Beanes are given in the Society's list, while in the reference "Liber 2, fol. 507" it is recorded that "Ralph Beane (2d), demanded land for transporting himself, Walter Beane and his wife *between the years 1640 and 1648*."

"Randall Revell," given in the list, "Liber A. B. H., page 79," is stated in that reference to have "demandeth 100 acres of land due to him by conditions of Plantations for transporting himself into the Province 1636."

"Nicholas Cawsin," given in the Society's list as "August 10, 1633," fol. 506, Liber 2," is shown in that reference to have received land through the widow of John Cockshutt, due him, John Cockshutt, for transporting himself and seven servants into the Province in the year 1642." This record was made "August 30, 1649-50," instead of 1633, proved by the signature of Governor Wm. Stone to have been made in that year or later.

By turning back to page 347 in the same Liber 2, the following is found: "Sept. 19th, 1646"—"Nicholas Cawsin demandeth 1000 acres of land for *transporting himself* and two men servants, viz: Julian Vernett and John Taylor into this Province, and for transporting at his own cost and charge two other persons, viz: Arthur La Hay and Thomas Peteet, all *in the year 1639*, and one able man servant viz: John Walter, in the year 1642."

"Robert Clark assigned 500 acres for transporting two men into the Province August 16th, 1633," Liber 1, fols. 38-61; Liber 2, fol. 506, their list.

In Liber 2, fol. 506, August 16 (margin on next page gives the year as 1649), the record reads: "Thomas Copley this day assigned to *Mr. Robert Clarke* 500 acres of land *due to the said Mr. Copley for transporting* two men servants in the year 1633."

"Ralph Crouch," given in the Society's list as (1633). Liber 2, fol. 506—the records there reads: "Thomas Copley Esq. this day *assigned to Mr. Ralph Crouch*, 400 acres of land due to the *said Mr. Copley* for transporting ten men servants into this Province in the year 1633." The date of this assignment to Crouch was August 16, 1649 (see margin).

"Thomas Pasmore, Liber A. B. H., page 13," the Society's list—The Record, on the contrary, gives April 9, 1648, by the Governor and Commissioners of Maryland, "Whereas Thomas Pasmore *of Virginia* is desirous and doth intend to transport himself and his family into the Province of Maryland to become a member of this Colony, these are for his encouragement to promote and assure the said Thomas Pasmore that he shall have 1000 acres of land in the Province, to him and his heirs forever.

Captain Henry Fleete shall make first choice; Given at St. Mary's 26th of June, Anno. 1634, signed

      LEONARD CALVERT,
      JERO. HAWLEY,
      THO. CORNWALLIS."

(The above shows that this grant was not recorded until April 9, 1648.)

"Thomas Pasmore came into the province from Virginia in the year 1634, and demanded land for transporting two men servants called Thomas Price and Richard Williams in the year 1634." See the Society's list for these as *Ark* and *Dove* colonists 1633, Liber 1–25 A. B. H., fol. 82.

"Thomas Thomas," "Henry Baker," "Taylor," given as original settlers in the Society's list, Liber A. B. H., fols. 82 and 66. Examination of these prove that the men were transported by Thomas Pasmore in the years 1634 and 1635 (evidently from Virginia).

"Samuel Barrett, Edward Ebbs, Thomas Occley, Matthew Rodam, Nicholas Polhampton, William Harrington, William Pinley, Thomas Mosse, and Richard Smith are all given in the Society's list of *Ark* and *Dove* colonists under reference A. B. H., fol. 61." Reference to this Liber 61 discloses the following: "Feb. 17th, 1641, Leonard Calvert, Esq., demands 5000 acres of land for transporting 25 able men into the province *since the year* 1633." Among those names are "Richard Smith, Thomas Occley, Samuel Barrett, Nicholas Polhampton, Matthew Rodam, Thomas Ebbs, William Harrington, William Pinley, Thomas Mosse," proving that none of them are entitled to be in the list.

"Stephen Sammon," given by the Society, "Liber A. B. H. 94," and "Stephen Tammion, Liber 1, page 110," as two different men, by examination of these references prove to be one and the same man.

"William Wolfe," the Society's List, Liber 1, fol. 121, appears on page 88 instead, in a list of men transported by Giles Basha, Sept. 7th, 1640.

"Thomas Willis," given by this list as a 1633 settler, Liber A. B. H., fol. 67," is in reality "entered by Mr. Thomas Green, Oct. 15th, 1639," "as one servant Thomas Wills brought into the province 1634."

"Thomas Grigston, 1633, Liber 1-38," and "Thomas Gregston, Liber A. B. H., fol. 66," are entered separately, and therefore as two different original settlers in the Society's list, while careful comparison in these transcribed records and "assigned land rights" prove that there was but one man intended.

"Mathias Susa, molatta, in 1633, Liber 1, fol. 37," and "Mathia Tusa, 1633, A. B. H. 65," and "Mathia Zause, 1633, Liber 1, fol. 166," and "Francis Molit, 1633, fol. 166, Liber 1" are given in the Society's list as four original settlers, whereas examination of these references prove that "Mathias Susa" and "Mathia Tusa" and "Mathias Zause" are really variations of spelling of the same name the capital letter in the last case being made peculiarly, and an attempt at the designation "ffra molito'" intended for "a molatto," being interpreted by them as a man's name—hence, the egregious error of interpreting the original settler, "Matthias Tousa," a mulatto, into four original settlers!

"Robert Sherly, 1633, Liber 1-20, 37, 166," and "Liber

A. B. H., fol. 65," is given by this list as different from "Robert Shoeley, 1633, Liber 1, fol. 37." Reference to these prove them to have been the same man.

"Capt. Robt. Wintour," Liber 2, fol. 161, the Society's list. Examination of this shows "The estate of Capt. Robert Winter, late of St. Mary's Esq., delivered by John Lewger, secretary, fourth of September, 1639." The author can add a further entry in Liber 1, page 18, "Jan. 12th, 1637, came into the province Captain Robert Wintour, who transported Richard Brown, Arthur Webb, John Speed, Bartholamew Phillips, Thomas White."

"Garrett Fitzwalters, 1633, Liber 1, page 171," the Society's list. According to the entry referred to, in the year 1650, it is stated that "Garrett Fitzwalters was brought in 'about nine years since,' which eliminates him also as an *Ark* and *Dove* settler.

"Francis Gray, Liber 1, page 222," the Society's list is mentioned in a suit in which Nicholas Keylin demanded three hundred pounds of tobacco for the price of a hog. This was after the year 1634, as reference to the preceding page in Liber 1 shows that court had been held in August, 1634.

"Thomas Matthews, Liber 2, page 500, 1633," the Society's list. An examination of this reference proves that on Aug. 17th, 1649, "Thomas Matthews demanded 4000 acres of land due to him by assignment from Mr. Thomas Copely."

"Fernando Pulton, 1633, Liber 1, fol. 27," the Society's list. The author finds Liber A. B. H., pages 65 and 66, "Mr. Fernando Pulton demandeth land due by conditions of plantations under these several titles for men brought in by the several persons whose assign the said Fernando

Pulton is, and for men brought in in his own right; those in his own right brought in by himself Ano. 1638," proving that Fernando Pulton did not come in the *Ark* and the *Dove.*

"John Norton, Sr., John Norton, Jr., Christopher Martin and Cuthbert Fenwick, 1633, A. B. H. Liber 244," are entered in the Society's list, but upon reference it is seen that the entry reads "Anodom 1634" "brought the same year and exported from Virginia four servants, viz: Cuthbert Fenwick, Christopher Martin, John Norton, Sr., John Norton, Jr."

Cuthbert Fenwick's name being one of the few names erroneously included in the author's first collection is, no doubt, responsible for his name appearing in the Society's list.

"Thomas Price, 1633, Liber A. B. H., fol. 82," the Society's list, proves to be one of the men transported in the year 1634 by Thomas Pasmore, evidently from Virginia.

"John Elbin, A. B. H., fol. 65-66, John Elkin, 1633, Liber 1, fol. 20, John Elkins, 1633, fol. 38, Liber 1," the Society's list. Upon careful examination the name is John Elkin on each folio quoted, and the engrosser's error which appeared in the executive list, i.e., "John Elbin," is evidently responsible for the mistake giving two names for one man.

"John Sanders, immigrant, 1633, Liber 1, fol. 30, A. B. H. fol. 65, fol. 244. Sanders, John, servant, Liber 1, fol. 38 (1633)," the Society's list. These names and entries indicate two men, one a gentleman and one a servant, but in reality the references prove that on page 65 Mr. John Saunders is mentioned, and on page 244 it is stated that Thomas Cornwallis, Esq., received from his partner,

Mr. John Sanders, who, dying in the *Ark* " "gave him five servants," and in Liber 1, page 38, Fernando Pulton demands land as assignee of Mr. John Sanders, Anno. 1633. These assignments prove that there was but one man intended, and *that* Mr. John Saunders, who died on the *Ark*. It must be noted that although Fernando Pulton is entered here as an assignee of Mr. John Sanders, it does not mean that he received these men personally from Mr. Sanders, but that the men under whom he claimed land had been transported by Mr. Sanders, as Pulton is shown above to have stated the year 1638 as being the date of his own arrival.

"Francis Rogers, Liber 1, page 38, in their list, 1633," should be Francis Rabnett.

"Thomas Stratham, Liber 1-19, etc.," should be "Statham."

"Thomas Hawley," entered in their list as one of the Commissioners in connection with his brother, Jerome Hawley, *was not a commissioner*, as he was the Governor in Barbadoes when visited by Leonard Calvert en route, for the purpose of buying corn.

After the above analysis the author regrets to say that not a single one of the forty or more "additional names" claimed in their list as first (1633) adventurers, has stood the test of critical investigation.

CHAPTER LXXV

MARYLAND EXECUTIVE EXHIBIT

"Collected and Arranged by Mrs. Hester Dorsey Richardson, Special Executive Historian; exhibited at the Jamestown Exposition 1907"

GOVERNOR WARFIELD has, during his entire administration, grasped every opportunity to honor the people of Maryland, and to preserve and perpetuate the history of the State.

His tribute to Maryland's part in the making of our national history, in his famous speech at the St. Louis Exposition, gave the State a national recognition and status never before enjoyed.

His successful effort to restore to its original condition the historic old Senate Chamber in the State House at Annapolis has added a vital interest to our Capitol which it has not possessed since its dismantling in 1876. This room hallowed by the most sublime act in the history of America—the resignation of his commission as Commander-in-Chief of the American Army by General Washington, December 23, 1783—has with the two adjoining rooms been dedicated as a memorial hall of Maryland history. A place in which to preserve and exploit all that lends interest and lustre to the old Commonwealth.

As a part of his plan and purpose, Governor Warfield desired a collection which would demonstrate the status of the founders of Maryland, morally, educationally and socially, this collection to be made from original sources, and as an offset to the many generally accepted errors regarding the early settlers of Maryland.

When the officials of the Jamestown Exposition announced that History would have first place at the tercentennial celebration, Governor Warfield recognized this as an opportunity to have Maryland's early history emphasized and full justice done her first settlers, should he have exhibited there the memorial collection which he was making for the State House at Annapolis.

Realizing that a collection of this kind could be made most quickly and satisfactorily by one thoroughly familiar with the original records of the State, and one who had demonstrated a desire to bring to light all that would reflect honor on Maryland, Governor Warfield issued a Commission bearing date at Annapolis, November 9, 1906, to Mrs. Hester Dorsey Richardson, which reads: "Be it known that you are hereby appointed Special Executive Historian to represent the Executive Department of the State of Maryland, in connection with the historic work of the Jamestown Exposition. To collect and put in shape such historic data and documents as will redound to the fame and glory of Maryland."

Accompanying this Commission, Colonel Oswald Tilghman, Secretary of State, wrote—"Dear Madam: By direction of His Excellency Governor Edwin Warfield, I have the honor to transmit to you herewith a Commission as Special Executive Historian, etc. . . . The Governor sincerely hopes that you will accept this position, as he well knows and thoroughly appreciates your exceptional capabilities for satisfactorily performing this critical literary work."

Accepting with keen appreciation this Commission, as unique in its form as it is gracious and loyal to the people of Maryland, Mrs. Richardson entered with enthusiasm into the work of bringing together all that would redound "to the fame and glory of Maryland"—and has given to the State the results of much special knowledge and original research covering many years of investigation in the ancient records of Maryland, which could not otherwise have been brought to light at this time.

None who sees this demonstration of Maryland history can ever again believe that this "Land of Sanctuary," as Maryland was called, was settled by convicts.

The purpose of the Executive Exhibit is educational. It demonstrates:

1. The high moral and religious character of the settlers in their official acts.

2. Their educational status in the hundreds of autographs of those who came before 1700.

3. Their social status in the use of heraldic seals and the erecting of lands into manors.

The Executive Exhibit is placed in a mahogany case, which consists of a heavy central column on which are hung 24 double-glass wings, each 37x28 inches, making 48 exposures, the surface amounting to 345 square feet.

The Exhibit includes the following object lesson in Maryland history:

The names of 110 of those who came in the *Ark* and the *Dove* with Governor Leonard Calvert—nearly a hundred of which names have never been published in any history.

Fac-simile of original letter sent back on the *Ark's* return trip to England giving an account of the voyage over. Also one of the receipts for the two Indian arrows paid at Windsor Castle each Tuesday in Easter Week by the Proprietary as fealty to the King, illustrating Maryland's exemption from taxation by King or Parliament as her chartered right. These are the most uniquely valuable historical survivals in this country. The originals, which are owned by the Maryland Historical Society, were photographed for the Executive Exhibit.

Cæcilius Calvert's instructions for the erecting of land into manors, dated 1636.

An original bill of lading of Colonial date beginning "Shipped by the Grace of God," etc., illustrating the religious tone of the Maryland colonists.

That part of the "Act Concerning Religion" ensuring freedom of conscience, passed by the Assembly of Maryland in the year 1649, records the fact that Maryland was at that time the only place in the known world where persons of all faiths were at liberty to worship God according to their own consciences.

The autographs of those who passed the Act are attached to it and are shown for the first time.

Many names of the earliest settlers for whom lands were surveyed in the twelve oldest counties, giving the name of their first surveys—not all of their patents or grants. This roll of honor includes over a thousand names of the progenitors of Maryland's oldest families, in many of which these original lands have descended to the present generation. Their status as independent settlers is thus established.

Under the head—"Lords of the Manor in Maryland"—are given the names of forty-six of those who had granted them manors, with all the privileges of Lords of the Manor in England—giving the names of the Manors and the acreage. These have never before been collected.

The Act "for erecting a pryson in this Province," 1662, is made to point the lesson that Maryland was without a prison for twenty-eight years after the settlement, a law-abiding condition unique in the history of colonization, which is supplemented by a quotaton from George Alsop, written in 1660, stating that "as there is no prison in Maryland, so the merit of the country deserves none."

The "Act against the Importation of Convicted persons into this Province," passed 1676, is displayed to prove that we had no convicts among our settlers, as this Act imposes a heavy fine on "some captains of merchant vessels" who smuggled in "several" felons and sold them for their own profit. The Early Settlers' list in the Land Office records twenty thousand original emigrants who received warrants for land in Maryland prior to 1681. Every one had to prove "his right," by stating how he came—not one instance gives a convict!

The Act for "the founding and erecting of a school or college within this Province for the Education of Youth in Learning and Virtue," April, 1671, and the Act establishing King William's School, 1696, are displayed to show that Maryland passed the first Act for a free school in this country—and perhaps in the world.

Fac-simile of Washington's letter "To The General Assembly of Maryland," after his election to the Presidency of the United States, in which he makes pleasant reference to Maryland. (Maryland State Papers.)

Washington's eulogy of his aide, Lieutenant-Colonel Tench Tilghman, of Maryland, who bore the official news of Cornwallis' surrender from Yorktown to the Congress at Philadelphia, October 19, 1781.

A curious document entitled "Jeremiah Riley's Scheme for destroying Ships of War" sent to the Council of Safety about 1776—the first plan for coast defense ever considered by the Council in Revolutionary times. (Maryland Original Research Society.)

An original Commission signed by Hon. Matthew Tilghman, President of the Maryland Convention, appointing Thomas Richardson Captain of a Company in Revolutionary service, January 3, 1776.

Photograph of the patriot, Dr. Charles Alexander Warfield, with a correct account of the "Burning of the *Peggy Stewart*," October 19, 1774.

Fac-simile of "The Star-Spangled Banner," also photograph of one of the first printed copies distributed and sung in Baltimore the day after it was written off Fort McHenry, September 14, 1814. A photograph of Francis Scott Key, the author of this national song, and a St. Memin's engraving of Judge Joseph Hopper Nicholson, brother-in-law of Key, who had the words printed and set to music September 15, 1814. The original descended to his granddaughter, Mrs. Rebecca Lloyd Shippen.

Photographic fac-simile of the autographs and seal of about 600 early settlers and important Colonial personages, taken from original wills and other legal documents in ancient Court Houses and the Land Office— many show heraldic seals of interest. These autographs are shown to illustrate the educational status of our early settlers who are believed by many to have been illiterate. To each autograph is attached some data regarding the writer, giving a vital personal interest to the collection and representing much original research. The seals have identified many of the early settlers.

Traced autographs of 160 of the very earliest settlers, including many who came in the *Ark* and the *Dove*, besides Leonard Calvert and his Commissioners, such interesting characters as Henry Fleete, of the Jamestown colony, who acted as interpreter between Governor Calvert and the Indians, from whom he bought the site of the first permanent landing in Maryland. Other autographs of special interest in this collection are those of Captain James Neale, a favorite of King Charles I; Richard Ingle, "Pirate and Rebel;" Mistress Margaret Brent, first woman suffragist in America and the Portia of Colonial Maryland.

Fac-simile of the unrecorded will of Charles, third Lord Baltimore, dated in 1714 and shown for the first time.

Survivals of mills employed in Colonial Maryland, also typical household implements used in early days in Maryland, photographed in Dorchester county by Miss Mary V. Dorsey, of that county.

Photograph of superb Communion service engraved with Royal Arms of England, presented to St. Anne's Church, Annapolis, by King William III, and inscribed with his signet.

Photograph of the memorial ring given by Queen Henrietta Maria to her maid of honor, wife of an early Maryland settler, Captain James Neale, still owned by a descendant, Mrs. Clara Tilghman Earle, of Maryland.

Shown through the courtesy of the Land Commissioner, Hon. E. Stanley Toadvin:

Original Charter of Annapolis, given by Queen Anne, 1708, in which are named the first Mayor and Alderman.

The Original Boundary Agreement between the Penns and Frederick, sixth Lord Baltimore (1760).

Frederick Calvert's instructions to Governor Horatio Sharpe about Boundary question, showing map of land in dispute.

Ratification of Federal Constitution with autographs of Maryland signers, April 28, 1788.

Tripartite Indenture between Frederick, sixth Lord Baltimore, his uncle Cæcilius Calvert and others, showing miniature of Lord Baltimore done in ink, also Royal Arms of England.

Typical Indenture executed at London, 10th May, 1684, showing Royal Arms of King Charles II.

This is the assignment of "Resurrection Manor" in Maryland by Richard Perry, of London, late of Patuxent, Maryland, to Thomas and George Plowden, of Lasham, Southampton, England.

Plat of Baltimore and Jones Town in the year 1747.

The pictures of Mt. Airy and the silver service of Benedict Leonard Calvert, with photographs of Eleanor, Elizabeth and Benedict Leonard Calvert, were lent by Miss Rebecca Lynn Webster, a descendant of the Calverts. Miss Webster photographed the original portraits and silver at Mt. Airy.

The wonderfully valuable and interesting collection of signatures and seals of Maryland's Colonial settlers was made by long and patient research among the original manuscript records of the State. With a special camera made to reproduce in fac-simile at short range, the Executive Historian went to the old counties and photographed all that were available, thus preserving these fast decaying autographs of our pioneers and makers of Maryland's Colonial history.

The traced autographs were found in the earliest record books of the day when the provincial officials lived mainly at the Capital, old "St. Maries," and affixed their signatures to the Acts in which they were concerned. To this custom we are indebted for many of our most interesting autographs.

The entire Executive Exhibit was made by gleaning from original sources all that could link the individuality of our early settlers with their public acts, and thus preserve to all time the names of those who braved the dangers and hardships of pioneer life to help lay the cornerstone of this great nation.

MANUSCRIPT AND RARE BIBLIOGRAPHY

USED IN THE PREPARATION OF SIDE-LIGHTS ON MARYLAND HISTORY, VOLUME I

"A Relation of the Successful Beginnings of Lord Baltemore's Plantation in Maryland, Being an extract of certaine letters written from thence, by some of the Adventurers to their friends in England, Anno Domini 1634," reprinted as "Shea's Early Southern Tracts No. 1." A still rarer, early printed book issued at London, September 8, 1635, entitled "A Relation of Maryland," together with a map of the Country, the Conditions of Plantations; His Majesty's Charter to Lord Baltimore, translated into English."

Sabin's reprint of the above, No. 2.

Father White's "Relatio Itineris."

Letters and account of voyage from Leonard Calvert, with receipts for Indian arrows paid by Lord Baltimore to the King at Windsor Castle every Easter week.

Caecilius Calvert's original instructions to the first settlers, 1633.

Original records of Maryland of all classes, familiar and unfamiliar.

Archives of Maryland, Original and Printed.

"Hammond versus Heamans."

George Alsop's "A Character of the Province of Maryland," published 1666.

Peter Force's "Historical Tracts."
"Leah and Rachel."
"Babylon's Fall," 1655.
"Langford's Refutation," 1655, etc.
Calvert letters, Maryland Historical Society.
Original Calvert papers and printed collections of same, Maryland Historical Society.
"Eddis' letters"—1769–1777.
Sabin's reprints.
Archives of Pennsylvania, and Delaware, printed and original.
Calendar of State Papers (Great Britain).
Printed and original collections in the Dioscesan library, Baltimore.
"Oldmixon."
Speed's "Prospect of the Most Famous Parts of the World."
Stevens' manuscripts.
Chalmers papers.
Documents relating to Maryland in the Public Record Office, London.

Printed Histories Consulted

Kilty's "Landholder's Assistant."
Davis' "Day Star of American Freedom."
Riley's "Ancient City."
Neill's "Founders."
Scharf's "History of Maryland."
Brown's "Maryland, A Palatinate."
J. Johnson Jr.'s "Old Maryland Manors."
Thomas' "Chronicles of Colonial Maryland."
And many others.

INDEX OF PROPER NAMES

Abbington, John............... 265, 304
Abbott, George..................... 333
Abington, Andrew.................. 290
Able, Edward...................... 274
Acero, Mr.......................... 21
Ackworth, Richard................. 319
Acton, Richard.................... 328
Adair, R.......................... 360
Adams, James................ 269, 345
Adams, John............ 279, 388, 392
Adams, Peter...................... 374
Adams, Samuel..................... 391
Adams, Thomas..................... 264
Addison, Colonel John............. 173
Adolphus, King Gustavus........... 188
Aires, Jacob...................... 280
Aisquith, George.................. 273
Aisquith, Thomas.................. 273
Aisquith, William............ 290, 360
Albert, Peter..................... 269
Alcome, John.................. 13, 412
Alexander, James.................. 283
Alexander, Moses.................. 283
Alexander, Robert............ 374, 377
Alexander, Sir William............ 151
Alexander, William................ 281
Alfred, King....................... 55
Allanson, Thomas.............. 265, 312
Allein, James..................... 214
Allen, Francis.................... 279
Allen, Michael.................... 360
Allen, Thomas.................... 9, 13
Alley, John....................... 346
Allnutt, William.................. 275
Alricks, Governor................. 130
Alsop, George................. 191, 423
Althem, Mr. John......9, 10, 11, 13, 412
Althcum, John..................... 412
Altome, John...................... 412
Anderson, John.................... 334
Anderton, John.................... 345
Andrews, John...................... 13
Andrews, William................... 9
Andros, Sir Edmund................ 260
Andy, John C...................... 377
Anketill, Francis................. 349
Anne, Queen....................... 425
Archer, Peter..................... 304
Archer, Thos...................... 269
Archihoe........................... 23
Armstrong, Francis............ 346, 351
Armstrong, Matthew................ 315
Arnold, Richard................... 327
Ashbrook, Thomas.................. 312

Ashbury, Francis.................. 107
Ashbury, Mary..................... 107
Ashcomb, John..................... 303
Ashcomb, Nathaniel................ 303
Ashcomb, Samuel................... 303
Ashmore, John................... 9, 13
Ashmore, William...... 9, 11, 12, 13, 154
Athee, John....................... 305
Atkinson, Law..................... 269
Austin, Ann....................... 220
Ayeres, James..................... 377
Ayleward, William................. 335
Ayers, William.................... 322
Anne, Queen........................ 80
Alsop, George...................... 62

Bacon, Mr. Anthony................. 93
Baden, Thomas..................... 277
Bagby, John....................... 304
Baker, Henry...................... 414
Baker, Thomas..................... 309
Baker, William.................... 360
Bailey, Godfrey................... 295
Bailliere, Laurence............... 204
Ballard, Charles.................. 278
Ball, Benjamin.................... 301
Ball, Richard..................... 338
Balye, James...................... 374
Baldwin, Henry.................... 391
Baldwin, Captain John............. 282
Baldwin, John..................... 328
Barnaby, Edm'd.................... 269
Baltimore, Lord.............. 153, 265
Baltimore, Lord and Lady.......... 253
Baltimore, Lady Jane.............. 253
Baltimore, Caecilius C............ 126
Baltimore, Frederick, Lord........ 426
Banks, Lieutenant Richard......... 181
Banister, James................... 335
Barber, Dr. Luke.................. 132
Barber, Luke...................... 261
Barbier, Luke..................... 266
Barber, James..................... 349
Bard, John........................ 203
Barker, John...................... 312
Barker, Thos...................... 269
Barkley, Nicholas................. 346
Barefoot, Mr..................... 8, 9
Barefoot, Wm...................... 269
Barnes, Abraham................... 273
Barnes, Richard................... 373
Barnes, Wever..................... 276
Barre, Colonel.................... 356
Barry, David...................... 269

431

432 INDEX OF PROPER NAMES

Barey, Edward.................. 283
Barry, William.................. 283
Barton, William................. 312
Barrett, Samuel................. 414
Barwell, John................... 326
Basha, Giles.................... 415
Batchellor, Thomas.............. 309
Battee, Ferdinando.............. 203
Batten, William............. 312, 338
Battin, Mrs..................... 149
Bateman, Secretary John......... 64
Bateman, John................... 342
Bateman, Mary.............. 291, 354
Batson, Thomas.................. 290
Boston, Henry................... 314
Baxter, John.................... 7, 9
Bayard, James................... 284
Bayard, Peter................... 284
Bayard, Samuel.................. 284
Bayne, Captain John............. 233
Bearfoot, Thomas................ 311
Beauchampe, Edmond.............. 254
Beauchamp, Marcey............... 278
Beachampe, O. T................. 254
Beauchamp, Thomas............... 278
Beane, Eleanore................. 311
Beane, Ralph............... 9, 13, 412
Beane, Walter................... 412
Beall, Alexander................ 277
Beall, Captain George........... 276
Beall, Jos...................... 374
Beall, Josias................... 373
Beall, Lloyd.................... 391
Beall, Ninian................... 305
Beall, Samuel................... 277
Beall, Samuel B................. 391
Beall, William.................. 276
Beall, William D................ 391
Beaston, William................ 282
Bell, James..................... 269
Bell, Ninian.................... 333
Beard, John..................... 212
Beard, Richard.................. 327
Beatty, Thomas.................. 391
Beckwith, Henry................. 352
Beckworth, Thomas........... 9, 12, 14
Beck, Captain Anthony........... 202
Beck, Edward.................... 294
Beck, Matt'w.................... 269
Bedel, Josiah................... 277
Belcher, Mrs.................... 149
Beggs, Miles.................... 215
Beekman, Governor............... 131
Bellson, John................... 154
Belt, John...................... 223
Belt, Nehemiah Jr............... 276
Belt, Captain Tobias............ 276
Berry, Thomas................... 215
Berry, William.............. 75, 349
Benson, Perry,.................. 391
Benson, Stephen................. 322
Bentley, Richard................ 351
Bennett, Henrietta Maria........ 295

Bennett, Mr. John............... 88
Bennett, Richard...... 75, 76, 262, 310
Bennett, Mr. Richard............ 182
Bennett, Richard, Esq.... 295, 317, 322
Bennett Susanna Maria........... 295
Bennett, Truman................. 300
Besson, Thomas.................. 327
Best, Dr. J. W. F............... 204
Biggs, Ambrose.............. 302, 303
Bigger, John.................... 173
Billingsley, Francis............ 301
Billingsley, Thomas............. 352
Birkhead, Christopher........... 323
Bishop, Henry........ 11, 12, 13, 321
Bishop, Joseph.................. 285
Bishop, Robert.................. 350
Bishop, T. S.................... 377
Bevans, Cornelius............... 286
Bevins, John.................... 339
Bevan, Roland................... 319
Blank, Mrs...................... 73
Blankinson, William............. 333
Blakstone, ——................... 107
Blackston, Ebenezer......... 293, 296
Blakistone, Nehemiah............ 262
Blakiston, Nathaniel............ 260
Bladen, Thomas.................. 261
Bladen, William................. 339
Blake, Levin.................... 377
Blake, Joel..................... 319
Blay, Edward................ 295, 296
Blondell, John.................. 214
Boarman, William................ 288
Body, Captain John.............. 338
Bordley, Beale.................. 91
Bond, John...................... 273
Bond, Peregrine................. 274
Bonnefield, Christiana.......... 219
Bonam, Anam................. 9, 10, 11
Bonham, Malakiah................ 391
Bonner, James................... 325
Bostic, Samuel.................. 294
Boston, Thomas.................. 334
Bonvier ——..................... 106
Bosworth, Mr. John.............. 141
Bowen, Rev. L. P................ 118
Bowe, James..................... 215
Bowie, John..................... 377
Bowie, W........................ 374
Bowles, James................... 334
Bowles, John.................... 298
Bowley, Daniel.................. 360
Bowdel, Thomas.................. 306
Bowlter, John................... 7, 8
Boyce, William.................. 314
Boyd, Michael................... 391
Boyd, Thomas.................... 391
Boyle, James.................... 204
Bozman ——...................... 76
Bozman, John.................... 319
Bozman, William................. 317
Booker, John.................... 274
Booker, Richard................. 341

INDEX OF PROPER NAMES 433

Boothby, Edward.............. 173, 335
Buchanan, Archibald............... 360
Buchanan, Wm..................... 374
Bullen, Mr. John.................. 91
Bullen, John....................... 342
Bullen, Robert..................... 346
Burchell, Adam.................... 335
Burk, William...................... 304
Burdett, Mr. and Mrs.............. 146
Burdit, Thomas.................... 312
Burgess, Basil..................... 391
Burgess, George............. 324, 334
Burgess, Richard.................. 203
Burgess, Samuel................... 202
Burgess, William........ 75, 222, 261, 326
Burrage, John..................... 323
Burly, Robert...................... 339
Burnham, Samuel.................. 269
Burnham, William................. 309
Burrows, John..................... 273
Burrowes, Mathew............ 9, 12, 14
Butler, Francis.................... 326
Butter, Thomas.................... 214
Butterworth, Hezekiah............. 56
Butterworth, Mr................... 57
Bushnell, Edw'd................... 269
Bushnells, Peter.................. 283
Bussey, Mrs....................... 149
Bradley, Henry.................... 353
Bradley, Richard.................. 9
Bradford, Colonel William......... 356
Bragg, B.......................... 243
Brainthwayt, William.............. 261
Bramble, Thomas.................. 352
Brannock, Edmond................ 353
Brandt, Randell................... 310
Bray, Dr. Thomas.................. 119
Brent, Colonel Giles............... 67
Brent, Giles.......... 114, 252, 264, 287
Brent, Captain Giles.............. 261
Brent, Margaret............... 67, 287
Brent, Mrs. Margaret.............. 70
Brent, Mistress Margaret........ 252, 425
Brent, Mary................... 67, 287
Brereton, William............. 318, 342
Brevitt, John..................... 391
Bresseuir, Benojs................. 229
Brewer, Elizabeth................. 347
Brewer, Mr. John.................. 199
Brewer, John.................. 202, 327
Brewer, Joseph.................... 203
Brice, John.................... 334, 359
Brick, Richard.................... 215
Bridgen, Thos..................... 269
Brightwell, Richard............... 307
Briestow, George.................. 283
Briscoe, Henry............... 9, 11, 13
Briscoe, James.................... 274
Briscoe, John..................... 297
Briscoe, Samuel................... 273
Briant, John............ 11, 14, 106, 107
Bridges, Joseph................... 319
Brittingham, William.............. 280

Broadnox, Thomas................. 297
Brogden, David McC............... 204
Brogden, Mr. Harry H............. 198
Brogden, John L................... 203
Brogden, Major William............ 203
Brogden, Rev. Mr. William......... 199
Brogden, Dr. William.............. 203
Brogden, Rev. William............. 202
Brooksby, Cornelius............... 267
Brooksby, Lieut. Corns............ 268
Brookes, Baker, Esq............... 64
Brooke, Baker................ 261, 305
Brooke, Colonel Baker............. 132
Brookes, Benjamin................. 277
Brookes, Francis.................. 288
Brookes, Henry.................... 277
Brooke, Mr. Michael....... 149, 262, 351
Brooke, Mrs....................... 149
Brooke, Rich...................... 374
Brooke, Robert... 126, 257, 264, 291, 303
Brooke, Mr. Robert................ 181
Brooke, Robert, Esq............... 305
Brooke, Samuel.................... 204
Brooke, Thomas.................... 307
Brooke, Thomas, Esq............... 233
Brooke, Major Thomas............. 301
Brooke, Rodger.................... 305
Brown, Ellis...................... 326
Brown, James.................. 285, 307
Brown, John............. 320, 325, 339
Brown, Capt. John................. 281
Brown, Ninian..................... 215
Brown, Perigrine.................. 296
Brown, Richard.................... 416
Brown, Sidney..................... 278
Browne, Capt. Turner.............. 280
Browne, William........... 9, 12, 14, 390
Browning, James............... 292, 339
Browning, John.................... 341
Bruce, William.................... 391
Bruff, James...................... 391
Bruff, Richard.................... 281
Brumal, William................... 304
Bruton, John...................... 329
Bryant, John...................... 9
Bryant, John...................... 11
Bryan, Mathias.................... 309

Calvert, Anne..................... 112
Calvert, Benedict Leonard, 260, 261, 426
Calvert, Caecilius, 1, 2, 6, 7, 17, 30, 34, 36,
    39, 49, 53, 56, 57, 66, 71, 111, 124, 125,
    129, 234, 260, 257, 407, 422, 426.
Calvert, Charles......... 109, 234, 260, 261
Calvert, Charles, Esq...... 63, 301, 326
Calvert, Captain Charles.......... 261
Calvert, Charles Gov.............. 111
Calvert, Governor................. 408
Charles, 3rd. Lord Baltimore...... 6
Calvert, Eleanor.................. 426
Calvert, Elizabeth................ 426
Calvert, Frederick............ 260, 426
Calvert, George............ 2, 7, 8, 57

INDEX OF PROPER NAMES

Calvert, Sir George............... 1, 153
Calvert, Mr. Leonard.............. 70
Calvert, Governor Leonard...... 67, 421
Calvert, Leonard, 2, 6, 7, 8, 13, 16, 30 32, 33, 34, 50, 111, 260, 263, 407, 409, 411, 414, 418, 425.
Calvert, Philip............ 126, 261, 352
Calvert, Phillip, Esq., 63, 263, 288, 291, 340, 343, 345.
Calvert, Governor Philip....... 126, 261
Calvert, William................... 261
Calverts, the..................... 5, 60
Calder, Mr. James................. 91
Calhoun, James................... 360
Camber, John..................... 325
Carmichall, Neall.................282
Cameron, Finley.................. 214
Cameron, John.................... 215
Campbell, John................... 334
Canady, Mrs...................... 149
Cane, John....................... 310
Carleton, Thomas................. 307
Carnall, Daniel................... 342
Carinton, Thomas................. 12
Carnot, Christopher............... 14
Carnock, Xtofer.................. 11
Carnock, Christopher............. 9, 11
Carroll, Charles (the emigrant)..... 307
Carroll, Charles, Esq.............. 339
Carroll, Mr. Charles B............ 367
Carroll, Charles... 265, 336, 337, 374, 376
Carroll, Mr. Daniel................ 384
Carroll, James................... 401
Castor, Edward................... 300
Caton, Mr. Thomas................ 199
Caton, Thomas................... 202
Carvill, John..................... 293
Carvel, Richard................... 95
Carvile, Robert............... 107, 306
Carville, Mr. Robert............... 147
Carr, Nicholas.................... 302
Cartwright, John.................. 273
Cartwright, Demetrious............ 306
Carter, Colonel Edward............ 292
Carter, Edward........... 265, 322, 331
Carter, John..................... 316
Cary, John Dow................... 391
Catlin, Henry.................... 346
Cattlin, Robert................... 314
Cate, William.................... 289
Cassimir, John................... 189
Cawsin, Nicholas............ 412, 413
Causeen, Nicholas............ 265, 310
Cawood, Stephen................. 311
Caxton, Elizabeth................. 149
Cecil, Joshua.................... 334
Chaille, Peter.................... 377
Chambers, The................... 252
Chambers, John.................. 215
Chamberlaine, Jas. Lloyd.......... 374
Champ, John..................... 327
Chambers, Samuel................ 202
Champ, William................... 344

Chandler, Mr. Job................. 181
Chandler, Richard......... 266, 298, 310
Chaplain, Mrs..................... 149
Chapline, Joseph.................. 374
Chaplin, William.................. 351
Chapman, Henry N................ 391
Chapman, Samuel................. 203
Chapman, Thomas................ 221
Chapman, William................. 202
Chapman, William, Jr............. 202
Charinton, Thomas............ 9, 11, 14
Charles I......................... 36
Charles I, King. 25, 27, 45, 49, 56, 59, 76
Charles, King................. 3, 50, 57
Charles II........................ 76
Charles II, King............. 28, 75, 426
Chas., Hon., Esq.................. 92
Chase, Jo. H'y................... 374
Chase, Samuel............ 374, 375, 376
Clarkson, Robert.................. 220
Clare, Mark...................... 301
Cramphin, Thos., Jr............... 374
Crampson, James................. 215
Cranfield, Edward................. 9
Cratock, John.................... 374
Crawfurd, David.................. 374
Chelsey, Robert.................. 274
Cheney, Richard.................. 327
Cheseldyn, Kenelm........... 173, 291
Cheesman, William................ 315
Cheston, Dr. D. Murray............ 204
Cheston, Mr. Robert Murray....... 204
Cheever, Captain Samuel.......... 275
Chew, Joseph.................... 307
Chew, Samuel..... 222, 264, 324, 338, 373
Childs, Benjamin.................. 283
Child, Francis.................... 340
Chilman, Robert.................. 290
Chilton, Stephen.................. 273
Chipshem, Mr.................... 141
Christison, Wenlock........... 223, 224
Clabourne, William................ 151
Clabourne, Captaine............... 22
Claiborne, Mr. William............. 182
Claiborne, William......... 76, 152, 262
Clebornne, William................ 158
Cleburne, Thomas................ 153
Clagett, Thomas.................. 266
Clagett, Edward.................. 204
Clark, George.................... 273
Clark, John.................. 310, 325
Clarke, Joshua................... 374
Clark, Samuel.................... 276
Clark, Robert................ 289, 413
Clarke, Robert................... 261
Claxon, Robert................... 339
Clayland, Rev. James.............. 349
Clayton, George D................ 204
Claywell, Peter................... 280
Clayton, Solomon................. 284
Clegate, Thomas................. 303
Clemm, William.................. 360
Clements, Henry................. 391

INDEX OF PROPER NAMES 435

Clemerson, Andrew.................. 341
Cleave, Nathaniel................... 285
Clickett, Thos...................... 269
Clinton, Honourable George... 267, 268
Cloberry, William............... 152, 158
Cloberry and Clayborne............. 151
Clocker, Daniel..................... 288
Coode, John................. 237, 260, 262
Cobreth, John....................... 301
Cockshutt, John..................... 412
Cockey, William..................... 337
Coleburn, William...............313, 316
Coulbourns, The..................... 256
Coke, Lord.......................... 3
Colden, Junr. Com. Cadr............ 268
Colgate, Richard.................... 335
Coal, Thomas.................. 303, 332
Cole, Mr. Charles................. 91, 92
Cole, Josiah........................ 221
Cole, Josias........................ 185
Cole, Richard............... 9, 11, 12, 14
Cole, William....................... 318
Colengs, Thomas.................... 286
Collings, John...................... 284
Collins, Thomas.................... 296
Collett, Richard................... 342
Collier, Douty..................... 279
Collier, Robert................ 279, 353
Combs, William..................... 349
Comegys, Cornelius................. 297
Compton, Bishop Henry............. 170
Compton, John...................... 313
Conant, Robert..................... 324
Conneway, James.................... 330
Conner, Sarah...................... 297
Cony, Rev. Mr. Peregrine........... 173
Constable, Henry................... 336
Contee, Charles S.................. 204
Contee, John....................... 374
Contee, Thos....................... 373
Copley, Sir Lionel......... 169, 237, 260
Copley, Father Thomas............. 15
Copley, Mr..................... 10, 413
Copley, Thomas....... 13, 15, 66, 67, 416
Covel, Ann......................... 327
Corbet, Hutton..................... 287
Corbyn, Mr. Henry.................. 141
Cornish, Jno....................... 269
Corwin, William.................... 349
Cornwalleys, Captain Thomas, 13, 154, 261.
Cornwalleys, Thomas, Esq.,.. 11, 12, 14
Cornwallis, Captain Thomas... 292, 294
Cornwallis, Thomas, Esq.......... 8, 417
Cornwallis, Thomas, 7, 114, 264, 288, 290, 291, 414.
Cornwallis, William................ 333
Cosden, Thomas..................... 304
Costin, Henry...................... 349
Costin, Stephen.............. 316, 319
Cottingham, Thomas................ 315
Cotton, Richard.................... 322
Couchan, John...................... 214

Coursey, Henry............ 261, 173, 304
Coursey, James..................... 296
Coursey, William................... 298
Courtney, Hercules................. 360
Courtney, Thomas............. 288, 290
Courts, Colonel John............... 233
Courts, John....................... 308
Cowley, George..................... 348
Cowman, Captain Joseph............ 202
Cowman, Joseph..................... 203
Cowman, Joseph E................... 204
Cook, Miles........................ 350
Cook, Thos......................... 269
Cooke, Captain Andrew........ 244, 561
Cooke, Anne........................ 244
Cooke, Ebenezer.................... 243
Cooke, John Esten.................. 153
Cooper, James...................... 269
Cooper, Patrick.................... 214
Cooper, Samuel..................... 320
Cooper, Thomas................... 9, 10
Covington, Nehemiah................ 317
Covingtons, The.................... 256
Cox, Mrs. Ann...................... 9
Cox, Edward........................ 326
Cox, James......................... 360
Cox, John.......................... 374
Craik, James....................... 391
Creak, Jo.......................... 269
Crato, John........................ 131
Crafts, Captain Dudley............. 268
Crafts, Dud................... 267, 268
Cromwell, Oliver.............. 181, 262
Cromwell, Richard.................. 338
Crouch, Ralph...................... 413
Crouch, John....................... 294
Crouch, William.................... 328
Crosby, William.................... 323
Crow, James........................ 276
Crowley, Chas...................... 374
Cumin, William..................... 214
Cummings, William, Esq............. 91
Curke, John...................... 8, 9
Currer, William.................... 283
Curtis, Edmund..................... 262
Curtis, Robert..................... 347

Daborn, Thomas..................... 324
Dailey, Mr.........................146
Dale, Thomas....................... 295
Daley, Bryan....................... 340
Dallam, Richd...................... 374
Darby, Mr.......................... 146
Darcey, William.................... 355
Dare, Captain John................. 203
Dare, Cleaverly.................... 276
Dare, Samuel....................... 276
Dare, William...................... 343
Darnell, Colonel Henry, 236, 261, 266, 290, 306, 323.
Darnall, John, Esq................. 236
Dashield, James............... 279, 322
Dashiell, Clement.................. 278

INDEX OF PROPER NAMES

Dashiell, George.................. 374
Dashiell, Henry................... 279
Dashiell, Joseph.................. 377
Dashiell, Louther................. 279
Dashield, Thomas.................. 322
Dashiells, The.................... 256
Dashiell, William..................278
Davenant, Sir William............ 76, 77
Davenport, Humphrey............... 297
Davidson, Andrew..................214
Davidson, John.................... 390
Davidson, William................. 214
Davies, Thomas.................... 282
Davis, Captain Allen.............. 274
Davis, George Lachlan............. 219
Davis, James................. 318, 377
Davis, John.................. 276, 298
Davis, Thomas................ 300, 323
Davis, William.................... 277
Daw, Andrew....................... 214
Dawson, Anthony................... 353
Dawson, Impy...................... 281
Dawson, William................... 154
Day, Dorothy...................... 149
Day, Edward....................... 321
Day, George....................... 289
Day, Richard...................... 276
Day, Samuel....................... 202
Deale, David...................... 355
Deale, Franklin................... 204
Dean, William..................... 299
De Courcy, William................ 228
d'Eestaing, Count................. 390
de Falstaff, Aubrey............... 207
Degedy, John...................... 214
de Grasse, Count............. 379, 390
d, Hinoyosa, Alexander............ 131
Delabar, John................ 152, 158
de la Rock, Charles............... 290
Denahoe, Daniel................... 315
Dent, George...................... 275
Dent, Jno.................... 231, 309, 373
Dent, William................ 173, 307
Denwood, Levin.................... 321
de Somerville, Sir Philip.... 205, 206
Derholme, James................... 214
Devall, Marien.................... 327
Dever, John....................... 360
Devoir, Richard................... 324
Dick, James....................... 202
Dick, Jean........................ 406
Dick, Mr.......................... 367
Dickinson, Captain Charles........ 281
Dickinson, Edward................. 314
Dickinson, Henry.................. 374
Dickenson, Walter................. 354
Dickinson, William................ 350
Digges, William........... 236, 261, 266
Diggs, Colonel William............ 340
Dixon, Ambrose.................... 313
Dixon, John.................. 202, 337
Dixon, Mr. James............. 215, 255
Dixon, Robert..................... 352
Dixon, Thomas................ 254, 278
Dixon, William............... 300, 349
Dodd, Wm.......................... 269
Donalson, Charles................. 214
Done, John........................ 377
Done, Robert...................... 377
Donaldson, Thomas................. 214
Dorrell, Thomas.................. 7, 9
Dorrington, William............... 351
Dorsey, Captain John.............. 337
Dorsey, Edward.... 88, 91, 173, 329, 338
Dorsey, Miss Mary V............... 425
Dorsey, Mr. John................... 88
Dorsey, Mr. Speaker................ 94
Dorsey, Richard................... 391
Dorseys, the....................... 79
Dorsey, John...................... 274
Dorsey, William................... 355
Douglass, John............... 266, 309
Downes, George.................... 377
Downes, Henry..................... 341
Downes, Mitchell.................. 377
Doyn, Isaac....................... 274
Draper, Alexander................. 315
Draper, Peter.................... 9, 13
Drummond, Alex.................... 269
Dryer, Samuel..................... 330
Dryson, Thomas A.................. 391
Dyer, Edward...................... 391
Duckett, Thomas A................. 204
Dudley, Richard................... 349
Duke, Richard............. 9, 11, 12, 14
Duke, James....................... 304
Dukes, Robert..................... 315
Dulany, H. Rozier................. 402
Dulany, Mr. Grafton............... 402
Dulaney, Walter.................... 91
Dunbarr, Jeremiah................. 214
Durand, Alice..................... 330
Durand, William.............. 181, 262
Duvall, Dr. Howard M.............. 204
Duvall, George.................... 360
Duvall, John...................... 328
Duvall, Mareen............... 277, 327

Eagleston, Bernard................ 330
Earle, James, Jr.................. 284
Earle, Jos........................ 374
Earle, Mrs. Clara Tilghman........ 425
Earle, R. T....................... 373
Eason, John....................... 352
Eaton, James...................... 351
Ebbert, Edward.................... 245
Ebbs, Edward...................... 414
Ebbs, Thomas...................... 414
Eccleston, Captain John E......... 281
Eccleston, Hugh................... 354
Eccleston, John, Lieutenant-Colonel, 390, 391.
Edd, —............................. 88
Eddis, —..................... 145, 374
Eden, Captain Robert.............. 261
Eden, Governor.................... 371

INDEX OF PROPER NAMES 437

Edlowe, Joseph.................... 304
Edminston, Samuel............... 391
Edmonds, Richard................ 342
Edmondson, John.......... 223, 347, 355
Edmonson, John............... 302, 351
Edward the Confessor............. 68
Edwards, Richard................ 7, 9
Edwards, Robert.......... 9, 11, 12, 14
Edwin, William................ 9, 12, 14
Edwyn, William................. 9, 11
Eisley, Jno....................... 269
Elbert, John L.................... 391
Elbin, John....................... 417
Eldridge, William................ 346
Elgate, William.................. 318
Elkin, John............ 9, 11, 12, 14, 417
Elkins, John...................... 417
Ellicotts, the..................... 98
Ellis, Joseph..................... 279
Ellis, Peter...................... 333
Elliott, Vincent.................. 293
Elliott, William.............. 203, 284
Elit, Benjamin................... 276
Ellys, Robert.................... 290
Elmes, William.................. 294
Eltonhead, Edward............... 303
Eltonhead, Madame.............. 184
Eltonhead, William......... 182, 291
Elston, Ralph.................... 348
Elzey, John...................... 317
Elzy, John....................... 319
Emerson, Thomas................ 344
Emerton, Humphrey.............. 324
Emmett, John.................... 316
Emory, Arthur................... 348
Enelegh, James.................. 162
English, James.................. 269
Ennalls, Bartholomew............ 353
Ennalls, Captain Henry.......... 280
Ennalls, Thos................ 173, 374
Evans, Anthony.................. 290
Evans, Captain William.......... 261
Evans, Ebenezer................. 285
Evans, Job....................... 338
Evans, John................. 285, 286
Evans, Walter................... 277
Evanson, Mr..................... 146
Evelyn, Captain George.......... 160
Evelyn, George.................. 264
Everett, John.................... 222
Ewen, Richard............... 262, 325
Ewens, William.................. 262
Ewing, William.................. 282
Ewins, John..................... 333
Exon, Henry..................... 289

Fairfax, Mr...................... 11
Fairfax, Nicholas.............. 7, 9, 11
Fairweather, Richard............. 269
Farchaser, Henry................ 214
Farguson, Joshua................ 270
Fay, Prof. William Wirt.......... 204
Farsett, Daniel.................. 377

Fenance, Auto................... 269
Fendall, Governor................ 72
Fendall, Josias. 73, 126, 260, 265, 292, 306,
Fenwick, Cuthbert, 12, 14, 15, 263, 288, 291, 417.
Fenwick, Madame................ 184
Fenwick, Mrs..................... 73
Ffitter, William................. 9, 12
Ferguson, Duncan................ 215
Ferguson, William............... 215
Fickle, Benjamin................. 391
Finch, Thomas................... 277
Fisher, Mary.................... 220
Fisher, Philip................... 15
Fisher, Thomas.................. 264
Fisher, William............. 294, 341
Fitspatrick, David............... 281
Fitter, William.................. 14
Fitzwalters, Garrett............. 416
Fleete, Captain Henry..... 137, 408, 425
Fleete, Edward,................. 106
Fleming, Wm.................... 279
Floyd, James.................... 338
Foard, Hezekiah................. 391
Forbus, Thomas................. 214
Force, Colonel Peter.............. 94
Ford, Josias..................... 224
Ford, Mr........................ 255
Ford, Rebecca................... 224
Ford, Samuel.................... 224
Ford, Sarah..................... 224
Ford, Thomas.................... 323
Ford, Widow..................... 223
Ford, William................... 354
Fossett, Jno..................... 270
Foster, Seth.................... 344
Fountain, Marcy................. 278
Fountain, Nicholas............... 318
Fowke, Gerard................... 311
Fowler, Benoi................... 276
Fowler, Jeremiah................ 276
Fox, George..................... 223
Franklin, Benjamin............... 392
Franklin, Thomas................ 106
Franklyn, John.................. 322
Franklyn, Robert................ 326
Franks, Matt.................... 270
Frazier, James.................. 269
Frazier, Ensign Jno.............. 268
Frazier, John................... 267
Freckle, Alison.................. 207
Freckle, Stephen................ 207
Freeman, John................... 327
Freeman, William................ 294
Freemond, Lewis.......... 9, 11, 12, 13
Frisby, James............... 296, 340
Fuller, Captain William...... 149, 262
Fulton, Robert.................. 195
Furnace, William................ 315
Furnis, James................... 280

Gage, General................... 372
Gaines, Richard................. 302

INDEX OF PROPER NAMES

Gaither, George R., Jr.............. 204
Gaither, Henry E................... 391
Gale, George....................... 204
Gale, Madam Elizabeth............. 255
Galloway, John................ 366, 368
Galloway, Richard.................. 325
Galloway, Samuel.............. 223, 366
Galloway, William.................. 293
Games, John...................... 8, 9
Gantt, Edwd.................. 275, 373
Gantt, Dr. Thomas..................203
Gantt, Thos., Jr.................... 374
Gardiner, Luke..................... 292
Gardiner, Richard.............. 263, 308
Garey, William..................... 281
Garrett, John...................... 316
Gary, John.................... 302, 351
Gater, John........................ 327
Gates, Major-General Horatio...... 390
Garnett, Richard................... 106
Garrett, Richard................... 291
Gassaway, Captain Thomas........ 203
Gassaway, Henry................... 202
Gassaway, John....... 202, 203, 270, 391
Gassaway, L. Dorsey............... 204
Gassaway, Mr. Louis Dorsey....... 198
Gasham, William.................... 377
Geddes, Mr. Andrew................ 172
George III.......................... 27
George, John....................... 295
Gerrard, Dr. Thomas, 71, 113, 132 263, 287, 291.
Gerrard, Justinian.................. 291
Gerard, Richard.............. 7, 10, 14
Gerard, Sir Thomas, Knight........ 7
Gerry, Elbridge............ 391, 402, 407
Gervais, Thomas.................... 9
Gervaise, "Brother" Thomas....... 15
Gibson, David...................... 270
Gibson, James...................... 277
Gibson, Miles................. 331, 336
Gibson, Woolman................... 281
Gilbert, Richard................ 10, 13
Gill, Benjamin..................... 308
Gill, Edward....................... 337
Gill, Mr. Benjamin................. 148
Gillett, German.................... 319
Gillis, Captain Thomas............. 278
Gillis, Thomas..................... 322
Gillis, William.................... 279
Gittine, John...................... 289
Gittings, W. R. S.................. 204
Gist, Mordecai, Brigadier-General.. 371
Glaney, John....................... 214
Glanvill, William.................. 318
Glass, John........................ 321
Glover, Wm........................ 270
Godden, John....................... 321
Godlington, Thomas.......... 264, 297
Godson, Peter...................... 142
Godwin, William.................... 348
Goldsborough, Robert......253, 281, 374
Goldsbury, Robert.................. 326

Goldsmith, George 342
Goldsmith, Harekins............... 331
Goldsmith, Samuel................. 331
Goldsmith, Thomas................. 331
Goldson, Daniel.................... 304
Goned, James....................... 285
Goodman, John..................... 277
Goodridge, Timothy............ 348, 351
Goodman, Edward................... 332
Gordon, Alexander............. 214, 322
Gordon, Daniel..................... 312
Gordon, Rev. Mr. John.............. 91
Gordon, Robert, Esq................ 91
Gore, Stephen................. 10, 12, 14
Gorsuch, Charles................... 337
Goulden, Gabriel................... 302
Gothery, Moses.................... 377
Gover, Robert...................... 324
Graham, David..................... 215
Granger, William................... 343
Grant, Daniel...................... 215
Grant, William..................... 214
Grantham, Cap. William........... 281
Gray, Allen........................ 278
Gray, Francis...................... 416
Gray, John......................... 327
Gray, Joseph....................... 316
Gray, Richard...................... 342
Gregston, Thomas.............. 12, 415
Green, Francis..................... 311
Greene, Henry...................... 7
Green, John................... 270, 377
Green, Jonas, Esq.................. 93
Green, Leonard..................... 311
Green, Mich'l...................... 269
Green, Mr. Jonas................... 91
Green, Mr. Thomas, 10, 11, 261, 266, 287, 415.
Green, Nicholas Harwood.......... 204
Green, Robert...................... 311
Green, William................ 94, 316
Greenberry, Nicholas....... 88, 261, 330
Greenfield, Kenelyn Truman....... 274
Greenfield, Thomas................. 273
Greenland, Jno..................... 270
Greenway, Robert.................. 216
Greenwood, Armiger................ 323
Greyson, Thomas.............. 10, 12, 14
Grendall, Captain Christopher..... 202
Grenville, Lord.................... 363
Groom, Moses...................... 334
Gross, Roger.................. 325, 346
Griffin, Anthony................... 344
Griffis, Edward.................... 275
Griffith, Benjamin................. 360
Griffith, Thomas.............. 336, 342
Griffith, H........................ 374
Grigsta............................ 11
Grigsta, Thomas.................... 10
Greene, Henry...................... 10
Grist, Isaac....................... 360
Grundy, Joseph.................... 296
Grundy, Robert.................... 350

INDEX OF PROPER NAMES 439

Gullock, Thomas.................. 324
Gunby, Kirk..................... 278

Hack, Stephen.................... 340
Haddoway, Captain............... 282
Hagner, Judge Alexander B.... 198, 204
Hailes, James.................... 270
Halfehide, John.................. 106
Halfhead, John................... 289
Hall, Banjamin............ 233, 313, 374
Hall, Benj. Edw.................. 374
Hall, Caleb...................... 360
Hall, Charles....................314
Hall, David...................... 278
Hall, J.......................... 374
Hall, James...................... 202
Hall, John....................... 331
Hall, Hamilton................... 204
Hall, Mr......................... 254
Hall, Peter...................... 377
Hall, Robert..................... 281
Hall, Stephen.................... 285
Hallam, Mr. and Mrs..............146
Hallowes, John...................   9
Hambleton, Phillimon............. 281
Hambleton, William............... 344
Hamblin, George.................. 321
Hamerton, Thos................... 270
Hamilton, Dr. Alexander........ 90, 91
Hamilton, George................. 391
Hamilton, John................... 391
Hammond, Charles................. 331
Hammond, Edward.................. 320
Hammond, Major John.............. 88
Hammond, Matthias................ 374
Hammond, Mr. T................... 367
Hammond, Rezin.............. 203, 374
Hammond, Richard................. 301
Hammond, Thomas............. 347, 329
Hamon, Benjamin.................. 70
Hamon, Cybil..................... 70
Handcock, J. F................... 272
Hands, Th. B..................... 374
Handy, —......................... 377
Handy, Levin..................... 377
Handy, Samuel.................... 377
Handy, Wm. Saml.................. 374
Hanson, Captain William.......... 274
Hanson, Hans..................... 298
Hanson, Isaac.................... 391
Hanson, John, Jr.................374
Hanson, S........................ 373
Hanson, Samuel................... 391
Hardesty, George................. 305
Hardesty, Richard C.............. 203
Harding, Charles................. 277
Harding, Robert.................. 202
Hardman, Major Henry............. 390
Harford, Henry.............. 164, 260
Hargess, Thomas.................. 312
Hargess, William................. 312
Harlow, Thos..................... 270
Harper, Jacob.................... 284

Harper, James.................... 204
Harpin, Thomas................... 289
Harrington, Thomas............... 12
Harrington, William.............. 414
Harris, Arthur................... 391
Harris, Benton................... 377
Harris, Elizabeth................ 220
Harris, John................ 266, 345
Harris, Richard.................. 304
Harris, Samuel................... 70
Harris, Thomas................... 309
Harris, William........ 281, 297, 320, 333
Harrison, Henry.................. 275
Harrison, Richard.......... 274, 308, 324
Harrison, Samuel................. 203
Harrison, Thomas................. 374
Harrison, Will.............. 274, 373
Hart, Captain John............... 260
Hart, Governor John......... 210, 212
Hart, Mr. Samuel................. 91
Harvey, Newman................... 275
Harvey, Nicholas....... 14, 106, 264, 291
Harvie, Governor................. 34
Harwood, Benjamin................ 203
Harwood, Captain Thomas.... 203, 334
Harwood, Colonel Richard......... 203
Harwood, Colonel Richard, Jr..... 203
Harwood Dr. Richard.............. 204
Harwood, James H................. 203
Harwood, Joseph.................. 203
Harwood, Major O. S.............. 203
Harwood, Major Thomas............ 203
Harwood, Osborn S................ 203
Harwood, Phill................... 304
Harwood, Richard................. 276
Harwood, Robert............. 325, 352
Harwood, Thomas, Jr.............. 203
Harwood, William................. 203
Hatch, John................. 262, 308
Hathaway, John................... 335
Hatton, Thomas.......... 261, 288, 308
Hatton, William.................. 344
Haupt, Dr........................ 400
Hawkins, Ernault................. 284
Hawkins, Henry.............. 297, 348
Hawkins, Ralph................... 330
Hawley, Captain William.......... 263
Hawley, Jerome........ 7, 8, 414, 418
Hawley, Mr. Hierom............... 21
Hawley, Thomas................... 418
Hay, John........................ 214
Hay, Thomas......................281
Hayes, "Father" Timothy.......... 15
Hayman, Henry.................... 317
Haynie, Ezekiel.................. 391
Hays, Timothy (Father)...........   9
Hayward, Captain Francis......... 280
Haywood, William................. 297
Heath, James............ 294, 297, 325
Heath, Thomas.......... 9, 11, 12, 13
Heckley, James................ 9, 13
Hedge, Thomas.................... 333
Heleger, Philip.................. 295

Hemmet, McKelvie................ 273
Hemmet, Robert.................. 273
Hempstead, William............... 289
Hemsley, John.................... 283
Hemsley, William...... 284, 298, 346, 350
Henderson, James................. 319
Henderson, Robert................ 214
Henrietta, Maria.................. 56
Henly, Israel..................... 268
Henly, Robert.................... 309
Henrys, The..................... 256
Herbert, Mr...................... 146
Herman, Augustin........ 131, 265, 341
Herman, Casparus................ 343
Herrings, Barito.................. 143
Hervey, Nicholas................ 9, 11
Hewett, Mr. John................. 173
Heyburn, Law.................... 270
Hickman, Arthur.................. 278
Hicks, Captain Levin.............. 281
Hicks, Thomas................... 354
Highland, John................... 343
Hill, Captain Edward.............. 261
Hill, Captain Richard.............. 88
Hill, Clement................ 261, 308
Hill, Dr. Richard S................ 204
Hill, Richard..................... 293
Hill, James...................... 214
Hill, John........... 7, 9, 10, 11, 14, 315
Hill, Thos....................... 270
Hill, William S................... 285
Hillary, Thomas.................. 307
Hillerd, John..................... 10
Hilliard, John.................. 13, 106
Hillierd, John.................... 9
Hills, Richard.................... 13
Hinderson, Bartlett................ 340
Hindman, Wm................... 374
Hindry, James................... 214
Hinman, Zadoch.................. 377
Hodges, Benjamin............ 11, 12, 14
Hodges, John T.................. 203
Hodges, the..................... 98
Hodges, Thomas............... 9, 11, 204
Hodgkins, John.................. 302
Hodgson, George................. 215
Hodson, John................ 280, 355
Holdern, John.................. 9, 11
Holdman, Abraham............... 333
Holey, Robert.................... 283
Holland, Arthur.................. 338
Holland, Francis.................. 323
Holland, George.............. 299, 332
Holland, Isaac................... 280
Holland, John................ 283, 318
Holland, Judge Charles F.......... 256
Holland, Nehemiah............... 377
Holland, Richard................. 353
Holland, Captain William.......... 87
Hollbrook, Thomas................ 318
Holliday, Henry.................. 268
Holliday, Thomas................. 306
Hollingsworth, George............. 337
Hollingsworth, S................. 360
Hollingsworth, Zebulon........... 283
Hollis, John.................... 9, 11
Hollis, William.................. 332
Hollman, William................ 294
Hollowes, John................... 11
Holt, Robert.................... 219
Hollyday, Colonel Henry C........ 255
Hollyday, Jr..................... 373
Hollyday, William Mcade.......... 204
Homewood, James................ 330
Homewood, John................. 336
Hooker, Francis.................. 222
Hooker Thomas.......... 325, 326, 337
Hooper, Captain Roger............ 281
Hooper, Henry........ 281, 302, 355, 374
Hooper, Richard.................. 355
Hooper, Wm..................... 374
Hopewell, Hugh.................. 273
Hopewell, Joseph.............. 273, 299
Hopewell, Richard............ 293, 299
Hopkins, Gerard.................. 360
Hopkins, Joseph.............. 292, 296
Hopkins, Robert.................. 345
Hopkins, Samuel................. 281
Hopkins, Wm................. 270, 352
Horn, Edward................... 288
Horn, Winifride.................. 290
Horsey, John.................... 314
Horsey, Stephen.................. 314
Horseys, The.................... 256
Hoskins, Bennett................. 311
Hoskins, Captain Philip............ 233
Hooe, R........................ 373
Howard, Cornelius................ 329
Howard, Edmond................. 319
Howard, Ephraim................. 374
Howard, Francis.................. 354
Howard, General John Eager....... 385
Howard, George.................. 286
Howard, Henry.................. 334
Howard, John................ 202, 329
Howard, Joshua.................. 337
Howard, Mathew................. 328
Howard, Mr. Philip............... 88
Howard, Samuel................. 329
Howard, William................. 286
Howell, John.................... 296
Howell, Thomas.................. 292
Howerton, John.................. 306
Howgate, James.................. 331
Hudson, John.................... 329
Hughes, Colonel G. W............ 204
Hull, Edward.................... 348
Hume, Thomas.................. 215
Humphreys, Mary................ 337
Humphreys, Robert............... 351
Hunt, William................... 323
Hunter, Lord.................... 363
Hunter, Patrick.................. 214
Hurlock, George.................. 350
Hutchins, Charles................ 353
Hutchins, Colonel Charles......... 173

INDEX OF PROPER NAMES 441

Hutchins, James..................... 284
Hutchinson, Thomas............... 350
Hutchinson, William................ 307
Hyland, Nicholas..................... 283
Hynsons, The 252
Hynson, Thomas..................... 298

Iglehart, Dr. James D.............. 204
Iglehart, Paul........................ 204
Iglehart, Richard W................ 204
Iglehart, Thomas S................. 204
Ijams, John............................ 203
Ijams, William........................ 276
Illingsworth, William............ 301, 348
Impey, Thomas...................... 296
Ingle, Richard.................. 262, 425
Ingram, Robert....................... 317
Innis, Thomas........................ 288
Insley, Captain James............. 281
Insull, Thos........................... 270
Isaacks, Captain Sutton........... 275
Isaac, Edward........................ 306
Ives, James........................... 335

Jackson, Barnaby 288
Jackson, Captain Edward........... 282
Jackson, Henry...................... 282
Jackson, James...................... 377
Jackson, Richard.................... 366
Jackson, Samuel..................... 322
Jackson, William H................. 256
Jacobs, John J....................... 391
Jacobs, Samuel...................... 202
Jacobson, Peter..................... 339
Jacque, Mr............................ 367
Jadwin, John......................... 347
James, Charles............. 293, 295, 296
James, Henry................... 9, 12, 14
James I................................ 25
James I, King........................ 45
James, John.................... 296, 332
James, William.................. 300, 366
Jammison, Stephen................. 12
Jarbo, John........................... 310
Jay, John............................. 392
Jefferson, Mr........................ 146
Jefferson, Thomas................... 392
Jenifer, Danl................ 289, 346, 373
Jenkins, Francis................. 173, 320
Jenkins, Thomas..................... 281
Jenkins, William..................... 315
Jenkinson, Charles.................. 363
Jennings, Mary.................. 9, 10, 13
Jennings, Richard................... 345
Johns, Richard.................. 301, 303
Johnson, Bradley T................. 380
Johnson, John............... 28, 314, 342
Johnson, Ths. Junr....... 374, 375, 377
Johnson, William.................... 215
Jones, Captain William............. 279
Jones, Daniel........................ 279
Jones, David......................... 333
Jones, Edward.................. 296, 340

Jones, Elisha........................ 286
Jones, Henry.................... 203, 295
Jones, Leonard...................... 315
Jones, Mrs........................... 146
Jones, Owen......................... 311
Jones, Robert.............. 270, 341, 345
Jones, Thomas....................... 279
Jones, William.................. 328, 353
Jordan, Jeremiah.................... 273
Jordan, Jno.......................... 373
Jordan, Justinian................... 273
Jordan, Theodorus................... 273
Jordan, Thomas...................... 351
Joseph, William................ 260, 321
Julian, Steven....................... 284
Jump, William....................... 284
Jumphry, And'w..................... 270

Kean, Mr............................. 146
Keech, Captain James............... 233
Keen, Edward........................ 304
Keen, Richard................... 302, 355
Keene, Richard...................... 266
Keen, William....................... 318
Keener, Melchoir.................... 360
Kager, Robert....................... 297
Kelly, Lot and Company........... 366
Kelly, Thos.......................... 270
Kemp, William....................... 301
Kendall, Richard.................... 353
Kennards, the....................... 98
Kennedy, Daniel..................... 215
Kennery, John....................... 215
Kent, Colonel Robert W............ 203
Kent, James......................... 204
Kenton, Richard.................... 8, 9
Key, Francis Scott.................. 424
Key, Peter........................... 289
Key, Richard Ward.................. 274
Keylin, Nicholas.................... 416
Kilty, John.......................... 391
Kilty, William...................... 391
King, Charles....................... 273
King, Colonel Robert................ 118
King, Elias.......................... 293
King, Honorable Colonel Robert... 278
King, Jesse.......................... 280
King of Pascatoway.................. 22
King of the Patuxent................ 33
Kings, The........................... 256
King, Thomson M.................... 204
King, Whittington................... 279
King, Yoacomaco..................... 24
Kinnemount, John.................... 346
Kinnemont, Samuel.................. 281
Kinsey, Paul........................ 336
Kirby, William...................... 290
Kirk, John..................... 315, 316
Kirk, Martin................. 67, 68, 344
Kirshaw, James..................... 276
Knight, William..................... 283
Knightleye, Robert.................. 205
Knighton, Thomas.................... 324

INDEX OF PROPER NAMES

Knox, Major-General Henry........ 390
Knox, General Henry............... 388
Krugier, Captain Martin........... 131

Lackey, Jno....................... 270
Lacy, Thomas...................... 348
La Hay, Arthur.................... 413
Lamar, William.................... 391
Lamax, Thomas..................... 313
Lamb, Pierce...................... 296
Lambert, Josias................... 347
Lancaster, Jo..................... 270
Lane, Captain William..............286
Lane, Dutton...................... 336
Lane, Rob't....................... 270
Lane, Tobias...................... 282
Langford, John.............. 162, 298
Langley, Robert................... 333
Lansdale, Isaac................... 276
Lansdle, Richard.................. 276
Larkins, Jeremiah................. 284
Larkin, John................ 295, 327
Larkin, Mr......................... 98
Larkin, Thomas.................... 306
Latham, John...................... 284
Latrobe, Henry.................... 204
Latrobe, Honorable John H. B..... 195
Lauder, David..................... 215
Lawrence, Benjamin................ 303
Lawrence, Honorable Sir Thomas, 88,
    170, 173, 237, 261.
Laws, Elijah...................... 286
Laws, Panter...................... 279
Lawson, David......................270
Lawson, John............. 262, 277, 307
Lawson, Peter..................... 374
Lawson, Samuel................... 8, 9
Leak, Richard..................... 295
Leake, Rob't...................... 270
Lechford, Sir Richard.......... 7, 30, 32
Le Compt, Anthony................. 354
Lee, Captain Arthur............... 274
Lee, Edward....................... 203
Lee, James........................ 312
Lee, John.................... 332, 353
Lee, Mary......................... 141
Lee, Peter........................ 271
Lee, Richard...................... 261
Lee, Tho. Sim..................... 374
Lee, William...................... 309
Leitchwoorth, Thomas.............. 301
Lemare, John...................... 311
Letchford, Sir Richard.............. 8
Leverly, George................... 360
Levington, Aaron.................. 360
Lewellin, John.................... 299
Lewger, John............. 261, 287, 416
Lewis, Henry...................... 330
Lewis, William.................... 287
Lightfoot, Thomas................. 329
Lincoln, Jonathan................. 297
Lindenberger, George.............. 360
Lingan, George............... 305, 339

Lingan, Mr. George................. 98
Littleton, Southby................ 320
Llewellyn, John................... 234
Lloyd, Col. Edward............91, 253
Lloyd, Edward, 75, 126, 132, 149, 181, 261
    262, 330, 344, 374
Lloyd, Henrietta Maria............ 350
Lloyd, Madam Henrietta Maria..... 255
Lloyd, Philemon..............299, 348
Lloyd, Rachel..................... 186
Lloyd, Thomas..................... 186
Lock, Mevell...................... 273
Lockerman, Jacob.................. 281
Lockwood, Robert............. 326, 332
Loe, Richard.................9, 12, 14
Lomas, Mr. John.................... 91
London, Ambrose................... 315
Long, Colonel Charles Challie..... 377
Long, Samuel...................... 316
Lookerman, Jacob.................. 354
Love, Robert...................... 336
Lovely, Deliverance............... 298
Lowe, Abraham..................... 214
Lowe, Captain Richard............... 7
Lowe, Colonel Henry............... 300
Lowe, Colonel Vincent............. 253
Lowe, Henry....................... 261
Lowe, Hon. Nicholas, Esq.......... 243
Lowe, James....................... 214
Lowe, John T...................... 391
Lowe, Nicholas.................... 350
Lowe, Richard.................... 3, 8
Lowe, Vincent................ 261, 332
Lowey, Thomas..................... 214
Lowndes, Charles................... 91
Lowndes, Christopher............... 91
Lowther, Lady Agnes............... 153
Lowther, Sir Richard.............. 153
Lumboldt, Annie................... 223
Lunsdale, Henry................... 214
Lusby, John....................... 282
Lusted, Richard.................... 13
Lusthead, Richard..... 9, 11, 12, 13, 106
Lux, Darby................... 202, 374
Lux, William...................... 360
Lyle, Sabret...................... 275
Lyle, William..................... 275
Lyne, Philip...................... 354
Lyon, William..................... 360

Macbayn, John..................... 214
Macbean, Francis.................. 215
McBean, William................... 214
Maclean, John..................... 214
McCarty, Alex..................... 270
McCarty, Jno...................... 270
McClamy, Captain Wm............... 279
McClery, Samuel................... 284
McCloster, Samuel................. 278
Maccollum, John................... 215
McCormack, Edw'd.................. 270
Maccubbin, Mr. Samuel............. 203
Maccubbin, Zachariah.............. 202

INDEX OF PROPER NAMES 443

Macdermott, Angus	215
Macdonall, Arch.	214
Macdonall, Arch. alias Kennedy	214
Macdonald, John	214
MacDougall, Major-General Alexander	390
Macdugall, Alexander	214
Macdugall, Hugh	215
McEllond, Roger	271
Macferson, William	215
Macgiffin, Alexander	215
Macgiloary, Farq	214
MacGiloray, William	214
MacGregor, Allestra	213
Macgregrier, John	215
McHenry, James	384
MacIntire, Finloe	215
MacIntire, Hugh	215
MacIntire, John	214
MacIntosh, Alexander	215
MacIntosh, James	215
McIntosh, Laughlin	215
McKean, Thomas	380
McKeele, Capt. Thomas	281
Mackeel, John	353
Makemie, Francis	116
Mackewan, John	215
Mackey, Daniel	341
Mackey, James	313
Mackey, Patrick	215
McKinly, Dan'l	270
Maclearn, James	215
MacLaughlin, Margaret	210
McLoad, Alex	271
MacNabb, Thomas	214
Macnemarra, Thomas	334
McPherson, Mark	391
McPherson, Samuel	391
Macqueen, Alexander	214
Macqueen, Dugall	214
McQueen, Phitt	270
Macqueen, David	214
Macqueen, Hector	214
Malcolm, Malcolm	215
Mabbery, William	214
Machen, Allen	214
Macculloh, James	203
Maddox, John	280
Maddox, Lazarus	314
Magruder, Alexander	277, 301
Magruder, Hezekiah	277
Magruder, Jeremiah	277
Magruder, James	277
Magruder, Capt. Samuel	277
Maitland, Hon. Frederick W.	133
Major, Chris	270
Mallone, James	215
Malone, Mrs.	146
Mankin, Michael	210
Manion, Wm.	270
Manlove, Mark	320
Manning, Thomas	316, 346
Mansell, John	70
Mansfield, Walter	326
Manship, Richard	142
Maplis, Jno.	270
Martin, Christopher	417
Martin, Xpofer	106
Martin, Ludwick	332
Martin, Thomas	293, 349
Mare, William	214
Marr, William	296
Maria, Queen Henrietta	425
Marlburgh, John	9, 12, 14
Marley, Joseph	323
Marloe, William	312
Marriott, John	329
Marsden, R. T.	151, 155
Marshe, Mr. Secretary	89
Marshe, Mr. William	91
Marsh, Thomas	262, 300, 325
Marshall, Benj.	373
Marshall, William	309
Martin, Christopher	15
Marvin, N.	377
Masse, Thomas	414
Mason, Mathew	299
Mason, Richd.	374
Mason, Thomas	281, 391
Mattenly, Thomas	311
Mattershead, Zachary	106
Matthews, Thomas	265, 310, 416
Mattson, Andrew	333
Mauld, John	332
Mauldin, Francis	302
Mayo, Captain Isaac	204
Mayo, William	204
Meakines, Joshua	283
Medcalfe, John	7
Mercer, Major John	203
Mercer, John	204
Mercer, R. S.	204
Mercer, Dr. Thomas	204
Mears, Thomas	222
Meeres, Thomas	262, 300
Meredith, William	284
Merryday, Rich.	337
Mertison, John	214
Metcalf, John	9
Mew, Chris.	270
Michaellson, Clement	339
Michell, Randall	316
Middleton, Chas.	9, 13
Middleton, Robert	308
Miller and Beacham	404
Miller, James	273
Miller, Captain Joseph	286
Miller, Michael	293, 294
Miller, Thomas	282
Miles, Francis	289
Miles, Henry	319
Miles, John	331, 336
Miles, Thomas	344
Miles, Tobias	302
Mills, David	214
Mills, Moses	286

INDEX OF PROPER NAMES

Mills, Nathaniel.................... 286
Mills, Smyth....................... 286
Mimus, Black...................... 12
Mimus, Thomas................... 9, 14
Minuit, Peter...................... 189
Mitchell, Henry.................... 347
Mitchell, James.................... 214
Mitchell, Josiah.................... 377
Mitchell, Captain Joseph........... 280
Mitchell, Joseph................... 377
Mitchell, Randall.................. 280
Mitchell, Thomas.................. 308
Moale, John....................... 374
Moale, Richard.................... 360
Mond, Thos....................... 374
Molton, John...................... 286
Monat, James..................... 202
Monat, Mr. John.................. 199
Money, Robert.................... 340
Molit, Francis..................... 415
Molleston, Wm.................... 374
Moreland, Captain Jacob........... 233
Monroe, James M.................. 204
Morgan, Anne..................... 341
Morgan, Edward................... 283
Morgan, Henry.............. 344, 345
Morgan, Jarvis................ 295, 340
Morgan, John..................... 348
Morgan, Phill..................... 302
Morgan, Perry.................... 286
Morgan, Philip.................... 262
Morgan, Roger................... 9, 11
Morgan, William.................. 283
Morgan, Mr....................... 255
Morrill, William................... 377
Morris, Mr........................ 146
Morris, Jonathan.................. 391
Morris, John...................... 273
Morris, Richard................... 313
Morris, Captain Robert.....266, 334, 345
Morris, Mr. Robert............. 91, 94
Morris, Robert............... 216, 217
Morris, Wm....................... 374
Morris, William............... 322, 377
Moor, Daniel...................... 353
Moore, Henry..................... 311
More, James...................... 305
Moor, Dr. Mordy.................. 339
Moore, Richard................... 202
Moore, Dr. Samuel Preston........ 202
Moore, William.................... 347
Montague, Stephen................ 313
Mortimer, Alexander............... 214
Moseby, John..................... 325
Moxey, Virgil..................... 203
Mudd, Thomas.................... 313
Mullican, Patrick.................. 347
Murray, James................ 337, 374
Murray, Henry.................... 214
Murray, Dr. William............... 203
Murray, Captain Willie............. 404
Muuns, Thomas................... 12
Murphy, James................... 296

Nave, Alexander................... 214
Neale, Captain James..148, 261, 265, 308
Neale, Ann Gill................... 148
Neale, Captain James.............. 425
Neille, John....................... 377
Nelson, John...................... 318
Nelson, Mary..................... 313
Nelson, Richard................... 313
Nelson, Robert.................... 285
Nelson, William................279, 285
Nethery, James.................... 214
Neulson, George.................. 215
Nevill, John.................. 9, 13, 309
Nevill, Richard........... 9, 11, 12, 14
Nevitt, John...................... 310
Newman, John.................... 349
Newton, John..................... 274
Newman, Jno..................... 271
Nicholson, Benj................... 374
Nicholson, Colonel Francis......... 169
Nicholson, Governor Francis.....86, 87, 88, 165, 173
Nicholson, James.................. 202
Nicholson, Joseph................. 279
Nicholson, J., Jr.................. 374
Nicholson, Joshua................. 271
Nicholson, Judge Joseph Hopper 401, 424
Nicholson, Rebecca Lloyd......... 401
Nicholson, Sir Francis............. 260
Nicholson, William................ 266
Niefe, Robert..................... 292
Niell ——......................... 165
Noble, Isaac...................... 279
Noble, Robert..................... 348
Nock, William.................... 321
Norfolke, John.................... 275
Norman, John.................... 326
Norris, James Lyon................ 402
Norris, Mr. James E................ 255
Norris, Mr. Owen................. 402
Norris, Mr. Samuel................ 402
Norris, Mrs. William Henry......... 402
Norris, William................... 271
Norris, Thomas................... 298
Norton, John, Jr............... 15, 417
Norton, John, Sr............... 15, 417
Norton, Rob...................... 271
North, Lord....................... 363
Norwood, John................... 302
Norwood, Mr. Andrew............. 88
Notley, Thomas............... 260, 261
Nuthead, Dinah................... 147
Nuthead, William................. 147
Nutt, Job......................... 346
Nutt, John........................ 303
Nutter, Christopher............... 319

Occley, Thomas................... 414
O'Dwyer, Edmund................ 343
Ogle, Samuel................. 261, 282
Oglesby, John..................... 284
Oldham, Edward.................. 391
O'Hara, William................... 204

INDEX OF PROPER NAMES 445

Oldcastle, Sir John................ 91, 93
Odell, James......................... 276
Oliphant, Matthew................. 278
O'Maly, Bryan...................... 296
Onam, William...................... 214
Orchard, Richard................... 8, 9
Orrach, Alexander.................. 215
Osborn, John........................ 321
Osborne, Mr. and Mrs............. 146
Osbourn, William................... 335
Oulton, John........................ 337
Overton, Thomas................... 331
Owen, Captain Richard............ 336
Owen, Richard...................... 330
Owens, Dr. Augustus G. W........ 204
Ozburn, Henry...................... 355

Paca, Aquila........................ 335
Paca, Robert........................ 323
Paca, William.............374, 375, 376
Packer, Edward..................... 292
Padison, John....................... 281
Page, Henry......................... 256
Page, Mrs........................... 146
Paget, William...................... 322
Pain, Thomas....................... 340
Painter, Nicholas.............. 298, 338
Palmer, Edward..................... 166
Palmer, John, Esq.................. 166
Palmer, William..................... 332
Palmson, Simon, Jr................. 283
Pardoe, John........................ 302
Parish, Edward................ 324, 338
Parker, George................ 328, 333
Parker, John........................ 318
Parker, William........... 262, 300, 328
Parker, Mr. and Mrs................ 146
Parks, William...................... 245
Parramour, John.................... 320
Parran, Alexander................... 305
Parrie, Nicholas..................... 9
Parrott, Gabriel.................... 307
Parrott, John T..................... 204
Parrott, William............... 262, 303
Parsons, John................. 299, 300
Pascall, George..................... 323
Pasmore, Thomas......... 413, 414, 417
Pate, John..................... 264, 342
Pattison, Thomas................... 353
Patton, George..................... 360
Patton, Robert..................... 284
Paulson, Jacobus................... 283
Peacock, Richard................... 341
Peale, Charles Wilson.............. 385
Peck, James........................ 271
Pendall, Dr. William N............. 204
Pendergast, William................ 391
Penfax, Samuel..................... 264
Penn, William....................... 253
Pennington, Admiral................ 3
Pennington, Henry.................. 340
Pennington, John.............. 282, 283

Penymore, Wm...................... 271
Perkins, The........................ 252
Perri, Nicholas..................... 8
Perry, John.................... 97, 276
Perry, Richard...................... 426
Peteet, Thomas..................... 413
Peterson, Adam..................... 97
Peterson, Jacob.................... 311
Petit, Thomas...................... 308
Peverell, Daniel.................... 335
Pew (Pue), Thomas................. 97
Phelps, Cuthbert................... 344
Phillips, Bartholomew.............. 416
Phillips, James................ 283, 332
Phillips, John...................... 283
Phillips, Thomas.............. 347, 354
Pickard, Nicholas.................. 344
Pierce, Daniel...................... 294
Pierce, John....................... 338
Pierce, William................ 295, 296
Pight, Richard..................... 125
Pike, Robert....................... 9, 13
Pile, Joseph........................ 313
Pincke, Henry...................... 153
Pindall, Jacob..................... 271
Pindall, Thomas.................... 271
Pinder, Edward.................... 224
Pinley, William..................... 414
Piper, Christopher................. 278
Pitt, John.................... 347, 352
Pitt, William.................. 364, 385
Pitter, John........................ 214
Pitts, Robert...................... 319
Plater, Coll. George................ 273
Plowden, George................... 426
Plowden, Sir Edmund.............. 190
Plowden, Thomas.................. 426
Poacher, Gervase................... 207
Polhampton, Nicholas.............. 414
Polk, David........................ 278
Polk, John......................... 278
Polk, Mr. James.................... 279
Polock, Sir Frederick............... 133
Pope, Mathew................. 293, 294
Pope, Nathaniel.................... 287
Porter, Hugh....................... 321
Porter, Peter...................... 328
Porter, Captain Thomas............ 282
Poss, John......................... 214
Postly, John....................... 377
Pott, Mr. John..................... 149
Pott, Robert....................... 262
Potter, Elizabeth.................. 149
Potter, Nath....................... 374
Potts, John........................ 262
Potts, Thomas..................... 214
Pountney, Henry................... 288
Powell, Howell..................... 352
Powell, John....................... 293
Powell, Thomas............... 336, 355
Powell, Walter..................... 321
Pratt, Thomas..................... 326

446 INDEX OF PROPER NAMES

Prescott, Edward............... 72, 74
Preston, Richard, 75, 85, 86, 181, 185 222, 262, 302, 351
Preston, Samuel..................... 186
Preston, Thomas.................... 334
Price, Benjamin.................... 391
Price, Captain Andrew......... 284, 285
Price, Jacob........................ 391
Price, James........................ 315
Price, John (Black)............ 9, 12, 14
Price, John (white)............ 9, 12, 14
Price, John, Jr..................... 12
Price, John, Sr..................... 12
Price, Lodowick.................... 9, 13
Price, Thomas......... 290, 314, 414, 417
Price, Thomas, Jr................... 391
Price, William...................... 283
Prince, Caesar...................... 293
Prince, James...................... 283
Printz, John....................... 190
Prior, Thomas...................... 295
Proctor, Robert.................... 327
Prudy, Thomas...................... 203
Puddington, George................. 326
Pullen, Richard.................... 296
Pulton, Fernando....11, 12, 13, 416, 418
Purnell ———........................ 377
Purnell, John...................... 320
Purnell, Thomas............ 321, 324, 377
Purnell, Zadock............ 285, 374, 377
Pye, Edward........................ 261
Pyle, Howard....................... 381

Queny, Sutton...................... 294
Quigley, Charles................... 343
Quinton, James..................... 377
Quyn, Mr........................... 368

Rabnet, Francis.......... 10, 12, 14, 418
Ramsay, Colonel Nathaniel, 374, 390, 391
Ramsey, John....................... 214
Randall, Blanchard................. 204
Randall, Daniel R.................. 204
Randall, John Wirt................. 204
Randall, Mr........................ 403
Randall, Richard................... 312
Randall, Wyatt W................... 204
Ranger, Charles.................... 334
Ravan, Luke........................ 334
Rawles, William.................... 297
Rawlins, Aaron..................... 336
Rawlins, John...................... 354
Rawlings, Isaac.................... 391
Ray, Nicholas...................... 356
Read, Abraham...................... 290
Read, Elizabeth.................... 329
Read, John......................... 282
Read, Thomas....................... 344
Reed, Obediah...................... 278
Read, William...................... 277
Reed, Philip,...................... 391
Reeder, John, Jr................... 373
Reily, William..................... 391

Reind, Alexander................... 214
Renton, James...................... 215
Reveley, Francis................... 391
Revell, Randall............... 106, 412
Revell, Randolph................... 316
Reynolds, Edwd..................... 373
Reynolds, Thomas......... 265, 284, 307
Reynolds, William.................. 203
Rhodeson, John..................... 314
Rice, Nicholas..................... 317
Richardson, Captain Joseph......... 364
Richardson, George........ 352, 354, 355
Richardson, John...... 223, 280, 337, 338 348, 350, 355
Richardson, Kath................... 245
Richardson, Lawrence............... 328
Richardson, Mary................... 339
Richardson, Mrs. Hester Dorsey..... 420
Richardson, Mark............. 306, 331
Richardson, Thomas........... 330, 424
Richardson, William................ 222
Richardson, Sr., William........... 223
Richardson, Will................... 374
Richmond, Christopher.............. 391
Richards, Samuel................... 276
Richardson, Robert................. 320
Ricketts, Lieutenant Nicholas...... 391
Ridgely, Henry............... 297, 329
Ridgley, Robert.................... 318
Ridgley, Thomas.................... 374
Rigby, James....................... 331
Riley, Jeremiah.................... 424
Ringgold, James.................... 298
Ringgold, John..................... 298
Ringgold, Thos.............. 369, 374
Ringgold, Wm., Jr.................. 374
Ripp, Hendrick..................... 131
Roach, John........................ 314
Robbins, Robert.................... 309
Roberson, George................... 377
Roberson, William.................. 279
Roberts, John, Jr.................. 283
Roberts, Mr. William............... 255
Roberts, Thomas.................... 336
Robertson, Donald.................. 214
Robertson, James................... 214
Robertson, John.................... 214
Robertson, Rowland................. 215
Robins, George..................... 349
Robins, John.................. 319, 320
Robins, John Purnell............... 377
Robinson, And'w.................... 271
Robinson, David.................... 281
Robinson, Henry.................... 301
Robinson, John...... 10, 12, 14, 106, 311
Robinson, Leonard.................. 214
Robinson, William.................. 346
Robotham, Colonel George........... 173
Robson, Capt. John................. 281
Robson, William.................... 354
Rochambeau, Count............ 390, 392
Rockson, John...................... 316
Rodam, Matthew..................... 414

INDEX OF PROPER NAMES 447

Roe, Edward 348
Rogers ——— 374
Rogers, Captain William 91
Rogers, Francis 418
Rogers, John 271, 376, 377
Rogers, John C. 204
Rogers, Mr. 10, 11, 14
Rogers, Robert 271, 336
Roosevelt, Nicholas 195
Roper, William 328
Rose, Wm. 271
Rowe, Thomas 285
Rowles, Christopher 325
Rowse, Thomas 391
Ruly, Michael 283
Rumley, Thomas 341
Rumsey, Captain William 283
Rumsey, Chas. 374
Rumsey, James 193
Rusk, David 360
Russell, Christopher 310
Russell, Michael 350
Rutherford, James 215
Ryder, John 355
Ryly, Hugh 306

Saire, William 7, 9
Salisbury, William 293
Salter, John 300, 343
Sammon, Stephen 9, 14, 415
Sampson, Thomas 332
Sanders, James 328
Sanders, John 307, 417
Sanders, Mr. James 88
Sanders, Mr. John 15, 88, 418
Sanders, Robert 296
Sanders, William 203
Sappington, Captain Thomas 276
Saunders, John 7, 9, 417
Saunders, Mr. John 11, 14
Saunders, Robert 202
Saunders, William 203
Sayer, Major Peter 264, 342, 350
Scarborough, John 285
Scarborough, Mathew 320
Scott, Captain Day 278
Scott, Daniel 335
Scott, Gustavus 374
Scott, James 344
Scott, John 299, 306
Scott, William 293, 316
Sears, John 391
Sedgwick, James 299
Sefton, Edward 203
Seimn, William 214
Selby, Daniel 280, 320
Selby, Edward 300, 324
Selby, John 280, 377
Selby, William, Jr. 377
Sellman, Alfred 204
Sellman, Dr. John H. 204
Sellman, Frank Stockett 204
Sellman, John Stevens 203

Sellman, Jonathan 202
Sellman, Major Jonathan 203
Sellman, Mr. Richard Parran 198
Sellman, Richard 203
Sellman, Richard B. 204
Sellman, William 203
Sergison, William 289
Seton, Thompson 136
Sewall, Major Nicholas 236, 307
Sewall, Nicholas 264
Sewell, Henry 330
Sewell, Henry, Esq. 64
Sewell, John 306
Sewell, Nicholas 261
Seymour, John 260
Seymour, Thomas 345
Shacklady, James 301
Shaftal, John 215
Shakespeare, William 76
Shanks, Thomas 273
Sharp, Peter 303, 347, 351
Sharp, Walter 283
Sharpe, Governor 362
Sharpe, Governor Horatio 426
Sharpe, Horatio 261
Shaw, James 214, 215
Shaw, John 327
Shaw, Ralph 311
Shaw, Thomas 215
Shaw, William 215, 346
Sheppard, Nicholas 330
Sheridan, Upton 374
Sherlock, Nich's. 271
Sherley Robert 11, 12, 13
Sherly, Robert 9, 10, 14, 415
Sherrin, Rob't. 271
Sherwood, Philip 350
Shields, David 360
Shields, Nathaniel 333
Shipley, Adam 337
Shipley, N. H. 204
Shippen, Mrs. Rebecca Lloyd 424
Shirt, William 348
Shocley, Robert 416
Shore, James 271
Silcock, Valentine 283
Sim, Joseph 373
Simmonds, Edw'd. 271
Simpson, Alexander 310
Simpson, Robert 10, 11, 12, 13
Simpson, William 215
Sinclair, John 214
Sinclare, James 215
Sisson, Elizaeth 329
Siverson, Marcus 339
Skidmore, Edward 292
Skillington, Thomas 352
Skinner, Andrew 297, 345
Skinner, Mackall 277
Skinner, Thomas 352
Sly, Captain Robert 262
Slye, Mr. 125
Slye, Thomas 313

448 INDEX OF PROPER NAMES

Slyter, Benjamin.................. 283
Small, James..................... 214
Smallwood, James............. 96, 311
Smallwood, General............... 390
Smallwood, Major-General......... 391
Smallwood, W..................... 373
Smith ——........................ 9
Smith, A..................... 11, 14
Smith, Alexander................. 214
Smith, Captain Richard...... 296, 339
Smith, Colonel Samuel............ 318
Smith, Eman'l.................... 271
Smith, Henry..................... 271
Smith, James..................... 391
Smith, James B................... 204
Smith, John................. 262, 346
Smith, Matthew................... 340
Smith, Mr........................ 11
Smith, Nathan.................... 324
Smith, Pott...................... 215
Smith, Richard...... 300, 304, 308, 414
Smith, Robert.................... 173
Smith, Robert John............... 203
Smith, Rose...................... 149
Smith, Thomas...... 9, 12, 14, 173, 214
Smith, Thos...................... 374
Smith, Walter.................... 335
Smith, Webster................... 377
Smith, William.... 10, 289, 294, 351, 355
Smithson, Mr. Robert............. 8
Smithson, Robt................... 9
Smoot, William.............. 308, 391
Snow, Abell................. 263, 287
Snowden, Richard................. 328
Snowden, Richards................ 266
Snowden, Thomas.................. 203
Sollers, Captain Robert.......... 276
Somers, The...................... 256
Somerset, Lady Mary......... 254, 256
Sousa, Mathias................... 11
South, Thomas.................... 298
Southern, Edward................. 318
Southern, Samuel................. 274
Spalding, Alexander.............. 214
Spark, Thomas.................... 214
Sparrow, Solomon, Jr............. 203
Sparrow, Thomas............. 202, 325
Spear, William................... 360
Speed, John...................... 416
Spence, Captain Adam............. 285
Spence, David.................... 317
Spencer, George.................. 341
Spencer, Mr...................... 146
Spencer, Rev. Archibald.......... 203
Spencer, Robert.................. 281
Spencer, Samuel.................. 298
Spoene, Nicholas................. 343
Sprie, Oliver.................... 331
Sprigg, O........................ 374
Sprigg, Thomas.............. 266, 307
Spry, Oliver..................... 340
Spurrier, Edward................. 391
Stafford, Earl of................ 5

Stainer James.................... 281
Stallings, Absalom............... 275
Stanfield, John.................. 273
Stanley, Hugh.................... 320
Stanley, William................. 295
Stansbury, Elijah................ 268
Stapleford, Raymond.............. 353
Staples, Henry................... 293
Starkey, George.................. 162
Start, Ephraim................... 281
Statham, Thomas............. 10, 11, 13
Staveley, James.................. 296
Stedman, James................... 271
Steele, Nevitt................... 204
Sterling, James.................. 91
Sterrett, James.................. 360
Sterrett, John................... 360
Steuart, General George H........ 204
Steuart, George.................. 359
Steuart, Mr. William Donaldson... 198
Stevens, John.................... 374
Stevens, Judge William........... 116
Stevenses, The................... 256
Stevens, Thos.................... 271
Stevens, William............ 315, 316
Stevenson, Philip................ 348
Stevenson, Robert................ 286
Steward, Charles................. 202
Steward, Daniel.................. 215
Steward, John.................... 352
Stewart, Anthony............ 366, 369
Stewart, Caleb................... 203
Stewart, Charles C............... 204
Stewart, David.............. 203, 214
Stewart, Peggy................... 365
Stewart, John.............. 215, 374
Stewart, Mr...................... 254
Stewart, Richard................. 203
Stewart, William................. 203
Stewart, William D............... 204
Stiles, Nathan................... 292
Stiles, Nathaniel................ 303
Stinson, John.................... 307
Stinson, Wm...................... 271
Stirling, Thomas................. 301
Stoakley, Woodman................ 304
Stobbs, Robert................... 214
Stockett, Benjamin............... 202
Stockett, Dr. John S............. 203
Stockett, Dr. Thomas Noble....... 203
Stockett, Francis................ 332
Stockett, Frank H................ 204
Stockett, Frank H. Jr............ 204
Stockett, James Noble............ 203
Stockett, Joseph Noble........... 204
Stockett, Lewis.................. 203
Stockett, Mr. Thomas......... 62, 191
Stockett, Thomas........ 202, 203, 327
Stockley, Woodman................ 262
Stodert, Jr., Captain............ 275
Stone, Captain William........... 132
Stone, J. H...................... 373
Stone, John...................... 275

INDEX OF PROPER NAMES

Stone, Governor William....... 181, 412
Stone, Matthew..................... 303
Stone, Mrs. Verlinda............... 312
Stone, Richard..................... 294
Stone, Thomas...................... 376
Stone, Thos........................ 374
Stone, William................ 260, 262
Stoey, Robert...................... 282
Strachan, Captain William.......... 203
Stratham, Thomas................... 418
Strong, Elizabeth.................. 330
Strong, Leonard............... 262, 300
Sturgis, Captain Joshua............ 286
Stuyvesant, Governor........... 27, 131
Sullivan, Daniel................... 343
Summers, Benjamin.................. 314
Summers, John...................... 328
Summers, Samuel.................... 377
Summerville, James................. 215
Susa, Mathias...................... 415
Sutton, Ashby...................... 271
Swan, Edward....................... 310
Swinfens, Francis.................. 301
Swinger, Alexander................. 214
Sword, Humphrey.................... 215
Symms, Marmduke.................... 343

Talbott, Colonel George....... 266, 343
Talbot, Edward................ 323, 338
Talbott, Richard................... 325
Tammion, Stephen................... 415
Taney, John........................ 274
Tannehill, Adamson................. 391
Tapper, Jno........................ 271
Tarkinton, John.................... 332
Tasker, Benjamin................... 261
Taskers, Thomas.................... 173
Taylard, William................... 147
Taylor ——.......................... 414
Taylor, Capt. Peter................ 280
Taylor, Edmund..................... 311
Taylor, John.................. 317, 413
Taylor, Robert..................... 305
Taylor, Samuel..................... 286
Taylor, Thomas........... 325, 333, 354
Taylor, William............... 286, 345
Teague, John....................... 280
Tench, John........................ 353
Tench, Thomas, Esq........ 88, 261, 335
Terrill, Jno....................... 271
Travers, Captain Thomas............ 280
Travers, Capt. Henry............... 280
Traverse, William.................. 352
Trippe, Henry...................... 352
Troth, William..................... 349
Troth, Mr. Samuel.................. 185
True, Richard...................... 309
Truitt, Samuel..................... 377
Truman, Thomas................ 291, 292
Theobald, Captain William.......... 274
Thomas, Jn. V...................... 373
Thomas, John.................. 274, 335
Thomas, James...................... 274

Thomas, Mr. Robert W............... 255
Thomas, Nl......................... 374
Thomas, Phill................. 262, 300
Thomas, Thomas........ 262, 303, 338, 414
Thomas, Tristram................... 281
Thomas, W.......................... 162
Thomas, William.................... 317
Thompson, Arthur................... 301
Thompson, Augustine................ 285
Thompson, Doctor................... 368
Thompson, Dr James................. 203
Thompson, George......... 214, 342, 353
Thompson, Henry F.................. 7
Thompson, Jno. D......... 173, 271, 374
Thompson, Marris................... 158
Thompson, Maurice.................. 152
Thompson, Richard.... 9, 11, 12, 13, 264
Thompson, William.................. 310
Thomson, John.................... 9, 11
Thornbury, Rowland................. 336
Tborne, William.................... 317
Thornton, James.................. 9, 11
Thornton, Mr. William, Esq...... 91, 92
Thornton, Richard.................. 296
Thundergen, Wm..................... 282
Thurston, Thomas.............. 221, 335
Thurstone, Thomas.................. 185
Tilghman, Colonel Oswald........... 253
Tilghman, Hon. Matthew..... 373, 375 377, 424
Tilghman, Lieutenant-Colonel
  Tench......................... 253, 423
Tilghman, Mary..................... 299
Tilghman, R........................ 285
Tilghman, R., Jun.................. 374
Tilghman, Richard........ 266, 299, 345
Tilghman, Samuel................... 345
Tilghmans, the..................... 98
Tilghman, Ja....................... 373
Tilghman, Peregrine................ 374
Tilman, Aaron...................... 279
Tingle, Daniel..................... 285
Tingle, Hugh....................... 286
Toadvin, Hon. E. Stanley...... 256, 425
Toas, Daniell...................... 97
Todd, Thomas......... 303, 328, 336, 345
Tolson, William.................... 294
Tomlinson, Groves.................. 277
Tomkinson, John.................... 312
Tongood, Major..................... 377
Tool, Thos......................... 271
Tousa, Mathias............. 9, 10, 12, 13
Tovey, Samuel...................... 299
Towle, Roger....................... 290
Townhill, Edward................... 327
Townsend, I. Spence................ 377
Townsend, Solomon.................. 286
Tracey, Rev. William P............. 15
Trent, James....................... 271
True, Fran's....................... 271
Tuchstone, Christopher............. 282
Tuckbury, William.................. 324
Tucker, Edm'd Thos................. 271

INDEX OF PROPER NAMES

Tucker, Walter 332
Tull, Samuel 280
Tull, Sollomon 280
Tully, John 297
Turbitt, William 284
Turbutt, Major 284
Turner, Gideon 276
Turner, Robert 304
Turner, Thomas 292
Turner, William 345, 374
Turpin, John 280
Turpin, Whittey 278
Turpin, William 278
Turgis, Simon 158
Turgus, Simon 152
Tusa, Mathia 415
Tweeg, John 294
Tyler, Robt. 373

Uhler, Erasmus 360
Usseling, William 188
Utie, Col. Nathaniel 130, 132, 331
Utye, Nathaniel, Esq 294

Van Ruyven, Cornelius 131
Vansweringen, Garrett 131, 289
Van Twiller, Wouter 189
Vaughan, Robert 298
Vaughan, Thomas 347
Vankak, John 317
Veazey, Captain John 283
Veazey, George 282
Veazey, John, Jr 374
Verling, Mr. 146
Vernett, Julian 413
Vickers, Wm. Brown 281
Virgen, James 281
von Steuben, Major-General Baron. 388

Wade, Zachary 308, 344
Waldren, Resolved 131
Wales, Levin 277
Walker, Captain John 318
Walker, Daniel 350
Walker, George 327
Walker, James 309
Walkers, The 256
Wall, Edward 321
Wall, Mr. 146
Wallace, Samuel 300
Waller, John 317
Waller, Mr. Sidney 254
Waller, Nathaniel 277, 278
Walley, Thomas 317
Walter, Daniel 278
Walter, John 413
Walter, Roger 9, 11
Walters, Samuel 306
Walton, William 280
Wamsley, Thomas 341
Ward, Captain Francis 275
Ward, Cornelius 315
Ward, John 10, 12, 14, 284, 312

Ward, Thomas 283
Ward, William 340
Warfield, Benjamin 337
Warfield, Charles 337
Warfield, Dr. Charles, Alexander. 359
  368, 406, 424
Warfield, Frank 337
Warfield, Governor 204, 385, 411, 419
  420
Warfield, John 329, 337
Warfield, Richard 329, 337
Warfield, Thomas 309
Waring, Basil 276
Waring, Sampson 262
Warner, George 296
Warner, James 328
Warren, Captain Barton 275
Warren, Humphrey 310
Warren, John 377
Warren, Lieutenant Ratcliffe... 115, 154
Washington, Colonel John 74
Washington, General 194, 384, 390
  392, 419
Washington, Mr. 73
Washington, Mr. John 72
Wastill, George 326
Waterman, Nicholas 325
Waters, Edward 279
Waters, John 279, 321, 374
Waters, Ramsey 203
Waters, Richard 321
Waters, Wm. 313, 374
Waterses, The 256
Watkins, Benjamin 203, 204
Watkins, Captain Joseph 203
Watkins, Edward   3
Watkins, Evan 10, 13
Watkins, Samuel 203
Watkins, Captain Thomas 203
Watkins, Dr. Benjamin 203
Watkins, John 202, 203, 326
Watkins, Nicholas of Stephen 203
Watkins, Richard 203
Watkins, Stephen 203
Watson, Andrew 312
Watts, George 346
Weasey, Thos. 272
Webb, Arthur 416
Webb, Edward 299
Webb, Mark 277
Webb, Solomon 286
Webb, Wm. 374
Webster, James 214
Webster, Miss Rebecca Lynn 426
Webster, P. Selby 377
Weems, Captain John B. 203
Weems, Franklin 204
Weems, Rev. Mason Locke 203
Well, Richard 322
Wells, Colonel, George 331
Wells, Nathan 276
Wells, Richard 323
Wells, Robert 305

INDEX OF PROPER NAMES   451

Welsh, Benjamin... 203
Welsh, Dr. Robert... 203
Welsh, Thomas... 203
Wells, Benjamin... 306
Wells, Cyprian... 360
Wells, George... 360
Wells, Richard... 262
Wentworth, Thomas... 312
West, Benjamin... 276
West, Stephen, Jr... 203
West, Stephen... 374
Weston, Thomas... 263, 291
Wetherly, James... 320
Wharton, Elizabeth... 313
Wharton, Henry... 347
Wharton, Jesse... 261
Wheatley, John... 290
Wheeler, Anna... 342
Wheeler, Ignatius, Jr... 374
Wheeler, John... 308, 339
Whetstone, Thomas... 347
White, Ambrose... 286
White, Father... 5, 8, 11, 411
White, Hugh... 215
White, James... 214
White, Jerome... 261, 288, 266, 323
White, John... 203, 316, 354
White, Mr... 111
White, Mr. Andrew... 9, 10, 11, 13
White, Peter... 377
White, Thomas... 416
Whittington, John... 349
Whittington, William... 321
Whittle, George... 302
Wicks, Edm'd... 272
Wicks, John... 293
Wickses, The... 252
Wilkie, Andrew... 203
Wilkinson, Rev. William... 219
Wilkinson, William... 314
Willen, Robert... 342
Willett, Thomas... 285
Willett, William... 285
William III, King... 425
Williams, Basil... 276
Williams, Boruch... 276
Williams, Captain John... 278
Williams, Geo... 272
Williams, James... 369
Williams, John... 310
Williams, Joseph... 366, 369
Williams, Michael... 314
Williams, Otho Holland, Brigadier-General... 390, 391
Williams, Ralph... 338, 347
Williams, Richard... 414
Williams, Thomas... 313, 366
Wiliamson, David... 317
Williamson, John... 131
Williamsons, The... 252
Willis, James... 272
Willis, John... 294
Wills, Thomas... 10, 11

Wilmer, Simon... 299
Wilmers, The... 252
Wilmot, John... 338
Wilson, Captain James... 277
Wilson, Ephraim... 322
Wilson, Henry... 214
Wilson, Hillary... 275
Wilson, J... 277
Wilson, James... 274, 294
Wilson, John... 294, 324
Wilson. Lieutenant Joe... 275
Wilson, Lingan... 277
Wilson, Margaret... 210
Willis, Thomas... 415
Wills, Thomas... 415
Wilson, John... 332
Wilson, Robert... 292
Wilsons, The... 256
Wilson, Thomas... 320
Wilson, William... 360
Windham, Captain Edward... 181
Winder, John... 318
Winder, William... 279
Winders, The... 256
Wing, Capt. Thomas... 281
Winn, Achsah... 401
Winn, Ida... 401
Winn, Mary... 401
Winslow, Joseph... 346
Winters, E... 360
Wintour, Captain... 3, 7, 9
Wintour, Capt. Robert... 50, 416
Wintour, Edward... 7, 10, 12, 14
Wintour, Frederick... 7, 10, 14
Wintour, Lady Anne... 7
Wise, Matthew... 286
Wise, Samuel... 377
Wise, William... 377
Withers, Samuel... 262
Wiseman, Henry... 7, 10
Wiseman, Sir Thomas... 7
Withgott, Joseph... 349
Withington, Richard... 215
Wolfe, William... 415
Woodfield, W. H... 204
Wood, Gerard... 391
Woodland, Jo... 272
Wright, Benjamin N... 204
Wright, Edward... 284, 285
Wright, Richard... 342
Wright, Sol... 374
Wright, Turbutt... 373
Wright, Th... 373
Wright, Thomas... 295
Wrightson, Mr. F. G... 255
Wood, Nicholas... 284
Wood, Sam'l... 268
Woodward, Henry... 203
Woodward, John... 354
Woolchurch, Henry... 299, 346
Woolford, Capt. James... 280
Woolford, Roger... 319
Woolfords, The... 256

Woolman, Richard.................. 262
Wooten, Turner.................... 202
Wootters, John.................... 349
Wootton, W. Sprigg................ 374
Worth, John....................... 299
Worthington, Beale................ 204
Worthington, Brice John........... 374
Worthington, Thomas............... 330
Wyatt, John....................... 106
Wyatt, Nicholas................... 329
Wyley, George..................... 275
Wynne, Thomas..................... 289

Yapp, William..................... 294
Yardley, Colonel Francis.......... 181
Yate, George...................... 328

Yeates, James..................... 272
Yelhelin, Simon................... 123
Yeoman, Jno....................... 272
Yoe, John......................... 333
York, William..................... 334
Young, Elizabeth.................. 309
Young, Joan....................... 153
Youngblood, Thos.................. 272
Young, John....................... 330
Young, Rob........................ 272
Young, Samuel..................... 335

Zause, Mathia.................. 13, 415
Zealand, Geo...................... 272
Zelipow, Andrew................... 283

GENERAL INDEX

Academia Virginiensis et Oxoniensis 166
A Character of Maryland........... 191
Act Against the Importation of Convicted Persons into Maryland—1676............................. 423
Act Concerning Religion ...102, 104, 422
Act Establishing King William's School........................... 423
Act for Erecting a Prison in Maryland, 1662........................ 423
Act for Founding a College in Maryland, 1671....................... 423
Adventurers, First......... 8, 9, 20, 22
Adventurers on the *Ark* and *Dove*—Inaccurate List of................. 411
Agreement Between Claiborne and Cloberry......................... 157
Aladdin's Lamp.................... 177
Albany............................. 122
Allegorical Portrait of William Pitt, by Peale......................... 385
Allen's Mill........................ 98
All Hallows........................ 226
All Saints' Parish.................. 172
Altoona............................ 130
American Archaeological School at Assos............................ 400
American Company, The...... 145, 146
American Empire................... 389
American Nation Born into the World............................ 381
Amstel, New....................... 130
Ancient Bill of Lading............... 7
Ancient City, The.................. 146
Ancient Temple.................... 33
Annapolis, 75, 89, 144, 145, 212, 245, 363 366
Annapolis Land Records......... 13, 14
Anne Arundell County............. 359
Anne Arundell Town............ 87, 174
Anne's, St......................... 226
Archbishop of Canterbury.......... 254
Archihatt.......................... 358
Archihoe.......................... 23
Ark and *Dove* Passengers, 7, 8, 9, 10, 11 12, 13, 14, 15
Ark and *Dove* Society's List Analyzed..... 412, 413, 414, 415, 416, 417, 418
Ark, The, 2, 6, 8, 14, 15, 16, 20, 25, 30, 33 36, 39, 40, 60, 216, 407, 409, 411, 412, 414 416, 417, 418, 421, 425
Armintzes......................... 174
Articles of Confederation.......... 371
A Satyr in Burlesque Verse......... 243

Assignment of "Resurrection Manor"............................ 374, 426
Association of Freemen, Declaration of................ 371, 373, 374, 377
Associators in Somerset County.... 377
Augusta Carolina............... 24, 137
Autographs of Those Who Passed the Act of Religious Toleration... 422
Avalon............................ 250

Bacon's Laws, Incorrect Seal on Copied........................... 410
Baltimore Chapter D. A. R........ 378
Baltimore Town.................... 367
Banished Huguenots................ 250
Barbadoes......................... 21
Barren Island...................... 186
Bath, Town of..................... 194
Battle Creek....................... 257
"Battle of the Severn".......... 86, 184
Battle Town....................... 257
Beggar's Opera, The............... 144
Birthplace of Religious Liberty..... 102
Bishop of London.................. 78
Bishop of Maryland First Elected... 227
"Blessed Virgin Mary and St. Michael the Archangel"............. 163
Bohemia River..................... 193
Boston......................... 87, 224
Boston, Handsome Contribution from Maryland................... 362
Boston Tea Party.................. 361
Bothwell Bridge, Battle of......... 209
Branding Irons.................... 64
Bricks Made in Maryland and Virginia............................ 35
Bricks Not Imported............... 34
Bridewells........................ 63
British Subjects................... 164
British Troops.................... 372
Burning of the *Peggy Stewart*, 361, 405 424

Cæcelius Calvert's Instructions for Erecting Land into Manors....... 422
Calvert County.................... 181
Calvert Papers.................... 400
Capital, Old St. Maries............ 427
Captain-General................... 86
Castle of Windsor................. 162
Catholic Families.................. 399
Catholic Marriages Kept Secret..... 400
Catholic Priest Forbidden to officiate................................. 399

453

GENERAL INDEX

Catholiques.......................... 20
"Cato"............................. 144
Cavalier and Round Head..... 183, 184
Cavaliers........................... 45
Cecil County....................... 109
Charles County..................... 231
Charleston, S. C................... 122
Charter and Constitution of Massachusetts Bay....................... 373
Charter of Maryland................ 1
Charybbies Isles................... 21
Cherry Tree........................ 244
Chesapeake Bay.................... 22
Chestertown........................ 251
Chilham Castle..................... 257
Chippendale Tables................. 177
Choptank Parish.................... 79
Choptank River................. 78, 244
Christina.......................... 190
Christmas, English................. 25
Christmas on the *Ark*......... 20, 25
Christian Martyr................... 64
Church Creek....................... 78
Cincinnati Insignia worn at Court.. 392
Cincinnati Society Members of Maryland Branch....................... 390
Cincinnati Society, Officers of..... 390
Cinquack........................... 129
Citie of St. Maries............ 109, 182
City of St. Marys.................. 62
Claiborne's Claim to Kent Island, New Light on...................... 151
Claiborne Rebellion................ 153
Claiborne, Trial of................ 152
Cloberrye and Companie... 158, 159, 160
Clubhouse—The South River....... 199
Coat of Arms....................... 50
College, William and Mary.......... 169
Colonial Aristocracy............... 361
Colonial Business Woman........... 147
Colonial Christening............... 72
Colonial Churches.................. 80
Colonial Currency.................. 124
Colonial Dames..................... 183
Colonial Dames of America, Society of................................ 187
Colonial Dames of Maryland........ 43
Colonial Doorways, A Glimpse Through........................... 49
Colonial Furniture................. 177
Colonial Gentleman's Writing desk. 216
Colonial Life and Aristocracy...... 45
Colonial Maryland.................. 65
Colonial Maryland Women........... 149
Colonial Maxim..................... 205
Colonial Militia................... 99
Colonial Militia Officers in Maryland, 272, 273, 274, 275, 276, 277, 278, 279 280, 281, 282, 283, 284, 285, 286
Colonial Sanitarium................ 231
Colonial Sanitarium, Trustees of.... 233
Colony of Virginia................. 151
Colors of the Counties............. 99
Columbian Order.................... 393

Commander-in-Chief of the American Army......................... 419
Commander of the Patuxent........ 85
Comedians from Virginia........... 144
Commissary of Maryland............ 120
Commission to Mrs. Hester Dorsey Richardson, Special Executive Historian......................... 420
Commission to Thomas Richardson as Captain in Revolutionary War.. 424
Committee of Observation.......... 373
Common Ale Houses................. 63
Communion Service sent by King William III....................... 425
Concessions made by Anthony Stewart........................... 369
Condemned Catholics............... 250
Conditions of Plantations...6, 41, 70, 164
Confederate Soldiers, Making Garments for....................... 401
Congress Invited to Sit at Annapolis, 383
Continental Congress.......... 373, 375
Contribution to Boston............. 362
Convention of Maryland............ 371
Convict Settlers, So-called........ 209
Cooke's Point...................... 244
Cool Springs....................... 232
Coole Springs.................. 231, 232
Corn Planting...................... 33
Corn Sallet........................ 43
Cornwallis' Surrender, News of, 378, 379 380, 424
Council for Land................... 236
Council of Nineteen................ 132
Council of Safety.................. 373
Covenanters Persecuted............. 210
Coventry........................... 226
Creek, Salem....................... 190
Crimping Officers.................. 248
Crimps............................. 209
Curious Law of Deodand............ 106
Custom House....................... 251

Daughters of American Revolution, Insignia.......................... 395
Declaration of Independence....... 371
Declaration of Independence to be Engrossed and Signed........ 376, 377
Declaration of Independence Signed August 2d......................... 376
Dedication......................... v
Delaware........................... 129
Denization of Foreigners........... 164
Deposition of Henry Corbyn........ 141
Deputies........................... 110
Deputy-Governors list of........... 261
Deputy Receiver General............ 243
Detestable Weed.................... 366
Diversity in Spelling Colonial Names......................... 228, 229
Divorce Law—Colonial......... 194, 218
Divorce Never Granted in Colonial Maryland.......................... 219
Dorchester......................... 226

GENERAL INDEX 455

Dorchester County.................. 244
Dorchester County Records......... 243
Dorchester Parish.................... 79
Dorchester Town.................... 79
Dove. The, 3, 7, 8, 16, 36, 39, 40, 60, 409
411, 412, 414, 416, 417, 420, 425
Ducking Stool....................... 64
Dumblane........................... 258
Dundee............................. 258
Durham............................. 226
Dutch.............................. 103
Dutch Descent...................... 164
Dutch from New Amsterdam....... 238
Dutch on the Delaware......... 129, 130
Dutch of Manhattan................. 27
Dutch West India Company... 188, 189

Early Jesuits in Maryland........... 15
Early Settlers of Maryland, Errors
  Regarding Them Corrected....... 420
Early Settlers of Maryland, Names
  of One Thousand with Their Land
  Grants.................. 287 to 355, 422
Early Settlers, Status of 420, 421
Early Inventories................... 49
Early Parishes, Names of...... 225, 226
Eastern Neck Manor................ 252
Eastern Shore............. 170, 223, 394
East India Goods................... 366
Edinborough....................... 258
Education in the Province......... 148
Elk Ridge.......................... 367
Emperor of Pascatoway.......... 23, 31
England.... 19, 26, 27, 29, 54, 122, 123, 249
English Christmas.................. 25
English Church.................... 219
English Crown..................... 164
English Parliament............ 181, 182
English Settlers.......... 53, 135, 137
Entailed Hat....................... 256
Episcopal Convention.............. 218
Everlasting Club................... 197
Executive Department of Maryland
  at Jamestown Exposition.......... 411
Executive Exhibit.................. 427
Executive Exhibit is Educational, 421
422, 423, 424, 425, 426, 427
Executive Exhibit in State House,
  Annapolis........................ 411
Expedition Against Canada........ 267

False Claims to Property........... 148
Family Records Destroyed.......... 399
Family Traditions.................. 397
Felons............................. 63
Feudal Service and Customs... 112, 114
Fifeshire........................... 258
First Adventurers, 8, 9, 10, 11. 12, 13, 14
15
First Battle Between Englishmen on
  American Soil.................... 181
First Club in America.............. 197
First Free School in Maryland...... 169
First Patent for Town Land........ 67

First Settlers, List of, 8, 9, 10, 11, 12, 13
14, 15
First Steamboat............... 193, 195
First Theatre in America........... 144
First University in America........ 165
Fish in Maryland Waters........... 240
Fitch and Rumsey.................. 173
Foreword........................... vii
Fountain Pen...................... 216
Fort Duquesne..................... 361
Fort Kent Manor................... 252
Fort McHenry...................... 403
Fort William....................... 212
Founders of Maryland, Their Moral,
  Educational, and Social Status
  Proven..................... 419, 420
Founder of Quakerism............. 223
France............................ 249
Frederick Calvert's Instructions to
  Governor Sharpe................. 426
Freeholders....................... 110
Free Will Servants................. 246
French Descent....................164
French Huguenots.................. 103
French and Indian Wars............ 363
Friends' Quarterly Meeting.........223
Friends at Treadhaven............. 223
Free School.................. 169, 173
Freemen of Maryland 371, 372
Fulton ——......................... 196

"Gazette," The.................... 144
General Washington's Aide......... 253
Gentle Hearted Indian............. 135
Gentlemen Adventurer's Supplies.. 37
Gentlemen of Very Good Fashion, 7, 209
George Fox, the Founder of Quaker-
  ism............................. 198
Germany........................... 249
Gilbert Stuart of Washington...... 385
Giving Names to Land.............. 257
Goods Brought by First Settlers, 36, 37
38, 39
Gossips........................ 73, 74
Governors—List of................. 261
Governor of Maryland.......... 76, 261
Governor's Pinnance *Dove*......... 409
Great Ball Given in Honor of Wash-
  ington.......................... 384
Great Choptank River.............. 244
Great Spirit...................... 138
Ground Rent, Origin of............ 161

Halberteers........................ 63
Hart's (Governor) Proclamation.... 213
Healing Fountains................. 231
Heir of Frederick Calvert.........:. 164
Herne Island....................... 22
Herring Creek................ 220, 222
Herring Creek Meeting House...... 222
High Court of Admiralty Records.. 151
155
Hill, Snow........................ 226
Holland Windmill.................. 238

GENERAL INDEX

"Hott Waters"...... 139
Hudson, The...... 196
Hue and Cry...... 133
Hurste Castle...... 17

Imperial Court...... 87
Indian Arrows as Rent...... 58
Indian Blue Water...... 244
Indian Corn at Christmas...... 163
Indian Kings on Governor's Pinnace Dove...... 409
Indian, Native, Noble...... 139
Indian Wheat (Maize)...... 33
Indians, First Description of...... 135
Indians' Houses...... 33
Indians of Yaocomico...... 137
Indians' Skill in Healing...... 241
Indicted for Bigamy...... 219
Ingle's Raid...... 252
Inverness...... 212
Irish Subjects...... 164
Island, Kent...... 156, 226
Italian Descent...... 164

Jacobite Uprising...... 210
Jamaica...... 87
James II...... 210
Jamestown...... 87
John's, St....... 114, 226
St. John's, Palace of...... 109, 111, 114
Jury of Women...... 148, 149

Kecoughtan...... 153
"Keeper of His Majesty's Wardrobe"...... 162
Kent Isle...... 252
Kenty County Families...... 251
Ketches and Barkes...... 241
King Charles I, 3, 5, 25, 26, 27, 34, 36 45, 49, 56, 57, 59, 76, 184.
King Charles II, 28, 75, 76, 77, 120, 182 184
King James I...... 25
King of Pascatoway...... 22, 135
King of Patuxent...... 33
King of Yoacomaco...... 24
King Richard III...... 144
King William's School...... 165, 173
King's Army, No Appropriation for, 361
King's Council...... 2
King's Party, The...... 182
"King's Pleasure"...... 161
King's Rebels...... 209, 214, 215
King's Suit Against Claiborne...... 156
King's Surveyor of Customs...... 145
King's Treasury...... 363

Labor Saving Invention in Maryland, The First...... 238
Lady Baltimore...... 123, 253
Lady Mary Somerset...... 254
Lady's Wardrobe...... 47
Land of Legendary Lore...... 253
Land Office Established...... 234

Land of Sanctuary...... 407, 421, 103
Land of the Persecuted...... 249
Land Surveys, One Thousand Earliest...... 287, 355
Land Tenements...... 174
Land of Valleys...... 258
Land Warrants...... 13
Lauriger, Horatius...... 402, 403
"Leah and Rachel"...... 169
Leamington...... 166
Leisurely Ways of Colonial Court... 72
Lending Library, Colonial. 119, 121, 122
Leonard Calvert at St. Clement's Island...... 407
Leonard Calvert's Treaty with the Indians...... 407, 409
Leonard Town...... 98
Letter from Scotch Rebel...... 212
Library at Herring Creek...... 123
Life on Colonial Plantations...... 246
London...... 87, 236
London Public Record Office...... 215
London Searcher...... 3
Londontown...... 198
Lord Archbishop of Canterbury.... 173
Lord Baltimore...... 223, 237, 238
Lord Baltimore Deposed...... 237
Lord Bishop of London...... 171
Lord Proprietaries Lands...... 359
Lord Protector...... 182
Lords and Ladies of Manors...... 65
Lords of Manors...... 110, 251, 263, 371
Lords of the Manor in Colonial Maryland, with Their Original Land Surveys, taken from Lord Baltimore's Rent Rolls, 263, 264, 265 266
Lords of the Manor in England..... 423
Lordship's Commissioners...... 154
Losing the Flitch of Bacon...... 182
Ludgates...... 63
Lying Valet, The...... 144

Magna Charta...... 161
Mail Service in Provincial Times... 95
Majesty's Pleasure...... 211
Manokin...... 116, 117
Manor Houses...... 27, 45
Manors...... 69
Man's Meeting...... 224
Mar and Derwentwater, Defeat of, 215
"Marianna"...... 57
Market House, Baltimore Town.... 356
"Marseillaise, The, of the South".. 401
"Maryland Boys"...... 404
Maryland Colonial Militia...... 267
Maryland Executive Exhibit...... 419
Maryland Flag Adopted...... 385
Maryland "Gazette"...... 197, 369
Maryland Girls, Description of..... 149
Maryland's Glorious Bonfire off Windmill Point...... 361
Maryland in Virginia...... 221
Maryland Legislature...... 193

GENERAL INDEX 457

"Maryland, My Maryland"......... 401
Maryland Not a Penal Colony...... 56
"Maryland, Prince of".............. 111
Maryland Proprietary, Invitation of, 190
Maryland Society of The Order of the Cincinnati, Officers and Members of.................... 387, 390, 391
Maryland, the Promised Land to the Persecuted......................... 249
Maryland Youth..................... 406
Maryland's Declaration of Independence........................ 371
Maryland's Poet Laureate.......... 244
Maryland's Proclamation of Freedom.............................. 126
Maryland's Settlement.............. 209
Marylander's Birthright............ 365
Marylanders who Voted For but did not Sign the Declaration of Independence......................... 376
Massachusetts Bay.................. 372
Massawameckes..................... 33
Master of Life...................... 138
Matrimonial Felicity................ 205
Mattapient......................... 106
Mattapony.......................... 110
Mattapony Sewall................... 236
Medeira Wines..................... 242
Memorial Hall of Maryland History 411
Michael's, St....................... 226
Middlesex, County of............... 244
Mint, The.......................... 125
"Money to Burn".................... 124
Monocacy.......................... 163
"Monument Street Girls," The..... 401
"Mother of Waters"................. 115
Municipal Art Society.............. 410
Mural Paintings in Baltimore Court House............................. 405
Muscipula, The Mouse Trap........ 245
Muster Roll of Colonial Militia Found in England, 267, 268, 269, 270 271, 272
Myrtle Grove.................. 47, 253

Names of One Thousand Early Settlers in Maryland, with Their Earliest Land Surveys, as Recorded in Lord Baltimore's Rent Rolls for the Various Counties... 256
Nanticoke.......................... 163
Nanticokes, The.................... 178
Natural Love and Affection......... 179
Newburg-on-the-Hudson........... 388
New England.............. 152, 166, 242
Newgates........................... 63
New Netherlands, Governor of..... 189
New Scotland....................... 152
Newton's Point..................... 97
New York.................. 97, 122, 194
New York Sons of Liberty......... 356
Noah, Tradition of................. 138
Northern Governments............. 357

Officers of Cecil County Colonial Militia Foot................... 283, 284
Officers of Colonial Militia Horse and Foot, Charles County... 274, 275
Officers of Dorchester County Militia Horse and Foot........... 280, 281
Officers of Foot, Calvert County, 275, 276
Officers of Horse and Foot, Charles County.................... 274, 275
Officers of Horse and Foot, St. Marys County................ 272, 273, 274
Officers of Prince George's County Militia, Foot and Horse........... 276
Officers of Queen Anne's County Militia, Horse and Foot....... 284, 285
Officers of Somerset County Militia, Foot and Horse......277, 278, 279, 280
Officers of Talbot County Militia, Foot and Horse............... 281, 282
Officers of the French Navy in the Revolution..................... 392, 393
Officers of Worcester County Colonial Militia, Foot.............. 285, 286
Old Dominion.................. 47, 169
Old Eastern Shore Families......... 253
Old Eastern Shore Towns........... 251
Oldest Building in Maryland....... 187
Oldest Church in Maryland...... 78, 79
Old Families in Office.............. 255
Old Senate Chamber................ 383
Oldmixon........................... 127
Opposition to the British Ministry. 361
Original Bill of Lading............. 422
Original Boundary Agreement Between Penn and Lord Baltimore.. 426
Original Charter of Annapolis....... 425
Origin of Lynch Law............... 133
Orphans, The....................... 145
Oxford............................. 170
Oxford University.................. 167

Palace of St. John's....109, 110, 111, 114
Palace of Westminster.............. 15
Palatinate of Durham........... 45, 126
Palatinate Government............. 60
Palatinate of Maryland............. 257
Palmer's Island.................... 166
Parishes, Erection of............78, 225
Parishes, Names of................. 226
Parish of St. Giles in the Fields.... 244
Parliamentary Commissioner to Govern Maryland................ 262
Pascatoway 22, 23, 31
Paschattoways..................... 135
Passengers for Virginia............ 153
Passengers on the Ark and Dove, 8, 9, 10 11, 12, 13, 14 15
Postrider........................... 97
Patents............................ 109
Pater Noster Row.................. 243
Patomecke.............. 22, 24, 66, 196
Patowmeck Towne................. 408
Patuxent........ 66, 86, 110, 182, 183, 366

GENERAL INDEX

Paul's, St............................ 226
Pay of Colonial Officers......... 100, 101
Peace Treaty Signed at Annapolis.. 381
Peggy Stewart............. 361, 365, 371
Penn's Visit........................ 223
Pennsylvania....................... 129
"Pennsylvania Historical Magazine"............................. 366
Pensions............................ 174
People of Maryland Honored........ 419
Persecuted French.................. 250
Pewter Platters.................... 50
Philadelphia............... 122, 253, 375
Photographic Facsimile of Autographs, 424
Pillory............................. 64
Piscataway......................... 408
Planter, The....................... 241
Plat of Baltimore Town, 1747....... 426
Plimhimmon......................... 258
Plumtree Street.................... 244
Plymouth........................... 224
Poet Laureate, Colonial..........93, 243
Point Comfort...................... 30
Point Paradise..................... 190
Point Patience..................... 96
Political Prisoners in Maryland.... 210
Poplar Hill Church................. 225
Port Royal......................... 87
Portia of Maryland Bar............. 148
Portraits of Maryland Signers, by Peale............................. 385
Potomac Navigation Committee..... 193
Prato Musicus...................... 92
Presbyterian Churches.............. 116
Presbyterians from Scotland, and Ireland............................ 254
Preservation of Historic Relics of Maryland.......................... 385
President of the Maryland Convention.............................. 424
Preston, 181, 182, 183, 184, 185, 186, 187
Preston in Lancashire.............. 210
Preston Mansion............... 181, 182
Priests Deported from England..... 249
Prime Minister..................... 189
Princess Anne...................... 117
Proclamation of Governor Hart..... 210
Propagation of the Gospel.......... 173
Property Qualification............. 82
Proprietaries and their Representatives............................. 260
Proprietaries of Maryland.......... 260
Protection of American Liberty..... 357
Protestant Church Established. 225, 227
Protestant Revolution.............. 225
Protestant Succession.............. 211
Providence...................... 75, 183
Provincial Court............... 85, 205
Provincial Poet's Lines......... 191, 192
Provision for Adventurer's House... 37
Public Instruments................. 110
Public Letters..................... 96
Public Post........................ 97

Public Printer..................... 147
Public Records Commission........ 385
Publishing of "Maryland My Maryland"............................ 403
Puritan Group...................... 406
Puritan Leaders.................... 181
Puritans....................... 103, 209
Puritans from Virginia............. 75
Puritan Soldiery................... 186
Puritan Stronghold................. 183

Quaker Meeting..................... 186
Quakers........................ 209, 254
Quakers in Maryland.. 209, 220, 221, 254
Quakers Not Persecuted in Maryland.............................. 220
Queen Anne's County.......... 252, 253
Queen Anne's Cushion............... 80
Quicksetts......................... 88
Quit Rents......................... 164
Quit Rent.......................... 163

Raid, Ingle's...................... 252
Rangers, The Kings................. 88
Rangers, Triangular Houses......... 88
Ratification of Federal Constitution, 426
Ratification of Peace Treaty....... 383
Receipts for Two Indian Arrows Paid at Windsor Castle, by Lord Baltimore..................... 162, 422
Redemptioners...................... 246
Red House Club..................... 90
Rehoboth........................... 116
Religious Toleration, Birthplace of.. 102
Removal of the Capital to Annapolis. 85
Renaissance of Antiques............ 177
Repeal of the Stamp Act............ 364
Restoration of King Charles II..... 28
Revolutionary War......... 168, 179, 193
Ride of Lt.-Col Tench Tilghman... 378
Ridge, The......................... 85
Ringan............................. 258
Roade River........................ 220
Rockawalkin Church................. 117
Royal Governors............... 237, 260
Rumseian Society................... 194
"Rumsey-Crazy"..................... 194
Rumsey's Steamboat................. 193
Rumsey's Patent.................... 194
Rumsey's Petition.................. 193
Rumsey's Work...................... 196
Rural Dean......................... 122

Salem Creek........................ 190
"Sallarys" of School Teachers...... 174
Sasquasahannockos.................. 24
Sasquesa-hanoughs.................. 137
Scheme for Destroying Ships of War, Jeremiah Riley's.................. 424
School, King William's............. 173
Scilley Isles...................... 19
Scotland........................... 249
Scots, Banished, Names of..... 214, 215
Scotch............................. 103

GENERAL INDEX 459

Scotch Exiles........................ 213
Scotch Type........................ 405
Scotch Uprisings.................... 213
Scutage Tax........................ 161
Seal of Maryland................... 385
Seat of Trade...................... 109
Sevearne River..................... 174
Severn............................. 170
Senate Chamber at Annapolis of National Interest........ 378, 383, 419
Signet Rings........................ 49
Silver Skillet....................... 51
Snow Hill.......................... 116
Socage Rent........................ 58
Social Athens of America........ 77, 144
Society of Arts..................... 195
Society of The Cincinnati, 387, 388, 389 390, 392, 393
Society of the Cincinnati First General Officers......................... 390
Society's (*Ark* and *Dove*) List....... 412
Somerset........................... 226
Somerset County and the Presbyterians............................ 115
Sons of American Revolutions Insignia........................... 396
Sons of Liberty, 356, 357, 358, 359, 360 371
Sons of the American Revolutions the Insignia of..................... 396
South River........................ 220
South River Club.......... 197, 198, 202
South River Club House............ 199
South River Club Members, 202, 203, 204
South River Club Rules, 199, 200, 201 202
Special Executive Exhibit.......... 420
Special Executive Historian, 411, 419, 420
Speed's Prospect of Famous Parts of the World...................... 109
Spelling of Names, variation in, 228, 229
"Spells and Tokens"................ 143
Staffordshire...................... 205
Stamp Act Opposed................. 363
"Star Spangled Banner, The".. 401, 424
State House, Annapolis......... 419, 420
State House and Circle Offered to Congress........................... 383
Statue of Chatham Erected......... 364
Stepney............................ 226
St. Christophers.................... 20
St. Clement's Day.................. 17
St. George's.................... 24, 226
St. Gregories....................22, 24
St. James,......................... 226
St. Johns........................... 95
St. Margaret's..................... 226
St. Maries........ 24, 68, 86, 87, 109, 163
St. Maries, Forte of................ 111
Stocks............................. 64
Suit Against Richard Ingle.
"Summoned by Special writt"...... 113
Susquehanna Fort.................. 222
Swedes, The Coming of............ 188

Talbot County................. 224, 253
Tammany Society.................. 393
"Tannenbaum, O Tannenbaum"... 402
Tax Collector Put to Flight......... 371
Tea Burnt.......................... 370
Teackle Mansion.................... 256
Tench Tilghman's Ride............. 378
Tench Tilghman, Tablet Erected to 378
Terra Mariae..................... 56, 57
Theatre, Earliest................... 145
Treadhaven........................ 223
"The Engagement"................. 220
"The Hermitage".................. 253
"The Marseillaise of the South".... 401
"The Sanctuary".................... 63
The Sot-Weed Factor............... 243
"The Sot-Weed Redivivus or the Planters' Looking Glass"......... 245
The Tercentenary................... 411
Their Majesties' Province of Maryland.............................. 86
Tin Candle Sticks.................. 242
Tobacco port....................... 226
Toll for Grinding Grain............ 240
"Town Land at Proctors".......... 88
Traced Autographs................. 425
Trading Company.................. 152
Transported Settlers................ 53
Treaty at Paris................ 362, 363
Tred Haven Meetings............... 253
Trinity............................ 79
Tripartite Indenture Showing Miniature of Sixth Lord Baltimore.... 426
Tuesday Club......... 89, 90, 91, 92, 93 366
Tulip Hill.......................... 366
Turkes.......................... 18, 20
Two Indian Arrows, Calvert's Feudal Rent to King.................. 162
Two Most Usual Feasts of the Year, 163
Typical Indenture, 1684............ 426

United Colonies.................... 372
University—First in America....... 165
Unrecorded Will of Third Lord Baltimore............................ 426
Unsung Heroes of the Revolution.. 394

Valuable Collection of Signatures, 426 427
Violet Sallet....................... 43
Virginia, 2, 20, 21, 33, 97, 129, 152, 153 166, 169, 193, 220, 407
Virginia Commissioners............ 182
Virginia Committee of Correspondence............................. 375
Virginia Company.............. 146, 166
Virginia's Annulled Charter........ 76
Visitors of Free Schools............ 175

Warrants........................... 109
Washington College................ 168
Washington's Eulogy of Lt.-Col. Tench Tilghman.................. 423
Washington's (Col. John) Excuse... 73

460 GENERAL INDEX

Washington, George.................. 194
Washington's Letter to the General Assembly of Maryland............ 423
Water Mills........................ 239
Water-Mill set up.................. 238
Watkin's Point...................... 129
Werowance Invited to Parley with Leonard Calvert.................. 408
Westminster........................ 226
Westmoreland County, Virginia..... 72
West River......................... 223
Where Washington Resigned His Commission.................. 383, 384
Whichenovre, Lord of............... 205
Whichenovre, Manor of.............. 206
Whig Club.......................... 359
Whipping Post...................... 64
Wicker Chairs...................... 242
Wicomico........................... 116
Widow's Lott....................... 224
Wighco............................. 129
William and Mary College...... 169, 237

William Penn....................... 253
William, Prince of Orange.......... 212
William Stadt...................... 97
Will of Andrew Cooke............... 224
Windmill Point..................... 361
Wind Mills......................... 238
Windsor Castle..................... 258
Witchcraft......................... 141
Witchcraft in Maryland............. 141
Woman Printer...................... 147
Writs, Special..................... 110
Wye House.......................... 253

Yale Book of Songs................. 402
Yaocomico.......................... 137
Yoacomaca, Governor Calvert Visits It........................... 408
Yoacomoco Indians.................. 33
Yorktown...................... 253, 380
Younger Sons Came to Maryland... 397
Yule Log........................... 26

EARLY SHIPS TO MARYLAND

Africa, The........................ 153
Charity of London.................. 141
Friendship, The............... 210, 215
Golden Fortune..................... 182
Grip, The Bird..................... 189
Helen, St.......................... 154

Longtail, The................. 115, 153
Sarah Artch, The................... 74
Svan, The.......................... 190
St. Helen.......................... 115
St. Margaret.................. 115, 154

LANDS

Earliest Land Surveys in *Anne Arundel County*.........322, 323, 324, 325, 326, 327, 328, 329, 330, 331.

Earliest Land Surveys in *Baltimore County*...........331, 332, 333, 334, 335, 336, 337, 338, 339.

Earliest Land Surveys in *Cecil County*..........339, 340, 341, 342, 343

Earliest Land Surveys in *Charles County*......308, 309, 310, 311, 312, 313

Earliest Land Surveys in *Dorchester County*........351, 352, 353, 354, 355

Earliest Land Surveys in *Kent County*......292, 293, 294, 295, 296, 297, 298, 299, 300, 301, 302, 303, 304, 305.

Earliest Land Surveys in *Prince George's County*......305, 306, 307, 308

Earliest Land Surveys in *St. Mary's County*.......287, 288, 289, 290, 291, 292

Earliest Land Surveys in *Somerset County*......313, 314, 315, 316, 317, 318, 319, 320, 321, 322.

Land Surveys Earliest in *Talbot County*......... 343, 344, 345, 346, 347, 348, 349, 350, 351.

Manors, List of..........263, 264, 265, 266

ERRATA

Page 24, fifteenth line from the bottom, "Carolino" should read *Carolina*.

Page 27, eighth line from the bottom, "when" should read *with*.

Page 30, sixth line from the top, and eleventh line from the bottom on page 32, "Lechford," should read *Letchford*.

Page 31, seventh line from the bottom of page, "which" should read *with*.

Page 107, fourth line from top of page, "sayd" should read *says*.

Page 127, fourth line from bottom of page, "Old Mixon" should read *Oldmixon*.

Page 160, fourth line from bottom, "in" should read *to*.

Page 220, fifth line from top of page, "lineage" should read *lineages*.

Page 223, twelfth line from top of page, "name" should read *names*.

Page 226, third line from top of page, a period should follow Eastern.

Page 255, sixteenth line from bottom of page, "country" should read *County*.

Page 257, eighth line from the bottom of page, "Sotterly" should read *Sotterley*.